Studies in Eighteenth-Century Culture

VOLUME 24

Studies in Eighteenth-Century Culture

VOLUME 24

Edited by

Carla H. Hay
Marquette University

and

Syndy M. Conger
Western Illinois University

Published by The Johns Hopkins University Press for the
American Society for Eighteenth-Century Studies

The Johns Hopkins University Press
Baltimore and London

This book is printed on recycled, acid-free paper

The Johns Hopkins University Press
2715 North Charles Street
Baltimore, Maryland 21218-4319
The Johns Hopkins Press Ltd., London

ISBN 0-8018-5136-X
ISSN 0013-2586
LC 95-79551

Editorial Readers for Volume Twenty-Four

JUDITH FRANK / *English* / *Amherst College*
ELLEN FRANCES GARDINER / *English* / *University of Mississippi*
ALEXANDER S. GOURLAY / *English* / *Rhode Island School of Design*
LANCE GRAHN / *History* / *Marquette University*
LILA V. GRAVES / *English* / *University of Alabama at Birmingham*
KATHERINE S. GREEN / *English* / *Western Kentucky University*
DONALD J. GREENE / *English Emeritus* / *University of Southern California*
ISOBEL GRUNDY / *English* / *University of Alberta*
MADELYN GUTWIRTH / *Women's Studies* / *University of Pennsylvania*
GEORGE HAGGERTY / *English* / *University of California, Riverside*
ELIZABETH HARRIES / *English* / *Smith College*
JOCELYN HARRIS / *English* / *University of Otago, New Zealand*
MARY JACKSON HARVEY / *Corporate and Foundation Relations* / *University of Chicago*
JULIE C. HAYES / *French* / *University of Richmond*
HAROLD M. HYMAN / *History* / *Rice University*
SUSAN K. JACKSON / *Modern Foreign Languages* / *Boston University*
ANNIBEL JENKINS / *English* / *Georgia Tech University*
DANIELLE JOHNSON-COUSIN / *Modern Languages* / *Florida International University*
DORIS Y. KADISH / *Romance Languages* / *University of Georgia*
MADELEINE KAHN / *English* / *Mills College*
JON KLANCHER / *English* / *Boston University*
BETH KOWALESKI-WALLACE / *English* / *Boston College*
ELIZABETH KRAFT / *English* / *University of Georgia*
ISAAC KRAMNICK / *Government* / *Cornell University*
ANNE K. KROOK / *English* / *University of Michigan*
MANFRED KUSCH / *French and Italian* / *University of California, Davis*
DONNA LANDRY / *English* / *Wayne State University*
LAWRENCE LIPKING / *English* / *Northwestern University*
CHRISTOPHER LOOBY / *English* / *University of Chicago*
RICHARD C. LOUNSBURY / *Humanities* / *Brigham Young University*
CYNTHIA LOWENTHAL / *English* / *Tulane University*
SANDRA RUDNICK LUFF / *Humanities* / *San Francisco State University*
MARK LUSSIER / *English* / *Western Illinois University*
DEIDRE S. LYNCH / *English* / *State University of New York at Buffalo*
ELIZABETH J. MACARTHUR / *French and Italian* / *University of California at Santa Barbara*
STEVEN D. MARTINSON / *German* / *University of Arizona*
SHAWN L. MAURER / *English* / *Texas A&M University*
BRIAN MCCREA / *English* / *University of Florida*
ARNOLD MILLER / *French and Italian* / *University of Wisconsin-Madison*

WENDY MOTOOKA */ English / Harvard University*
MITZI MYERS */ Women's Studies / Unversity of California, Los Angeles*
DEBORAH J. NESTOR */ English / University of California, Los Angeles*
GREGORY S. O'DEA */ English / University of Tennessee at Chattanooga*
FRANK PALMERI */ English / University of Miami*
JULIE STONE PETERS */ English / Columbia University*
WILLIAM PIPER */ English / Rice University*
ELLEN POLLACK */ English / Michigan State University*
SUZANNE PUCCI */ French / State University of New York at Buffalo*
MARTHA M. RAINBOLT */ English / DePauw University*
RHONDA J. RAY */ English / East Stroudsburg University*
WALTER E. REX */ French / University of California, Berkeley*
JOHN RIELY */ English / Boston University*
ALBERT J. RIVERO */ English / Marquette University*
SHIRLEY A. ROE */ History / University of Connecticut*
MARTIN ROSENBERG */ Art / University of Nebraska at Omaha*
LAURA J. ROSENTHAL */ English / Florida State University*
WENDY WASSYNG ROWORTH */ Art / University of Rhode Island*
PETER SABOR */ English / Queens University*
BARBARA BRANDON SCHNORRENBERG */ History of Science / Independent*
Scholar
MANUEL SCHONHORN */ English / Southern Illinois University*
E. JOANNE SHATTOCK */ English / University of Leicester*
DANIEL SHERMAN */ French Studies / Rice University*
KENNETH D. SHIELDS */ English / Southern Methodist University*
DONALD T. SIEBERT */ English / University of South Carolina*
ALEX A. SOKALSKI */ French and Spanish / University of Saskatchewan*
JOAN HINDE STEWART */ French / North Carolina State University*
ROBERT D. STOCK */ English / University of Nebraska-Lincoln*
KRISTINA STRAUB */ English / Carnegie Mellon University*
CHARLOTTE SUSSMAN */ English / University of Colorado at Boulder*
CORLISS SWAIN */ Philosophy / St. Olaf University*
CLAUDIA THOMAS */ English / Wake Forest*
ROBERT TOMLINSON */ French / Emory University*
DAVID TROTT / French */ University of Toronto, Mississauga*
ROBERT W. UPHAUS */ English / Michigan State University*
ALBERT VAN HELDEN */ History / Rice University*
JANIE VANPÉE */ French / Smith College*
MARY VERMILLION */ English / University of Iowa*
ANNE C. VILA */ French and Italian / University of Wisconsin-Madison*
DROR WAHRMAN */ History / University of Michigan*
TARA GHOSHAL WALLACE */ English / George Washington University*

Contents

Preface

Volume twenty-four of *Studies in Eighteenth-Century Culture* inaugurates what promises to be an exciting period in the history of the series. With the support of its new publisher, The Johns Hopkins University Press, *SECC* can build on its already solid record for publishing innovative inter-disciplinary scholarship on the interpretative edge of research on the "long" eighteenth century.

Representing the diversity of interests within the eighteenth-century studies community, the eighteen essays in this volume range chronologi-cally from the mid-seventeenth century to the early nineteenth century and geographically from the Italian peninsula to the American colonies on the eve of revolution. Revolution serves as political context for several of the essays: Backscheider's study of "The Cavalier Woman" in early Restora-tion England, Farrell's study of American patriot, John Adams, during the revolutionary war, Tenger and Trolander's analysis of English literary periodicals at the time of the French Revolution, a seminal event which also serves as the context for Coleman's study of Germaine de Staël. Different time periods and locales notwithstanding, several themes resonate through-out the volume. Alienation and exile figure prominently in the essays of Backscheider, Coleman, Farrell, Ferguson, and Levine. The Rise of the Novel as a genre are referenced by Cantrell, Edmiston, Harkin, Ingrassia, and Turner. Challenges to Enlightenment rationalism are foregrounded by Crease and Tenger and Trolander. Issues of gender and the Other are framed in various ways: on the stage (Backscheider and Koch), in Exchange Alley (Ingrassia), the classroom (Wilner), or the world of the prostitute and libertine (Edmiston and Turner), from the vantage point of the gods (Maresca and Rizzo), a moral philosopher (Harkin), or a "scribbling lass" (Ferguson). The role of the New Science (Crease), sympathy (Harkin), the libertine (Edmiston), poet (Levine), or virtuoso (Brown) in bringing "cognitive value" to the "confusion and obscurity" (Barnouw) of a changing social and commercial world peopled by figures as disparate as cavalier women (Backscheider), a milkmaid poet (Ferguson), French playwrights (Koch), and stockjobbers (Ingrassia) are explored in creative ways by our authors who collectively advance our understanding of the dynamic world of eighteenth-century studies.

Editing two volumes of *Studies in Eighteenth-Century Culture* has been a gratifying experience in no small measure because of the tremendous cooperation of the authors, readers, members of the Editorial Board, and associate editor, Syndy Conger. I am particularly indebted to my graduate assistant, Justin Hoffman, who indexed and formatted camera-ready copy of the manuscript. Finally, my thanks to Marquette University for its financial support of this endeavor.

Carla H. Hay

Studies in Eighteenth-Century Culture

VOLUME 24

The Cavalier Woman

PAULA R. BACKSCHEIDER

In 1993 we do not often hear expressed the opinion that literature performs "urgent" work in society. Yet it does; a major contribution of recent cultural studies and reception theory is increased understanding of how literature functions in different cultures and also how individual elements of texts can be temporary sites for the expression and negotiation of the most pressing concerns of a consuming community.

It is a commonplace to note the number of kinds of writing, including major literary genres, born or largely shaped in the Restoration and eighteenth century. Many of these forms are blatantly political, even propagandistic. The history of the novel might easily be written as a shift from the political and economic propaganda of *Oroonoko*, *Love-Letters between a Nobleman and his Sister*, *Robinson Crusoe*, and *A Journal of the Plague Year* to the moral propaganda of *Tom Jones*, *Evelina*, and the novels of sensibility. The novel's evolution has received much critical attention; in contrast, some forms of Restoration and eighteenth-century drama have received very little in spite of the fact that the major kinds of modern drama can be traced to them.

In this paper, I want to concentrate on a single genre, drama, and a very limited group of plays—comedies and a few tragi-comedies primarily produced between 1660 and 1663.[1] I shall point out some of the "urgent" work that they had to do and concentrate upon a single kind of character, the cavalier woman. I shall argue that this character was a new type, that it illustrates one of the ways the "feminine" functions in the social reproduction of a dominant male culture, and that it did urgent work in the early Restoration. Within the argument regarding the cultural effort expended to maintain male hegemony, I include a brief revisionary consideration of the breeches part, a part that gained enormous popularity

3

shortly after the production of the plays that are the subject of this study and a part that I see as one of the outgrowths of the cavalier woman plot. My conclusion points even more sketchily to the way this character type remained available for reaccentuation and new cultural uses.

* * * * * * * * *

In the years immediately following the Restoration, "cavalier" had a complex meaning. Obviously inseparable from the distinction between the Cavaliers and the Roundheads during the Civil War, the cavaliers of 1660 were royalists, many returning from abroad and evoking stories of young noblemen riding spirited horses into glorious battle. "Cavalier" had long meant knight and "a gay sprightly military man who was also a courtly gentleman," but it had also been pejoratively used to describe "swash-bucklers on the king's side who hailed the prospect of war" and was consistently joined to adjectives such as "haughty, domineering" and "careless in manner."[2] Martin Butler points out that the images of cavaliers were "heroic Prince Ruperts or debauched devil-may-cares."[3] Long, curling hair, a horse, and a sword maintained the class overtones that were both respected and reviled.

In 1660 and 1661, the associations of gallant young loyalists and of arrogant, privileged men spoiling for a fight were overlaid with the reality of defeat, exile, and the sequestration of their property. The cavaliers of 1660 were more often than not in straitened circumstances and facing a world in which they had no secure place. The first thing that the reader notices about Robert Howard's *Committee* and the other original plays of these years is how poor many of the characters are, that money is the controlling obsession, and that the women are more likely to have it than the men. Ragged soldiers in bedraggled capes walk the streets and meet in cheap taverns to pool their resources and speculate on means to secure their next meal. Using the plays of the 1662–63 season alone, we find many examples.

Burr in John Dryden's *The Wild Gallant* hopes that his buff coat will cover his tattered clothes and exposed skin. Howard's Blunt and Careless are destitute. Corbulo in Robert Stapylton's *The Slighted Maid* says, "The times are chang'd . . . War into Peace, and Soldiers into Beggars."[4] Often identified as belonging to the Flanders troops, these penniless characters would have been identified by the audience with the men quartered at the charity of the Spanish in the year before Charles' return and now being cashiered out of the army at great expense to the nation.[5] Characters in *The Wild Gallant* and Samuel Tuke's hit, *The Adventures of Five Hours,*[6] are from Flanders. Several characters mention that they are considering going to the New World or trying their fortunes as mercenaries in Candy, the royal city in Ceylon that the Portuguese were unable to take when they held the rest of the country. (In the 1630s, the king of Candy invited the Dutch to help him drive out the Portuguese in exchange for extensive trading privileges; by 1656, the Portuguese had lost their last forts in Ceylon.)[7] A few leave to fight the Turks.[8]

All of this complexity and these ambivalences are captured in the comedies of 1660–63, and the cavalier woman character reveals several major tensions in the culture.[9] Claudine Herrmann has argued that literature allows women to dream a utopian man and that sometimes this is the "man of the future."[10] As I have argued elsewhere,[11] women of this same period were indeed creating a new literary character of their own, a character I have called the domesticated hero. It is possible to read the cavalier woman of these plays as a disturbing prefiguration of "the woman of the future."

The cavalier woman shares with the cavalier hero courage, gallantry, loyalty, flair, and a certain *fin de ère* consciousness that adds poignancy and even theatricality to many gestures. In ways that sometimes seem to romanticize an earlier time even as older symbols were used to re-establish the power of the monarchy's hierarchy, the upper classes made cavalier synonymous with "royalist-loyalist." Tradesmen were quick to provide emblems for the part of the nation that embraced the Restoration and the hopes inherent in it. For example, the cavalier hat quickly became a popular fashion for women. Perhaps encouraged by a very public gesture made by Barbara Palmer, Lady Castlemaine, the king's then-favorite mistress, by 1666 the hats were as common as the sacque[12] and the embroidered shoe. As a spectator at the royal entrée of Queen Catherine of Braganza in 1662, Lady Castlemaine had hurried down to the street to see if a child bumped by a horse was hurt. Pepys commented admiringly on her gesture and dashing appearance: She alone "of all the great ladies" had gone to see if the child had been hurt, "which methought was so noble"; "one there, booted and spurred, . . . she talked long with" in the wind and sun. "And . . . being in her haire, she put on his hat. . . . it became her mightily."[13] In 1666, John Evelyn would remark casually, "The *Queene* was now in her *Cavaliers* riding habite, hat & feather & horsemans Coate, going to take the aire."[14] Castlemaine, the king's loyal mistress, acted out the flair of the cavaliers and the heterosexual aggressiveness of the court but also expressed the propagandistic message of the Restoration, that the king would be genuinely concerned with his people.

What sets this new heroine apart from the early seventeenth-century romantic-comedy heroine and the later Restoration one are her maturity, money, and engagement in the public sphere. The cavalier women express opinions about *public* affairs and events, believe they have the right and ability to speak about these issues, and display other signs identified by Ernesto Laclau as "deliberative behavior."[15] In Robert Howard's Ruth (*The Committee*), in Dryden's Lady Constance (*Wild Gallant*), and Samuel Tuke's Porcia (*Adventure of Five Hours*), the audience could recognize behaviors associated with women during the Interregnum. Left alone to face hardship and even, perhaps, an army, this clever woman shared the men's loyalty and flair and perhaps even enjoyed "playing the man." And, while the men had been away with the army or across the channel, the women had had to live and, therefore, make compromises with the victors at home. Again realistically, many of these earliest heroines are widows, and they guard their money and themselves alertly.[16] A typical example is the heroine of James Howard's *The English Mounsieur* (performed 1663, published 1674), the widow, Lady Wealthy. She is tricky, businesslike, and gets what she wants. Even the selection of plays to be revived shows an affinity for such heroines. Madam Beaufield in William Cavendish's *The Varietie* is called "the Lady of spirit and entertainment . . . the Magnetick widdow."[17] George Etherege's Widow Rich and her witty exchanges with Sir Frolick helped make *The Comical Revenge* (1664) one of the two greatest successes of the decade; Peter Holland calls that play the "fruition of the widow-suitor" plot.[18]

It has been observed many times, "in every war, women fight when there are no more men left to defend them."[19] More commonly, they manage estates and households, take the place of absent men in almost every occupation, and are forced to secret and protect resources for the future. They read the papers avidly, discuss events, and feel compelling reasons to attempt to insert themselves into political processes. As historians have demonstrated, civil war women did these things and coped, in Margaret George's words, "with ingenuity, intelligence, and courage." She describes women such as Lady Mary Verney routinely doing "the difficult political and financial business"—what she calls "the man's work." The way the Days have appropriated Ruth and her property and that Arbella must petition for hers in *The Committee* would have been familiar to the audience. Lieutenant Story's praise of his wife also gives a glimpse of the life of such historical women: "A most violent cavalier," she has traded food and tobacco for news of the army.[20] In order to survive, Ruth and women like her depended on their wits and waited their chances.

I will use Robert Howard's *The Committee*, which was performed in 1662, to provide a touchstone for much of my argument.[21] The play is a well-constructed city comedy, and city comedies were popular.[22] Howard's sympathetic treatment of the cavaliers is of a piece with these plays, but there are major differences. A more skillful dramatist and by 1662 part of a group of playwrights who collaborated formally and informally, he created somewhat deeper characters with the potential for expressing more of the experiences and emotions of the cavaliers. He makes the cavaliers seem to be exiles in their own country. Faced with demands, oaths, rules, and codes of conduct as foreign to their own past as those of an alien nation, confronted by kitchen maids turned ladies, and arrested without warrants, they consider real exile; at one point in the negotiations, Careless exclaims, "Why then hoist Sails for a new World" (76).

Howard cleverly uses Teague, that favorite character of Charles II, to develop this aspect of the play.[23] Like the cavaliers, Teague has no occupation, is seeking a new economic and social place, and will jockey for years with the merchant class that would continue to be associated with Nonconformist religion and Whig conceptions of the monarchy.[24] As the Days attempt to hold on to their wealth and secure the estates they have appropriated, Careless, Blunt, Arbella, and Ruth struggle to regain what the Civil War and Interregnum have taken from them. The shift in power, of course, put the royalist survivors in direct competition with the gentry and city men who had prospered and held power during the Interregnum. Another level of characters—Lieutenant Story, Obadiah, Teague, and others—find the ground shifting beneath their feet and search for a new place and a new orientation to those in power.

Ruth lays bare the stratified, competing, and stratifying forces in society that are reproduced in the languages of the characters.[25] In *The Long Revolution*, Raymond Williams borrows Erich Fromm's term and writes of the importance of the analysis of the interaction among simultaneously existing "social characters," by which he means "valued systems of behavior and attitudes."[26] Howard's play is one of the first post-Restoration plays to capture the experience of conflicting social characters and of competing residual and emergent structures of feeling; Ruth, as the character who can move among them successfully, reveals major elements in the social characters. On one level she functions as a bridge between the Days, the City couple who control the Committee of Sequestrations, and the cavaliers,[27] and it is her energy and ingenuity—and willingness to coerce and blackmail—that rescue the cavaliers and bring about the happy ending. And that happy ending lays bare one of the processes at work to re-order society.

The stories of guilt, entitlement, and moral imperatives compete visibly in *The Committee*, and Ruth is sharply distinguished from the male cavaliers. In order to bring about the happy ending, Ruth must steal documents and use threats. She triumphs in the Days' world, and her conduct has usually been described as making her look clever and practical, but there is no denying the fact that Careless and Blunt, not Ruth, survive as the idealistic people of uncompromising honor—the real cavaliers. In one of the richest scenes in the play, Careless asks her, "Do but swear then, that thou art not the issue of Mr. Day; and tho' I know 'tis a lie, I'll be content to be cozened, and believe" (89) and again, "do but swear me into a pretence" (104). He asks her to do for love what he cannot do for property. She does, and he responds, "Poor kind perjured pretty one, I am beholden to thee; wouldst damn thyself for me?"

By housing the unwillingness to swear in the man, by having Careless willing to accept *her* love of him as worth damnation, Howard uses gendered categories to illustrate additional contradictions inherent in contemporary oath taking but also in demands on male and female behavior.[28] Cowley's Truman rejects Lucia when he thinks she is being less than honorable and chaste. As they had in earlier plays and pamphlets, female characters represent unauthorized behaviors and structures of feeling. They are, in short, in no danger of making honor an idol, as Day accuses the cavaliers of doing (75). As Susan Staves and others have said, the male cavaliers are idealized: they are "the creatures of wish-fulfillment dreams. They always behave well and always preserve honor intact under kaleidoscopically shifting circumstances. . . . [They] behave as their creators and their audiences would like to have behaved, but, for the most part, did not." They "take oaths seriously, reject material considerations for the pursuit of their ideals, and are finally rewarded with both money and women."[29]

At this stage, when a new man—one prepared to negotiate rather than fight—is being created, the cavaliers and the puritans are still often portrayed as inflexible. Ruth's character serves to bring out the uncompromising rigidity of the Cromwellians and cavaliers. Both groups seem to be hypnotized by the past and adhere stubbornly to prejudices and positions.[30]

The uncompromising demands of the characters in *The Committee* are found in many plays. Filomarini tells Salerno in *The Slighted Maid*, "Kill me first; I would not live to see you . . . marry the Daughter of a Cheat" (61). The men take the stance that no matter what happens, they will remain essentially the same and continue to resist; Careless asks Ruth, "D'ye think a prison takes away blood and fight?" (103). In language and gesture, the cavalier woman, like her male counterpart, could soar above the wealthy cits; in contrast to the men's obsession with the past, she adapts to the present and builds a future. The songs that the men sing in act 4 have a nostalgia that jars with the gritty pragmatism of Ruth's final lines. Later playwrights who often drew upon or even adapted these plays recognized the contrast. Lois Potter points out that "heroick" became "virtually synonymous" with cavalier,[31] and this kind of drama and stance quickly became identified with a past time and attitude.

The deconstruction of this rigid ideal of honor is evident as early as Tuke's *Adventures of Five Hours*. In this play Don Antonio finds moral imperatives lead him to attack Don Octavio one moment and, almost instantly, to protect him against Don Henrique. The people and causes to which he finds himself called to be loyal are hilariously divided and conflicting, and honor makes him and the other male character appear confused and ineffectual. In this play, a woman, Porcia, has the information, perspective, and calm temper to steer characters bent on mayhem from room to room and to keep the plot going toward its happy resolution; and at the conclusion Don Antonio is valorized and rewarded. As Robert Hume has said, Tuke succeeds "in investing his characters with a certain potty nobility."[32]

Unlike the men on both sides who act out the moods of those who have known oppression, injustice, and defeat, Ruth is one of the first of a group of characters that would be part of the construction of the myth of the cavalier woman. The cavalier has been described as that "merry, fearless, improvident good fellow," "that perennial gallant, wearing with an air his tattered finery, and cracking broad jests with his penniless comrades."[33] Merry, fearless, and even gallant, the cavalier woman is far from improvident. John Lilburne praised his wife's civil war efforts for the "gallant and true masculine spirit" that she displayed.[34] Cavalier women can stand firm, but they prefer to fight with persuasion and, if necessary, flanking maneuvers rather than direct confrontation. Arbella says, "I have no need to compound for what's my own," but she recognizes that the Days are "marriage-jobbers" and joins Ruth's scheme (75).

To some extent, Howard and the other playwrights of these two years participate in, even as they dramatize, the struggle for control of representation. Each group of characters has a narrative, and each needs to control what is represented as history and as present entitlement. The centrality of the theme that things and people are not what they seem in the new plays and even in those chosen for revival is a natural expression of the problem of control of representation and a variant on what Michael McKeon has labeled "questions of virtue." As we have seen, Ruth also bears the weight of this major theme. She is a wonderful mimic and actress; once she acts Blunt to perfection (80). The Days, who have appropriated more than adopted her, think her obedient and enlist her in such causes as tutoring Abel in the art of lovers' language; Careless who loves her cannot believe that she is not the Days' daughter. Thus, those who use her think better of her while those who love her think worse.

The cavalier-woman types in these plays are distinguished as much by their alertness to trickery and to opportunity as by their more-discussed dashing, witty personalities. Wise in the ways of a corrupt world, they often seem to be lonely figures and can appear cold and harsh. When Loveby asks Lady Constance what he lacks to appeal to her, she tells him, "A good estate, that makes every thing handsome; nothing can look well without it."[35] In the same play, Isabella has one of her suitors beaten. Lady Ample chides Lucy severely for selling her gold, jewelry, and even her caudle cup and spoons in order to give Pallatine Younger money: "This, Lucey, is such Apostacy in Wit, / As Nature must degrade herself in Woman / To forgive it."[36] She takes Lucy into her home but only on condition that she "redeem the credit of your Sex" by getting "more Feathers than you lost to *Pallatine*" (77). Stapylton's Ericina, disguised as her brother Decio, allows the man who has humiliated her to believe that she has poisoned him and his beloved.

It is in the contrasting of details with the well-known "Restoration heroine" that the significance of the cavalier woman's differences becomes starkly evident.[37] This woman's "masculine spirt"—her courage, self-reliance, resourcefulness, and endurance—are admired. Many of these earliest heroines are widows, but as quickly as five years later, widows become obstacles to young lovers rather than heroines and are often portrayed as sexually starved and ludicrous women. By the end of these plays, the widows have been stripped of their money and their dignity;

some, such as Farquhar's Lady Bountiful, are not figured in the conclusions at all. The early Restoration woman was passionate by nature, but her sexuality was integrated into her personality. Almost immediately this passionateness became a dominant, strongly gendered characteristic: in older women ridiculous and pathetic, and in younger heroines titillating and risqué, or in villainesses inseparable from their crimes and downfall.

In the first years of the Restoration, however, the hero pursued the young widow and admired her mature beauty, independence, and "wit." The wit of the earlier heroines, although less dramatic and lively, not only tested the hero and protected her from seduction but also was part of her defense against falling victim to "the way of the world." She and her suitors openly claim to have "wit." The issues are often appearance/reality, coaxing or battering out truth, and demonstrating the ability to disguise and dissemble. It is easy to elide differences and see these women as the shrewd and randy widows of later Restoration plays *or* to make no distinctions between these characters' wit and that of the heroines of the fully developed "witty couple" of the later decades.[38] In fact, however, Howard, Dryden, and even Etherege recognize that the stakes are higher and different tests and rewards are in force. The witty couples are testing each other and parading for the audience their suitability for union; they meet their matches, and, of course, that is intended to go beyond the representation of the war between the sexes to suggest that they may be happy together. Women's wit is deployed not so much in repartée as in recognizing hypocrisy and ferreting out schemes to defraud.

* * * * * * * * *

In the early plays, survival, the securing of economic security, is the issue more than sex, and the resolution is the return of property to the royalists and the positioning of women in what will come to be called "the private sphere." Part of the social process at the end of every major war is the reintegration of men into the worlds of home and work and the re-establishment of the "balance" of power, which really means of the subordination of women. This process is inscribed in *The Committee* and the other cavalier woman plays. A number of feminist historians and critics have identified what Phyllis Mack calls "the aggressive promiscuity of the Restoration court"[39] as but one sign of the misogyny and domination strategies alive in the royalist culture. Riding on a powerful, genuinely patriarchal ideology, the royalist male became the site again of wit, language, and money. In the post-Restoration world, the only satisfying victory was a willing surrender, an embrace, and Ruth and the other cavalier women comply. They are uniformly portrayed as willingly turning over their power, authority, and money.

The conclusion of *The Committee* returns Ruth and Arbella to the position that is "right," the way the world ought to be both in public sense of property and in the private sense of marriage. Tellingly, all of the closing lines of the play are the male character's pronouncements and commands. In this play, the audience had found a wealth of lived experience, but also saw a utopian image emerging. The royalist characters are genuinely cooperative and caring; for instance, they converge on the prison to rescue Careless, and even the soldiers within help. The resolution of the play goes beyond what could be dismissed as part of the sympathetic portrait of the cavaliers to deliver a glimpse of a dreamlike, magic ending: a blending of people, an end to hostility (albeit forced on the Days), a harmonious dance in honor of the king.

The contrast between the royalist men and women is suggestive of social change, including the reassessment of the position of women. The women in "committee" or "parliament" plays and pamphlets of the decades of the 1630s through 1650s were objects of ridicule because they aspired to influence in the public sphere; Mrs. Day busies herself with her husband's business, but Ruth and Arbella are almost wholly concerned with the private, domestic sphere. Their goals are not power or wealth but happy marriages and economic security. They have a strong sense of property and of justice, but at the end, their power and property belong to Blunt and Careless. The rapid change can be mapped easily. For instance, Mistress Barebottle in the slightly earlier *Cutter of Coleman-Street* has bought Col. Jolly's estate from the Committee of Sequestrations; he marries her for it, and Cutter marries her daughter to get the rest.[40]

Perhaps most interesting for the literary critic is the triumph of male royalist discourse over puritan, city, and even female cavalier. As Bakhtin says, "Consciousness finds itself inevitably facing the necessity of *having to choose a language.*" Phallic power cannot be separated from woman's access to language.[41] Mid-seventeenth-century women display the signs of deliberative behavior, and that means above all a sense of having the right and the ability to use language. That they published and petitioned in unprecedented and remarkable numbers, that they even traveled to spread and gain support for their causes and attempted to speak in parliament is of a piece with the portrayal of Ruth and other cavalier women characters.[42] Their language is often that of war. Pyramena challenges Iberio,

> I laugh,
> To see so great a Soldier fool himself
> With a belief, that th' Enemy (the Traitor,
> As you were graciously pleas'd to call me)
> Would yield without a Summons: true it is,
> To work your Hope up to a Confidence,
> My white Flag I hung out, courted a Treaty,
> As if I held a Fort untenable,
> You'l find it Man'd, the Woman so well Man'd,
> That you may sooner take *Constantinople.*
> (*Slighted Maid*, 31)

In facing Decio, she is as articulate and forceful as Iberio. Cavendish's Voluble conducts a school for other women, and she and Madam Beaufield orchestrate the plot and its episodes. The fact that these characters are active and unrestrained associates them with the masculine rather than the feminine as these terms were being rapidly defined.

Freedom of movement as well as speech became an issue. The early playwrights gave it to women, and slightly later the breeches part appeared to allow it but actually became a strategy of ruthless control. Among the familiar marks of male misogyny and fear of women's powers are the playwrights' recurrent portrayals of women's ability to disguise themselves, to shift shapes, and to be willing to do things that the cavalier men will not. It is no accident, I think, that the breeches part gained in popularity at the moment society was attempting to re-negotiate the position of women in the private and public spheres.[43] From the bold, determined, sometimes impudent young women with masculine spirit evolved the character who was "very piquant and voluptuous in the uniform" of men. As Janet Todd says, "at least since the days when Queen Henrietta Maria went abroad in breeches," female cross-dressing "had a royalist, foreign and naughty flavour to it. The image of spiritedness, calculation and delicacy is complex."[44] Ruth moves freely about the city, goes to the prison several times, waits beneath a window with the rope ladder for the cavaliers' escape—all actions that a slightly later playwright might have written as scenes in which she wore a masculine disguise.

Men's clothes can be functional, expressions of internal character or signs of creative responses to restrictions.[45] Breeches parts, however, rather than protecting or disguising women or helping them effect a scheme, became, on the level of plot, an expression of woman as huntress, as in need of a man, and, on the level of theatrical event, an emphasis on the sex and secondary sexual characteristics of the woman, on sexual *difference*, and on what the woman did not have. It became common for playwrights to emphasize this characteristic of the cross-dressed actresses. In Dryden's *Rival Ladies* (late 1663?), Hippolito (Honoria) and Amideo (Angellina), who have been disguised as men throughout most of the play, delighted the audience by revealing "swelling Breasts" when they remove their doublets in order to duel. In contrast to Stapylton's Decio, the stereotypical female characteristics are foregrounded. Jealousy not honor motivates them, and they prefer to scratch and bite, and they use their swords so awkwardly as to be comic (act 4, sc. 3).

Soon the revelation of inadequacy became conventional. For instance, in the epilogue to Catherine Trotter's *Agnes de Castro* (1695), the actress mentions that her disguise "promises more than I can do." The episodes and plots of the plays come to emphasize that the woman has neither penis nor phallic power and privileges.[46] By the early eighteenth century, expressions of genuine disapproval of breeches parts became fairly common. Although some of these objections resurrected the Renaissance citing of Deuteronomy

22:5 and 1 Corinthians 11:14–15, others are evidence of cultural changes regarding sex and gender.[47] Just as the breeches part would come to represent something quite different by the late seventeenth century, in the post-Glorious Revolution reign of Queen Anne, so did the cavalier woman. In *The New Atalantis* (1709), Delarivière Manley describes the widow of a member of the New Cabal as typical of those who "do not in reality love *Men*; but doat on the Representation of *Men* in *Women*. Hence it is that those Ladies are so fond of the Dress *En Cavaliere*; tho' it is extremly against my liking, I would have the *Sex* distinguish'd as well by their *Garb* as by their *Manner*."[48] She especially condemns the "*bold* . . . Air of the *Hat, Feather* and *Peruke*" (2:207). The identification of the fashion with boldness and masculine freedom, in explicit contrast to feminine "modesty" and the wearing of veils, underscores the underlying issues of gender and natural order.

Dryden's brilliant Florimel as played by Nell Gwyn pointed the direction that the breeches part and the active woman would go. John Downes says that Jane Long first appeared in "Man's Habit" on the stage, perhaps as early as 1662, and that "prov'd as Beneficial to the Company, as several succeeding new Plays" (as Dulcino in Shirley's *The Grateful Servant*).[49] In fact, Thomas Killigrew, who lacked the theatrical flair and resources of his rival William Davenant, had cast an actress as Parthenia and then sent her out after the performance of Henry Glapthorne's *Argalus and Parthenia* on 28 October 1661. Pepys commented that she had the "best legs that ever I saw."[50] By 1664 the commodification of the cross-dressed and cross-cast woman was a perceptible trend. Judith Milhous has argued that economic successes such as Long's and especially Gwyn's fueled the increase in breeches parts, and Kristina Straub has pointed out how rapidly the actress's sexuality came to play an important part in the establishment of what became the dominant ideology associated with "oppositional, separate spheres for men and women."[51]

What was touted in 1660 as a trend toward a more morally uplifting theatre, the introduction of actresses, became associated with the licentiousness and immorality still identified with Restoration and eighteenth-century theatre. The prologue sometimes titled "A Prologue to introduce the first Woman that came to Act on the Stage in the Tragedy, call'd *The Moor of Venice*," concluded, "We shall purge every thing that is unclean, / Lascivious, scurrilous, impious or obscene; / And when we've put all things in this fair way / *Barebones* himself may come to see a Play."[52] By 1667 when Long played Hippolito in the Dryden-Davenant adaptation of *The Tempest*, the prologue highlighted this cross-over part and stimulated the audience's imagination:

> But, if for Shakespear we your grace implore,
> We for our Theatre shall want it more:
> Who by our dearth of Youths are forc'd t' employ

One of our Women to present a Boy.
And that's a transformation, you will say,
Exceeding all the Magick in the Play.
Let none expect in the last Act to find,
Her Sex transform'd from Man to Woman-kind.
What e'r she was before the Play began,
All you shall see of her is perfect Man.
Or if your fancy will be farther led
To find her Woman, it must be abed.

In 1672 three plays in a single season were produced with all female casts, and, again, the audience is invited to strip away the disguise.[53] The prologue to Dryden's *Secret Love* begins, "Accept us these bad times in any dress. / You'l find the sweet on't, now old Pantaloons, / Will go as far, as formerly new gowns."

Between these titillating characters and the mature cavalier women was Celestina-Florio, the creation of Thomas Killigrew's brother William and the heroine of *The Siege of Urbin*.[54] Unquestionably part of Thomas' continued commodification of the female body, Celestina was played by Ann Marshall, perhaps the first actress in a Restoration play; Nell Gwyn, then still a neophyte and just before her success as Florimel, played her maid, Melinda-Pedro. *The Siege of Urbin* is a fascinating amalgam of old ideas of human sexuality and contemporary anxieties. The prologue promises the women that the playwright will put their "reserv'd Virtues" on display to the world. After a beautiful, feminine bedchamber scene, Celestina disguises herself as a warrior to avoid a forced marriage. Through her, Killigrew evokes most of the existing and emergent objections to cross-dressing. Celestina is not motivated to dress as a man by patriotism or love, the most commonly sanctioned Renaissance excuses. Rather she hopes to die—a sinful, even damnable motive. She rejects mental and physical gendered categories. She says, "Why should not Womens hearts agree with such a strength, as our Arms have to mannage this Sword? 'tis only custome, and a tender Education, makes us lesse bold, and active, then the bravest men;—the *Amazons* we read, have done great things" (6). Her brave speeches become equally courageous deeds. Not only does she rescue Fernando from bandits, but she helps him save the Duke of Urbin in battle, and as just reward is offered the command of his guards. Later she slips into the enemy camp to rescuc the captured Fernando and once again rallies the Duke's troops and rescues him: an officer says, "the all conquering Florio, with his guards . . . with such vigour, and such force renew'd the fight, that the amaz'd Enemy, ran headlong from the Walls againe" (49).

As Florio, Celestina also attracts the love of men. The Duke seems so obsessed with "him," that he neglects all other men and women and attempts to marry Florio to his sister or another close associate in order to keep him close. At one point, the Duke says, "This storme which I have rais'd [in you] is more bewitching lovely, then thy calme gentle looks were" (9). The fire and heat, the masculine qualities, are what attract the Duke. He calls Florio "some divine substance, I have no name for!" (11) and says, "There must be something more then I discerne in this new kind of passion, which I have no name for . . . Florio captivates my heart, beyond all the beauteous Women I have seen!" (15).

Literary historians have pointed out how theories of the unfixed nature of sex as well as gender can explain such scenes, and others have found homoerotic or homosocial propensities to be stronger than heterosexual ones in Renaissance plays and their adaptations and imitations.[55] In the second half of the seventeenth century, the growing awareness and public discussion of gendered spheres naturally led to heightened awareness of the existence of masculine and feminine behaviors and characteristics within each person. In the court circle, bisexuality was widely accepted and neither unusual nor threatening and, within the circle of those influenced by the court, continued to be depicted without stigma throughout the century.[56] To a considerable extent, *The Siege of Urbin* draws upon all of these ideas.

The transitional nature of the play, however, is evident in the resolution. By the fourth act, Celestina believes she has made a mistake. Killigrew has her believe that she would have showed more courage to remain at home and remain firm "even at the altar" (37), but she also says she has become a "monster" and a "scandal" (41). From this point on, Killigrew rapidly reinscribes her femininity while allowing the masculine to appear in crises. Once she confesses to Fernando, she says that telling him "has reduc'd me to a Woman, I can now tremble at my own shadow, my courage is quite gone, and I now shake, to thinke, what I have done" (42). Even after this, however, Celestina "scatter'd [the 'enemy'] like frighted Birds, at an approaching storme" (49).

Rather than "reducing" her to woman, Killigrew elevates her with masculine charateristics even as he makes these traits ones she assumes, puts on like her armor, rather than the ones that are her essential nature and revealed in her private moments. Her shame and fear of disgrace because of her disguise give way to a happy engagement, and the Duke pronounces that he should have known her a woman because of his "sympathetic Love" and her particular kind of virtue.[57] In one adept move, Killigrew obscures the homosexual attaction and presents the female representation as the emblem of virtue that, like Dante's Beatrice, leads men to virtue and, like the domestic woman to come, is the family caretaker of moral values. Killigrew gave his audience the comforting image of a woman like the Commonwealth women who could *rise* to great feats but *was* a "real woman" at the core—one who after a crisis would "tremble" and "shake at what she had done."

This tension between the ability to assume masculine characteristics, to rise to masculine conduct, and the security of belief in an unalterable, essential, feminine nature increased with the rise of the concept of the sexes as binary oppositions. By mid-eighteenth century, critics remarked on Dorothy

Jordan kicking her dress's train "hastily out of her way."[58] Here she openly expresses the restriction that women's clothing was and calls attention to— and drew criticism for—the possibility that her most notable parts were breeches parts because the roles revealed her repressed sexual preference. Reviews of her performances often mention the "ease and elegance" with which she played the part of a man, and James Quin noted that she had "dispossessed herself of that awkward stiffness and effeminacy which so commonly attend the fair sex in breeches."[59] The recognition that women's clothing acted as "shackles of modesty"[60] and the growing condemnation of breeches parts testify to the monumental social change in beliefs and attitudes about sex and gender.

What had partaken of the anxieties over appearance/reality and of the fluidity of gender roles became an enforcement of patriarchal structures and of gendered limitations. Ann Gibbs, who had played Decio in *The Slighted Maid* in 1663, said in the epilogue, "Gentlemen, Resembling you in Shape and Courage" (lines 1–2). In contrast, no one who has watched the famous scene in which Horner pretends to believe the disguised Margery Pinchwife a "pretty boy" can miss the way she is humiliated and her sex and feminine powerlessness emphasized.[61] Indeed, she is surrounded by men, every type of man, bent on controlling her sexuality, confining her within a repressive, even repulsive marriage. Jacqueline Pearson has pointed out the number of cross-dressed heroines who disguise themselves in order to be near and serve "myopically unappreciative lovers with masochistic self-abasement," thereby reinforcing the image of woman as "passive and self-punishing."[62] Both types of breeches parts were cast to emphasize woman as sex object. Many of the actresses whose reputations were heavily based on cross-gender parts were the best-known mistresses, as Nell Gwyn, Margaret Woffington, and Dorothy Jordan were. Most were excellent dancers, and jigs and other dances could be used to accentuate the bouncing breasts and feminine hips. Competitors quickly grumbled about Nell Gwyn's jigs, and Woffington had been a rope dancer and was known into old age as an extraordinary dancer. As with Sarah Bernhardt, Marlene Dietrich, and Greta Garbo, these actresses' most attractive sexual qualities (legs, brooding eyes, body symmetry) could be foregrounded even as the audience is teased by the knowledge of the female anatomy beneath the male trousers. Sandra Gilbert and Susan Gubar offer a remarkable quotation: "they are sure of themselves; their . . . voluptuous bodies are strong, hard, slim, long, and smooth, i.e., phallic."[63]

Ursula Heise has pointed out that theatrical "transvestism," as she calls it, was perceived as threatening and disruptive in Spain where women had acted on the public stage since the mid-fourteenth century. She demonstrates that authorities attempted to repress it and finds in cross-dressing "the moment which projects an alternative structure as a viable possibility."[64] On the English stage, it usually emphatically portrayed the impossibility of escape from sex, of an "alternative structure," and, thus, served the purposes of the patriarchal ideology. There is never a question of "identity" with the disguised woman—the issue is in the minds (and sight) of everyone else. She must at every moment "act" like a man, and the audience is constantly judging her *performance*. This fact takes away the emphasis on the audience judging her effectiveness in a difficult, adult situation in (usually) the public sphere and foregrounds that she is playing a double part. As Garber says of the modern transvestite theatre, the performance becomes "a recuperative structure for the social control of sexual behavior, but also a critique of the possibility of 'representation' itself."[65]

The work of the Restoration was to restore order, and for the royalist that meant that money and property had to be restored to men, and so did discourse and wit. Thus, a hegemonic plot is exposed, and we can see the idea that structured the play and animated it, that was the "urgent work" to which the dramatists attached to the royal theatres contributed. The work of Nancy Armstrong and others has traced the establishment of the "domestic woman," and in these plays we can see this "woman of the future" pre-figured. As Raymond Williams says, art "works a social character through to its reality,"[66] and sometimes that means creating plots and solutions that the society is not yet able to recognize and articulate. The formation of clearly defined public and private spheres lurks in the shadows of the first Restoration plays, and women characters are depicted as choosing to leave the public for the private.

The competing economic and ideological languages come into play, and conclusions reveal the tensions that must be resolved. As Bakhtin points out, "A language is revealed in all its distinctiveness only when it is brought into relationship with other languages, entering with them into one single heteroglot unity of societal becoming."[67] In these plays, woman functioned as sign of the displacement of wealth, power, and language, and glimpses of the "woman of the future" emerge as testimony to the power of a patriarchal culture to re-establish itself and re-define and restrict the Other. It is also possible to argue that the suppression of women was part of the returning royalists accommodation with the indigenous power structure. As Lois Potter has demonstrated, the activity and visibility of "women on the royalist side . . . inspired hostility from parliamentarians."[68] And royalists expressed similar hostility by consistently depicting women as contributors to the disorder and turmoil caused by the parliamentarians. Susan Staves quotes a ballad by Thomas Jordan: "Then let's ha' King Charles, sayes George / Nay we'll have his son, sayes Hugh / Nay then let's ha' none says jabbering Joan, / Nay lets be all Kings, sayes Prue."[69] In the early years of the Restoration, the feminine funtioned to justify a social order and to hold together an imaginary world in which the royalist man could win the battles lost to Cromwell.

For a brief time, one of the rare moments that feminists have identified when "having an intelligent woman is fashionable" existed. Men praised women, as John Lilburne did his wife, for having "a gallant and true masculine spirit."[70] Claudine Hermann writes cynically that economics often motivate such times and continues, "let us not fool ourselves: in each of these cases, the woman will be appreciated only insofar as she *reflects*, if not a specific man, at least virile values."[71] So the cavalier woman. The Restoration theatre was licensed by the King and all the players were his servants; appropriately the stage became a vehicle for an ideology struggling for dominance, the site of hegemonic representations intended to "foster forms of consciousness" that encouraged some people to accept a position of subordination.[72] The behavior of women during the Civil War and Interregnum challenged the foundation of patriarchal assumptions and the institution of the family. Accompanied by such things as a campaign against entails and primogeniture, the Civil Marriage Act, and the shift in economic power from the country estate and household to the city and the individual, women's activities appeared to be part of a powerful challenge to social order. These plays repressed this challenge.

* * * * * * * * *

The cavalier woman remained, however, an available device for playwrights. Especially in the breeches part and in the heroine of the gay couple, vestiges survived. Both removed constraints on the representation of movement outside the home and on physical movement and language. Both provided a means for the expression of women's perspectives. Etherege's *She Would if She Could* (1668) is often cited as an archetypal Restoration comedy, and it does consolidate many major strains in the plays of the years immediately before it and anticipate those of the next decades. Peter Holland remarks that Ariana and Gatty "usurp the rake's normal role," and they foreground some of the characteristics of the cavalier woman that Ariana desires and gains only through a series of disguises.[73] She says, men "can run and ramble here and there, and everywhere."[74] Gatty and Ariana have been praised for their "clear-eyed view of the world and the people in it" and are never the victims of the forged letters. Like Ruth, these characters are aware of their need to make decisions about their own lives. In a passage with a significant choice of words, Wycherley's Hippolita admonishes herself, "Courage, Hippolita, make use of the only opportunity thou canst have to *enfranchize* thy self . . . shift for thy self."[75]

As the heroine of the "gay couple," women had equal access to language for an interlude, and the proviso scene reached its height as the true cavalier woman faded. Dryden's *Wild Gallant* sets a precedent in the scene between Isabelle and Timorous (3.1). Isabelle says forthrightly to the audience: "I'll make my own conditions." She demands to have "all the money in my disposing" and insists she can manage it better than he. As playwrights learned to exploit these parts as played by Nell Gwyn and Charles Hart, contractual agreements and repartée based upon the conflicts between men's and women's needs and desires multiplied and took on central prominence in productions.[76]

In the 1690s with a flowering of what we would call feminist activity, the cavalier-woman type was reaccentuated. In the wake of the Glorious Revolution, a number of royalist playwrights drew upon the early plays and evoked something of the poignant mood of these plays. Thomas D'Urfey's Sir Charles says, "The World's an arrant Cheat, a very Rook that never obliges you . . . he that is honest, and has no money, is no man of this world." But Philippa, who will send £20,000 to rescue the king, says, "You live . . . and are a man of it, 'till you come to a better."[77] D'Urfey exploits the potential for the breeches part to emphasize sex and vulnerability, but he gives Philippa the freedom, economic means, and public sphere involvement of the earlier heroines.

It was the new group of women playwrights, however, that found the cavalier-woman device most useful. Aphra Behn realized that economics and ideology made women subordinate, and her plays often demand the audience consider gender issues. She has one of her many unconventional women characters say that she was "pleased with the cavalier in herself."[78] Ruth, whose metaphors come from war more often than from the home, had been created to feel the cavalier in herself before the type was confirmed, and her opinions and language invigorate Behn's Hellena, Florinda, Lady Desbro (a "cavalier in her heart," *The Roundheads*, 1:349), Hippolita (whose soul is "all man," *Dutch Lover*, 1:293), and Laura Lucretia (*Feign'd Courtesan*). Her Cloris in *The Amorous Prince* goes out to find the prince who has "ruined" her, wins him, and he says that he will "still" receive her as "a gift from Heaven." The heroine of Ariadne's *She Ventures and He Wins*, Charlot, takes to the streets dressed as a man in hope of meeting "the Man I can find in my heart to take for better or worse." Her disguise will allow her, she says the liberty she needs to move through the city safely and "Besides, should I meet with the Man whose outside pleases me, 'twill be impossible by any other means to discover his Humour; for they are so used to flatter and deceive our Sex, that there's nothing but the Angel appears, tho' the Devil lies lurking within, and never so much as shews his Paw till he has got his Prey fast in his Clutches" (1). Within a short time, this heroine was again a prominent established type, and the clear association with the cavalier mind and experience lingered, even as it was used as a device to give another means of examining the issues being discussed in the work of Mary Astell and others regarding the appropriate limits and kinds of authority husbands had over wives and parents had over children.

* * * * * * * * *

The early Restoration plays that I have analyzed here are almost never read, and some, including Cowley's *Cutter of Coleman Street* and Dryden's *Wild Gallant*, have had strikingly mixed receptions from the time of their first performances.[79] They are, however, essential parts of women's history and of the history of dramatic forms, especially of the rise and development of bourgeois tragedy and the "problem play." They are a case of a changing society leading directly to radical innovations in form and, as Raymond Williams says of later plays, specifically those of Farquhar and Lillo, this development was "an obvious and necessary basis for all serious modern drama."[80] The theatre turned from the Renaissance concern with exploring human existence within an inexorable, majestic natural order toward becoming a place for eloquent critiques of love, commerce, and marriage, what Pierre Macherey calls "the basic categories of society."[81] Here, too, we can see the construction of "man" and "woman," those who would become what Armstrong identifies as "middle-class love, the stuff that modern marriages are made of."[82] The marxist critical process has been described as reaching "the heart of a text at the very moment you pass beyond it to its social context."[83] Sometimes this "heart" will be one sex's "treasure," and not the other sex's—or at least not that of another historical period's other sex. In any event, however, the "urgent work" of a cultural text is revealed, and that is what happens upon close analysis of the cavalier woman and the earliest original plays of the Restoration.

NOTES

This essay is a slightly revised version of my 1993 ASECS Presidential Address. I would like to thank my research assistant Elaine Posanka for her ingenious detective work and many trips to the library.

1. One of the few in-depth studies of the original drama of this period is Robert D. Hume's essay "Diversity and Development in Restoration Comedy," *Eighteenth-Century Studies* 5 (1972): 365–97. In it he argues correctly that the idea that the Etheregean mode dominated is unsound, and that considerable variety existed, perhaps with romantic tragicomedies and comedies of London city life in a slight majority.
2. *OED.*
3. Martin Butler, *Theatre and Crisis 1632–1642* (New York: Cambridge University Press), 161.
4. Robert Stapylton, *The Slighted Maid* (London: Thomas Dring, 1663), 17. Citations hereafter appear in the text.
5. Ronald Hutton, *Charles the Second* (New York: Oxford University Press, 1989), 100–105 and *The Restoration* (New York: Clarendon Press, 1985), 58; James R. Jones, *Country and Court* (Cambridge: Harvard University Press, 1978), 58; also much of the navy had to be paid off.
6. It had an almost unheard of initial run of thirteen nights.
7. S. A. Pakeman, *Ceylon* (London: Ernest Benn, 1964), 42–44.
8. History teaches us that these portrayals are accurate. The ordinary men of the king's forces often owned nothing and had nowhere to live. Of those who had stayed in England, some had managed to pay the fines and penalties and hold on to their property; some had enterprising family members who

had protected at least some of their estates; others had purchased their own estates at inflated rates. Up to two-thirds had been re-purchased in the north. Hutton, *Charles the Second*, 146. Those returning often had to sue in the courts or in Commons or Lords to regain their estates. City corporations resisted granting royalists restitution, and the king and parliament wrangled over writs of *quo warranto* and other means of "persuading" corporations to restore royalists' property and positions. Even the earl of Clarendon mentioned being able to afford but one meal a day and having so little fuel that his hands were sometimes too cold to hold a pen. Ibid., 74–75, 146–47. Some saw permanent national change. Sir John Oglander wrote, "most of the ancient gentry were either extinct or undone . . . so that none of them could appear again as gentlemen. Death, plunder, sales and sequestrations sent them to another world or beggar's bush." He went on to say that "base men" had taken their places, and Swift saw "the Noblest Blood of England" shed in the rebellion, leaving only "Minors" or lesser families. Quoted in Michael McKeon, *The Origins of the English Novel* (Baltimore: Johns Hopkins University Press, 1987), 228.

9. The character may, in fact, be what Antonio Gramsci has identified as a hegemonic apparatus. The term is Gramsci's and is usefully explained by Raymond Williams in *Marxism and Literature* (Oxford: Oxford University Press, 1988). Briefly, it is any cultural form or institution that participates in important ways in the dynamic process that is "hegemony," what Gramsci calls "a moving equilibrium," and that emphasizes the fact that the dominant culture is, in Williams' words, always in the state of being "resisted, limited, altered, challenged" (112). Throughout this paper I am extending and applying some of the theories of Gramsci and of a configuration of social and literary theoretical books, the most important of which are Gramsci's *Selections from the Prison Notebooks* (New York: International, 1992), Raymond Williams' *Marxism and Literature*, Fredric Jameson's *The Political Unconscious* (Ithaca: Cornell University Press, 1986) and "Metacommentary," *PMLA* 86 (1971): 9–18, and Mikhail Bakhtin's *The Dialogic Imagination* (Austin: University of Texas Press, 1981).

10. Claudine Hermann, *The Tongue Snatchers*, trans. Nancy Kline (Lincoln: University of Nebraska Press, 1989), 38.

11. "'The Woman's Part': Richardson, Defoe, and the Horrors of Marriage" in *The Past as Prologue*, ed. Carla H. Hay and Syndy Conger (New York: AMS Press, 1994), 205–31.

12. On the popularity and changes in the sacque in the Restoration and eighteenth century see Aileen Ribeiro, *A Visual History of Costume: The Eighteenth Century* (London: Batsford, 1983), 44, 56, 58, 61, 72, 74, and 144. The cavalier hat had been popular in the 1630s and after the Restoration went through several modifications, first as a riding hat, and then in increasingly feminine styles; it is still recognizable in the Gainsborough or Marlborough hat of the late eighteenth century. See Marion Sichel, *Costume Reference 3: Jacobean, Stuart and Restoration* (Boston: Plays, Inc., 1977), 31, and R. Turner Wilcox, *The Mode in Hats and Headdress* (New York: Scribners, 1948), 108 and illustrations. Compare, for example, Van Dyck's "Queen Henrietta Maria" in hunting

clothes (c. 1634) and Gainsborough's portrait of Elizabeth Hallett, "The Morning Walk" (c. 1785).

13. Samuel Pepys, *Diary*, 11 vols. (Berkeley: University of California Press, 1970–1983), 3:175–75.

14. *The Diary of John Evelyn* (Oxford: Clarendon Press, 1955) 3:463. The note mentions that the maids of honor and others had been wearing the fashion years earlier, 463 n. 3.

15. See Ernesto Laclau, *Politics and Ideology in Marxist Theory* (London: NLB, 1977), 148–49. He defines this behavior as interventions in national life, which may take such forms as protest movements and legalized activity, such as petitioning. Historians have documented many examples of women's behavior between 1630 and 1665 that fit Laclau's description. See, for example, Patricia Higgins, "The Reactions of Women" in *Politics, Religion, and the English Civil War*, ed. Brian Manning (London: Edward Arnold, 1973), especially 214–17; Margaret Ezell, *The Patriarch's Wife* (Chapel Hill: University of North Carolina, 1987), 83–92; Keith Thomas, "Women and the Civil War Sects," *Past and Present* 13 (1958): 55. There was an important exhibit, "The Weaker Vessel," at the Nottingham Castle Museum in the summer of 1992 that celebrated women's activities during the mid-seventeenth century.

16. Among the widows were Lady Constance Nonesuch in *The Wild Gallant*, Lady Wealthy in *The English Monsieur*, Lady Cockwood in *She Would if She Cou'd*, Mistress Barebottle in *Cutter of Coleman Street*, Madame Beaufield and Mrs. Simpleton in *The Variety*, and Lady Ample in *The Wits*.

17. This play was often performed as *The French Dancing Master* in the Restoration because of the popularity of the part of Galliard, played by John Lacy. The quotation is from the Moseley edition of 1649, pp. 1–2.

18. Peter Holland, *The Ornament of Action* (Cambridge: Cambridge University Press, 1979), 83.

19. Rosalind Miles, "Sisters under the armour plating," article in the *London Times*, 29 July 1992, 5a.

20. Margaret George, *Women in the First Capitalist Society* (Urbana: University of Illinois Press, 1988), 30, 37–39. It was usual, of course, for women to manage the home and the estate during times when the husband was absent. Moreover, it was common for women to be sent to work with the Committee of Sequestration; in fact, men advised other men to send their wives. In addition to George, see Elaine Hobby, *Virtue of Necessity* (Ann Arbor: University of Michigan Press, 1989), 14–15; Thomas Knyvett's letters reprinted in *Politics, Religion, and Literature in the Seventeenth Century*, eds., William Lamont and Sybil Oldfield (London: Dent, 1975), 95–96, and Hilda Smith, *Reason's Disciples* (Urbana: University of Illinois Press, 1982), 54–55. Women's armed defenses of their estates were not unknown, cf., George, 192–93. Feminist scholars and historians as a group would agree with Phyllis Mack that "the burgeoning feminism of the seventeenth century" was "squelched" by "the cult of sentimentalism" and the "rise of the domestic woman." "The History of Women in Early Modern Britain," *Comparative Studies in Society and History* 28 (1986): 719.

21. Robert Howard, *The Commitee* (London: 1692). Citations in the text are to this edition. John Evelyn saw the play 27 November 1662 at the Queen

Mother's Court, *Diary* 3:345. Evelyn called the play "ridiculous," but admired Lacy's performance. Pepys saw the King's Company perform it at their new Bridges Street Theatre on 12 June 1663, *London Stage*. This section grew out of my discussion of the early Restoration theatre as hegemonic apparatus in *Spectacular Politics: Theatrical Power and Mass Culture in Early Modern England* (Baltimore: Johns Hopkins University Press, 1993); a few of the ideas are repeated.

22. I base this statement in part on the pre-Restoration plays that were most successfully revived. Among the city comedies were Beaumont and Fletcher's *Wit without Money*; Jonson's *Epicoene, Bartholomew Fair*, and *Alchemist*; Massinger's *New Way to Pay Old Debts*; Davenant's *The Wits*, and Shirley's *The Changes* (as *Love in a Maze*). Wendy Griswold points out that 54 of the 58 productions in 1661–62 were pre-Restoration plays, *Renaissance Revivals* (Chicago: University of Chicago Press, 1986), 115.

23. John Lacy, the original Teague, was a great favorite of the king, who had his portrait painted in the characters of Teague, Scruple (*The Cheats*), and Galliard (*Variety*). The portrait by Michael Wright is at Windsor Castle.

24. Robert D. Hume, *The Development of English Drama in the Seventeenth Century* (Oxford: Clarendon Press, 1976), 114; Arthur H. Scouten, "Plays and Playwrights" in *The Revels History of Drama in English*, 7 vols. (London: Methuen, 1975–78), 5:166–69.

25. As cultural theorists have pointed out, every speech "tastes of the context and contexts in which it has lived its socially charged life." Bakhtin, *The Dialogic Imagination*, 293.

26. Raymond Williams, *The Long Revolution* (New York: Columbia University Press, 1961), 47; the term is from Erich Fromm's *Escape from Freedom* (1941; New York: Avon, 1966), see especially 304–9.

27. Other characters, such as Lucia in *Cutter of Coleman Street*, Constance in *The English Mounsieur*, Lady Constance in *The Wild Gallant*, Portia in *The Adventures of Five Hours*, Graciana in *The Comical Revenge*, and even Pyramena in *The Slighted Maid*, are cavalier women who both bridge and lay bare social groups.

28. By that time, of course, the audience and Ruth know that she is the daughter of a royalist, and her oath is honest. Things are not what they seem to Careless, and Careless calls himself, rightly, a compounder. Like two popular revived plays, *Epicoene* and *The Scornful Lady*, *The Committee* through Ruth gives the audience the pleasure of knowing that things are as they ought to be. Like Epicoene and Welford who can move successfully in both the male and female worlds, Ruth can move in both the puritan and the cavalier societies.

29. Susan Staves, *Players' Scepters* (Lincoln: University of Nebraska Press, 1979), 52, 203.

30. Historians often comment on this behavior; Arthur Bryant, for instance, says, "The Cavaliers in Parliament in no way shared their sovereign's capacity for forgetting the past," *King Charles II* (London: Longmans, Green, 1932), 140.

31. Lois Potter also calls it "a comic ending to a tragic sequence," *Secret Rites and Secret Writing*, (New York: Cambridge University Press, 1990), 111.

32. Hume, "Diversity and Development in Restoration Comedy," 370.

33. Alfred Harbage, *Cavalier Drama*, (New York: Modern Language Association, 1936), 188.
34. Quoted in Smith, *Reason's Disciples*, 54–55.
35. *The Wild Gallant* in *The Works of John Dryden*, vol. 8, ed. John Harrington Smith, Dougold MacMillan, et al. (Berkeley: University of California Press, 1967), 3.1.28–29. Citations hereafter in the text are to this edition.
36. William Davenant, *The Wits* in *The Works of Sir William Davenant*, 2 vols. (London, 1673), 2:76. Citations hereafter in the text are to this edition and volume.
37. On somewhat similar female characters in early seventeenth-century plays, see Simon Shepherd, *Amazons and Warrior Women* (New York: St. Martin's, 1981), 67–92 and 151–67.
38. Shepherd discusses Shakespeare's witty women and contrasts them to other seventeenth-century playwrights' characters. His work suggests that the gay couple of the 1670s draws closer to Shakespeare's *Amazons and Warrior Women*; see especially 162–67. Peter Holland, however, demonstrates that the "gay couple" was "the most distinctive new contribution to comedy of the 1660s." *The Ornament of Action*, 82–86.
39. Mack, "The History of Women in Early Modern Britain," 716; see also Elaine Hobby on signs of misogyny in the Restoration court circle, *Virtue of Necessity*, 85–88 and 190–91. In *The First English Actresses*, (New York: Cambridge University Press, 1992), 43ff, Elizabeth Howe notes the amount of violence against women and associates it with the control strategies Susan Brownmiller has identified in rape.
40. Susan Staves notes that "marriage was . . . used by both sides to get control of property" and that Buckingham had married Mary Fairfax and recovered his property, *Players' Scepters*, 205.
41. Bakhtin, *The Dialogic Imagination*, 295; Herrmann, *The Tongue Snatchers*, 23, 58–61, 97.
42. See Hobby, *Virtue of Necessity*, 11–21, 60, 85–88; she remarks upon women's considerable mobility. See also Thomas, "Women and the Civil War Sects," 55; Ezell, *The Patriarch's Wife*, 82–100. Janet Todd discusses a parallel example of a woman, that of Mary Carleton, who "reveals her strength by her writing in trouble and by her general outrage at woman's oppressed situation," *The Sign of Angellica* (New York: Columbia University Press, 1989), 53–55.
43. On the growing popularity see Pat Rogers, "The Breeches Part" in Paul-Gabriel Boucé, *Sexuality in Eighteenth-Century Britain*, (Tototowa: Manchester University Press, 1982), 248–50. On the functions of cross-dressing, see Jacqueline Pearson, *The Prostituted Muse* (New York: St. Martin's, 1988), 100–101; her examples are almost entirely from plays after 1675. J. H. Wilson calculates that of the 300 plays first performed in London between 1660 and 1700, eighty-nine contained breeches parts; cited in Pearson, 101, and most other studies of cross-dressing.
44. Todd, *The Sign of Angellica*, 55.
45. See Michelene Wandor, *Carry On, Understudies: Theatre and Sexual Politics* (London: Routledge and Kegan Paul, 1981), 25–26. Dorothy Jordan may be an example of an actress who made cross-dressing seem a double expression of internal character—hers and her character's. James Boaden described her

acting as "NATURE herself shewing us the *heart of her own mystery*," quoted in Marsden, "Modesty Unshackled," in *Studies in Eighteenth-Century Culture*, ed. Patricia Craddock and Carla H. Hay (East Lansing, MI: Colleagues Press, 1992), 29.

46. Hélène Cixous, *The Newly Born Woman* (Minneapolis: University of Minnesota Press, 1975), 95–96. Augustin Daly quotes a poem about Peg Woffington, "Your very sex receives the Dart / And almost thinks there's nothing wanting," *Woffington: A Tribute to the Actress and the Woman* (1888; New York: Blom, 1972), 28. Moll Flanders is always afraid she will "betray" herself—show what she lacks—when she is disguised as a man.

47. Among the critics who have discussed this change in some detail are Rudolf M. Dekker and Lotte van de Pol, who also trace reactions to historical women discovered in men's clothing, *The Tradition of Female Transvestism in Early Modern Europe* (New York: St. Martin's Press, 1989), see especially 85–90; Kristina Straub, *Sexual Suspects: Eighteenth-Century Players and Sexual Ideology* (Princeton: Princeton University Press, 1992), 48, 127, 131; Terry Castle, *Masquerade and Civilization* (Palo Alto, CA: Stanford University Press, 1986), 46-47, 73-74, and Marsden, "Modesty Unshackled," 21–23 and 25.

48. Delarivière Manley, *Secret Memoirs and Manners of Several Persons of Quality, of both Sexes. from the New Atalantis*, ed. Patricia Köster (Gainesville, FL: Scholars' Facsimiles and Reprints, 1971), 2:206.

49. The footnote to this part of the text points out the problems with this identification and the date. In addition to the ambiguity of the wording, Hume and Milhous note that the paragraph giving the information was added in the margin of the 1708 edition. See John Downes, *Roscius Anglicanus*, ed. Robert Hume and Judith Milhous (London: Society for Theatre Research, 1987), 60, notes 169 and 170.

50. Pepys, *Diary* 2:203; Judith Milhous, *Thomas Betterton and the Management of Lincoln's Inn Fields 1695-1708* (Carbondale: Southern Illinois University Press, 1979), 22. Milhous also cites Killigrew's October 1664 all-female production of his *Parson's Wedding* and a "series" of play revivals "acted all by Women" in 1672; see 22 and 31.

51. Straub, *Sexual Suspects*, 88 et passim; see also Howe, *First English Actresses*, 36–37.

52. Pierre Danchin, *The Prologues and Epilogues of the Restoration*, 4 vols. (Nancy: Presses Universitaires de Nancy, 1981), 1:56.

53. Howe, *The First English Actresses*, 57–59.

54. This play was probably performed in 1664; it was published in *Four New Playes* (Oxford, 1666). Peter Holland assumes its performance, *The Ornament of Action*, 83; the *London Stage* prints the Bodleian manuscript cast list, 1:82.

55. Stephen Orgel gives many examples of the Renaissance fear of sex changes, "Nobody's Perfect: Or Why Did the English Stage Take Boys for Women?" *South Atlantic Quarterly* 88 (1989): 10-16, and on homosexual elements, 17, 20–24; J. W. Binns, "Women or Transvestites on the Elizabethan Stage?" *Sixteenth-Century Journal* 5 (1974): 95–96, 101–3; Jean Howard, "Crossdressing, The Theatre, and Gender Struggle in Earluy Modern England," *Shakespeare Quarterly* 39 (1988): 421–24; Stephen Greenblatt,

"Fiction and Friction" in *Shakespearean Negotiations* (Berkeley: University of California Press, 1988), 66–93.

56. This is particularly true earlier; for instance, Orgel points out that "there is no indication whatever that Shakespeare is doing something sexually daring" with Ganymede-Rosalind, "Nobody's Perfect," 22. Although not so prominent, the theme of the cross-dressed player able to arouse sexual feelings in both sexes continued throughout the century. A poem addressed to Woffington ends, "Would lavish nature, who her gave / This double pow'r to please, / In Pity give her both to save / A double power to ease," quoted in Daly, *Woffington*, 19.

57. Joe Cady argues that seventeenth-century language shows an awareness of "different sexual orientations" and discriminated among kinds of heterosexual love. "Renaissance Awareness and Language for Heterosexuality" in *Renaissance Discourses of Desire*, ed. Claude J. Summers and Ted-Larry Pebworth (Columbia: University of Missouri Press, 1993), 143–58.

58. Quoted from James Boaden's biography in Marsden, "Modesty Unshackled," 30, and see her useful discussion, 21–35. This section has been influenced by her article. Kristina Straub also notes that "erasure of sexual ambiguity" is common by mid-eighteenth century, *Sexual Suspects*, 134 et passim. Madeleine Kahn finds anxiety expressed about the "instability of gender categories in the many cross-narrated novels of the same period, *Narrative Transvestism* (Ithaca: Cornell University Press, 1991).

59. Quoted in Rogers, "The Breeches Part," 256.

60. Sandra M. Gilbert and Susan Gubar note episodes in later novels, including James Joyce's *Ulysses* in which boys are disciplined in schools in which they were dressed as girls and confined in tightly laced corsets, *Sexchanges*, vol. 2 of *No Man's Land* (New Haven: Yale University Press, 1984), 332–33.

61. Wandor describes how cross-dressing can function by way of responses such as ridicule as a way of containing rebellion. She alludes to the way it allows misogynist jokes, *Carry On, Understudies*, 25.

62. Pearson, *Prostituted Muse*, 102.

63. Gilbert and Gubar, *Sexchanges*, 350; the quotation, p. 335, is from Robert Stoller. As I have argued in *Spectacular Politics*, the greatest players may have bisexual characteristics and fascination; along the same lines, Marjorie Garber describes Sir Laurence Olivier's "sinister amalgam of male power-hunger and female seductivenss," *Vested Interests: Cross-Dressing and Cultural Anxiety* (New York: Routledge, 1992), 34.

64. Ursula Heise, "Transvestism and the Stage Controversy in Spain and England 1580–1680," *Theatre Journal* 44 (1992): 372. There is evidence that the same kinds of responses occurred in England by the last quarter of the eighteenth century. See Straub, *Sexual Suspects*; Marsden, "Modesty Unshackled"; and Rogers, "The Breeches Part," 244–57.

65. Garber, *Vested Interests*, 353.

66. Williams, *The Long Revolution*, 69.

67. Bakhtin, *The Dialogic Imagination*, 411.

68. Potter, *Secret Rites and Secret Writing*, 79–80.

69. Staves, *Players' Scepters*, 6.

70. Quoted in Hilda Smith, *Reason's Disciples*, 54-55.

71. Hermann, *The Tongue Snatchers*, 63, emphasis mine.
72. Morag Shiach, *Discourse on Popular Culture* (Palo Alto: Stanford University Press, 1989), 17.
73. Holland works their role out in terms of their control of the forestage area, *The Ornament of Action*, 52–54.
74. *She Would if She Could*, 1.2.166–67, in *The Plays of Sir George Etherege*, ed. Michael Cordner (Cambridge: Cambridge University Press, 1982), 126.
75. *The Gentleman Dancing Master* (1672), 2.1, emphasis mine, in *The Complete Plays of William Wycherley*, ed. Gerald Weales (New York: Norton, 1977), 155.
76. The performance of Hart and Gwyn in James Howard's *All Mistaken* (1665) is usually cited as a watershed, and the revivals of a series of original Restoration plays as evidence of how Gwyn's performances, personality, and well-publicized personal life brought the part of the witty woman to its height; see, for instance, Howe, *First English Actresses*, 67–68. This later repartée was more like the "verbal tennis match" Shepherd identifies in early seventeenth-century plays than like the dialogue in the earliest Restoration plays; see *Amazons and Warrior Women*, 151–59.
77. Thomas D'Urfey, *The Royalist* [1682], 16.
78. Aphra Behn, *Love-Letters between a Nobleman and his Sister*, (London: Virago, 1987), 117–18. Marilyn Williams calls this character, Sylvia, a sign that Behn is "male-identified" and finds Sylvia the representation of libertine ideology, *Raising their Voices*, (Detroit: Wayne State University, 1990), 216. Citations in the text to Behn's plays are from *The Works of Aphra Behn*, ed. Montagu Summers, 6 vols. (London: Heineman, 1915).
79. Dryden's play, for instance, failed in 1663 and again in 1667; we possess only the text of the revision, Hume, "Diversity and Development in Restoration Comedy," 371.
80. Williams, *The Long Revolution*, 256 and 261.
81. Pierre Macherey, *A Theory of Literary Production* (London: Routledge & Kegan Paul, 1986), 247; he is speaking of Defoe's *Moll Flanders*.
82. Nancy Armstrong, *Desire and Domestic Fiction* (New York: Oxford University Press, 1987), 6 passim.
83. Fredric Jameson, "Criticism in History" in *The Ideologies of Theory* (Minneapolis: University of Minnesota Press, 1988) 1:121.

The Cognitive Value of Confusion and Obscurity in the German Enlightenment: Leibniz, Baumgarten, and Herder

JEFFREY BARNOUW

The Cartesian identification of rational thought with knowledge grounded in clear and distinct 'ideas' (representations in and to the mind) at first cast a shadow of opprobrium on obscure and confused representations,[1] but eventually it provoked a reaction which brought light and definition to dark and indistinct mental phenomena and powers. These make up by far the greater part not only of our mental activity but of our thinking. Two principal impulses of this reaction were Leibniz's reconceiving the intrinsic confusion of sensation and Baumgarten's use of this innovative conception as the basis of a new science and art, aesthetics. The purpose of this discipline was originally "perfecting sensuous cognition as such,"[2] that is, as confused.

Aesthetics would therefore not seek to improve sensuous ideas by rendering them less confused, let alone making them distinct (which would undermine their very constitution), but rather to discover what the virtues of confusion itself were and see that they were exercised and appreciated. In earlier essays I have elucidated some advantages of the inherent confusion of sensation as recognized by Leibniz and Baumgarten[3] and discerned a grudging and back-handed acknowledgement of analogous virtues of passion as 'confused' perception or thought on the part of Descartes, Malebranche, and Hutcheson.[4]

Might a similar case be made for representations that do not attain clarity, namely, that their obscurity is not a deficiency but has cognitive value? There are many passages in Herder's writings where 'dark' or 'obscure ideas' take on a particular power and resonance. Is this part of an irrationalist reaction against Enlightenment epistemology? I will argue, on the contrary, that Herder's positive evaluation of the obscure carries forward a main theme of Leibniz's insight into the virtues of confused ideas. First, however, an analysis of the Leibnizian conception of sensation as confused will illuminate Baumgarten's intention in founding aesthetics.

Leibniz on Confused Ideas

In the first published philosophical paper reflecting his mature philosophy, Leibniz began by improving on Descartes' characterization of "the different kinds and the criteria of ideas."

> Knowledge is *clear*, therefore, when it makes it possible for me to recognize the thing represented. Clear knowledge, in turn, is either confused or distinct. It is *confused* when I cannot enumerate one by one the marks [*notas*] which are sufficient to distinguish the thing from others, even though the thing may in truth have such marks and constituents into which its concept [*notio*] can be resolved. Thus we know colors, odors, flavors, and other particular objects of the senses clearly enough and discern them from each other but only by the simple evidence of the senses and not by marks that can be stated.[5]

Confused knowledge takes ideas simply as they are given, as unanalyzed wholes which may include many undifferentiated elements fused together. When Leibniz repeated this explanation two years later, he added, "In this way we sometimes know *clearly*, . . . if a poem or a picture is well done or badly, because it has a certain 'something, I know not what' which either satisfies or repels us. But when I can explain [*expliquer*, perhaps better rendered 'make explicit'] the marks I have, my knowledge is called distinct."[6]

The *je ne sais quoi* offers an analogy for the confused nature of sensation. We cannot explain to a blind man what red is; it has to be experienced. But the 'idea' of red is not therefore logically simple.

> The concepts of these qualities are composite and can be resolved, for they certainly have their causes. Likewise we sometimes see painters and other artists correctly judge what has been done well or done badly; yet they are often unable to give a reason for their judgment but tell the inquirer that the work which displeases them lacks "something, I know not what."[7]

The composite nature of color is a 'con-fusion' constituting sensation in a way similar to the unformulated judgments on which artistic creation and appreciation rely. Yet the constitution of color obviously depends on the constitution of human sensibility. In *Nouveaux Essais sur l'Entendement Humain*, Philalèthe, who stands for and quotes from Locke, says "If our senses were acute enough, sensible qualities such as 'the yellow color of gold, would then disappear, and instead of it we should see an admirable texture of parts.'" Théophile, speaking for Leibniz, answers that "the color yellow is a reality, all the same, like the rainbow," and that "if our eyes became better equipped or more penetrating, so that some colors or other qualities disappeared from our view, others would apparently [that is, appearingly] arise out of them."[8] By extension the condensation implied in con-fused representation can occur at various levels, and the wholes we grasp as simple, by ignoring or being ignorant of their composition, have their own reality and validity.

For Leibniz, sensation is perception accompanied by awareness: "Not all perception is sensation, but . . . there is also insensible perception. For example, I could not have the sensation of [*sentire*] green unless I perceived the blue and yellow from which it results. At the same time I do not have the sensation of blue and yellow, unless a microscope is used."[9] In the *Nouveaux Essais* this is put in terms of the idea of green being composed of the ideas of blue and of yellow, but the point is, once again, that the idea of green appears as simple as that of blue, so the latter must also be "regarded as simple only in appearance."[10] It is evident that this conception of sensation as constitutively confused is intimately connected with Leibniz's seminal idea of "minute perceptions" which we become aware of or sense only in a cumulative aggregate.

Leibniz holds that confused knowledge is opposed to distinct only as a relative differentiation within a continuum. Distinct "is the knowledge of an assayer who discerns the true gold from the false by means of certain tests or marks which make up the definition of gold. But distinct knowledge has degrees, because ordinarily the conceptions which enter into the definitions will themselves be in need of definition, and are only known confusedly."[11] No concept is ever wholly free of a residual confusion from its sensuous origin.

A nice expression of the advantage presented by the holism or con-fusion of sense is Leibniz's answer to Bayle's criticism of his "system of pre-established harmony" in which Leibniz uses the analogy of reading a musical score and perceiving the melody. Bayle argues that the soul must recognize the sequence of notes and thus perceive them individually. Leibniz answers, "it suffices that the soul has included them in its confused thoughts in the same way that it has a thousand things in its memory without thinking of them distinctly."[12] What is sensed or consciously perceived is the melody; if we attend to the individual notes, we lose the melody, the *sense* of the whole.

The context of this example is a vindication of Leibniz's idea that "the present is pregnant with the future" on the grounds that our thoughts are never simple and the mind is accordingly led from one to the next. It is "present perceptions, along with their regulated tendency to change in conformity to what is outside, which form the musical score which the soul reads." This fine analogy for perception as an ongoing process implies that any (artifically isolated) sensation, whatever its apparent immediacy, will be the cumulative result of innumerable infinitessimal contributions from past perceptions. Memory is articulated, below the reach of language, by fine networks of association. The confusion of sense is a token of its continuity with past and future; what is present in sensation has a depth or penumbra that has accrued to it through associations.

In this connection Leibniz grants "spontaneity to confused and involuntary thoughts," while recognizing how directly this differs from the traditional view, "there is spontaneity in the confused as well as the distinct. In another sense, however, we are justified in speaking, as did the ancients, of that which consists of confused thoughts, where there is an element of the involuntary and unknown, as perturbations or passions." On the one hand, 'confused thoughts', taken as including sense qualities, constitute wholes which are aesthetically or practically advantageous even though (or perhaps because) they do not enable or even allow us to know what they are composed of. They afford a kind of spontaneity or facilitation to human action. On the other hand, 'confused thoughts' are clouded by passion which restricts freedom. Leibniz evokes a Platonic Christian version of this: "Our confused thoughts represent the body or the flesh and constitute our imperfection."[13]

In another context Leibniz explicitly qualifies the Cartesian and Malebranchian view that:

> confused thoughts mark our imperfection, passions, and dependence on a mass of external things or matter, while the perfection, force, empire, liberty and action of the soul consist principally in our distinct thoughts. However it does not cease to be true that at bottom confused thoughts are nothing else than a multitude of thoughts which are in themselves like the distinct, but which are so small that each separately does not excite our attention and cause itself to be distinguished. We can even say that there is all at once a virtually infinite number of them contained in our sensations. It is in this that the great difference between confused and distinct thoughts really consists.[14]

This appraisal reveals advantages for human practice in the confused character of sensuous ideas, even where it stems from their relation to appetites and passions. Leibniz's conception of 'minute perceptions' serves to show how restricted and restrictive the exclusive Cartesian focus on clear and distinct ideas is:

> At every moment there is in us an infinity of perceptions, unaccompanied by awareness or reflection; that is, of alterations in the soul itself, of which we are unaware because these impressions are either too minute and too numerous, or else too *united*, so that they are not sufficiently distinctive on their own. But when they are combined with others they do nevertheless have their effect and make themselves felt, at least confusedly, within the whole.[15]

Every sensation is a *"assemblage confus,"* emerging in consciousness. "By virtue of these minute perceptions the present is big with the future and burdened [*chargé*] with the past."[16]

The indistinctness of sensation creates relative wholes that can be dealt with far more easily in practical life than the constituent elements taken singly. Leibniz's conception of the development of character and motivation suggests that, taken strictly, no action is completely voluntary (informed solely by distinct ideas), nor would it be a reasonable ideal. "All our undeliberated actions result from a conjunction of minute perceptions; and even our customs and passions, which have so much influence when we do deliberate, come from the same source; for these tendencies come into being gradually, and so without the minute perceptions we would not have acquired these noticeable dispositions.[17]

A final illustration of the way in which sensations which seem immediate are actually the result of compounding many others that were registered without being directly noticed is the contrast that Leibniz draws between two kinds of judgment—a distinction that is similar to Kant's later opposition of logical and aesthetic judgment.[18]

> A mathematician may have precise knowledge of the nature of nine- and ten-sided figures, because he has the means for constructing them, yet not be able to tell one from the other on sight. The fact is that a laborer or an engineer, perhaps knowing little enough of the nature of the figures, may have an advantage over a great geometrician in being able to tell them apart just by looking and without counting; just as there are porters and pedlars who will say what their loads weigh, to within a pound—the world's ablest expert in statics could not do as well. It is true that this empiric's kind of knowledge, gained through long practice, can greatly facilitate swift action such as the engineer often needs in emergencies where any delay would put him in danger. Still, this clear image that one may have of a regular ten-sided figure or of a 99-pound weight—this accurate sense that one may have of them—consists merely in a confused idea.[19]

Such a sense of the whole works, in Leibniz's view, in much the same way sensation itself does. The same readiness of response comes with sensation, not because sensation is something immediate, instinctual, but, on the contrary, because sensation imperceptibly—like an empiric's knowing—draws on a distillation of past experience in the form of myriad minute perceptions. This is an insight into sensation which is developed by Baumgarten under the heading of confused ideas and taken further, under a different description, by Herder.

Baumgarten on Confused Ideas

In his 1735 dissertation Baumgarten held that poetry represented a sensuous knowledge complementary to the rational mode exemplified by philosophy, and he identified sensuous ideas with confused ones, alluding to Christian Wolff's usage as a precedent: "since an appetite which follows from a confused representation of the good [that is, its object] is called sensuous, and a confused representation is gained through the lower part of the cognitive faculty just as an obscure one is, one can apply the same term to the representations."[20] Wolff had divided the cognitive faculty into upper and lower parts, granting sensuous knowledge a certain status. Baumgarten enhanced its worth by arguing that only confused ideas could be poetic.

Following Leibniz's definitions, Baumgarten held that because obscure ideas do not contain sufficient marks or identifying features to allow us to recognize their objects and to distinguish them from others, clear representations are more poetic than obscure ones. Conversely, however, distinct ones are not sensuous and thus not at all poetic.[21] The dissertation, focusing on expressive more than epistemological value but still affirming that poetry is a form of knowledge, found advantages in confused but not in obscure ideas. Baumgarten called for a new science "which might direct the lower cognitive faculty in knowing things sensuously," just as logic guides rational cognition. Referring to a classical Greek opposition between *aistheta* (things perceived) and *noeta* (things known) and identifying the latter with the object of logic, he dubbed the new science "*aesthetica*," the discipline of *aisthesis* or sensuous knowledge, including sense perception and sensuous imagination.[22]

In later lectures on aesthetics Baumgarten claimed to find the notion of confusion in the Greek root of his term: "In Plato *aistheta* are opposed to *noetois* as indistinct to distinct representations. . . . As they made *logike*, the science of the distinct, from *logikos*, the distinct, so from *aisthetos* we make *aisthetike*, the science of all that is sensuous."[23] There was precedent for these ideas in Plato. Baumgarten may well have been thinking of *Republic* 523–25, concerning the knowledge which leads the philosopher up out of becoming and toward being and rationality. Socrates distinguishes between the cases in which perception does not lead to thought because we are satisfied with the "judgment of the senses," and others in which sense perception gives conflicting reports that call for reflection and reasoning in the form of calculation. *Aisthesis*, sense perception, can discriminate relatively between bigger and smaller, softer and harder; but nothing is essentially big or small, soft or hard, and the same object is big or small, soft or hard, depending on the context. Sight perceives large and small "not separated but confused [*sungkechumenon*]," and intellect is therefore forced to distinguish big from small and view them as distinct from one another. This is the point, Socrates says, at which we first ask what the big and the small are (essentially or by definition) and are led to distinguish the intelligble (*noeton*) from the visible, a crucial step in the progress toward being and truth and rationality.

Aristotle also characterizes what is known by *aisthesis* as being confused, but he is less dismissive of it than Plato. The beginning of the

Physics defines scientific knowledge as knowledge of the principles, causes, or elements of the matter in question, but adds that acquisition of such knowledge cannot start from these. We must start from things that are clearer to us, though they are confused (*sungkechumena*) and less clear in their own nature, and progress by gradual steps to what is intrinsically more knowable. The whole is best known to sense perception but contains many elements which must remain undifferentiated for sense. It is only through analysis of what is compounded or confused, though taken at first as a whole, that we come to know it through its constituent factors.[24] It is this sense of confusion particularly that Leibniz developed further.

Baumgarten referred to *aesthetica* in his *Metaphysica* of 1739 as the science of sensuously knowing and presenting what one knows (*sensitive cognoscendi et proponendi*). The Leibnizian background of this was evident where "*repraesentatio non distincta*" was called *sensitiva*, and "confused thinking" (*confuse cogito*) defined as that in which one does not distinguish the marks (*notas*) of the object of thought.[25] Baumgarten does not directly address the question, nor overtly use the analogy or example of the confused constitution of sense itself, although it is contained in the very definition he gives aesthetics, insofar as 'sensuous' is equated with 'confused'. Still he affirms in a general way, that an idea may be lively, rich, and fruitful in proportion to its confusion. The kind of advantage he will draw from the 'confusion' of sensuous ideas is shown in §517 of *Metaphysica*: "The more marks a perception contains, the stronger it is," and "a confused perception which includes more than a distinct one is stronger than it" and is thus called 'pregnant'.[26]

Baumgarten answered his own call for the new science in 1750 with the first volume of his *Aesthetica*. In its first paragraph he defined aesthetics as "the science of sensitive cognition," and as "the theory of the liberal arts, low-level epistemology [*gnoseologia inferior*], the art of fine thinking [*ars pulchre cogitandi*] and the art of the 'analogue of reason'."[27] This last expression was first used by Christian Wolff to designate the reason-like capacity in animals (and human beings) which Leibniz characterized as "a kind of inference [*consécution*] which imitates reason" by anticipating the recurrence of similar cases from past associations of ideas.[28]

Leibniz compares this mode of inference to that of Empiricist physicians (presumably in the Hellenistic methodological debates) and remarks, "in three quarters of our actions we are but empiricists."[29] Like these Empiricists, Hobbes had analyzed this capacity in terms of natural signs, showing that the "succession of conceptions in the mind" follows "experience, which is nothing else but remembrance of what antecedents have been followed by what consequents."[30]

> When a man hath so often observed like antecedents to be followed by like consequents, that whensoever he seeth the antecedent, he looketh again for the consequent; or when he seeth the consequent, maketh account there hath been the like antecedent; then he calleth both the

antecedent and the consequent, *signs* one of another, as clouds are signs of rain to come, and rain of clouds past.[31]

Without referring to Hobbes, Baumgarten elaborates the *analogon rationis* in terms of natural signs, a fact which is often obscured by the proximity, in Baumgarten's presentation, of remarks concerning the expression of ideas through artificial signs. In *Aesthetica* §36 he considers the capacity of foresight and anticipation (*praevidendum et praesagiendum*), which is not reserved for a rare aesthetic oracle but is rather required for every vital or vivid moment of knowledge (*cognitionis vitam*). He follows this immediately with a discussion of the capacity of signifying one's perceptions, "*dispositio ad significandas perceptiones*," with cross-reference to *Metaphysica* on the *facultas characteristica*. A closer look at the latter suggests that this does not concern a faculty of designation or expression in signs so much as a cognitive capacity to perceive through signs.

> I perceive signs together with what they signify [*Signa cum signatis una percipio*]; thus I have the capacity to conjoin the sign with the signified in representation [*representando*, representingly], which can be called *facultas charcteristica*. And since there is in this world a significative nexus, perceptions of the 'characteristic faculty' are brought about by the power of the soul to represent the universe. The significative nexus is known either distinctly or indistinctly, and thus the characteristic faculty is either intellectual or sensuous.[32]

The 'characteristic faculty' does not re-present ideas in signs such as words or symbols, but represents (that is, sensuously grasps) the world in and through its natural sign relations.[33] Baumgarten's lectures on the *aesthetica* justify calling it '*ars analogi rationis*' in similar terms: "Since it is known from psychology that our insight into the overall connection of things is partly distinct, partly confused, the first is by reason, the second by *analogon rationis*."[34]

The nexus is a network of signs that can alternatively be seen as one of efficient causes or of final causes (purposes).[35] Signs reflect the links between associated ideas. Sensation and imagination represent things "in a universal context [*in universali nexu*]; thus the law of imagination is that when one represents an idea to oneself partially, the whole of the representation returns. This proposition is also called the association of ideas."[36]

Sensuous anticipation (*praesagitio*) is an expectation of similar cases (*exspectatio casuum similium*, a phrase that Wolff used to gloss the *analogon rationis*), and Baumgarten spells out its rule in another variation of the law of association of ideas, which supplies the basis for a *facultas praesumendi*.[37] The related law of foresight (*lex praevisionis*) is also a variation of the principle of association, and its statement leads, most significantly, to the reformulation of a Leibnizian dictum: "This means, from the present impregnated by the past [*per praeteritum*] the future is born."[38] This impregnation is in effect the unnoted presence of ideas associated with those ideas that are noted. Such association can even involve one idea signifying another without this being noted, as the signifying is absorbed in confusion. This seems to be the burden of *Metaphysica* §620:

> If the sign and the signified are conjoined in perception [*percipiendo*, perceivingly] and the perception of the sign is greater than that of the signified, the cognition is called *symbolic*, but if the representation of the signified is greater than that of the sign, the cognition is *intuitive*. In both cases the law of the 'characteristic faculty' is that one of the associated perceptions becomes the means for knowing the existence of the other.[39]

The distinction between symbolic and intuitive knowledge is generally taken to be a question of representation in artificial signs as opposed to some cognitive immediacy, and the *facultas characteristica* is understood accordingly. But here it seems that the natural signs which constitute the *nexus significativum* of the world through their associative linkings underlie the distinction, and that intuitive cognition is itself mediated by signs, but unconsciously. In intuition the signified is greater (*maior*) and the sign is "seen through" and disappears into what it signifies.[40] The fact that the signs are indexical, that each perception can serve to signify the *existence* of the other, supports the view that they are natural. This is the most basic sense of sign for Baumgarten, "A means of knowing the existence of another thing is a sign, the purpose of the sign is the signified. So the sign is the basis for knowing the signified."[41]

Another dimension of classical sign theory is also involved in the constitution of confusion. Drawing on the idea that marks (*notae*, but also *characteres*)[42] within representations determine not only types and classes but also unique individual identities (a Stoic idea presented in Cicero's *Academica* or *Lucullus* and revived by Leibniz), Baumgarten argues that it is precisely the richness of particularity that must be sacrificed to attain general concepts. The universals of demonstrative knowledge are gained through abstraction at the cost of a great loss in material fullness and perfection of representation. "What is abstraction," Baumgarten asks, "if not loss [*iactura*]?"[43]

At the outset of *Aesthetica* Baumgarten anticipated an objection to his conception of aesthetic as a logic of sensuous or confused thought, namely that confusion is the mother of error, and answered that it is rather "a *conditio sine qua non* for the discovery of truth, since nature makes no leap from the obscure into the distinct. The way out of the night into midday must go by way of dawn."[44] In fact he went on to show that the half-light of dawn has advantages when contrasted with the clarity and distinctness of noon. Although he introduced the term *fundus animae* (ground of the soul) for the manifold (*complexus*) of obscure perceptions contained in it,[45]

Baumgarten made nothing of the cognitive virtues to be found in the darkness of night.

Herder on Obscure Ideas

Herder greatly admired Baumgarten's dissertation, finding in it "the entire ground-plan of his metapoetic," as he wrote in a 1767 draft for a memorial to Baumgarten, adding, "I always regard the first products of a mind with a small shudder of awe before a human spirit."[46] "Psychological fruitfulness" makes Baumgarten's the most philosophical concept of poetry, "for this explanation leads furthest into the soul and allows us to derive the essence of poetry from the nature of the human mind."[47] In this context Herder quotes Moses Mendelssohn to the effect that aesthetics, as the study of artistic expression, is the most valuable resource for psychology, since it offers better access to the mind's innermost workings than any intellectual analysis, introspection, or external observation of everyday behavior. Significantly, the quoted passage begins, "If the philosopher follows the traces of sensations [or feelings, *Empfindungen*] along their obscure [*dunkel*] paths, new prospects must open up to him in the soul."[48] The association of the obscure with *Empfindungen* will prove crucial to Herder's theory.

The further development of Baumgarten's basic approach in his *Aesthetic* draws criticism rather than approval from Herder. Apropos of its opening paragraphs, Herder says that the aesthetic that is natural to humans differs from the artificial not only in degree but essentially, since the natural aesthetic is always a *habitus*, not *scientia*; it "operates [or has its effect] through sensation [or feeling] and obscure concepts; while artificial aesthetic teaches and convinces through propositions and distinct concepts."[49] The distinct is opposed to the dark, to "*dunklen Begriffen*," as Herder seems to conflate Leibniz's two distinctions: clear and obscure, distinct and confused. It is strange as well that Herder speaks of dark or obscure *concepts*, while opposing sensation or feeling to formulation or foundation, as '*Sätze*' could mean either propositions or principles, while '*Empfindung*' has much the same scope as the Greek '*aisthesis*', ranging from feeling to sense perception.

Herder has brought in a genetic viewpoint which fundamentally alters Baumgarten's balance of factors. The artificial aesthetic must develop out of the natural. Since all humans are born "sensuous animals" and are more animal than mind or spirit, their "connatural aesthetic is greater than their inborn logic." Thus the "sensuous feeling of beauty is common to all peoples," Herder concludes, and artificial aesthetic must draw all its strength from this, even as it extends and refines it. But, he complains, Baumgarten's aesthetic is merely a theory of the fine (*schöne*) sciences, rhetoric and poetics, while all the fine arts are neglected. Moreover, artificial aesthetic does not really enhance the natural but weakens and distracts it.

Conceived more broadly, as Herder would have it, aesthetic as a science would give up its claim to improve *Empfindung* and find its own value as a psychology and physiology affording knowledge of the powers of the soul. In this sense it would be "part of the most necessary anthropology, since our strength as humans consists in the ground [*Grunde*, cf. *fundus*] of the soul." Aesthetics then splits into a "subjective aspect, that part of psychology inquiring into sensuous feeling [*Gefühl*] in its drives and motions," and an objective one, developing the general concept of beauty and determining beauty "in expression," from which the fine arts and sciences all follow. Thus subjective aesthetic studies beauty "*in der Empfindung*."[50]

Herder would invert Baumgarten's notion that logic is the older sister of aesthetic in three respects: in its value, since the lower powers of cognition are always more practical and effective, in its age, since the natural aesthetic is the very beginning, and in its dignity, since logic is less imposing once one understands it. Logic must itself give up its normative pretension to show how we should think, since its only basis is experience of how the mind actually works. It has no *a priori* authority and its present weakness, as an inquiring (as opposed to an improving) discipline, is a result of its divorce from psychology. The deeper such inquiry goes into the powers of the soul, the further it must get from formulating any rules.

Fine, subtle, or beautiful *knowledge* cannot be the beginning of the aesthetic, as Baumgarten makes it seem. "Man, the animal, senses first, obscurely senses itself, and then vividly; and pleasure and pain obscurely in itself, and then pleasure and pain clearly outside itself; and then only does it know." *Empfindung* is at first purely subjective, even in its nascent reflexivity. Pleasure and pain are merely internal feelings and only gradually come to be referred to external causes, which is finally the beginning of knowledge.[51]

Clarity of sensation grows gradually from the dark or obscure inner senses, which remain its subjective ground. Herder calls this ground obscure in contexts that suggest depths that are dark to the human mind looking into itself, that is, what is obscure is not so much primal sensations themselves as our self-aware knowledge of them. At the same time, '*dunkel*' acquires a positive, mysteriously attractive connotation. To the "philosopher of feeling [*des Gefühls*]" who would go beyond Baumgarten, Herder dramatically intones,

> Look down into the dark abyss of the human soul where the sensations of the animal become sensations of a human being and mix themselves—from a distance as it were—with the soul; look down into the abyss of dark thoughts, from which drives and passions, pleasure and uneasiness will later arise.[52]

Herder objects to Baumgarten's characterizing sensuous knowlege as "not distinct" since he sees this as a purely negative description and ignores the positive Leibnizian conception of confusion. In the fourth of his *Critical*

Groves, a work discussed at some length below, Herder rejects Baumgarten's defense of 'confusion': aesthetics "does not like [*liebt*] confused [*verworrenen*] ideas, as *conditio sine qua non* or dawn to truth. . . . Aesthetics does not like confused [*confusen*] concepts at all; it only takes them as its object in order to make them distinct."[53] Much of what Leibniz accomplished, however, through his re-conceptualizing of confusion is undertaken by Herder through a transvaluation of obscurity. Although the rhetorical appeal of Herder's endorsement of the dark and abysmal seems to usher in a new world of sensibility, we will find that the essential point of his new idea of obscurity simply (but powerfully) restates a basic insight of Leibniz into the confused character of sense perception.[54]

Against Baumgarten he argues, "Sensuous clarity and intelligible distinctness are such different extremes that no progress is made by explaining one by means of the other."[55] But this error is only a consequence of the more basic one of making cognition primary and thus making beauty a part of sensuous knowledge instead of realizing that the feeling (*Gefühl*) of beauty is basic and its essence is not knowledge. "It is a fundamental power [*Grundkraft*] distinct from that power which forms representations, the bond that links body and soul, and which in pure spirits would link understanding and will."[56] What Herder says of Baumgarten's mentor, Wolff, "the darkest areas of the soul, from which the greater part of all inventions arise, remained unilluminated by him,"[57] would seem to apply to Baumgarten as well.

Baumgarten's privileging of cognition or representation as the essential activity of mind is countered by Herder's insistence on a mental power that is prior to—and remains crucial for—the differentiation of body and soul, of understanding and will. Like similar tendencies in Johann Nicholas Tetens and later in Friedrich Schiller, this emphasis on feeling as the root of aesthetic is faithful to Leibniz's teaching that every minute perception is at the same time a minute appetition or minute solicitation, an infinitessimal element of motivation. This intuition is inimical to any rigid faculty psychology.[58]

In "Truths out of Leibniz," notes and paraphrases of the *Nouveaux Essais sur l'Entendement humain* (first published in 1765) which seem to have followed the fragments on Baumgarten from 1767, it is unmistakable that Herder writes '*dunkle*' (and not '*verworren*', the German term for 'confused') where Leibniz has '*confus*', as in the sound of the sea compounded of the imperceptible sounds of individual waves ("*eine dunkle Vereinigung aller*") or "the weak and confused sensation" that is present in even the deepest sleep."[59] "Obscure representations [*dunkle Vorstellungen*]" (not, as in Leibniz, minute perceptions con-fused to a summation) determine us to move one way or another, where most people assume a perfect indifference, and cause that 'uneasiness' (*inquiétude*) which is distinguished from pain only in its minuteness and yet constitutes our desire and pleasure.[60]

Herder's conception of the value of the dark or obscure in the human mind comes into particular focus in the fourth of his *Critical Groves* (*Wäldchen*), written in 1769 but published only posthumously in 1846. It is a polemic confrontation with the ideas of Friedrich Just Riedel who elaborated a tendency of the "Common Sense" School of the Scottish Enlightenment in positing three primal internal senses: for the true, the good, and the beautiful, that is, common sense, conscience, and taste, each simply given and working as an instinct.

Herder counters this in just the way Diderot had attacked the notion of taste as a 'sixth sense', by showing the complex cumulative experience that goes into the formation of such an apparently innate or instinctual mental power and supposedly immediate experience. Diderot extended Leibniz's conception by speaking of myriad *petites expériences* or *essais*, which are integrated into taste and judgment. If we are aware of this genesis and background, that is, of the premises of our judgment, he says, we have what they call science; if the premises are not in our conscious memory, we have what they call instinct, (or more properly) taste or tact.[61]

In the same vein Herder analyzes what seems to be immediate sensation to find it subtly yet deeply prepared by past experience.

> We judge in dispatch and from habit; we draw conclusions and yet believe we are immediately sensing; we drop out the middle terms, and the conclusion seems a simple judgment: we obscure [*verdunkeln*] the connection of concepts, and the judgment seems an immediate sense perception [*Empfindung*]. Thus the first concepts of color, figure, distance of bodies were learned only through a long process of comparison [*Gegeneinanderhalten*] of single sensations. Precisely through such long comparison it became familiar to us. The middle terms between them became obscure [*verdunkelten sich*], they remain as simple immediate sensation, and we take them this way in use, in the oversight of application, in ready, quick and inattentive [*unbemerkenden*] habit.[62]

Here the obscurity of the mediating sensations is brought about by a kind of instinctual practical necessity. Despite the implication that they become or are made obscure, Herder continues to speak of the ground of the soul (or is it an abyss, *Ab-grund*?) as obscure in itself. "The entire ground of our soul are the obscure ideas [*dunkle Ideen*] which are the liveliest and most numerous, the mass from which the soul prepares its finer ones, the strongest drives of our lives and which contribute most to our happiness or unhappiness."[63]

The beginning and core of this ground of the soul is an organic sensation of self-awareness that precedes all consciousness of an object or an other, "the obscure idea of his I, as obscure as only a plant could feel it, but in which a concept of the entire cosmos lives."[64] This primal sense of self spreads itself into a sense of what has identity without, and here Herder suggests that the process by which primitive judgments are "obscured" into apparent sensations, is a means of removing them from reflection and ensuring they endure.

> With repeated identical sensations the first judgment is formed, that it is the *same* sensation. This judgment is obscure and must be so, because it must last all one's life and persist as an eternal basis in the soul. Thus it must attain the strength and so to speak consistency [*Consistenz*] of an inner feeling [*Gefühl*]; it is preserved as a sensation [*Empfindung*]. In its genesis it was already a judgment, a conclusion from the linking of several concepts; but since it arose through habituation, and it was habit which—in order to apply it right away— preserved it, therefore the form of its genesis was obscured [*verdunkelte sich*], leaving only the material, which became sensation.[65]

This explains the fundamental but natural error of those like Riedel who posit immediate moral and aesthetic senses. "All these ideas [order, agreement, perfection, beauty] are, in the first state of our existence, developments of our inner capacity of thought, but since they are obscure as to the form of their development, they remain, as *Empfindungen*, lying on the ground of our soul, and fold themselves so closely into our I, that we take them to be innate feelings."[66] This is just what Leibniz meant by 'confused ideas'.

This natural process of obscuring the perceptions that provide the premises of originary judgments which, for fundamental practical reasons, must appear to us as immediate, unmediated, gives a meaning to 'obscure ideas' which marks an advance in an important Leibnizian line of thought, previously associated with 'confused ideas'. But the force of this insight is overpowered immediately by a new theme in Herder, which takes 'feeling' and 'obscurity' in a different way.

Herder on Feeling as Touch, and as Inner Sense

Herder makes the point about obscuring the terms of an originary judgment of external existence once again in a different context in *Plastik*, written in 1768–70, recasting material from the second part of the fourth *Critical Grove*, and published with revisions in 1778.

> In this way the first judgment is formed, that what is repeated is the same sensation. The form of the judgment remained obscure and had to be extinguished, since it had to cease to be a judgment. It must take on the steadfastness [*Bestandheit*] of an immediate feeling [*Gefühl*], must become the basis, the eternally secured basis, of all the judgments and inferences that there is sensuous reality [*Wahrheit*] outside us.[67]

"In order to arrive at its first ideas of external bodies, of form, shape, size, distance, etc.," he continues, "the human soul acted and thought, judged and inferred, erred and discovered more than the greatest philosopher in a lifetime of abstractions." This labor of the mind essentially involved a cross-referencing of the imput of the different senses, correlating what the eye, the ear, touch etc. tell us, so that the perceptions of each sense would be informed by what has been learned from the others. Herder's new theme focuses on this integration (or con-fusion) but seeks to undo it.

The basic premise of part 2 of the fourth *Critical Grove* and of *Plastik* is a stark contrast between seeing, which senses only colors and surfaces, and feeling (*Gefühl*) or touch, which senses body, depth, solidity, contours and form. Painting is an art for vision, while sculpture is for touch. "There is absolutely no sculpture for the eye," he claims, "for the eye can see no body as a body."[68] The tendentiously exaggerated nature of the contrast may be motivated as correcting the bias of accounts which viewed sculpture too much in visual terms, but the effect on his underlying psychological ideas is distorting, and this is exacerbated when he exploits the double meaning of 'feeling' (*Gefühl*) as inner sense and external touch.[69]

Adapting a strict Berkeleyan dichotomy of the 'proper objects' of the two senses, Herder argues that much of what we think we see is derived from touch and transferred to sight by habitual association. But then we see (and must see) sculpture with eyes that have learned from touch, which Herder insistently ignores, as no sculptor would. The scanning movement of the eye viewing sculpture is no imitation of the palpating (*tastende*) hand, as he claims, but its natural motion, reading surfaces for figure, depth and volume,[70] and the idea that sight had to learn of form and gestalt from touch is far-fetched.[71]

It is not hard to see how Herder could have conflated the two meanings of feeling as inner sense and external touch. Sight is the most distinct (*deutlichste*) sense, while touch is the *gründlichste*, meaning most thorough and basic.[72] On the one hand this means sight is analytic or abstractive, it has its objects separated from each other and itself, but, on the other hand, it is also abstracted (*zerstreut*) because, as superficial (linked to surfaces, but only loosely from a distance), it is easily distracted, while touch patiently, experimentally palpates and finally reaches an unshakeable sense of substance, body, form, physical reality.[73]

Phrases like "*das innige Gefühl, in seiner dunkeln Kammer*" (the intimate feeling, in its dark chamber),[74] said of touch, show how one meaning of 'feeling' could slide into the other. Insights drawn from the experience of the blind and once blind are frequently cited here, following Diderot's *Lettre sur les Aveugles*, and touch is implicitly thought of as working in the dark. Obscurity draws added resonance from the pervasive shadowy presence of blind experience taken as a model to correct the false and unaware assumptions of the sighted.[75]

First Herder valued obscurity as allowing primal judgments to be taken as immediate sensations or feelings, a reduction which sealed them into the foundation of our perception. Then he recognized that the abstraction of sight works in the other direction, condensing the hard-earned haptic senses of resistance, density, volume, depth, etc. to associated visual signs which can be 'read off' in a fleeting glance.[76] In the final version of *Plastik* sight is said to bring clarity to what feeling grasped only obscurely, but this clarity is seen as a liability. "In the end we see so much and so fast, that we feel no more and cannot feel any more, but this sense must still be the foundation and security of the other."[77] The abstraction of sight is a process of con-fusion, as the reduction to immediate-seeming feeling is. Leibniz saw sensation in general as cognition because it was simplification, reducing many to one. But Herder deplores the reduction of qualities derived from touch to visual clues or cues.[78]

The focus on feeling as inner sense, linked functionally to all the external senses, returns in the mid-1770s with three versions of a psychological treatise on knowing and sensing (*Empfinden*) which Herder wrote in response to a contest question posed by the Berlin Academy (and framed by Johann Georg Sulzer): What is the influence of the two main powers of the human mind, knowing and sensing, on each other? Herder rejects the premise of the question and construes the two as aspects of a single power, with sensing or feeling seen as obscurely knowing (*dunkel erkennen*), while "knowing can be regarded as a distinct resultant [*deutliches Resultat*] of all the states of sensing."[79]

Again 'obscure' (not 'confused') is opposed to 'distinct',[80] although a new term, 'bright' (*helle*) is introduced which may fill in for both clear and distinct. Providence, Herder says, insures that "all representations, even the most obscure, are pregnant with truth in the womb of sensation," and "the natural progress leads from the obscure to the bright."[81] "The principal law by which nature organizes these two powers is that feeling must operate where no knowing can yet be, that it bring many things at once obscurely into the soul, so that the soul can enlighten it to a certain degree and find a resultant of its essence therein."[82]

By 'resultant' Herder means an abbreviation or distillation that emerges from a process in which

> knowledge becomes intuition and is preserved as habit [*Fertigkeit*] and thus perpetually applied as a deaf, encased [*zusammengehüllte*] knowledge, a symbolic sensation; we operate with previously acquired knowledge as with algebraic signs for which we may forget the meaning as long as they produce the result.[83]

This is a variant of the knowledge which Leibniz called blind (not deaf) and symbolic, and Leibniz is cited later in the paragraph for his idea of *petites perceptions* "which strive toward brightness." What is obscure is now valued because it contains the seeds of its own enlightenment. In the second essay Herder writes that people may speak of a moral sense, if they must, but they should remember that it is a narrow, obscure feeling, and he directs them, "brighten it [*helle es auf*] and raise it to knowledge."[84] Indeed, already in the fourth *Critical Grove* he had written, "the essence of philosophy is, as it were, to draw out ideas that lie within us, truths that we knew only obscurely, and to enlighten [*aufklären*] them to distinctness."[85] Is Herder offering a *post mortem* of the whole way of analyzing mental representations that has been studied here, when in the third essay he attacks a certain brand of 'deaf knowledge' in philosophy?

> Now our bright and clear philosophy dreads above all such an abyss of obscure sensations, powers and stimuli; it avoids it like the hell of the lowest powers of the soul and would rather play on the Leibnizian chessboard with a few deaf words and classifications like *obscure* and *clear, distinct* and *confused* ideas.[86]

Even granting that his own words were never devoid of sense, he has himself played several long games on that Leibnizian chessboard.

N O T E S

1. See for example *Discourse on Method*, part 4, *The Philosophical Writings of Descartes*, ed. John Cottingham, Robert Stoothoff, Dugald Murdoch, (Cambridge: Cambridge University Press, 1985), 1:130, "our ideas or notions, being real and coming from God, cannot be anything but true, in every respect in which they are clear and distinct. Thus, if we frequently have ideas containing some falsity, this can happen only because there is something confused and obscure in them, for in that respect they participate in nothingness."
2. A. G. Baumgarten, *Aesthetica*, ed. and trans. Hans Rudolf Schweizer, as *Theoretische Ästhetik* (Hamburg: Felix Meiner, 1983), §14, p. 10, "Aesthetices finis est perfectio cognitionis sensitivae, qua talis."
3. Jeffrey Barnouw, "The Beginnings of 'Aesthetics' and the Leibnizian Conception of Sensation," in *Eighteenth-Century Aesthetics and the Reconstruction of Art*, ed. Paul Mattick, Jr., (Cambridge: Cambridge University Press, 1993), 52–95.
4. Jeffrey Barnouw, "Passion as 'Confused' Perception or Thought in Descartes, Malebranche, and Hutcheson." *Journal of the History of Ideas* 53 (1992): 397–424.
5. "Meditations on Knowledge, Truth, and Ideas," (1684) in Leibniz, *Philosophical Papers and Letters*, ed. Leroy E. Loemker, (Dordrecht: Reidel, 1969), 291.
6. Leibniz, *Discourse on Metaphysics* §24, *Philosophical Papers*, 318–19. Loemker's rendering of the last part ("explain the criteria I use") makes it too intellectualistic. The translation in *Selections*, ed. Philip P. Wiener, (New York: Scribner, 1951), 325: "explain the peculiarities which a thing has," errs to the other side. Instead, "Expliquer les marques que j'ai," means make explicit the distinguishing marks which I have for a thing *in my idea of it*. In other contexts 'marques' are the criteria involved in a definition, as when Leibniz says it is useless to claim that whatever is conceived clearly

and distinctly is true, as Descartes does, unless one gives the *marques* of a
distinct conception. Letter to the Landgraf Ernst zu Hessen-Rheinfels,
December 24, 1684, *Sämtliche Schriften und Briefe*, ser. 1, vol. 4
(Berlin/Leipzig, 1950), 342.

7. Leibniz, *Philosophical Papers*, 291. In "The Beginnings of 'Aesthetics'
and the Leibnizian Conception of Sensation," 63–66, 68–71, I review
earlier usage of the 'je ne sais quoi'.

8. Leibniz, *New Essays on Human Understanding*, trans. Peter Remnant and
Jonathan Bennett, (Cambridge: Cambridge University Press, 1981),
2.23§11, p. 219, "il en naîtrait apparemment d'autres." Cf. 2.2§1, p. 120,
"these sensible ideas [such as warmth and softness of wax] appear simple
because they are confused and thus do not provide the mind with any way of
making discriminations within what they contain."

9. Leibniz, *Die philosophischen Werke*, ed. C. I. Gerhardt (Berlin 1875ff),
7:529, trans. in Robert McRae, *Leibniz: Perception, Apperception and
Thought* (Toronto: University of Toronto Press, 1976), 27. This concerns
a mixture of pigment, not light.

10. Leibniz, *New Essays* 2.2§1, p. 120.

11. Leibniz, *Discourse on Metaphysics* §24, *Selections*, 325; *Philosophical
Papers*, 319. See also §33, *Selections*, 338–39.

12. Leibniz, *Philosophical Papers*, 580.

13. Ibid., 581.

14. Leibniz, *Die philosophischen Werke* 4:574–75, in McRae, *Leibniz*, 127.

15. Leibniz, *New Essays*, preface, 53. Remnant and Bennett translated "*unies*"
as 'unvarying' where I substituted 'united' (cf. 'fused'). They may have been
anticipating a subsequent reference to impressions which lack "the appeal
of novelty" and therefore escape notice.

16. Ibid., 54–55.

17. Ibid. 2.1§15, pp. 115–16.

18. Immanuel Kant, *Critique of Judgment*, trans. J. H. Bernard, (New York:
Hafner, 1951), 25–27, 37–38 (§1); cf. 30, aesthetic is "the faculty of
judging . . . by means of the feeling of pleasure or pain"; logical judgment
works by means of understanding and reason. Unlike Leibniz, however,
Kant claims feeling tells us nothing about the object, so the point of his
distinction is different. Schiller reverses the implications of Kant's terms
by preserving a Leibnizian sense of the cognitive value of *aisthesis*
(*Empfindung, Gefühl*) in his conception of 'aesthetic' education.

19. Leibniz, *New Essays* 2.29§13, p. 262.

20. A. G. Baumgarten, *Meditationes philosophicae de nonnullis ad poema
pertinentibus*, trans. H. Paetzold as *Philosophische Betrachtungen über
einige Bedingungen des Gedichtes* (Hamburg: Meiner, 1983), 8 and xi;
Reflections on Poetry trans. Karl Aschenbrenner and W. B. Holther,
(Berkeley: University of California Press, 1954), 38.

21. Baumgarten, *Philosophische Betrachtungen*, 66, 14; *Reflections*, 68, 42.

22. Baumgarten, *Philosophische Betrachtungen*, 84–87; *Reflections*, 77–78.

23. Baumgarten, *Texte zur Grundlegung der Ästhetik*, ed. Hans Rudolf
Schweizer, (Hamburg: Meiner, 1983), 79–80.

24. Aristotle, *Physics* 184a1–26. See the further discussion and yet another
classical conception of sensation as confused (from Sextus Empiricus) in

Barnouw, "Passion as 'Confused' Perception," 399–401.

25. Baumgarten §§535, 521, 511, *Texte zur Grundlegung*, 16, 10 and 4.
26. Ibid., 8.
27. Baumgarten, *Aesthetica* §1, *Theoretische Ästhetik*, 3. In the second edition (1742) *Metaphysica* §533 added "logic of the lower cognitive faculty" to the definition of aesthetic.
28. Leibniz, *Monadology* §§26–28, in *Philosophical Papers and Letters*, 645. Cf. Wolff, *Psychologia rationalis* §765; *Psychologia empirica* §506. The importance of the 'analogue of reason' has been emphasized in Alfred Baeumler, *Das Irrationalitätsproblem in der Aesthetik und Logik des 18. Jahrhunderts* (Halle, 1923, repr. Tübingen: Niemeyer, 1967), 188–97, and Ursula Franke, *Kunst als Erkenntnis. Die Rolle der Sinnlichkeit in der Aesthetik des Alexander Gottlieb Baumgarten* (Wiesbaden: Steiner, 1972), 51–58. Neither, however, brings out the role of natural signs in the *analogon rationis*.
29. Leibniz, *Monadology* §28, p. 645.
30. Thomas Hobbes, *Humane Nature*, 4, §§1 & 6, in *The Elements of Law, Natural and Politic*, ed F. Toennies, (London: Frank Cass, 1969).
31. *Humane Nature*, chap. 4, §9. Hobbes also calls this knowledge based in natural signs 'prudence'. See my essay, "Prudence et Science chez Hobbes." in *Thomas Hobbes: Philosophie premiere, Théorie de la Science et Politique*, ed. J. Bernhardt and Y-Ch. Zarka, (Paris: Presses Universitaires de France, 1989), 107–17.
32. Baumgarten, *Metaphysica* §619, *Texte zur Grundlegung*, 62.
33. David Wellbery, *Lessing's* Laocoon. *Semiotics and Aesthetics in the Age of Reason* (Cambridge: Cambridge University Press, 1984), 26–28, catches a glimpse of this but then loses it in confusion with a very different conception of natural sign (e.g. 80–84.) See my review in *Eighteenth-Century Life* 10 (1986): 71–79, esp. 74–77.
34. Baumgarten, *Texte zur Grundlegung*, 80.
35. Baumgarten, *Metaphysica* §358.
36. Ibid. §561, *Texte zur Grundlegung*, 30. Associated (*sociae*) perceptions are defined in similar terms in §516, 6.
37. *Metaphysica* §612–13, ibid., 58, 60.
38. *Metaphysica* §596, ibid., 48.
39. *Metaphysica* §620, ibid., 62.
40. Although she does not connect it with the characteristic faculty or natural signs, Franke, *Kunst*, 58, nicely conveys the merging of past and present perception within perception, "In der empfindenden Vergegenwärtigung, die Vorstellung des jeweils Gegenwärtigen, wird auch das Vergangene durch die Einbildungskraft aufgrund einer Ideenassoziation in der Weise eingeholt, daß ein früher gehabte Vorstellung mit einer an sie erinnernden gegenwärtigen 'zusammenläuft'." This 'running together' constitutes one species of confusion. I have studied similar senses of confusion as condensed association in Malebranche and Hutcheson, "Passion as 'Confused' Perception," 411–12, 420–24.
41. Baumgarten, *Metaphysica* §347, *Texte zur Grundlegung*, 97 n. 212.
42. *Metaphysica* §522, ibid., 10, (affirming that a representation is distinct insofar as it has clear 'marks', sensuous insofar as it has obscure ones, and

the distinct have some admixture of confusion and darkness, while there is something distinct in the sensuous,) uses *'characteres'* and *'notas'* interchangeably.

43. Baumgarten, *Theoretische Ästhetik*, 142–44, §§559–560.

44. Ibid. 4, §7.

45. Baumgarten, *Metaphysica* §511, *Texte zur Grundlegung*, 4. Obscurity's rise to prominence is traced in Hans Adler, "Fundus Animae—der Grund der Seele. Zur Gnoseologie des Dunklen in der Aufklärung," *Deutsche Vierteljahrsschrift für Literaturwissenschaft und Geistesgeschichte*, 62 (1988), 197–220. Adler shows that Baumgarten's follower, Georg Friedrich Meier, went further in his claims for obscure cognition, but the most significant contributions before Herder, as passages quoted on 203 and 208 suggest, come from Johann Georg Sulzer.

46. Herder, *Werke*, ed. Wolfgang Pross, (Munich: Hanser, 1987), 2:20; cf. Herder, *Werke*, vol. 1, *Frühe Schriften 1764–1772*, ed. Ulrich Gaier, (Frankfurt: Deutsche Klassiker Verlag, 1985), 682.

47. Herder, *Werke*, ed. Pross, 2:21.

48. Ibid. 25. The quotation is from Mendelssohn, *Von den Quellen und Verbindungen der Schönen Künste* (1757).

49. Herder, *Werke*, ed. Gaier, 1:660.

50. Ibid. 664–66. On 661, Herder says that a universal artificial aesthetic was born from the *Gefühlslehre* or "doctrine of feeling" just as metaphysics was from logic.

51. Ibid. 670. Cf. 671, "Weg also cognitio: Gefühl macht eine besondere Gattung aus." Feeling is first, fineness of knowledge is last and weakest, "das letzte Schwächste."

52. Herder, "Von Baumgartens Denkart," *Werke*, ed. Pross, 2:23.

53. Ibid. 78.

54. Hans Adler, *Die Prägnanz des Dunklen. Gnoseologie—Aesthetik—Geschichtsphilosophie bei Johann Gottfried Herder* (Hamburg: Meiner, 1990), again traces lines linking Leibniz, Baumgarten and Herder, but despite the titles of his article (note 44 above) and book, he does not specifically examine the workings of the obscure in Herder or its relation to the functions of the confused in Leibniz and Baumgarten. His main point in this regard is that Herder grasps the obscure as an origin which all human development must remain tied to (65). "The obscure is introduced into philosophy by the path of metaphor," above all, that of pregnancy (91), but analysis of the Prägnanz-image leads far afield without illuminating the 'marks' of darkness.

55. Herder, *Werke*, ed. Gaier, 1:671–72.

56. Ibid. 672.

57. Herder, "Ueber Christian Wolfs Schriften," *Werke*, ed. Pross, 2:10.

58. See Jeffrey Barnouw "The Philosophical Achievement and Historical Significance of Johann Nicolas Tetens," *Studies in Eighteenth-Century Culture*, vol. 9, (Madison: University of Wisconsin Press, 1979), 301–35, esp. 306, 311–12, 320–24; and "'Aesthetic' for Schiller and Peirce: A Neglected Origin of Pragmatism." *Journal of the History of Ideas*, 49 (October 1988), 607–32, 615–26, reprinted in *Essays on the History of Aesthetics*, ed. Peter Kivy, Library of the History of Ideas, 5 (Rochester:

University of Rochester Press, 1992), 377–402.

59. Herder, *Werke*, ed. Pross, 2:35. Cf. *New Essays*, preface, 54.
60. Herder, *Werke*, ed. Pross, 2:36. Cf. *New Essays*, preface, 56, and 2.20§6, p. 165, on uneasiness, "That is why the infinitely wise Author of our being was acting in our interests when he brought it about that we are often ignorant and subject to confused perceptions—so that we could act the more quickly by instinct, and not be troubled by excessively distinct sensations of hosts of objects."
61. Denis Diderot, *Correspondance*, ed. Georges Roth, (Paris: Editions de Minuit, 1958 and 1962), 4:125 and 7:163–64; *Diderot's Letters to Sophie Volland*, trans. Peter France, (London: Oxford University Press, 1972) 112, 167. In the *Encyclopedia* article "Beau" Diderot writes, "Hutcheson and his followers try to establish the necessity of an internal sense of beauty but succeed only in demonstrating that there is something obscure [N.B.] and impenetrable in the pleasure which the beautiful causes us." *Oeuvres Esthétiques*, ed. P. Vernière, (Paris: Garnier, n.d.), 401, cf. 414. This passage is noted by Herder, *Werke*, ed. Pross, 2:194. Diderot goes on, 415–16, to say that expedients which we come up with in response to our needs are the source of our ideas of order, arrangement etc. "These notions are *expérimentales* like all the others; they came to us through the senses." Not explicitly, but in effect, this answers Hutcheson.
62. Herder, "Viertes Kritisches Wäldchen," *Werke*, ed. Pross, 2:63.
63. Ibid. 80.
64. Ibid. 81.
65. Ibid. 82.
66. Ibid. 83.
67. Herder, "Plastik" (1770), ibid. 408–9.
68. Herder, "Viertes Kritisches Wäldchen," ibid. 114. The version of *Plastik* revised for publication is less tendentious. I refer more to the first version because my purpose is not to assess Herder's comparison of painting and sculpture, but merely to show how one idea of 'obscure sensation' or feeling was swamped by another.
69. See ibid. 100 where Herder argues for the neglected importance of feeling-as-touch from the supposed etymological sense of 'aesthetics' as the philosophy of feeling (*des Gefühls*).
70. Ibid. 115–16.
71. Ibid. 102. Just as touch knows nothing of color or surface (?!), sight knows absolutely nothing of *Form* and *Gestalt*. Summing up, the final version of *Plastik*, 527, claims it is metaphysically and physically established that only bodily feeling (touch) can give us forms.
72. Ibid. 410. Cf. 422–23: touch is the "most obscure sense" and has been excluded from aesthetics until now. See also the beginning of the sketch, "Zum Sinn des Gefühls," ibid. 243–50, esp. 243–44: touch is the most sensuous of the senses, sight the least.
73. Ibid. 96–97, 99, 244, 409. Cf. 122, classical sculpture was meant for "feeling which (as it were) palpated in darkness in order not to be diffused (*zerstreut*) by sight."
74. Ibid. 122. This is not a reference (or is at best a paradoxical one) to the *camera obscura*, which Herder uses elsewhere (e.g. 468) as an obvious model

of vision.
75. Ibid. 417, the characterization of feelings as 'obscure' takes on negative associations (*"Dunkle unnütze* [useless] *Gefühle," "Dunkle, unbefriedigende* [unsatisfactory] *Gefühle"*) to convey the attitudes of those who do not understand what their sight owes to feeling, nor what they are missing in the experience of art.
76. Herder, "Plastik" (1770) and (1778), ibid. 410, 470.
77. Ibid. 470.
78. Herder, "Viertes Kritisches Wäldchen," ibid. 123, "In common life this abbreviation [sight as an abbreviated touch] should continue, it is convenient, adroit, quick, and (what counts the most with us) respectable; who would want to feel, when they could see? But for philosophy and the true theory of art an inauthentic abbreviation can never fully replace the true organ."
79. Herder, "Vom Erkennen und Empfinden" (1774), ibid. 546, 548–49.
80. Herder opens the first essay, "On Knowing and Sensing," of 1774, ibid. 545, with what was classically (Descartes, Malebranche, Leibniz) a case of *confused* knowing: "No knowledge is devoid of *Empfindung*, that is, a feeling [*Gefühl*] of good or evil, affirmation or negation, pleasure or pain," by which the soul knows *obscurely* (549) that the object is to be pursued or avoided. In his equally classical observation on the passions (*Affekte*), he sees them as "very strong, comprehensive [*vielfassend*] and lively concepts or images of what we take to be good or evil. Nature chose them as the easiest way to bring into the soul at once such strong impressions, such multiple knowledge, which would not have been possible by the means of distinct [*deutlichen*] knowledge" (554).
81. Herder, "Vom Erkennen und Empfinden" (1774), ibid. 552; cf. 555. An indication of how far he has come from *Plastik* is the statement, "The finer the sense, the more lasting and certain are its objects" (605). This clearly favors sight, as the most intellectual sense, and symptomatically, in the next paragraph, Herder manages to give a favorable turn to the notion that sight "disperses [*zerstreuet*] outside of ourselves."
82. Ibid. 558. Exceptionally, Herder uses '*verworren*' (confused) here together with and as a synonym for 'obscure'.
83. Ibid. 578.
84. Ibid. 620.
85. Herder, "Viertes Kritisches Wäldchen," ibid. 66.
86. Herder, "Vom Erkennen und Empfinden" (1778), ibid. 674.

The Idea of Life as a Work of Art in Scottish Enlightenment Discourse

LESLIE ELLEN BROWN

The writings of the eighteenth-century Scots *literati* that touch upon the area of sense theory treated considerably more than the scientific properties of sound and the psychology of perception. Rather, Scottish philosophy provided for a language in which aesthetic beauties could be discussed within the realm of polite learning. For instance, definitions and discussions associated with the subject of taste incorporated a rather conspicuous usage of words such as "virtuoso," "master," "maker," and similar terms that imply an act of exceptional creative skill. These labels do not appear to any considerable degree in formalized discourses on art or, specifically in the case of "virtuoso," in descriptions of the performance of music, as they would later in the nineteenth century. Rather, this terminology is found within writings on the subject of virtue and merit. Moreover, inclusion of the terminology in association with ideas about ethics contribute to the peculiarly Scottish tenor of such discourses.

The broad discussion of the correspondence between virtue and beauty which permeates much of the writings of Francis Hutcheson and the subsequent generation of Scottish moral philosophers is beyond the scope of this paper. Nevertheless, we can investigate one aspect of the correlation, the idea of life as a work of art. This idea—which for the purposes of this discussion will be called the life/art paradigm—may be regarded as the Scots' construction of a vocabulary and in turn a set of images in which moral excellence, as apparent in life and conduct, was not divorced from scholarly and artistic excellence. Specifically, the vocabulary and imagery suggest the artist himself as a shaper or molder of life. The argument, which links the man of virtue with the artist, draws us to yet another

51

correlation, one which connects eighteenth-century philosophical discourse with Scotland's ancient past.

The source for the life/art idea, Shaftesbury's *Characteristics*,[1] was an important one to the Scots in a number of respects. In the discourse entitled "An Inquiry Concerning Virtue or Merit," Shaftesbury draws objects of aesthetic sense into line with the evidences of moral sense. Specifically, Shaftesbury views the moral sense intuitively in that acts of moral judgment are discerned as either positive or negative, not unlike objects of aesthetic judgment discerned as either beautiful or ugly. Good taste, therefore, is important both to the aesthetic sense and the moral sense. In conjoining the good with the beautiful, Shaftesbury established an analogy between the fine arts and life and manners. To Shaftesbury, the central concept of both morality and aesthetics is harmony and proportion:

> For harmony is harmony by nature, let men judge ever so ridiculously of music. So is symmetry and proportion founded still in nature, let men's fancy prove ever so barbarous, or their fashions ever so Gothic in their architecture, sculpture, or whatever other designing art. 'Tis the same case where life and manners are concerned. Virtue has the same fixed standard. The same numbers, harmony, and proportions will have place in morals, and are discernable in the characters and affections of mankind; in which are laid the foundations of art and science superior to every other of human practice and comprehension. (*Characteristics*, 1:227–28)

Shaftesbury perceives this fixed standard to be beauty—uniformity and the relation of parts to the whole—and recognizes that there exists something virtuous within as the fixed standard becomes manifest in acts and attitudes.

Shaftesbury reinforces this thesis by establishing a correlation between a man of virtue and the artist, suggesting that the successful artist is a superior being who stands positioned above worldly affairs. Nor are there words to precisely describe the artist's inherently special position: "Though his [the artist's] intention be to please the world, he must nevertheless be, in a manner, above it and fix his eye upon the consummate grace, that beauty and Nature, and that perfection of numbers which the rest of mankind, feeling only by the effect whilst ignorant of the cause, term the *je ne scay quoy*, the unintelligible or the I know not what, and suppose to be a kind of charm or enchantment of which the artist himself can give no account" (ibid. 214). He relies on the term "virtuoso," stating that being a virtuoso and being virtuous are identical; both are based on an innate knowledge of proportion, sensitivity, and character. Shaftesbury regards this innate knowledge as an operation of the mind in which moral subjects are judged in the same manner as aesthetic subjects (ibid. 251–52): "And thus the sense of inward numbers, the knowledge and practice of the social virtues, and the familiarity and favour of the moral graces, are essential to the character of a deserving artist and just favourite of the Muses. Thus are the Arts and Virtues mutually friends; and thus the science of virtuosi and that of virtue itself become, in a manner, one and the same" (ibid. 217).

Apparently Shaftesbury accepted the term "virtuoso" in its most ancient literal sense, that is, in the equating of technical prowess and strength of character.[2] In the eighteenth century, the virtuoso—both in Britain and on the continent—was a connoisseur who pursued investigations in the arts and sciences in general and was therefore learned, scholarly, and skilled. Moreover, elements of the most obsolete usage of the word, that is, in reference to manly excellence, figure as a factor here, in that both virtuoso and virtue derive from the concept of strength, which in turn was equated with goodness and worth. Like the virtuous individual, the virtuoso was capable of producing significant effect, possessive of power or at least of influence, an idea which plays out in the writings of the Scots, as we will see.

Shaftesbury counters fashionable opinion with his contention that the source of virtue lies, not within formal academies of higher learning, but perhaps within the studios of the practicing artist: "But in this I am so fully satisfied I have reason on my side, that let custom be ever so strong against me, I had rather repair to these inferior schools to search for Truth and Nature than to some other places where higher arts and sciences are professed" (ibid. 214). With this gesture, he places the virtuoso as one possessed of morality to a greater degree than the student of learned discourse: "I am persuaded that to be a *virtuoso* (so far as befits a gentleman) is a higher step towards the becoming a man of virtue and good sense than the being what in this age we call a scholar" (ibid. 214–15). This argument unfolds in Shaftesbury's invocation for a "just and liberal education," and in his calling for institutions to reconsider the formation of the "genteel and liberal character" (ibid. 215n). To that end, Shaftesbury employs the domain of art to create a contrast with conventional philosophy, venturing so far as to shatter faith in age-old philosophical judgments. He scorns those philosophies which are in no way linked to the lively arts because they have grown "dronish, insipid, pedantic, useless, and directly opposite the real knowledge and practice of the world and mankind" (ibid.). To Shaftesbury, these kinds of philosophical writings signify mere pretense; they carry inadequate discussions of the true nature of moral virtue and vice, whereas the work of the painter or poet, for example, conveys sincerity and truth: "One would imagine that our philosophical writers, who pretend to treat morals, should far out-do mere poets in recommending virtue and representing what was fair and amiable in human actions. . . . But so far are our modern moralists from condemning any unnatural vices or corrupt manners, whether in our own or foreign climates, that they would have vice itself appear as natural as virtue." (ibid. 225–27).

Within this context, however, Shaftesbury reminds us of the responsibility of the artist—and again, particularly the poet—to the understanding of truth. He calls forth the ideal of liberal learning, which can be entirely useless if content is severed from feeling, sense, and aesthetic or moral judgments. The activities of pedantic authors do nothing for the act of creation unless true knowledge of humanity is present: "There can be no kind of writing which relates to men and manners where it is not necessary for the author to understand poetical and moral truth, the beauty of sentiments, the sublime of characters, and carry in his eye the model or exemplar of that natural grace which gives to every action its attractive charm. If he has naturally no eye or ear for these interior numbers, 'tis not likely he should be able to judge better of that exterior proportion and symmetry of composition which constitutes a legitimate piece" (ibid. 226). Shaftesbury's language is intriguing here in that he refers to the moral sense as "interior numbers," a figure of speech used also to describe an internal sense that dictates aesthetic judgments and which he discusses elsewhere in terms of taste. Further, moral grace and the variety of characters and human affections are those things which the artist imitates: "If he knows not this Venus, these graces, nor was ever struck with the beauty, the decorum of this inward kind, he can neither paint advantageously after the life nor in a feigned subject where he has full scope. For never can he, on these terms, represent merit and virtue, or mark deformity and blemish" (ibid. 217). Thus, it is hardly surprising that in discussing taste, Shaftesbury refers to the characteristics of civility and humanity as a type of taste, noting that in forming judgments in both the arts and manners, correct models of perfection are necessary (ibid. 217–18). From successful models derive rigid and rigorous rules governing the arts, the true knowledge of which is not an accident or a game. Shaftesbury identifies the individual who would imagine it so as a "mock-virtuoso" (ibid. 219–20).

Shaftesbury's method for imposing order on aesthetics was instrumental in the formation of Francis Hutcheson's theory of a parallel aesthetic and moral sense, one of the major contributions, it is often agreed, of Scottish Enlightenment thought in general. Indeed, it has been proposed that although Shaftesbury does relate sense perception to value judgment, he never ventures so far as to conclude that the two are the same; Hutcheson must be given his due for taking this step and particularly for identifying aesthetic and moral judgments as perceptual and emotive.[3] Nevertheless, Hutcheson himself acknowledges his debt to Shaftesbury: "This moral sense of beauty in actions and affections may appear strange at first view. Some of our moralists themselves are offended at it in my Lord Shaftesbury, so much are they accustomed to deduce every approbation or aversion from rational views of private interest (except it be merely in the simple ideas of the external sense) and have such a horror at *innate ideas*, which they imagine this borders upon."[4]

It is within the division of pleasures into the sensible and the rational that Hutcheson first introduces the idea of the living of life as an artistic process: "For there are many sorts of objects, which please or displease us as necessarily, as material objects do when they operate upon our Organs of Sense.

There is scarcely any object which our minds are employed about which is not thus constituted the necessary occasion of some pleasure or pain. Thus we shall find our selves pleased with a regular form, a piece of architecture or painting, a composition of notes, a theorem, an action, an affection, a character" (*Inquiry*, 24). Hutcheson here is referring to the rational pleasures, which he also calls "aesthetic"; these pleasures, whether they deal with the fine arts or human character, all involve collecting and contemplating simple ideas through an internal sense, in turn leading to the complex ideas of structure, proportion, and the like. In noting that pleasure derives from both artistic constructs and personal traits or acts, Hutcheson is finding value in both moral and aesthetic feeling. He continues by identifying this phenomenon as usual in life and based on a common faculty which permits man to recognize the nature of beauty and the nature of good and evil: "If the reader be convinced of such determinations of the mind to be pleased with forms, proportions, resemblances, theorems, it will be no difficult matter to apprehend another superior sense, natural to men, determining them to be pleased with actions, characters, affections" (ibid. 26).

Although Hutcheson does not use Shaftesbury's precise term "virtuoso" in this instance, he does retain the concept. Further, the concept in connection with the notion of a life/art paradigm is found in numerous writings of the authors of moral philosophy in Scotland and significantly those from the second half of the eighteenth century. The features of this argument vary. But for the most part, the Scots *literati* clearly viewed "virtuoso" as a title of honor, reserved for those distinguished in any intellectual or artistic discipline. A virtuoso in music was not only a skillful performer but one possessed of a solid theoretical expertise as well.[5] Thus the *literati* developed a particularly important feature of the life/art discussion: the role of the artist as philosopher. Hutcheson, for instance, constructs the image of a "master" in discussing the process of perceiving ideas of beauty as the work of an internal sense; he praises both the poet and the man of fine taste for successfully regarding objects of beauty, for seeing the whole, and for looking beyond the knowledge of external sensations: "Our external senses may, by measuring, teach us all the proportions of architecture to the tenth of an inch, and the situation of every muscle in the human body; and a good memory may retain these. And yet there is still something farther necessary, not only to make a man a complete master in architecture, painting, or statuary, but even a tolerable judge in these works, or capable of receiving the highest pleasure in contemplating them."[6] For Hutcheson, mastery requires not only true knowledge of the art form itself but also taste, judgment, and the recognition of value. Through the concept of virtuoso or master, the artist and connoisseur merge into one.

Yet another view of the artist as philosopher emphasizes the importance of reason over the senses, as is evident in the discourses of Lord Monboddo. In some respects, Monboddo might serve as an alternative voice to Hutcheson in a discussion of beauty in art and character, since he was a metaphysicist and not in sympathy with Hutcheson's approach to moral didacticism. Nevertheless, basing a belief in universal science on the works of Plato, Aristotle, and their successors, Monboddo discusses pleasure, intellect, and beauty in an essay entitled "Of the Several Kinds of Mind." He dispenses with the assumption that knowledge pleases for its own sake, contending that there must exist something within an object which creates pleasure in the mind. This something is beauty, the author notes, adding that truth, science, virtue, and the fine arts all create pleasure because they are beautiful. Monboddo also disdains the theory that knowledge pleases because it is useful, and instead assimilates the understanding of knowledge in general to the virtuoso's true understanding of the arts: "But a Man that loves Knowledge merely for the utility of it will never be esteemed a philosopher by those who know what philosophy is; any more that a Man, who loves Pictures and Statues merely for the money he will make of them, will be esteemed a Virtuoso."[7]

The life/art paradigm further emerges from various eighteenth-century Scottish writings, some addressed to a learned audience, others to a broader public of interested amateurs. This latter group was concerned with the artist as philosopher, as were Hutcheson and Monboddo's readers. In a letter to the editor of the popular periodical the *Scots Magazine*, one critic holds forth on the characteristics of valid artistry. He considers fine musicians—those capable of moving the more delicate passions—to be a rarity; fine actors, he expressly notes, perform successfully and arrive at the standard of virtue set by nature when the individual is an "absolute master of every passion of the mind, and a tolerable judge of men and things."[8] Again, the necessity of making valid value judgments, based on taste and rules, is implicit.

Yet another feature of the argument for a life/art paradigm unfolds in the use of specific terminology to delineate the acts of moving and affecting, a concept which recalls Shaftesbury's view of the term "virtuoso" in its ancient and literal sense. The classicist James Moor sets this forth in a discussion of Euripides and the high esteem in which Athenians held him for having directed the temperament of the mind, promoted happiness, and brought forth human feelings; Moor speaks of "masters of all their virtue." He places these observations in the context of sociability, noting Euripides' ability to convey "all of the finer springs of the human heart; every tender emotion, of love, affection, gratitude, friendship; every delicate occurrence; every thing truly amiable, or polite, in social life, or hospitable intercourse." Further, Moor specifies that the chief aim of the public arts—poetry, painting, and music—is to cultivate virtue and that their noblest enterprise is to "strike the heart, and make it glow with the most generous and manly sentiments,"[9] vocabulary suggestive of the obsolete meaning of the term "virtuoso" in which strength correlates with goodness. Typical here is Moor's sensitivity to his audience of male colleagues who, like himself, would have been well aware of the roots of English words.

Adam Smith advances like terminology in the essay entitled, "Of the Imitative Arts," in which he discusses instrumental music as effectively imitative when handled with expertise and by one who thoroughly understands the temper and character of the music: "It is an art which requires all the judgment, knowledge, and invention of the most consummate master."[10] What is significant in Smith's view is the belief that the master is one whose knowledge of the passions, and the ability to produce them, is as thorough as the knowledge of technique. To Smith, musicians without this understanding are inferior artists, capable of producing only tricks or imperfect imitations. Smith's concern with imitation in instrumental music lies not with representation but rather with the process of exciting the mind. In this regard, Smith does not fundamentally disagree with Shaftesbury and Hutcheson.

The idea of skill in manipulating the passions also prevails in creating standards for virtue, as reflected in Adam Ferguson's description of the artist as the "artificer": "We speak of art as distinguished from nature; but art itself is natural to man. He is in some measure the artificer in his own frame, as well as his fortune, and is destined, from the first of his being, to invent and contrive. He applies the same talents to a variety of purposes, and acts merely the same part in very different scenes."[11] Within this discussion of the general characteristics of human nature, Ferguson uses unusually expressive language in drawing a picture of man as an actor living through the various changing scenes of a drama and shaping life as an art form in the process. Certainly his characterization of man as an ingenious deviser is evidence of the strength of Shaftesbury's acclaim for the achievements of practicing artists.

It is frequently argued that one of the most important contributions of the Scottish moral philosophers was the investigation of the science of the mind, and this idea is also a feature of the argument for the life/art paradigm. Again, Shaftesbury's "An Inquiry Concerning Virtue and Merit" provides a model for the theory of moral subjects judged in the same way that aesthetic subjects are and for the argument that the mind makes these judgments, discerning the good or the bad in something (*Characteristics* 1:251–52). David Hume's well-known description of the anatomy of the mind establishes a slightly different point of reference from Shaftesbury's approach: "[T]here are different ways of examining the Mind as well as the Body. One may consider it either as an Anatomist or as a Painter; either to discover its most secret Springs & Principles or to describe the Grace & Beauty of its Actions. I imagine it impossible to conjoin these two views. . . . Any warm sentiment of Morals, I am afraid, wou'd have the Air of Declamation amidst abstract Reasonings & wou'd be esteem'd contrary to good Taste."[12] Hume highlights a contrast between the metaphysician and the moralist, professions which he argues are incompatible.[13] But in doing so, he parallels an aesthetic image (painter) with an ethical image (moral sentiment).

Thomas Reid likewise views the discipline of moral philosophy in terms of the various operations of the mind. While arguing that the senses and the intellect operate on the mind in different ways (the way of reflection versus the way of analogy), Reid ultimately sees considerable harmony between the two. Writing to refute Hume, among others, Reid regards philosophical thought on the various faculties of the human mind to be in a low state and criticizes overly narrow investigations: "But in the noblest arts, the mind is also the subject upon which we operate. The painter, the poet, the actor, the orator, the moralist, and the statesman, attempt to operate upon the mind in different ways, and for different ends; and they succeed, according as they touch properly the strings of the human frame."[14] The commonality of these diverse operations is effectiveness in moving the spectators. Reid's approach becomes clearer when, in a later instance, he specifies that as objects of sense, there exist beauties of color, sound, form, motion, speech, thought, actions, affections, and character.[15]

Both Hume's anatomist/painter imagery and Reid's operations-of-the-mind construct complement Shaftesbury's virtue/virtuoso model. The appeal of the idea of the life/art relationship is also demonstrated by its popularization in encyclopedic form. The *Encyclopaedia Britannica* article on "moral philosophy," authored in part by George Gleig, summarizes Shaftesbury and Hutcheson's supposition of moral actions and characters deriving from a common instinct. Gleig's essay opens with a definition of moral philosophy as both an "art" and a "science"; of these, the former is of particular significance in that it involves a system of rules relating to virtue and happiness. In this same article and within a discussion of man's duties to society, the aesthetic foundation is again brought forward as music is used as an analogy relevant to aptitude for human sociability or social union:

> Man is admirably formed for particular social attachments and duties. There is a particular and strong propensity in his nature to be affected with the sentiments and dispositions of others. Men, like certain musical instruments, are set to each other, so that the vibrations or notes excited in one raise correspondent notes and vibrations in the others. The impulses of pleasure or pain, joy or sorrow, made on one mind, are by an instantaneous sympathy of nature communicated in some degree to all; especially when hearts are (as an humane writer expresses it) in unison of kindness; the joy that vibrates in one communicates to the other also. We may add, that though joy thus imparted swells the harmony, yet grief vibrated to the heart of a friend, and rebounding from thence in sympathetic notes, melts as it were, and almost dies away.[16]

Human sociability as a feature of the life/art paradigm is also noted in a popular periodical article entitled "An Essay on Virtue and Harmony":

> Some of the ancient philosophers [i.e., Cicero] have considered the

order and harmony of the universe as a declaration of God's love of order and harmony. . . . They compared the just order of the human affections to a well-tuned harp. Agreeably to this, they called virtue *harmony*, and *virtutis quasi carmen*. . . . That as several parts of musick, and different musical instruments, jointly compose a concert; so the various sorts of beauty, order, proportion, and harmony in unorganized matter, and in the vegetable, animals, and intellectual kingdoms, constitute one universal harmony or concert; and that in it every man is bound to perform his part, in just consonance with the whole; which can be done only by the order and regularity of his affections and actions . . . for we feel a pleasure in moral harmony, as well as in musical numbers.[17]

Although addressing an entirely different audience, Adam Ferguson also utilizes the idea of human sociability within a discussion of the concept of progress. Despite the fact that artists are few in number, they are the most successful members of society in communicating the essence of the society and representing a nation's sentiments. Ferguson regards the individual living out his life as an artist fully involved in performance: "Man is formed for an artist; and he must be allowed, even when he mistakes the purpose of his work, to practice his calling, in order to find out for himself what is best for him to perform."[18]

The choice of language of these Scottish writers fully supports the premise that the living of life is not unlike an artistic performance and that artistic achievement supplements the very act of fashioning or shaping life itself, yet another feature of the life/art paradigm. Connections between theology and social philosophy illustrate this point. In discussing the importance of the "internal senses of life," Hutcheson, for instance, addresses the topic of divine goodness. He connects moral necessity with the sense of beauty, concluding that irregularity is not pleasing and that uniformity amidst variety—his definition of aesthetic beauty—derives from divine goodness. He then raises the question how it is that the Deity would choose to operate by the simplest means possible and through general laws to instill in nature uniformity, proportion, and similitude. Hutcheson answers himself:

perhaps there may be some real excellence in this manner of operation, and in these forms, which we know not. But this we may probably say, that since the divine goodness . . . has constituted our sense of beauty as it is at present, the same goodness might have determined the great Architect to adorn this stupendous theatre in a manner agreeable to the spectators, and that part which is exposed to the observation of men so as to be pleasant to them, especially if we suppose that he designed to discover himself to them as wise and good, as well as powerful. (*Inquiry*, 93)

Further, Hutcheson describes the presence of virtue by means of an aesthetic vocabulary, suggesting that the divinity has made the moral sense apparent and accessible in the same way that the artist creates: "The Author of nature has much better furnished us for a virtuous conduct than some moralists seem to imagine, by almost so quick and powerful instructions as we have for strong affections to be the springs of each form, that we may easily distinguish it from its contrary, and be made happy by the pursuit of it" (ibid., 25).

The argument in favor of the artist as a shaper of life is also dealt with by Ferguson, although he replaces Hutcheson's theological vantage point with that of the social scientist. Ferguson identifies utility in the arts as that which serves as the models of excellence and beauty presented in nature. The arts transcend mere usefulness, however, in that the artist pursues virtue well in excess of the boundaries of what is necessary for instruction and the communication of knowledge: "The human mind affects to create, and would furnish the matter as well as the form of its works. Such is the *Poet's* aim;—a name which, in its origin, signifies a *maker*, and implies a contradistinction to those who merely avail themselves of what is made. This disposition to the branch of arts, is such as to make mankind affect the merit of invention, in preference to that of observation or judgment, which are so much required to the successful conduct of the invention itself, and so essential to man, as an actor in the real scenes of human life" (*Principles* 1:286). It is through the arts that mankind exceeds the boundaries of mere empiricism and becomes a creator.

If art, therefore, is the act of shaping or directing life, it must carry an immense responsibility, an idea developed by the Scots which echoes Shaftesbury. For example, in his desire to construct a clear philosophical system for beauty, the aesthetician John Donaldson pursues an explanation of the connection between "outward elegance and virtue" and approaches art as transcending representation. Mere imitation in poetry, painting, and music is beneath the dignity of these three arts, and the artist should disdain the representation of objects as they are but rather seize them as they tend to strike the soul or enhance the imagination, which is already predisposed to sentiment and passion. Donaldson elaborates, describing music as "the means of soothing and exciting the virtuous dispositions of the soul; so far as it answers to this end, it is to be esteemed; otherwise it is fit only to tickle the ears of such as have no hearts, whose presumption is ever proportioned to their ignorance and want of feeling."[19] This conclusion hardly surprises when considering the dimension of Donaldson's treatise as a whole, which seeks to find a true balance between rationalism and emotionalism and which constructs an argument on the linking of taste with virtue: "Taste is the younger sister of Virtue; the offspring of Taste is Pleasure, that of Virtue is Happiness."[20] A life of virtue therefore is also a life of pleasure, if indeed refined and noble sentiments are cultivated and savored in context: "The virtuous man is he who has sense enough to enjoy the greatest pleasure."[21]

The virtuoso or master or maker as a conveyer of virtue undoubtedly held an esteemed role in eighteenth-century Scottish life and thought. The strength of this role, however, lay within the validation of the artist by the proponents of moral philosophy, and when the synergism between art and morality broke down, the result evoked criticism. Shaftesbury, as we have observed, views the virtuosi positively, yet injects a degree of caution based on inherent prejudices again the artisan, as demonstrated in his reference to "the rules of common artists, to the masters of exercise, to the academies of painters, statuaries, and to the rest of the *virtuoso* tribe" (*Characteristics* 1:114). Echoing Shaftesbury's caution, Hutcheson regards the virtuosi critically when they lack a finely tuned aesthetic sense:

> Let everyone here consider how different we must suppose the perception to be which a poet is transported upon the prospect of any of those objects of natural beauty which ravish us even in his description, from that cold lifeless conception which we imagine in a dull critic, or one of the *virtuosi*, without what we call a *fine taste*. This latter class of men may have greater perfection in that knowledge which is derived from external sensation. They can tell the specific differences of trees, herbs, minerals, metals; they know the form of every leaf, stalk, root, flower, and seed of all species about which the poet is ignorant. And yet the poet shall have a much more delightful perception of the whole, and not only the poet but the man of fine taste. (*Inquiry*, 2nd and 3rd eds., 35–36n.)

Of particular interest here is an image of death ("cold lifeless"), in opposition to the previously noted descriptions of the artist as the designer of life itself. Moreover, Hutcheson's comment, which appeared in the context of the perception of ideas of beauty as an internal sense, previews the tenor of Hume's anatomist/painter reference. Hutcheson suggests an incompatible dualism, indicating the virtuoso to be the flawed "anatomist" because he is solely dependent on the external senses or at least inattentive to his finer senses.

It is within a similar discussion of the arts and the sense of taste that John Gregory likewise warns of the breakdown between art and morality, a circumstance marked by superficiality or an over-great regard for fashion and caprice. He is critical of "practical musicians" as well as of "every private practitioner," setting these figures apart from those described as "artists" and "masters."[22] The virtuoso or connoisseur is the only one to carry ethical substance within his art. Like Moor before him, Gregory expressly emphasizes the necessity of music's power to affect the mind by raising passions and emotions, suggesting that failure to do so creates an entirely valueless product: "For in order to give Music any extensive influence over the Mind, the Composer and Performer must understand well the human heart, the various associations of the Passions, and the natural transitions from one to another, as to enable him to command them in consequence of his skill in musical Expression. No Science ever flourished, while it was confined to a set of Men who lived by it as a profession. Such Men have pursuits very different from the end and design of the Art. The interested views of a trade are far different from the enlarged and liberal prospects of Genius and Science."[23]

During the last two decades of the century in particular, the internal sense theory which placed virtue and the arts along side one another was accompanied by other currents within philosophical discourse. One of these was a theory of commercial property, positing that both the fine arts and the mechanical arts flourish because of a market demand for them. To that end, Archibald Arthur's essay, entitled "On the Causes That Have Promoted or Retarded the Growth of the Fine Arts," criticizes those who contend that artistic accomplishment emanates from divine sources. Without directly saying so, Arthur challenges Hutcheson's moral didactic point of view in favor of a more analytic vantage point, one in which progress and growth in the fine arts depend on available market and available providers:

> They persuaded themselves, that those elegant accomplishments which embellished human life, and afforded a most refined pleasure to delicate and cultivated minds, must have sprung from some more noble origin, than the mean occupation which furnished food to a mechanic. They were desirous of discovering a cause in some measure, proportioned to the dignity of the effect which they beheld. They thought it derogatory to those productions which fill the soul of man with enthusiasm, to imagine it possible that Demosthenes pleaded, and Raphael painted, and Corneille composed tragedies, from the vulgar motive which renders the meanest artisan industrious. They were disposed to believe, that those great accomplishments from which they derived the most lasting and rational pleasures, must have proceeded immediately from a heavenly origin.[24]

Arthur illustrates his argument with numerous examples of the fruitful cultivation of the fine arts within various civilizations which have in turn experienced commercial success in foreign commerce and domestic manufacturing. He further contends that the production of works of art throughout history have become tied to increasing demands for luxuries, as have escalating prices and the desire to surpass one's competitors.[25] Clearly the connection between the moral sense and the aesthetic sense holds no place here, nor does the concept of the virtuoso or artist as life's hero.

Clearly, the life/art paradigm played a significant role in eighteenth-century Scottish thought, because of the importance attached to the parallel between the aesthetic and moral senses. Yet I propose that another factor also contributed to the appeal of the life/art paradigm. In part its vitality is attributable to a revival of interest in Scotland's distant past which accompanied the country's move into the enterprises of polite and learned society. One aspect of this interest in Scottish history was a fascination with the sociological significance of the ancient Scottish bard. Several of the Scots *literati* and reformers promoted intense interest in the tools of the bard—the history, language, and song of the Highlands—as an aspect of the anglicized and gentrified ideal of improvement which developed during the second half of the century. The MacPherson-Ossian affair is certainly the most famous manifestation of this movement, and the fact that the controversy which began the 1760s prevailed into the nineteenth century substantiates its strength.[26]

Writings on the sense of beauty and the sense of virtue put forth by the Scots therefore were complemented by attention to the bard as a guardian of moral sensibility. The *literati* themselves—Ferguson, Lord Kames,[27] and Beattie[28] among them—were responsible to some degree for the complementary arrangement. Hugh Blair, for instance, addressed the importance of moral content to epic poetry and specifically noted its use in *Fingal*:[29]

> An epic poem is by its nature one of the most moral of all political compositions: But its moral tendency is by no means to be limited to some common-place maxim, which may be gathered from the strong. It arises from the admiration of heroic actions, which such a composition is peculiarly calculated to produce; from the virtuous emotions which the characters and incidents raise, whilst we read it; from the happy impression which all the parts separately, as well as the whole taken together, leave upon the mind.[30]

Similar currents appear in other writings. Ferguson discusses various types of literature with regard to imagination, delight, and movement of the heart; he cites the ancient poet as the first to combine the source of his stories with the experiences of the performer, suggesting that historic verse tied to the superstitions, glory, and enthusiasm of the bard is appropriate for arousing passions. The bard carved out subjects from his own history and culture: violent, brave, generous, and intrepid characters, trials of fortitude and fidelity, and simple passions of friendship, resentment, and love.[31] A periodical essay entitled "Observations on the Minstrel Profession" also discusses the occupation, once highly esteemed but currently held in contempt. Noting the original, now obsolete, sense of the title—an official—the article presents a romanticized and flattering view of the ancient bard and his importance.[32] Similarly, in defining the golden age of music and poetry in Scotland as the reign of James I through the reign of James V, William Tytler recognizes the role of the bard in maintaining clan history through songs which deal with the deeds, heroes, and ancestors of the chieftains.[33] Likewise, a curious anonymous manuscript dating from the end of century, entitled "An Essay Suggesting an Important Application of the Highland Music," identifies the bard not only as a transmitter of moral truth but a bearer of political influence: "It must be admitted indeed, that there is a period of Society, when the Offices of Legislator & Bard are united in the same person, & that the Songs proceeding from this lustred Character acquire in that connexion a degree of influence, which by no means descends to the poems of a succeeding period. . . . The separation of the Office of legislator & Bard, & the decline of this last profession, in the northern parts of Caledonia, denote some distance from that time."[34]

The bard could be viewed as a touchstone, so that, perhaps not surprisingly, the *literati's* discussion of the life/art idea referenced aspects of the bardic heritage. Ferguson in particular acknowledged that once a nation reached a position where conflict was absent, it was free to delve into the territory identified by sentiment and reason; the bard was the first to mold this process into a profession: "The songs of the bard, the harangues of the statesman and warrior, the tradition and the story of ancient times, are considered as the models, or the earliest production, of so many arts, which it becomes the object of different professions to copy or improve."[35] Although the role of the bard was no longer of any significance within the society which assigned to itself the tenets of modern moral philosophy, the romanticized revival of the image was. The end result was the triumph of the idea of the artist—the virtuoso or master or maker—as a conveyer of virtue, formulated through the language of a parallel aesthetic and moral sense.

NOTES

Funding for research for this essay was provided by the National Endowment for the Humanities and the Pennsylvania State University Arts and Humanistic Studies Institute.
 1. Anthony Ashley Cooper, third earl of Shaftesbury, *Characteristics of Men, Manner, Opinions, Times* (1711), ed. John Robertson, 2 vols. (London: Grant Richards, 1900; reprint with introduction by Stanley Grean, Indianapolis: Bobbs-Merrill, 1964). Hereafter cited in the text as *Characteristics*.
 2. *OED*, s.v. "virtuoso." See also "virtue" and "virtuous."
 3. An idea argued extensively by Peter Kivy, *The Seventh Sense: A Study of Francis Hutcheson's Aesthetics and Its Influence in Eighteenth-Century Britain* (New York: Burt Franklin, 1976), 1, 14, 22, 23. Kivy notes that Hutcheson's writings on aesthetics appeared at a time when the sense of beauty was regarded progressively—that is, when speculation turned away from the art object to the perception of the object and away from a rational approach to a perceptual one. Although George Turnbull's *The Principles of Moral Philosophy. An Enquiry into the Wise and Good Government of the Moral World* (London, 1740) is often cited as the work which introduces the tenets of moral philosophy—the application of the same principles of careful study of the natural world to the human mind—Hutcheson is regarded by Kivy as the first to apply these tenets to aesthetics.
 4. Francis Hutcheson, *An Inquiry into the Original Ideas of Beauty and Virtue, in Two Treatises* (London, 1725), and specifically the first treatise *An*

Inquiry Concerning Beauty, Order, Harmony, Design, ed. Peter Kivy (The Hague: Martinus Nijhoff, 1973), 25. Hereafter cited in text as *Inquiry*.

5. This concept is carried forward from sixteenth- and seventeenth-century Italian usage and may be found in such eighteenth-century musical sources as Sébastien de Brossard's *Dictionnaire de musique* (1701) and Johann Walther's *Musikalisches Lexicon* (1732). See *The New Grove Dictionary of Music and Musicians*, s.v. "virtuoso."

6. Hutcheson, *Inquiry* 35–36; the editor specifies that this material appears in the second and third editions only.

7. James Burnett, Lord Monboddo, *Antient Metaphysics or the Science of Universals*, 6 vols. (London, 1779–99), 2:104, 105.

8. *Scots Magazine* 1 (1739): 132.

9. James Moor, "An Essay on the Influence of Philosophy upon the Fine Arts," published in *Essays Read to a Literary Society* (Glasgow, 1759), 17, 14, 2.

10. Adam Smith, *Essays on Philosophical Subjects* (Dublin, 1795), 228.

11. Adam Ferguson, *An Essay on the History of Civil Society* (Edinburgh, 1767), 9–10.

12. David Hume, *The Letters of David Hume*, ed. Raymond Klibansky and Ernest C. Mosner (Oxford: Clarendon Press, 1954), 1:32–33. Letter dated 1739.

13. See Richard B. Sher, "Professors of Virtue: The Social History of the Edinburgh Moral Philosophy Chair in the Eighteenth Century," in *Studies in the Philosophy of the Scottish Enlightenment*, ed. M.A. Stewart (Oxford: Clarendon Press, 1990), 87–126.

14. Thomas Reid, *An Inquiry into the Human Mind, on the Principles of Common Sense* (Edinburgh, 1764), 2–3.

15. Thomas Reid, *Essay on the Intellectual Powers of Man* (1785). Printed in *Essays on the Powers of the Human Mind*, 3 vols. (Edinburgh, 1803), 1:527. Reid's writings lend support to the paradigm in other ways as well, one of which is the use of analogies between the harmony of a piece of music and the harmony of social intercourse ("If they have any just foundation, as they seem to me to have, they serve to account for the metaphysical application of the names of concord and discord to the relations of sounds; to account for the pleasure we have from harmony in music; and to show that the beauty of harmony is derived from the relation it has to agreeable affections of mind," 1:550).

16. *Encylopaedia Britannica or a Dictionary of Arts, Sciences, and Miscellaneous Literature: Constructed on a Plan*, 3rd ed., 18 vols. (Edinburgh, 1787–97), 12:272, 299. For a discussion of the philosophical foundation of moral judgment, aesthetic judgment, and social philosophy, see Susan M. Purviance, "Intersubjectivity and Sociable Relations in the Philosophy of Francis Hutcheson," *Sociability and Society in Eighteenth-Century Scotland*, ed. J. Dwyer and R. Sher, in *Eighteenth-Century Life*, 15, n.s. 1 & 2 (1991): 23–38. The author illustrates precisely how beauty and virtue both derive from the sorts of experiences that express natural human sociability.

17. *Scots Magazine*, 12 (1750): 422–23, 557.

18. Adam Ferguson, *Principles of Moral and Political Science* (Edinburgh, 1792), 1:289, 299. Hereafter cited in the text as *Principles*.

19. John Donaldson, *The Elements of Beauty. Also, Reflections on the Harmony of Sensibility and Reason* (Edinburgh, 1780), 87, 88.
20. Ibid., 83.
21. Ibid., 105.
22. John Gregory, *A Comparative View of the State and Faculties of Man with Those of the Animal World*, 2d ed. (London, 1766), 7, 78, 79. Gregory's publication consists of a set of discourses delivered at the Philosophical Society of Aberdeen.
23. Ibid., 78–79.
24. Archibald Arthur, *Discourses on Theological and Literary Subjects* (Glasgow, 1803), 363–90, quotation on 376. Arthur's work contains fourteen essays, several of which deal with sensations, beauty (comments on Burke and Hutcheson), the grand, taste, sensibility, the promotion of the fine arts, and the advancement of the fine arts.
25. Ibid., 379.
26. See David Daiches, *The Paradox of Scottish Culture: The Eighteenth-Century Experience* (London: Oxford University Press, 1964), 8–10; Bruce Lenman, *Integration, Enlightenment, and Industrialization: Scotland 1746–1832* (Toronto: University of Toronto Press, 1981), 120–21; and Peter Womack, *Improvement and Romance: Constructing the Myth of the Highlands* (Houndsmills, Basingstoke, Hampshire: MacMillan, 1989), 96, 107. For more varied and liberal treatments of the Ossian issue, see *Ossian Revisited*, ed. Howard Gaskill (Edinburgh: Edinburgh University Press, 1991). Of the numerous contemporary references, the best known is Hugh Blair's *A Critical Dissertation on the Poems of Ossian, the Son of Fingal*, 2d ed. (London, 1765; reprint, New York: Garland, 1970). One especially interesting source, Alexander Campbell's *An Introduction to the History of Poetry in Scotland* (Edinburgh, 1798), 25–26, condemns skepticism of Ossian authenticity as an anti-Stuart political intrigue.
27. See, for example, Henry Home, Lord Kames, *Sketches in the History of Man*, 2 vols. (Edinburgh, 1774), and especially the essay from volume 1 entitled "Progress of Taste and of the Fine Arts."
28. See, for example, James Beattie, *Essays: On Poetry and Music, as They Affect the Mind; on Laughter and Ludicrous Composition* (Edinburgh, 1778), and specfically the essay "Conjectures on Some Peculiarities of National Music."
29. See John Dwyer, "Enlightened Spectators and Classical Moralists: Sympathetic Relations in Eighteenth-Century Scotland," *Sociability and Society in Eighteenth-Century Scotland*, 96–118. Dwyer contends that Blair's thrust in the *Dissertation* was not only to recall civic virtues of the ancient Greeks and Romans (classical values of manliness) but to support the sentimental content of *Ossian*. This ability to produce pathos could then control the feelings of the readers for the purposes of being pleased and morally uplifted. The emotional manipulation for ethical effect was quite intriguing to Blair.
30. Blair, *Critical Dissertation*, 43.
31. Ferguson, *History of Civil Society*, 263, 266.
32. *Scots Magazine* 45 (1783): 583–84. An entry on the "Highlanders" in the *Encyclopaedia Britannica*, 8:506–8 also notes the refinement in sentiment

and manners of the ancient Scottish civilizations, addressing the significance of the bard in terms of this characteristic.

33. William Tytler, "A Dissertation of the Scottish Music," printed as an appendix to Hugo Arnot's *The History of Edinburgh*, (Edinburgh, 1779), 632–33.

34. University of Edinburgh Library Ms. La. II. 47, 17–18.

35. Ferguson, *History of Civil Society*, 289.

Writing the Picture: Fielding, Smollett, and Hogarthian Pictorialism

PAMELA CANTRELL

During the late seventeenth and early eighteenth centuries the expression of the sister-arts relationship had begun to shift from a shared system of traditional symbols and emblems to more universal sorts of relations between image and narrative. Invoking Mikhail Bakhtin, Ronald Paulson has recently seen the replacement of sacred images and biblical texts as an iconoclastic break with the past, a break from "literary and artistic precursors, or at least the canonical ones idolized by society's connoisseurs and critics."[1] Bakhtin in "Epic and Novel" relates this shift to the rise in prominence of the novel, a genre which exists outside the "high" literature of the ruling societal group. When the novel became the dominant genre in the eighteenth century, it "novelized" other genres, making them "more free and flexible."[2] Novelization was not limited to literary genres; a similar reaction is evident in the visual arts. As Paulson notes in *Emblem and Expression*, Renaissance emblems did not disappear, but were displaced to areas of lesser import, becoming in many instances no more than "topoi on the wall." The time had come for art's position as the "idol of the ruling culture," in Paulson's phrasing, to be replaced by its "subculture equivalent"—an art and literature aimed at the general public.[3] As a result, the relationship of painting to text as it had existed in the Renaissance tradition began to yield to new cultural and artistic sensibilities.

Just as eighteenth-century painters began to abandon the allegory and symbols of Renaissance art in favor of the more familiar narrative style of modern history painting, popular writers such as Henry Fielding, Laurence Sterne, and Tobias Smollett came to value the spatiality and pictorialism intrinsic to the visual arts. It became common practice to invoke the pencil of such contemporary artists as Thomas Rowlandson and William Hogarth when language seemed insufficient to express a vivid facial expression or physical trait.

Over the years an analogy has often been suggested between the art of William Hogarth and the novels of Henry Fielding, an analogy founded in Fielding's complimentary reference to Hogarth by name in the preface to *Joseph Andrews* (1742) and in Hogarth's response in his print *Characters and Caricaturas* (1743) where, as Martin C. Battestin notes, Hogarth actually repaid the compliment twice, both in the caption and within the print itself.[4] Robert Etheridge Moore some time ago cited several areas of similarity of character and incident between Hogarth and Fielding, and also noted the direct influence of Hogarth's imagery on Fielding's style.[5] And in a 1981 study, Peter Jan de Voogd argues strongly for a Hogarth-Fielding analogy based upon affinities in style and ideology, as well as in the many mutual references found within the works of both.[6] Ronald Paulson has dated the relationship between Hogarth and Fielding to 1728, upon the publication of Fielding's *The Masquerade*, which Paulson believes to have been directly inspired by Hogarth's *Masquerade Ticket*.[7]

In his famous preface to *Joseph Andrews*, Fielding describes Hogarth as his counterpart in the visual arts and claims to adopt Hogarth's artistic practice by divorcing the burlesque from comedy in literature as part of an attempt to elevate the lowly form of the novel to the generic level of the epic, just as Hogarth had raised the depiction of character above that of caricature.[8] Hogarth had taken the already established aristocratic form of history painting and tried to democratize it, replacing biblical and mythical scenes with realistic modern characters and events, thereby transforming history painting into a contemporary, middle-class genre. By contrast, Fielding used representational changes to raise the level of the comic novel from a mere burlesque into what Fielding calls "a comic epic poem in prose" after the lost comic epics of Homer.[9] Both Fielding and Hogarth publicly fostered a symbiotic influence that would serve to further the analogy between the novel and modern history painting, yet their affinity relies more on teleological approximation than ideology. I would like to suggest that Fielding's emphasis on epic in fact distances him ideologically from Hogarth who, rather than cling to ancient models, meant to break from tradition in order to create a composite modern form, and that a more fruitful correspondence with Hogarth may be charted in the works of Tobias Smollett.

Whether Fielding failed to recognize that he and Hogarth had actually set out to accomplish different goals or not, he consistently promoted the analogy between himself and Hogarth in calling upon the "inimitable pencil" of Hogarth when he wanted to illuminate a direct reference to a specific Hogarth print or when he felt that a particular facial expression was especially characteristic of Hogarth.[10] No doubt Fielding aimed to do in his novels what Hogarth accomplished visually, and succeeded in creating scenes of realistic characters placed in real-life situations. Here, however, the analogy begins to weaken. Paulson tells us that Fielding understood the "operation" of Hogarth's progresses and that he put it into practice in *Joseph Andrews*. In that work "delusions are constantly being exposed, though dreaded consequences are avoided."[11] The claim is true as far as it goes since the general movement of the story, the subject matter, and the Bakhtinian use of contemporary reality to create comedy all correspond to the literary aspect of Hogarth's technique.

And yet, Fielding rarely accomplishes in his prose fiction a truly visual Hogarthian scene. Fielding writes a sustained narrative incorporating well-developed but not individualized central characters who play an integral role in the action of the story. Hogarth's series move in a linear fashion with a focus on the main character[s], yet they also include activity and characters that serve as a secondary locus of satire. In *Marriage a la Mode* (1745), for example, plate 3 (figure 1) illustrates not only the need of a treatment for syphilis but serves also as a satire on the practice of medicine by quack doctors. While it advances the linear action of the series as a whole, the scene is both active and interesting when it stands alone. From the licentious movement by the skeleton in the closet, to the machines in the left foreground (more for torture, it appears, than for healing!), to the assortment of strange objects that line the wall overhead (including a crocodile on the ceiling), our gaze is free to wander, stop, examine and interpret the unique environment Hogarth creates for his protagonist. An abundance of visual detail augments the action at the center of the print, where the central drama of the earl and the results of his sexual escapades is rendered. Hogarth presents us with a variety of activity extending the parameters of the linear progress. By contrast, Paulson tells us,

> Fielding's picaresque, with the mediation of Augustan ideas of unity and economy, gives the impression of being single-minded, a straight line in which intensity of gaze makes up for variety. Every detail or encounter contributes to the development of an argument concerning the relationship between greatness and goodness or form and feeling.[12]

Another point of difference lies in the sense of "author" as mediator between the reader, or beholder, and the material. In Fielding, to quote Paulson, "the narrator's gravely ironic stance makes the reader aware at every step of an author standing between him and the material, preventing any irrelevant information from reaching him."[13] Hogarth's prints are relatively unmediated. Our eyes are free to take in every pictorial detail and arena of action within the print. This is not to say that Hogarth does not guide our gaze through the narrative, but rather that we are free to examine at our leisure all the nooks and nuances of the scene. It is as if we were on the inside poking about, able to explore our surroundings before moving on. Yet at the same time we are not integrally involved in the scene; we are not actually a part of the action as are such central characters of Fielding's as Tom Jones or Joseph Andrews. It is as though we were instead a minor character, able to observe and report the scene in all its detail from a closely involved point of view where we react to a situation rather than create it.

When we look beyond the more obvious points of relationship between Hogarth and Fielding—Fielding's direct appropriation of character and incident and his understanding of the basic working of a Hogarth series—we find that the analogy ends unsatisfactorily at the formal level and, although Fielding owes much to Hogarth's influence, he rarely achieves the visual acuity of a Hogarth print. Tobias Smollett on the other hand, often does. What Paulson sees as a weakness in Smollett, I would suggest links him, more so than Fielding, to Hogarth:

> Smollett's [satire] is centrifugal, away from the hero and toward a general exploration. Moreover, the central "I" who is seeing, being acted upon, and reacting produces a heightened reality. . . . He appears to be in the very middle of the chaotic action, describing what it feels like, while Fielding's normative and controlling narrator is on the periphery. . . . With Smollett's lack of detachment . . . comes a much greater sense of immediacy, or sensuous contact, almost totally lacking in Fielding's novels.[14]

In a Smollett novel, the reader assumes the point of view of the central character (or, in the case of *Humphry Clinker*, of the character who, as current letter-writer, is central at the time) without the author's mediating presence. Here the character often adopts the role of the viewer of a visual work of art. Guided by the character rather than by the author, we are able to peruse the written scene as we would a painting, taking in all of the peripheral objects and information because we are at the center looking out through the eyes of the character. Our gaze is guided but also diffuse. As in a print by Hogarth, the periphery becomes as important as the central action. J. Paul Hunter writes that "Smollett has more of the satirist's interests in confessional and exhibitionism . . . but here too are clear instances of the novel's tendency to try to get all of life by poking into the crevices and letting the nooks and crannies pop into view."[15] In a word, Smollett is ecphrastic; each scene is separate and complete within itself, yet contributes to the overall sense of the narrative. And periodically the satire can be more cutting and the characters better illustrated when the focus is more diffuse.

Smollett presents his protagonists' progress through a succession of dramatic vignettes, each related to the other by a thematic moral thread. Each has its own drama, created through caricature, verbal expression, and the spatial quality of the action. The descriptive language is active as well as precise; in Jerry Beasley's words, Smollett's description "throbs with energy and feeling."[16] Throughout his picaresque novels the protagonist travels from place to place, meeting interesting and unusual characters along the way. The ancillary characters rarely influence the linear action of the novel but serve instead as the occasion for Smollett to suspend the narrative

Figure 1. William Hogarth, *Marriage a la Mode* (Plate 3, 1745). Courtesy of the Huntington
Library.

momentarily in order to present a panorama of character and incident, where we are momentarily allowed to view the periphery and to witness an expanded arena of action and satire. Smollett's ecphrastic scenes are never static, and nowhere is the technique more skillfully used than in his final novel *The Expedition of Humphry Clinker* (1771).

Humphry Clinker is an epistolary novel and borrows more from the tradition of the travel book than do the sustained narratives of Smollett's earlier picaresque novels. Because the novel centers on the travels of the Bramble party, and especially on the people they meet and the places they visit, Smollett presents many scenes of local color and character. The novel is textured in such a way as to present what Beasley calls "composite pictures" of character, scene, and action.[17] Aside from the five principal letter writers, most of the characters in *Humphry Clinker* appear as subjects in one or two letters, that is, as figures in isolated scenes, and then, having served their function, they disappear. The pictorial quality of the novel arises from the ecphrases that occur when members of the Bramble party stop to observe the scenes around them. Although the Brambles do not always become involved in the action, neither do they become static, a paradox that Beasley has termed "dynamic stasis."[18] Through such a technique Smollett creates a novel that is pictorial in its underlying design.

A representative episode from *Humphry Clinker* may serve to illustrate. In a scene described in Jery Melford's letter of September 12, the Bramble party stops at a Scottish inn while waiting for their carriage to be repaired. Looking out the window they witness a scene that might easily be drawn from Hogarth. An old man is at work paving a street when a well-dressed stranger arrives on horseback. The stranger stops, gives his horse to the innkeeper, and asks the old man about his family. The old man tells him about his sons, that the eldest and youngest have gone to sea and that the second is locked in the prison across the way for his father's debts. While they talk, a young man extends his head between two bars of the prison window and immediately recognizes the stranger as his elder brother. With that, the young men's mother runs out of a house adjacent to the prison and they embrace. From the spatial arrangement of the scene to the dramatic activity, Smollett captures qualities one recognizes from Hogarth.

A close examination of the opening sentence of the passage reveals Smollett's ability to use verbal indices to create a sense of atemporality and spatiality:

> —As we stood at the window of an inn that fronted the public prison, a person arrived on horseback, genteelly, tho' plainly, dressed in a blue frock, with his own hair cut short, and a gold-laced hat upon his head.[19]

The opening clause, "as we stood," indicates simultaneity, and Smollett's use of the deictic mode gives the scene a sense of what Norman Bryson calls "relative temporality" which serves to draw in the reader as part of the "we."[20] The following phrase, "at the window," places the "we" in space.

The window itself serves a dual purpose: first, the reader becomes aware of the location of the Bramble party in the scene; second, the window becomes a frame for the action that is about to unfold outside. The "we" of the opening clause now becomes ambiguous, for the reader as part of the "we" witnesses the action outside the frame of the window, while simultaneously watching the Bramble party as they physically stand before it. In a very few words the larger scene is ordered in space: we see the Brambles, the window frame, and the arena outside. The opening sentence then begins to order exterior space, or what we might refer to as the space of the empty canvas. We learn initially that the inn faces a prison and that a person on horseback enters the scene. Visually, the prison would occupy a large space at the center of the canvas, serving as background to the arriving horseman. According to Paulson, the eye of a person "reading" a picture "moves from the lower left and into the depth of the picture and toward the right."[21] And as Jean Hagstrum has pointed out, "It is not necessary to paint out to the four corners of the 'canvas,'" to relate every detail of the scene, because a minor "hint of painterly structure . . . can evoke a train of controlled pictorial sensations."[22] In this case, although Smollett does not specify the direction of the horseman's entry, we can reasonably place him on our canvas as arriving from the left, the first place our eye would rest. Smollett also presents a brief visual image of the horseman—he has a "blue frock," short hair and a "gold-laced hat." Smollett has chosen just enough detail about the horseman to enable us to visualize him and to determine his social status while maintaining an economy of words. A longer description would occupy a more purely literary space;[23] by keeping the description terse Smollett from the moment of the opening clause maintains the pictorial impression of simultaneity.

Details of the scene continue to unfold as the passage progresses. Other characters arrive and, since the novel is by nature a temporal medium, we view them as they appear, in succession. Even here, Smollett maintains simultaneity through frequent use of gerundives to indicate one action occurring concurrently with another: "Alighting and giving," "So saying," "desiring," "thrusting," "bolting."[24] Other verbal cues of temporal unfolding, such as "At that instant" and "Before," also compress the temporal sense of the narrative. It is not that the action unfolds in one moment, of course, but rather that its successive dimension is compressed into a mood of simultaneity. While it's a temporal scene that the Brambles witness, it presents itself in the spatial form of a Hogarthian scene.

To visualize the previous scene more fully, let's now return to the canvas we began to paint earlier, a scene framed by the sash of the window through which we see in the foreground a street with its horseman and, in the background, a prison. If we were to capture the action at the moment of dramatic climax, we would see the innkeeper at the lower left holding a horse, the alighted horseman holding the paving instrument and speaking to the old man who points toward the prison; while another son's face, wearing a look of recognition, pokes out through the prison bars. From the right, emerging from a house adjacent to the prison, we would see the old woman beginning to run to embrace her eldest son. In the narrative, the frame functions to illuminate simultaneous action and surrounds the entire scene, presenting it in spatial rather than temporal terms.

Now where Smollett compresses the narrative into a single moment, Hogarth uses framing in an opposed, though complementary manner, to create a sense of narrative time in a pictorial mode. The narrative quality of a Hogarth print arises from the strategic placement of several temporal arenas of action within the same rectilinear frame. Any number of Hogarth's prints would exemplify this process, and here plate 5 of *Marriage a la Mode* (figure 2) will serve as an example. Within the larger frame many smaller frames are placed (picture frames, mirrors, doorways, windows) which, as Paulson explains, serve to "delimit and compartmentalize the scene into pieces of more or less accessible information."[25] Such a division of information permits an abundance of narrative action within a single print, actions which would occur naturally as linear and temporal in a written narrative but which must occur atemporally and spatially in a graphic medium. Hogarth captures the action at the precise moment of dramatic crisis. Aided by the frame, Hogarth simultaneously depicts the action that occurs immediately before and after the critical moment. And as our gaze travels across the print, we are able to read the narrative sequence through a series of spatial and temporal cues.

Plates 1–4 of *Marriage a la Mode* depict the deterioration of the marriage between the young earl of Squanderfield and his middle-class wife. Although not wealthy, the couple has assumed the trappings of aristocracy. Both of them have taken lovers (their marriage, arranged by their fathers, was loveless), and the earl has become suspicious of his wife's activities after having heard that she attended a masquerade without him. In a fit of false pride and foolish valor, the earl has decided to interrupt his wife and her lover in their indiscretion. Plate 5 serves as the dramatic climax of the series and involves a closet drama of its own. The scene can be read as a sequential narrative, beginning in the foreground with the central event and then moving along to the peripheral planes in the background and along the sides according to the conventions of the perspective box.[26] Before we enter the scene a duel occurs between the earl and his wife's lover, the lawyer Silvertongue. The drama of plate 5 begins with the earl in the center foreground dying of a wound which has just been inflicted by Silvertongue. We see the earl as he falls to the floor while his kneeling wife begs forgiveness. His sword has not yet fallen, indicating that the mortal blow has just been given. Our gaze then moves to the second arena of action, Silvertongue's escape at the window to the left, an action which occurs immediately after the duel. The painting of the prostitute and the tapestry depicting the Judgment of Solomon next capture our attention, allowing for a temporal pause between Silvertongue's escape and the entrance of the

Figure 2. William Hogarth, *Marriage a la Mode* (Plate 5, 1745). Courtesy of the Huntington Library.

authorities at the right, the third arena of action. The paintings also serve to confront us emotionally; the gaze of the prostitute on the wall is directed immediately at the viewer, as if to ask the beholder to pass moral judgment upon the participants in the drama. By the time the authorities enter, all that remains of the central action is the aftermath, the scene of the dying earl with his penitent wife at his side. As we move through the narrative of the print, through three distinct arenas of action, our experience is one of temporal succession rather than of simultaneity. Each scene, in other words, presents a different stage in the narrative. Hogarth draws our attention to these temporal stages by placing a frame around each area of activity: Squanderfield's head appears framed by the frame of a mirror on the wall behind him; Silvertongue's escape appears in the window frame; and the entering authorities are framed by the open door. Additionally, Hogarth uses the frame to call our attention to other areas that play secondary yet vital roles in the narrative: the toppled chair frames the ticket from the masquerade while the open curtain frames the mussed bed, taking us back in time to the circumstances that caused the current confrontation and to the sexual activity apparently interrupted by the entrance of the earl.

Character is at the heart of a Smollett novel just as in a Hogarth print. Hogarth creates character through physical appearance, facial expression, and action. His characters, like Smollett's, are rarely static, and the meaning of the print whether moral or satiric emerges from the action of the characters. For Hogarth, working in a visual field, physical image and facial expression must work together to develop a narrative without words; for Smollett, visual images can be evoked only through description (both of physical characteristics and action), dialogue (including occupational and class inflection), and an analogous reference to such visual masters of character as Hogarth. Smollett usually limits his allusion to the rare occasion when he needs to illustrate a particular facial expression, whereas Fielding frequently turns to Hogarth to bring to mind a complete character.[27]

Another difference in their innovative appropriation rests in the fact that Fielding often mentions Hogarth in conjunction with his appropriation, while Smollett does not. Moore has argued that Smollett's neglect on this count indicates "a fundamental difference" between his characters and those of Fielding, and that Smollett differs from Hogarth as well because Smollett's characters more resemble caricatures than "the characters of human life" drawn, as he sees them, by Fielding and Hogarth.[28] More recently, however, George Kahrl, who also calls Smollett a caricaturist, has employed the term to liken caricature to a kind of Hogarthian pictorialism rather than to satiric style.[29] Unlike Fielding, who prides himself on the expression of character, Smollett translates into language the visual quality of caricature. Despite his arguments to the contrary, Hogarth creates through the exaggeration of recognizable physical traits a technique bordering on caricature—that is the depiction of unique characters who each express a distinctive individuality. Smollett translates this sort of quasi-caricature into language through both physical description and dialogue, so that when Smollett's characters speak (or write, in the case of *Humphry Clinker*) they are as immediately recognizable as are Hogarth's Moll Hackabout or Tom Rakewell.[30]

The character of Tabitha Bramble from *Humphry Clinker* is a case in point. It seems quite likely that Smollett appropriated the character from Hogarth's *Morning*, the first plate of the series *The Four Times of the Day* (1738) (figure 3).[31] Physically, the two figures bear a striking resemblance. The initial physical description is provided by Jery Melford in his letter of May 6:

> Mrs. Bramble is a maiden of forty-five. In her person she is tall, raw-boned, aukward, flat-chested, and stooping; her complexion is sallow and freckled . . . her forehead low; her nose long, sharp, and, towards the extremity, always red in cool weather; her lips skinny, her mouth extensive, her teeth straggling and loose, of various colours and confirmation; and her long neck shrivelled into a thousand wrinkles.[32]

The image is strikingly visual and remarkably reminiscent of Hogarth; and although Smollett could simply have appropriated her physical appearance for the character of Tabitha, the development of her character appears remarkably similar as well. Both Hogarth and Smollett were making a more serious statement not only about the character of this one particular woman but of her type. Hogarth's lady appears remarkably vain—the weather is cold but she ignores it, preferring rather to expose her bony chest and fingers to the weather than to cover herself and her thin but fashionable dress with a warmer garment. She is on her way to church, and her face expresses a superiority to those she passes on the street. She is ignorant of the suffering of those around her; she disregards the discomfort of the page who freezes as he walks behind her and neither does she notice the outstretched hand of the beggar to her right. She does, however, notice the pair of lovers in front of her and is offended by their conduct, but it is more out of envy, it seems, than from a sense of moral self-righteousness. The lady believes she should be admired for her superiority but in fact she is, because of her narrow view of life and lack of human compassion, less honorable than the poor people who surround her. She suffers from a skewed sense of values, in other words, valuing wealth and appearance over kindness and empathy.

Smollett paints the character of Tabitha Bramble in much the same way. Our first introduction to Tabitha comes in her own words when we read her letter of April 2 to her housekeeper, Mrs. Gwyllim:

> When this cums to hand, be sure to pack up in the trunk male that stands in my closet, to be sent me in the Bristol waggon without loss of time, the following articles, viz. my rose collard neglejay, with green robins, my yellow damask, and my black velvet suit, with the

short hoop; my bloo quilted petticot, my green manteel, my laced
apron, my French commode, Macklin head and lappets, and the litel
box with my jowls.[33]

Tabitha is a static character in an active world, a world which she never
allows to act upon her or to enrich her experience. Her life revolves about
itself; never does she express a thought outside her own self-interest. As
John Sekora has pointed out, Tabitha "is concerned solely with her
possessions. In none of her letters does she remark journey, place, or
emotion. Nothing beyond self touches her. . . . She is oblivious."[34]
Tabitha is easily distinguished from the other letter writers in the novel for
her misspellings and malapropisms (often sexual in nature) as well as for
her lack of interest in the world around her. Like the lady in Hogarth's
Morning, Tabitha has no compassion for those less fortunate than she. In
his letter of April 20, Jery Melford relates an incident that had occurred
between his uncle Matthew and a poor woman he had been charitably
assisting. Matthew had just offered the woman a twenty pound note to help
ease the suffering of her dying child when Tabitha burst into the room and
snatched the note out of the woman's hand, crying, "Who gives twenty
pounds to charity? . . . Besides, charity begins at home—Twenty pounds
would buy me a complete suit of flowered silk, trimmings and all."[35]
Tabitha expresses a similar sentiment in her own letter (of June 14) to her
housekeeper after having been informed that her servants had been eating
more than their share of provisions: "God forbid that I should lack christian
charity; but charity begins at huom, and sure nothing can be a more
charitable work than to rid the family of such vermine."[36] Again, Tabitha
shows herself to be self-centered, petty, and vain, and although a pictorial
caricature, she, along with Hogarth's lady, is more than a type: she is an
individual, a character in her own right.

The relation of Hogarth to Smollett encompasses more than their
similarities in design and artistic vision. In many instances we can draw a
direct ideological and political connection between specific Hogarth prints
and individual scenes in a Smollett novel. One such connection is evident
in Hogarth's and Smollett's separate representations of events that occurred
during the Oxfordshire Election of 1754. Both Hogarth's series, *Four Prints
of an Election* (1754–58), and Smollett's chapters concerning an election in
The Life and Adventures of Sir Launcelot Greaves (1762) are based on
events of the Oxfordshire election. According to Sean Shesgreen, Hogarth's
work "aims to present a generalized picture of a violent, chaotic election."[37]
Although we cannot draw a direct pictorial analogy between Smollett's
depiction of the election and that of Hogarth's series, they are thematically
similar. We do know that Smollett was familiar with the series. James
Basker notes that in the April 1759, edition of the *Critical Review* Smollett
devoted an article in opposition to an "opportunistic poet who claimed to
have Hogarth's authorization for his 'Poetical description of Mr. Hogarth's
Election Prints.'" Hogarth and Smollett independently satirize the actual

Figure 3. William Hogarth, *Morning* (Plate 1 of *The Four Times of the Day*, 1738). Courtesy of the Huntington Library.

election that they each observed, yet, as Basker points out, "one sees detail after detail of correspondence" between them.[38]

Smollett's depiction of the election appears in chapters nine and ten of *Sir Launcelot Greaves*. Awakened from his sleep by a loud clatter outside his window, Launcelot looks out to see "a cavalcade of persons well-mounted, and distinguished by blue cockades."[39] The color blue, representative of the Tory faction, becomes an important motif in Smollett's chapters as well as in Hogarth's series. Smollett's horsemen wave a blue banner which declares "Liberty and the Landed Interest," and the phrase reminds us of the banner proclaiming "Liberty and Property" that passes outside the window in the first print of Hogarth's series. In order to illustrate the representative color blue, Hogarth includes the words "True Blue" in two of his prints: in plate 3 they appear on a ribbon worn by a dying man and in plate 4 we see them on a banner carried in the procession. In addition, the color orange plays an important role in both works to represent the opposing Whig faction. Although orange is not a motif in Hogarth's prints, the original paintings depict the Whig supporters wearing orange cockades. As in Hogarth's painting, Smollett also uses orange to represent the Whigs, placing the Whig candidate in a "procession of people on foot, adorned with bunches of orange ribbons." Orange was the symbol of Protestantism, from its defender, William of Orange. The slogan on Smollett's Whig banner, "Liberty and Conscience and the Protestant Succession" is analogous to the flag that leans against the wall in Hogarth's print of the Whig celebration (*An Election Entertainment*) which reads "Liberty and Loyalty." William Gaunt has noted that this is one of the many examples where "the novelist and the painter were . . . close in exuberance . . . where it might be said that the novel illustrated the picture."[40] Both express the themes of corruption and violence in party politics through active and dramatic comic scenes, sparing criticism of neither Whig nor Tory.

In *An Election Entertainment* (figure 4) Hogarth depicts the Whig celebration as an orgy of drunkenness, violence, gluttony, and bribery, a representation of the mob no more genteel indoors than when it conducts its riotous activity outdoors. The print is a flurry of activity—drinking, shouting, seduction, music, plotting, and overindulgence. As the more sedate Tory procession passes by the open window, we are struck by a contrast in decorum made even more pointed by two particular members of the Whig party, one of whom pours the contents of a chamber pot on the passing parade while the other prepares to attack it with a three-legged stool. In the second plate of the series, *Canvassing for Votes* (figure 5), the Tories are shown in an outdoor scene that again appears more refined than the celebration of the Whigs. Violence and corruption, however, are no less evident. Bribery, prostitution, and gluttony are similarly featured in the foreground, while in the distance an angry mob storms the Whig headquarters where shots are fired. In these scenes of mob violence, Hogarth captures Smollett's sentiment that the mob, "the base, unthinking rabble of

Figure 4. William Hogarth, *An Election Entertainment* (Plate 1 of *Four Prints of an Election*, 1755). Courtesy of the Huntington Library.

this metropolis, without principle, sentiment or understanding," hurt rather than helped the political process. Robin Fabel has pointed out that Smollett held little regard for party labels and came to feel "nothing but contempt for the men that bore them."[41] In *Sir Launcelot Greaves* Smollett criticizes both factions through Launcelot's heated speech to the crowd. He denounces the extremes of both parties while noting the presence of corruption in both.[42]

In chapter forty-four of *The Adventures of Peregrine Pickle* (1751), Smollett depicts a dinner given by the doctor "in the Manner of the Ancients,"[43] a comic culinary representation of a very real confrontation between ancient and modern aesthetics. The character of the doctor (recognized for his penchant for speaking in Latin and quoting Homer) prepares a feast for several coxcombs and for his friend, the artist Pallet. Pallet, a character modeled on Hogarth himself,[44] finds the feast abhorrent, and though Smollett treats the character of Pallet with satiric irreverence, it is clear that Pallet reflects Smollett's, as well as Hogarth's own, modernist ideology. The food served by the doctor consists of authentic ancient Roman delicacies literally unpalatable to people accustomed to living in the modern world. Pallet calls the Romans "beastly fellows" and claims that he "would not give one slice of the roast beef of Old England for all the dainties of a Roman emperor's table."[45] Pallet, like Hogarth, had little use for either the ancient or the foreign, espousing rather the art and culture of modern England. Smollett, too, supported modern British art and artists through his position as art critic for the *Critical Review*. According to Basker, Smollett's purpose was to promote "the emergence of a distinctly British school of artists equal to any on the Continent."[46] And Smollett extended his support to Hogarth, as well as to such artists as Gavin Hamilton, Sir Robert Strange, and Joseph Wilton. Despite the satiric depiction of Hogarth in *Peregrine Pickle*, Smollett admired Hogarth for his work in the genre of modern history painting. He extols Hogarth as standing alone, "unrivalled and inimitable."[47]

Unlike Fielding, Smollett saw the novel as an iconoclastic form, a new democratic model divorced from ancient values. Where Fielding adapted the form of the epic to his novels,[48] Smollett found his model in the picaresque, travel books, and letter-writers. Like Hogarth, Smollett discarded the forms of high genre in favor of a modern, more democratic mode. In Hogarth's manner of modern history painting, he found a model for his own work. Hogarth's ecphrastic scenes of realistic, often frenetic action are replicated in Smollett's novels in a way that Fielding, with his technique of a single, sustained action never assimilated. Fielding understood Hogarth, to be sure, but underlying differences prevented him from translating Hogarth's pictorialism into the deep structure of his novels. Part of the difference is aesthetic, deriving from Fielding's reliance on classical forms. At the same time, Fielding's attempt to force critical acceptance of the novel as a literary form and to extend its scope beyond Richardson's anti-pictorial

Figure 5. William Hogarth, *Canvassing for Votes* (Plate 2 of *Four Prints of an Election*, 1757). Courtesy of the Huntington Library.

stance was necessary to move the genre forward. By the time Smollett published *The Adventures of Roderick Random* in 1748, Fielding had already laid the groundwork for the assimilation of modern forms, such as the picaresque, into the developing genre of the novel. Smollett abandoned the high-heroic model of Fielding to work within a more modern composite form of narrative in much the same way that Hogarth early had imposed contemporary narrative and novelistic sequences on traditional history painting. Smollett's modern sensibility aptly reflects Hogarth's democratic style, an affinity which serves to establish a sound pictorial connection.

NOTES

I would like to thank Jeff Portnoy and Joanne Padderud for their comments on early drafts of this paper, and Timothy Erwin for his continued assistance and support.

1. Ronald Paulson, *Breaking and Remaking: Aesthetic Practice in England, 1700–1820* (New Brunswick: Rutgers University Press, 1989), 33.
2. M. M. Bakhtin, *The Dialogic Imagination: Four Essays by M. M. Bakhtin*, trans. Caryl Emerson and Michael Holquist, ed. Holquist (Austin: University of Texas Press, 1981), 4, 7.
3. Ronald Paulson, *Emblem and Expression: Meaning in English Art of the Eighteenth Century* (Cambridge: Harvard University Press, 1975) 36, 33.
4. Martin C. Battestin, "Pictures of Fielding," *Eighteenth-Century Studies* 17 (Fall 1983): 8–13.
5. Robert Etheridge Moore draws analogies between Mr. Wilson in *Joseph Andrews* and Rakewell in *A Rake's Progress*; and between Mrs. Bridget Allworthy and Thwackum in *Tom Jones* to the lady in *Morning* from *Four Times of the Day* and the man correcting the ladies in Bridewell prison in *A Harlot's Progress*. For a complete discussion of these analogies and others, see Moore's, *Hogarth's Literary Relationships* (Minneapolis: University of Minnesota Press, 1948), 122–46.
6. Peter Jan de Voogd, *Henry Fielding and William Hogarth: The Correspondences between the Arts*, Costerus New Series, vol. 30 (Amsterdam: Rodopi, 1981).
7. Ronald Paulson, *Hogarth: His Life, Art, and Times*, vol. 1 (New Haven: Yale University Press, 1971), 292. In the preface to his revision of volume one of *Hogarth* (New Brunswick and London: Rutgers University Press, 1991), Paulson writes that in his "rethinking" of Hogarth he has come to a new understanding of the artist, drawing us, I believe, closer to agreement. I am indebted to Paulson for his work on Hogarth and literary pictorialism, and commentaries such as this one owe much to his significant contribution.
8. Henry Fielding, *The History of the Adventures of Joseph Andrews*, intro. Howard Mumford Jones (New York: Random House, 1950), xxxiv–xxxv. See also note 31 below.

9. Ibid., xxxi–xxxii.
10. For Fielding's references to Hogarth, see Moore, *Hogarth's Literary Relationships*, 122–32.
11. Paulson, *Hogarth* 1:468.
12. Ronald Paulson, *Satire and the Novel in Eighteenth-Century England* (New Haven and London: Yale University Press, 1967), 177.
13. Ibid.
14. Ibid., 178.
15. J. Paul Hunter, *Before Novels: The Cultural Contexts of Eighteenth-Century English Fiction* (New York and London: W. W. Norton, 1990), 39.
16. Jerry C. Beasley, "Smollett's Art: The Novel as 'Picture,'" in *The First English Novelists: Essays in Understanding*, ed. J. M. Armistead (Knoxville: University of Tennessee Press, 1985), 153.
17. Ibid., 175.
18. Ibid.
19. Tobias Smollett, *The Expedition of Humphry Clinker, The Works of Tobias Smollett*, ed. O M Brack, Jr. (Athens and London: University of Georgia Press, 1990), 254.
20. Norman Bryson contrasts the deictic with the aoristic tenses: "the aoristic tenses (simple past, imperfect, pluperfect) are characteristically those of the historian," while the deictic tenses (the present and all of its compounds) "create and refer to their own perspective." According to Bryson: "The wider class of deixis therefore includes all those particles and forms of speech where the utterance incorporates into itself information about its own spatial position relative to its content (here, there, near, far off), and its own relative temporality (yesterday, today, tomorrow, sooner, later, long ago)." See *Vision and Painting: The Logic of the Gaze*, (New Haven: Yale University Press, 1983), 88.
21. Paulson, *Hogarth* 1:409.
22. Jean Hagstrum, *The Sister Arts: The Tradition of Literary Pictorialism and English Poetry from Dryden to Gray* (Chicago: University of Chicago Press, 1958), 140.
23. According to W. J. T. Mitchell, the text itself is a spatial form. As we read, our eyes follow a linear "track" which is "literally a spatial form, and only metaphorically a temporal one." "Spatial Form in Literature: Toward a General Theory" in *Critical Inquiry* 6 (Spring 1980): 539-67.
24. Smollett, *Humphry Clinker*, 254.
25. Ronald Paulson, *Emblem and Expression*, 36.
26. Hogarth largely maintained traditional pictorial conventions in the spatial construction of his paintings and prints. For one, he used the Renaissance convention of the perspective box in which architectural structures are used to delineate separate areas on the canvas. As Paulson explains: "The norms of axis and orthogonals directed inward draw the viewer's attention from all sides: as soon as the eye tries to move away it is caught by the orthogonals and forced into the depth of the composition. This is always from near to far, or from the periphery to the centre of perspective, the central axis." The perspective box also works to allow for temporal stages in the "story." By arranging events in space on separate areas of the canvas, several

actions depicted simultaneously in the picture can be read as occurring at different points in time. See ibid., 44–45.

27. Moore, *Hogarth's Literary Relationships*, 127.
28. Ibid., 167, 181.
29. George Kahrl's definition of caricature presents it in a positive light. He explains: "Caricature was primarily pictorial. When the subjects and the interpretations of these subjects were assimilated to another medium—to prose fiction—equivalencies in language had to be developed and perfected. Henry Fielding equated caricature with style, mistakenly with the burlesque style which he employed for narrative detachment and comment, not characterization." See "Smollett as a Caricaturist," *Tobias Smollett, Bicentennial Essays Presented to Lewis M. Knapp*, ed. G. S. Rousseau and P.-G. Bouce (New York: Oxford University Press, 1971), 183.
30. Ibid., 183–85.
31. In *Hogarth's Literary Relationships*, 127, Moore refers to Fielding's appropriation of the same figure for the character of Bridget Allworthy. He cites a passage from *Tom Jones*, book 4:

> I would attempt to draw her picture, but that is done already by a more able master, Mr. Hogarth himself, to whom she sat many years ago, and hath been lately exhibited by that gentleman in his print of a winter's morning, of which she was no improper emblem, and may be seen walking (for walk she doth in the print) to Covent Garden church, with a starved footboy behind carrying her prayer book.

32. Smollett, *Humphry Clinker*, 58–59.
33. Ibid., 8.
34. John Sekora, *Luxury: The Concept in Western Thought, Eden to Smollett* (Baltimore: Johns Hopkins University Press, 1977), 258.
35. Smollett, *Humphry Clinker*, 24.
36. Ibid., 153.
37. Sean Shesgreen, *Engravings by Hogarth: 101 Prints* (New York: Dover Publications, 1973), 86.
38. James Basker, *Tobias Smollett, Critic and Journalist*, (Newark: University of Delaware Press, 1988), 116.
39. Tobias Smollett, *The Life and Adventures of Sir Launcelot Greaves*, ed. David Evans (London: Oxford University Press, 1973), 71. All references are to this text.
40. William Gaunt, *The World of William Hogarth* (London: Jonathan Cape Ltd., 1978), 78.
41. Noted in Robin Fabel, "The Patriotic Briton: Tobias Smollett and English Politics, 1756–1771," *Eighteenth-Century Studies* 8 (Fall 1974): 110, 104.
42. Launcelot's speech appears on pages 75–78 of *Sir Launcelot Greaves*.
43. Tobias Smollett, *Peregrine Pickle* in two volumes, vol. 1 ([1930]; reprint London: J. M. Dent & Sons, Ltd., 1962), 217.
44. For a more complete discussion of Hogarth and Pallet, see Ronald Paulson, "Smollett and Hogarth: The Identification of Pallet" in *Studies in English Literature* 4 (1964): 351–59. See also Kahrl, "Smollett as a Caricaturist," 194–96. De Voogd argues against identification, claiming rather that "there may well have been more than one jingoistic, over-dressed, garrulous, semi-literate painter striving to paint in Paris in the modern sublime style," and that if Pallet was indeed to be identified with Hogarth,

his novelistic relationship to the character of Spondy (identified with Fielding) would have been closer. See *Fielding and Hogarth*, 11–12.

45. Smollett, *Peregrine Pickle*, 222. The obvious reference is to Hogarth's print *The Gate of Calais, or The Roast Beef of Old England* (1748).

46. Basker, *Tobias Smollett*, 113. Art reviews were a regular feature in the *Critical Review* during the first six months of 1756, but no further reviews appeared after the June issue. Two reviews appeared in 1757, in the February and May issues; only one appeared in 1758, in March.

47. *Critical Review* 1 (June 1756): 480. Basker attributes the authorship of this article to Smollett. *Tobias Smollett*, 39–40, 220.

48. Maurice Johnson first showed that Fielding's *Amelia* was patterned upon the *Aeneid* in a book-by-book comparative analysis. See *Fielding's Art of Fiction: Eleven Essays on* Shamela, Joseph Andrews, Tom Jones, and Amelia (Philadelphia: University of Pennsylvania Press, 1961), 139–64.

Exile and Narrative Voice in Corinne

PATRICK COLEMAN

Exile was a decisive experience for Germaine de Staël, shaping not only the course of her life but the character of her work as well. If women's fame, in Staël's phrase, can be defined as "le deuil éclatant du bonheur,"[1] her own reluctant career, out of which emerged such works as *Corinne* and *De l'Allemagne*, provides the most striking example of this intimate yet painful connection between separation and success. For in Staël's most important books the physical distancing of exile and the psychological separation of mourning combine to produce new connections between political, moral, and literary thought. In her masterpieces about Italy and Germany, geographical breadth goes hand in hand with a concern for the inner spirit of persons and nations. I want to suggest that Staël's response to exile may also help us understand her experiments with narrative voice. *Corinne* is in fact the first modern French novel to use an external narrator in what may be called the realist manner, anticipating in many respects the method of her nineteenth-century successors. Except for brief interventions in the first person (a device that will reappear in *Le Rouge et le noir* and *Madame Bovary*), Staël's narrator occupies a position close to but outside the world of the story. I would argue that the special intimacy of tone and the adoption of an external standpoint go together, and that the emergence of this influential novelistic attitude can be traced, at least in part, to the cultural dislocations that shaped Staël's career.

Staël gave her memoirs the title *Dix années d'exil*. In that work she compared exile to a kind of moral death, claiming that "on rencontre plus de braves contre l'échafaud que contre la perte de sa patrie."[2] She added that the threat of exile was particularly painful for women, "qui sont destinées à soutenir et à récompenser l'enthousiasme," for even more than men will

91

they stifle their "sentiments généreux, s'il doit en résulter ou qu'elles soient enlevées aux objets de leur tendresse, ou qu'ils leur sacrifient leur existence en les suivant en exil" (62). Yet, what is most significant about Staël's experience is that it does not conform to this rather conventional view of women's role. If we except the early episode of her father's banishment in 1787, Staël's forced departures resulted primarily from her own political and intellectual activity. Furthermore, while Paris would always be Staël's emotional and intellectual home, and while she would suffer because it was difficult for her to see the friends who continued to live there, her experience of other countries and cultures inspired a philosophy in which the notion of exile is redefined. In the pluralistic Europe imagined by the Coppet circle,[3] there is no one center. Staël's heroine Corinne, for example, is at home (and in exile) in both England and Italy. The pain of separation may not be less intense, but the sorrow, whether personal or political, can no longer be traced to a single source or relieved by pursuing a single goal.

The exaggerated conventionality of Staël's rhetoric in *Dix années d'exil* betrays the author's discomfort with a mode of expression that should also be left behind. Why does Staël not do so? One reason is that these memoirs were composed in 1811–1812 to rally European opposition to Napoleon. Under the circumstances, Staël felt obliged to minimize her own involvement in the French Revolution and in political activity generally. Another is Staël's ambivalence about women's presence on any public stage, even as witness and writer. She accepts the need to exile herself from her own work. "Je me flatte," she tells us, "de me faire souvent oublier en racontant ma propre histoire" (2). Staël's difficulties in negotiating her participation in the public sphere have been ably described by a number of scholars.[4] But I would also suggest a third reason that applies to some male authors as well. The sentence I have just quoted is echoed in other works of the period, for example in Benjamin Constant's *Adolphe*, which is also a tale of wandering and dispossession. Speaking of his earlier self, the narrator notes that "tout en ne m'intéressant qu'à moi, je m'intéressais faiblement à moi-même."[5] In a number of pre-romantic authors, talk of exile, mourning, or some other form of loss, becomes a way of expressing a discursive problem. How, in a dislocated world, can one accept the centrality of individual experience in artistic creation while asserting the subordination of that experience to the symbolic forms art must produce to help repair the damage, and which, to succeed, must transcend the limits of what Charles Taylor has called the "punctual" self?[6]

One influential solution was to view the writer's vocation as a kind of secular priesthood, endowing his experience with exemplary, even sacred meaning. Rousseau played a crucial role here, and Paul Bénichou has traced the extension of this idea in the late eighteenth and early nineteenth centuries.[7] But while post-revolutionary French culture may have produced the most inflated claims for the writer's mission, culminating in Victor Hugo's cosmic will, it also fostered the most sceptical, even systematically reductive conceptions of the scope of artistic action. This is most apparent in the long tradition of academic criticism which, from the Imperial period on, saw Romanticism as a pernicious foreign import for which Staël deserved much of the blame. But it also can be seen in the sometimes paralyzing self-doubt and second thoughts of those writers who, like Constant and Staël, wonder just how possible—or socially responsible—it is to enhance the ordinary with a higher, more privileged, poetic self. Her mixture of enthusiasm and scruple on this point has not helped Staël's literary reputation. French critics of the right dismissed her work as insufficiently objective and restrained; those of the left, as lacking in practical zeal. For more sympathetic critics steeped in English or German Romanticism, Staël is too hesitant about embracing the subjective impersonality of the poetic self. In an influential essay, Georges Poulet praised Staël's search for a new artistic consciousness in which the self's immediate concerns would be subordinated to a more authentic apprehension of human consciousness in time.[8] But critics close to Poulet, such as Jean Starobinski and Paul de Man, characterized Staël's reluctance to give up the empirical self's demands and commit herself to art as a serious flaw.[9]

More recent critics, writing from a feminist point of view, have asked whether the ideal of aesthetic transcendence was not a trap for a writer struggling to overcome the handicap of a gender role in which aesthetic categories themselves became a tool for cultural marginalization. Joan de Jean, for example, includes Staël in her study of the image of Sappho, the suffering woman whose transcendent lyricism has been praised at the expense of her female identity and whose work has suffered even more by the problematic and reductive equation of the two.[10] From this point of view, artistic authenticity, far from giving the self a new anchor in the deepest structures of consciousness, only masks another kind of exile. What is needed is to set Staël's work more firmly in its cultural context by analyzing its relationship to the circumstances of its time, to the vocabularies and images available to women for creative appropriation or subversion.

These two viewpoints may appear poles apart, but I suggest we keep them both in mind, for both derive in some degree from Staël's own discussion of literature in *De la littérature* and *De l'Allemagne*. Each of these works combines a sociological approach to literature with an idealist doctrine of art and attempts to reconcile them within a broad philosophy of history.[11] In sketching an interpretation of *Corinne*'s narrative form that seeks to relate the inner dynamic of the novel's form to its cultural context, I hope to be faithful to Staël's own example and to recover some of the literary-historical significance of her work.[12]

Staël's choice of an external narrator is particularly revealing in this regard because it seems to contradict rather than conform to her ideas about the relationship between fictional form and the progress of human sensibility. For Staël, the modern spirit finds its most advanced expression in the epistolary novel. This was the form she chose for her first full-length fiction, *Delphine*, and in *De l'Allemagne* she would claim that the epistolary narration is the truly modern form:

> Les romans par lettres supposent toujours plus de sentiments que de faits; jamais les Anciens n'auraient imaginé de donner cette forme à leurs fictions; et ce n'est même que depuis deux siècles que la philosophie s'est assez introduite en nous-mêmes pour que l'analyse de ce qu'on éprouve tienne une si grande place dans les livres. Cette manière de concevoir les romans n'est pas aussi poétique, sans doute, que celle qui consiste tout entière dans les récits; mais l'esprit humain est maintenant bien moins avide des événements même les mieux combinés, que des observations sur ce qui se passe dans le coeur.[13]

Staël's stark opposition between "récit" and "observation" may not be fair to the subtleties of a novel such as Lafayette's *La Princesse de Clèves* (1678), but it does reflect the broad history of novelistic techniques in France. In the seventeenth century, third-person narration was most often linked to a disenchanted view of life in which the chance and often blind acts of the characters were framed by a kind of transcendent, impersonal necessity. The form almost disappeared in the eighteenth century, replaced initially by the first-person, autobiographical novel that focused on the achievement of a limited but genuine self-knowledge, then by the epistolary novel, with its emphasis on what the characters thought and felt at particular moments in relation to each other. Of course, a controlling consciousness was at work in all these forms, but it is as if that consciousness could not be made explicit without spoiling the integrity of the fictional world. I speak here of France, because in England Frances Burney, to cite one writer known to Staël, had set an important example in moving from the epistolary form of *Evelina* (1778) to the external narrator of *Cecilia* (1782). Burney's novels, however, include a comic element, largely absent from Staël's work, that connects Burney's choice of narrator with a long-established use of the third person for comic commentary. The most famous eighteenth-century example was *Tom Jones*, a novel Staël admired,[14] but which was quite foreign to the French tradition in which old distinctions between comic and serious modes persisted much longer. Only in the ironic novels of Diderot and Sade (largely unappreciated, of course, in the post-revolutionary period) did this tradition start to break down.

Thus *Corinne*'s reintroduction of the distinction between the world of the characters and that of the commentary in a novel of sentiment marks a new stage in the evolution of French narrative. Staël's novel contains, it is true, a long letter in which the heroine tells her own story, as well as lengthy speeches in which the characters open their hearts, but its overall form does not foster a feeling of immediacy. The ebb and flow of correspondence is replaced by a series of twenty clearly divided "books," each with its own title. The narrator does enter the story at the very end of the novel, but this final, first-person remark only underscores the distance between narrator and character. Speaking of Oswald's regret at abandoning Corinne in favor of the more docile but vapid Lucile, the narrator asks: "se pardonna-t-il sa conduite passée? Le monde qui l'approuva le consola-t-il? Se contenta-t-il d'un sort commun, après ce qu'il avait perdu? Je l'ignore, et ne veux, à cet égard, ni le blâmer, ni l'absoudre."[15] Judged by Staël's "modern" standard, the inability to supply this information is a sign of aesthetic inadequacy, not only because we do not learn what Oswald feels, but because it is implied we do not need to know: the story is over. Although Corinne is hardly stingy in its "observations sur ce qui se passe dans le coeur," it ends by asserting the precedence of a "récit" with its own distinct coherence and closure.

The narrative perspective of *Corinne* is nonetheless very different from that of *La Princesse de Clèves*. Instead of chance and necessity, Staël's book dramatizes contingency and probability. The characters' actions are determined by any number of social or psychological causes, but their relative weight can be assessed and their probable effects, in other circumstances, could be predicted. The relation between the narrator and the characters is also different. Lafayette's authoritative narrator lays bare hidden motives only to show that the human heart remains unknowable.[16] The last lines of *Corinne* express a different relationship between ignorance and knowledge. One could, in theory, find out what Oswald felt. The limits to the narrator's knowledge do not reflect a necessary incapacity. Like everyone else's, the narrator's knowledge is real, but precisely because it is like everyone else's it is only a partial perspective, not the whole truth. Even within its sphere of competence, it suggests rather than defines absolutely.

Yet, Staël's strategy should also be distinguished from that of the fictional "editor" of an epistolary novel like *Les Liaisons dangereuses*. Was Valmont a libertine right to the end? Laclos' editor inserts a footnote saying that because nothing in the correspondence entrusted to him resolves this question he has decided to suppress a last letter by Valmont expressing remorse over his betrayal of Madame de Tourvel.[17] Here the uncertainty is ostensibly attributed to a lack of external evidence in the "society" which produced the correspondence. Laclos uses that uncertainty, however, to damn Valmont all the more effectively by excluding his letter which in itself is held to possess no evidential value. Staël's tentativeness is also ironic—Oswald *is* being judged—but the tenor of that irony is different. In Laclos, the absence of external evidence means paradoxically that the editor's decision cannot be appealed. Staël's narrator does not attribute her ignorance to the same definite cause. The kind of evidence that might or might not resolve the issue is left an open question. But although its narrator is less peremptory, *Corinne* is in one sense less dependent on its social intertext than *Les Liaisons*. Within the fictional terms of the "found" correspondence, the possibility that other evidence might turn up still exists—a pretext used by other novelists of the time to publish sequels to popular books. Laclos has done his best to forestall that possibility by composing a tightly-woven plot, but the eighteenth-century French novel situates itself within a larger communicative network in which stories are exchanged and revised.[18] The indeterminate basis for Staël's "je l'ignore," a statement whose social location cannot be identified—or, if so, only in the space between French, English, and Italian societies—really means we can only support or appeal the narrator's judgment by referring to the story itself. Incomplete and unrooted as it may be, the novel in an important sense becomes its own context.

Staël's narrator, at once inside and outside the world of the story, freely asserting an independent point of view yet refusing to assume a position of final authority, may be seen as an attempt to mediate between the central and the exiled, marginal self whose duality lies at the heart of pre-romantic French writing. The goal of this mediation is neither wholly aesthetic nor wholly practical. Rather, it is to redefine these fields through the symbolic construct of the work. Detailed evidence about the formal genesis of *Corinne* is still unavailable,[19] but we can get some insight into what was at stake from a review of the novel written by August Wilhelm Schlegel, who accompanied Staël throughout her travels in Italy and played an important role in her aesthetic education.[20] This little-known essay is significant in that Schlegel, perhaps mindful of the kind of thinking that led Staël to praise the epistolary novel as the form most expressive of "modern" interiority, tries to justify Staël's choice of form. He does so in the name of a literary imagination that has managed to combine what Staël earlier called the poetry of story with the insight of analysis.

The problem with *Delphine*, according to Schlegel, was that the heroine's "imagination of the heart" (and by implication, the author's identification with that imagination, expressed in the choice of the epistolary form) had overwhelmed every other form of imagination. The narrative form chosen in *Corinne* is "unquestionably preferable." First, because it is more "concise"—the implication being that otherwise the novel would have been much longer than it is! Second, and more important, because it allows for a presentation of the characters that is both clearer and more plausible.

> The constant use of the epistolary form is subject to many inconveniences: the characters have to be constrained by their individual situation, and yet they have to be endowed with a power that is incompatible with their condition, a power to observe themselves and others so that the reader can understand them and their illusions more clearly, and so the stage can be set for what comes next. Narrative on the other hand can allow itself to look down calmly and impartially on the players with a kind of poetic omniscience.[21]

At first glance, Schlegel's defence seems rather strained. In Richardson and Rousseau there was no incompatibility between the characters' limited awareness and their capacity for analysis. Indeed, their novels turn on the complex interplay between the two. Why would *Corinne* need to be more explicit? I think we have to read the issue of plausibility and the need to accommodate the reader's understanding as two aspects of the same problem, which is that of increasing cultural diversification. The unifying sociability of Ancien Régime culture which enabled one to appeal, beyond differences and disagreements, to a common realm of general opinion, has broken down. Staël is writing for a post-revolutionary Europe defined no longer as a homogeneous audience but as groups of readers reflecting distinct national cultures. Things may have to be explained that earlier could be taken for granted. The fictional world in which the characters move is also more radically diverse, too much so for the effects of cultural difference to be dramatized in a purely immanent way.

And yet, a unifying framework cannot simply be imposed from outside: that would be to reproduce Napoleon's oppressive parody of European unity. The relatively autonomous narrator Staël devises for *Corinne* offers a possible alternative. Schlegel speaks of poetic omniscience, but that omniscience is not simply assumed by the authorial consciousness. The latter strives to achieve it by a moral effort we can feel, and through which the narrative strives to overcome the limited "imagination of the heart" in favor of a more "serene and impartial" perspective. However detached and impersonal that perspective, it remains linked to the ordinary self, to the "moi-même" behind the "moi." To put it another way, the author is also a reader in search of clarity. It is to Schlegel's credit that he does not impute the author's difficulty to the fact that she is a woman, although the terms he uses could easily lend themselves to a gender-saturated discourse. Staël's struggle is interpreted instead, most suggestively I think, in a broad context of formal and cultural considerations. Again, according to Schlegel, a narrator is needed not only to explain the characters' situation to each other and to the reader, but also to "set the stage for what comes next." I think we can read this not only in terms of plot developments that have to be anticipated, but more broadly as a call to include within the novel a more explicit sense of the agency that shapes it.

In *Corinne*, this struggle for perspective is thematized in various ways. One is Corinne and Oswald's discussion of aesthetic principles as they examine the paintings and monuments of Rome. In spite of what Schlegel says, their clash of views, as modern critics have noted, provides an illuminating commentary on the novel's evolving articulation.[22] But Staël also resorts to a device that has not received the attention it deserves. At critical points in the book she includes excerpts from her father's writings.[23] Necker's comments on the consolations of religion, quoted extensively, are not simply illustrative. Rather, they are the interventions of a super-narrator who for a moment takes the place of the novel's own narrator, as if the latter were unable or unwilling to carry the full burden of omniscience.

Staël's adoption of a presiding external perspective is clearly made possible by her identification with her father.

The gesture is thus a problematic one, involving what to us is an all-too-enthusiastic idealization of paternal authority. Yet, on the level of the book's composition, if not of its themes, Necker is not primarily a symbol of law. The novel's reverence for his memory does not lead to the paralysis we see in Oswald's relationship with his father. Rather, it increases the novel's range of sympathy by allowing for a more nuanced portrayal of Oswald's weakness, despite the latter's injustice to Corinne. This achievement builds on the insight that in an important sense the two characters share a common father. That father is no longer the real father (good or bad), for the latter is no longer present (and we recall that Staël's own father died in between the writing of *Delphine* and *Corinne*). Paternity becomes a figure for the novel's own more inclusive understanding. This understanding, it seems, needs to be grounded in something more than the attempt to reconcile moral and aesthetic categories in Corinne and Oswald's debates. The latter, after all, lead to an impasse. The two lovers agree to disagree, but the differences in their viewpoints—Oswald looking more to moral energy and Corinne to ideal sympathy, the one accused of narrow-mindedness, the other of passive indulgence—anticipate a more serious emotional estrangement that will not be overcome.

The choice of narrative form can be read as an attempt to bridge the gap at a higher level: Not so much by subsuming art and morality together under religion[24] as by postulating an ideal point where sympathetic intimacy and an energizing distance of perspective no longer contradict each other. For while the quotations from Necker help establish a narrative perspective of broad sympathy, the way that perspective takes narrative form also sets limits to the characters' scope of action. The suspense plot chosen by Staël requires that many things not be said in the early parts of the book. Oswald and Corinne must long remain in ignorance of essential facts about each other. While their long discussions about historical monuments and art works give them clues about each other's state of mind, they cannot entirely replace those other, more ordinary opportunities to test their powers of self-observation that earlier novelists provided through interaction with other characters. The mute stones may speak, but, in the decorous world of *Corinne*, they don't talk back. Nor are the secondary characters granted any real access to the protagonists' thoughts or feelings.

From the point of view of today's reader, the effect is not always a happy one. Ellen Peel, for example, has expressed some scepticism about the novel's feminist thrust on the grounds that Corinne has no female friends.[25] We should recognize, however, that this is in part a formal problem. The move from the epistolary to the third-person form eliminates the structural need for confidantes, and so we should more correctly say that in this respect, as in some others, *Corinne* exploits too simplistically the powers its narrator enjoys. But these powers also play an essential role in giving the novel its integrity as a work of art. The form of Staël's novel underscores the contrast between the logic of its plot and the heroine's talent for improvisation. Now, it is true that Corinne's transcendent genius can be rendered only imperfectly. But it is significant that, in contrast to earlier aesthetic practice, which would either simply declare the impossibility of conveying perfection or epitomize it through brief quotation, Staël offers extended approximations of Corinne's Italian poems in French prose. In doing so, and perhaps despite herself, she gives the heroine's aesthetic expression a more conditional value.

This also applies, ironically, to Corinne's one sustained written composition: the narration of her own life story. Oswald has told her his story in person, but Corinne, out of consideration for his feelings as well as her own, refuses to do the same. She writes her story and compounds the distancing effect of her choice by postponing as long as she can its communication to Oswald. When the story finally reaches him, it is too late: the lovers' separation is inevitable. One could say that Corinne's narrative takes retrospection too far. It is prematurely posthumous, anticipating the final retrospection that belongs to a consciousness beyond the limits of the story's action. If Corinne can only improvise in the presence of admirers who look up to her, she can only narrate when the reply she seeks could only come from an ideal Oswald who didn't belong to the real, imperfect world, an Oswald who would incarnate within that world the transcendent paternal super-narrator. According to Margaret Waller, the fact that Corinne writes her confession "thematizes the link between conventional narrative imperatives and a repressive paternal line."[26] Waller's insight is suggestive, although formulated too broadly. Many women writers have, after all, used conventional narrative forms (the romance and the Gothic, for example) for their own subversive purposes. In the first instance, the figure of the father in *Corinne* is a liberating one, opening up the emotional range of the story. The problem, however, comes from identifying too much with that transcendent guarantee, to the point where the pluralism of outlook it initially made possible collapses into a self-destructive withdrawal from the ordinary world. For Corinne, as opposed to the character-narrators of earlier epistolary novels, there is no middle ground between unreflective action and a retrospective stance that renounces any further initiative on the practical level. To return to utilitarian calculation would undermine the authenticity of the reflective insight. This polarization of interest and "disinterest," it should be stressed, has to be understood in political as well as psychological terms, for it is part of Staël's response to the Terror's fusion of partisan interest and the rhetoric of disinterest in Robespierre's Republic of Virtue. As Corinne's fate shows, however, too strenuous a defence against that fusion leads to another kind of oppression.

The problems associated with Corinne as self-narrator support Schlegel's point about the suitability of the omniscient perspective for a novelist standing outside the story from the beginning. For what no longer works at the level of the character may be rearticulated at the level of the novel's overall composition. Because it is a fiction, the novel stands apart from the world of action. But not entirely. A novel that portrays realistic characters in the ordinary world involves, to the extent that it gives those characters a destiny, a series of decisions that readers (and often authors) may interpret as matters of craft but also as moral actions.[27] The key issue, on which Corinne and Oswald disagree in their discussions of various artworks mentioned in the novel, is to what extent aesthetic form relativizes and mediates moral imperatives, or is itself undercut by them. Looking again at the narrator's final words, we can read them as an attempt to establish a balance between the exercise and suspension of moral judgment, of intervention and reflection, that should characterize the work as a whole.

The sense of equilibrium in the narrator's final words depends for its effect, however, on the refusal to specify what happens to Oswald in the indefinite future. A negative gesture of this kind is not enough to resolve the problems raised by the closure of the story itself. For to complete the novel means finishing off the heroine. As Carla Peterson puts it, "the narrator . . . comes to displace Corinne as the center of the novel. If unity and singleness of personality are finally achieved, if morcellation is overcome, these accomplishments occur at the expense of Corinne herself, at the level of the narrator, not of the character."[28] Toward the end of the novel, when she has retired to Florence to waste away and die, Corinne tries to write, that is, to compose from day to day as an artist would for whom writing is part of life, a vocation or a career. But we are told her poetic gift has left her. Although art arises from melancholy, too strong a sadness destroys the capacity to create. At this point, we are made to reflect on the crucial artistic difference between the heroine and the narrator who is about to complete the story of Corinne.

In recent years, a number of critics have asked us to consider the death of a fictional character from an ethical point of view. Feminist critics in particular have questioned the relationship between Manon Lescaut's death, for example, and the sentimental lyricism it occasions. Is the one the price of the other? Or does such a question reflect a blurring of the boundary between life and literature?[29] Without pretending to answer this question, I would like to suggest that it is connected to the problems with which we began: about Staël's reluctance to abandon an instrumental view of art, and about the problematic distinction between the kinds of self displayed in French pre-romantic writing. It has been observed that while Staël's major works of criticism end optimistically, both her novels end on a mournful note with the death of the heroine.[30] What readers like to think of as the "natural" consequence of a broken heart and society's hostility must, in the light of Staël's own reflections on literature as moral action, be seen as no less—or no more—the result of an artistic decision than the death of, say, Constant's Éléonore.

Although in one sense *Corinne*'s conclusion is less tragic than that of *Delphine*, since something of her is transmitted to Oswald and Lucile's daughter Julie, through whom Corinne will live on, in another sense her death is more problematic precisely because of Staël's choice of narrative form. In an epistolary fiction like *Delphine*, the character seems in some degree to be in control, if not of her life, at least of her story. A third-person narrative like *Corinne*, however strong its investment in the character, subordinates the heroine's agency to its own logic. Because the narrator is now located outside the world of the story, the character may seem that much more the object of the writer's whim. This would be especially true in a literature that had earlier abandoned the external narrator because the transcendent authority that grounded it had come to appear arbitrary. Staël's gamble in *Corinne* is that the apparent concession to the centrality of the writing self will allow, on the contrary, for a more nuanced perspective in which specific actions can be productively contextualized within a larger, more differentiated symbolic world.

The appeal to a paternal super-narrator is one way Staël tries to achieve this perspective. But by itself it would have brought the novel too close to the model of *Wilhelm Meister*, a book Staël praised,[31] but with serious reservations about the disproportion between the impartial point of view and the sensibility of the Mignon story, whose pathos is sacrificed to Goethe's overarching scheme. A second kind of framework is therefore needed to mitigate the oppressive effect of premature closure. It is provided by the conception of Italy as a maternal world. Marie-Claire Vallois has very perceptively analyzed *Corinne*'s evocation of Italy as a pre-Oedipal containing context which is opposed to the harsh—yet in many ways admirable—world of English political virtue where the separation of private and public spheres is held to be vital to self-government in every sense of that term. She sees Corinne's exploration of Italy's ruins as an attempt to recover a creative maternal power that has been devastated by the laws of history.[32]

Vallois' insightful interpretation needs to be qualified, however: first, because Corinne's maternal Italy is not truly pre-symbolic. It is very much, in the Schillerian sense, a sentimental reconstruction. When Corinne dresses up as a sybil, for example, she imitates, not an ancient image, but Domenichino's painting.[33] Fusion with the maternal is never a real possibility. It is rehearsed, instead, so that the seductiveness of such a fusion can be felt but then put in perspective. Oswald's criticism of the sentimentalism of religion in Rome and the common people's superstitiousness clearly reflects Staël's own point of view, as does his praise of Britain's more masculine political energy. It is the containing rather than directly creative power of the maternal to which Staël appeals. Staël's survey of Italy emphasizes above all what endures beyond destruction—even the destruction caused by the heroine's (or the author's) own initiative.

If in giving shape, coherence, and closure to her story through the use of the external narrator Staël identifies with an image of the father, the maternal image of Italy allows us to put story-telling in perspective by showing us what remains beyond the drama of rise and fall. At first glance, what remains is a collection of ruins, but the pathos of fragmentation is to some extent compensated by the energizing appreciation of the way different layers of time and different cultural productions coexist for the observing eye. As Roland Mortier has pointed out, the ruin is "the meeting-point of nature and art, of determinism and freedom, of voluntaristic creation and fate."[34] But that meeting-point lies in the consciousness of the viewer, a consciousness that cannot rest on any one point, but must work to supply the missing pieces. Appreciation of Italy may in this sense be opposed to the prematurely posthumous closure of Corinne's self-narration, which was placed under the sign of the father. For better and for worse, Italy is a land of contradiction and diversity, where actions, as Corinne tries to show the stiff-mannered Oswald, may have more than one meaning. Italy's story is not a happy one, but it is unfinished. Italy provided a home for Corinne after Lady Edgermond, the wicked stepmother, demanded she accept the fiction of her death so as not to sully the family's reputation. One could say that Italy makes it possible for Staël to have Corinne die a second time for the sake of her novel without that gesture carrying the burden of authorial anxiety it might otherwise have done. As containing context, "Italy" inscribes that gesture in the *longue durée* and stumbling progress of the human spirit.

In the end, though, there is no one context. About the only thing we know about the shaping of *Corinne* is Staël's uncertainty whether her novel would be a love story contained in a travel book, or a travel book contained in a love story.[35] From the formal point of view, this can be seen as a hesitation between a unitary and a looser narrative logic. Similarly, *Corinne* depends on both a paternal and a maternal model, neither of which has any clear priority—if indeed we can clearly distinguish the contours of each. For one could say that, contrary to expectation, the inwardness of the love story belongs to the former, while the expansiveness of the travel book belongs to the latter. Staël's adoption and transformation of the external narrator is an attempt to relativize the hierarchy of these models without abandoning the ideal of an ultimate context of meaning. That context can no longer be apprehended immediately, still less inhabited as one would a home. Corinne's final wish, "tout dire et tout éprouver à la fois" (579), can only be realized in her dying song. The experience of exile cannot be erased. But if there is no single home, then exile loses its privilege as the definitive cultural metaphor. A more suitable analogy for the mobility and cross-fertilization of discursive contexts attempted in *Corinne* may be found in an activity whose broad cultural importance to the diversity of the modern world Staël was one of the first to recognize: translation.[36]

NOTES

I wish to thank Madelyn Gutwirth, Julie Hayes, and the *SECC* readers for their comments on this paper.

1. Germaine de Staël, *De l'Allemagne*, ed. Simone Balayé (Paris: Garnier-Flammarion, 1968), 2:218 (pt. 3, chap. 19).
2. Germaine de Staël, *Dix années d'exil*, preface by Emmanuel d'Astier, introduction and notes by Simone Balayé (Paris: Union générale d'éditions, 1966), 61. References to this edition will be included in the text. The work is available in English under the title *Ten Years of Exile*, trans. Doris Beik (New York: Saturday Review Press, 1972).
3. Coppet, Staël's home in Switzerland, attracted a circle of friends and admirers.
4. See especially Madelyn Gutwirth's pathbreaking *Madame de Staël, Novelist: The Emergence of the Artist as Woman* (Urbana: University of Illinois Press, 1978); Simone Balayé, *Madame de Staël: Lumières et liberté* (Paris: Klincksieck, 1979); and the various perspectives included in *Germaine de Staël: Crossing the Borders*, ed. Madelyn Gutwirth, Avriel Goldberger, and Karyna Szmurlo (New Brunswick, NJ: Rutgers University Press, 1991).
5. Benjamin Constant, *Oeuvres* (Paris: Gallimard, 1957), 14. The quotation is from the first chapter of Adolphe.
6. I take the expression "punctual self" from Charles Taylor's illuminating discussion of modernity in *Sources of the Self: The Making of the Modern Identity* (Cambridge: Harvard University Press, 1989), 159ff.
7. Paul Bénichou, *Le Sacre de l'écrivain* (Paris: Corti, 1973).
8. Georges Poulet, "Madame de Staël," in *Mesure de l'instant* (Paris: Plon, 1968), 193–212.
9. Jean Starobinski, "Suicide et mélancolie chez Mme de Staël," *Madame de Staël et l'Europe. Colloque de Coppet (18–24 juillet 1966)* (Paris: Klincksieck, 1970), 242–52; Paul de Man, "Madame de Staël and Jean-Jacques Rousseau," in *Critical Writings 1953–1978*, ed. Lindsay Waters (Minneapolis: University of Minnesota Press, 1989), 171–78 (originally published in French in *Preuves* 190 [Dec. 1966]: 35–40).
10. Joan de Jean, *Fictions of Sappho 1546–1937* (Chicago: University of Chicago Press, 1989), especially 161–86.
11. For a suggestive recent introduction to Staël's views on literary history, see the introduction to Madame de Staël, *De la littérature*, ed. Gérard Gengembre and Jean Goldzink (Paris: Flammarion, 1991).
12. Marie-Claire Vallois' *Fictions féminines: Mme de Staël et les voix de la Sibylle* (Saratogo, CA: Anima Libri, 1987) includes some valuable remarks on the third person in *Corinne* as an "autobiographie dédoublée" (165–69). Susan Sniader Lanser, in *Fictions of Authority: Women Writers and Narrative Voice* (Ithaca: Cornell University Press, 1992), 162–64, argues on the contrary that the third-person voice of the novel means that Corinne is prevented from becoming a full Romantic subject. Carla Peterson, in *The*

Determined Reader: Gender and Culture in the Novel from Napoleon to Victoria (New Brunswick, NJ: Rutgers University Press, 1986), asserts instead that "Staël attests to the indomitability of the female genius in her creation of an omniscient narrator, superior to Corinne, who strives to heal madness, reconcile conflict . . . in her own narrative" (59). My own approach is closest to Peterson's and has been influenced by the discussions of novelistic realism in Michael Bell, *The Sentiment of Reality* (London: George Allen and Unwin, 1983), and Marshall Brown, "The Logic of Realism: A Hegelian Approach," *PMLA* 96 (1981): 224–41.

13. *De l'Allemagne*, 2:43 (pt. 2, chap. 28).

14. *De la littérature*, 244.

15. Germaine de Staël, *Corinne ou l'Italie*, ed. Simone Balayé (Paris: Galliamrd, 1985), 587. For the English text, see *Corinne, or Italy*, trans. Avriel Goldberger (New Brunswick, NJ: Rutgers University Press, 1987), 419.

16. As J. W. Scott points out in *Madame de Lafayette: La Princesse de Clèves* (London, 1983), the narrator uses the word "perhaps" only ironically, when the unflattering truth is obvious. But I would claim the irony is double-edged, pointing to the fundamental untrustworthiness of one's own ability to achieve a clear understanding of human affairs.

17. Choderlos de Laclos, *Oeuvres complètes,* ed. Laurent Versini (Paris: Gallimard, 1979), 352n (note to letter 154).

18. See William Ray, *Story and History* (Oxford: Blackwell, 1990). A good example of such supplementary exchange is the "préface dialoguée" Rousseau himself added to *Julie*.

19. According to Avriel Goldberger, *Corinne, or Italy*, xxxvii and n. 21, fragments of early drafts do exist, but they have yet to be published. The edition of Staël's complete correspondence, which is progressing very slowly, does not cover the period of *Corinne*'s revision and publication.

20. A. W. Schlegel, review of *Corinne*, in *Werke* (Leipzig, 1846), 12:188–206. It originally appeared in the *Jenaischen allgemeinen Literatur-Zeitung* no. 152, in 1807. The text is also available in Emil Staiger's selection of Schlegel's *Kritische Schriften* (Zürich: Artemis, 1962), 326–41. It has been translated into French as "Une étude critique de Corinne ou l'Italie," by A. Blschke and J. Arnaud, *Cahiers staëliens* n.s. 16 (June 1973): 57–71.

21. "Die in der Corinna gewälte erzählende Form ist unstreitig der Abfassung eines Roman in Briefen vorzuziehen. Erstlich ist sie weit gedrängter; ferner ist der durchgängige Gebrauch der Briefform vielen Unbequemlichkeiten unterworfen: die Personen sollen in ihrer jedesmaligen Lage Befangen sein, und doch muss ihnen eine damit unverträgliche Beobachtung ihrer selbst und anderer verliehen werden, um den Leser über sie und ihre Täuchungen ins klare zu setzen und die Zukunft vorzubereiten. Die Erzählung hingegen darf mit einer gewissen dichterischen Allwissenheit ruhig und unparteiisch auf die Mithandelnden herabschauen." Staiger edition, 339–40, my translation.

22. In addition to the books by Gutwirth and Balayé, see the articles listed in the latter's edition of *Corinne*.

23. See bk. 8, chap. 1, and bk. 12, chap. 2.

24. Staël was inclined to such a view, but her views on this point, which need to be studied alongside and against those of Chateaubriand and others of the period, cannot be discussed here.

25. Ellen Peel, "Contradictions of Form and Feminism in *Corinne, ou l'Italie*," *Essays in Literature* 14 (1987): 281–98. I am not sure Staël meant to give this impression, but it is significant that the only woman in Rome we are told Corinne visits is referred to as the "wife of a friend" (*Corinne*, 125).

26. Margaret Waller, *The Male Malady: Fictions of Impotence in the French Romantic Novel* (New Brunswick, NJ: Rutgers University Press, 1993), 76.

27. For a discussion of the perplexed, often unproductive attempts to establish the cultural status of the novel in France, see Georges May, *Le Dilemme du roman au XVIIIe siècle* (Paris: Presses universitaires de France, 1963). A good example of the attempt in Staël's circle to modify the terms of the debate is Constant's discussion of *Corinne* in "De Madame de Staël et de ses ouvrages," *Oeuvres*, 834: "Un ouvrage d'imagination ne doit pas avoir un but moral, mais un résultat moral."

28. Peterson, *The Determined Reader*, 61.

29. See for example Naomi Segal, *The Unintended Reader: Feminism and Manon Lescaut* (Cambridge: Cambridge University Press, 1986); Nancy K. Miller, "1735: The Gender of the Memoir Novel," in *A New History of French Literature*, ed. Denis Hollier (Cambridge: Harvard University Press, 1989), 436–42; and Patrick Coleman, "From the *Mémoires* to *Manon*: Mourning and Narrative Control in Prévost," *Nottingham French Studies* 29:2 (1990): 3–11.

30. Balayé, *Madame de Staël*, 136.

31. Staël, *De l'Allemagne* 2:44–45.

32. Vallois, *Fictions féminines*, chap. 3.

33. *Corinne*, 52 (bk. 2, chap. 1).

34. Roland Mortier, *La Poétique des ruines en France* (Geneva: Droz, 1970), 10.

35. For the genesis of the novel, see Simone Balayé, *Les Carnets de voyage de Madame de Staël: contribution àla genèse de ses oeuvres* (Geneva: Droz, 1971), 93–103, and Staël's letter of 9 April 1805 to Jean-Baptiste Suard in *Madame de Staël, Correspondance générale*, ed. Beatrice W. Jasinski, vol. 5, pt. 2 (Paris: Hachette, 1985), 531–32 and notes.

36. See "De l'esprit des traductions," in Staël's *Oeuvres* (Paris, 1821), 17:387–99.

Narrative, the Scienza Nuova, and the Barbarism of Reflection

ROBERT P. CREASE

Giambattista Vico (1688–1744) stands at the crossroads of two formidable but conflicting intellectual traditions: Renaissance humanism and the Enlightenment, which partly explains why he is an ambiguous figure amid eighteenth-century thinkers. He can be read either as an Enlightenment (or at least proto-Enlightenment) thinker attempting to develop an epistemological response to Descartes that validates a *science* of history and philology—and thus as someone who attempts to extend and elaborate modernism—or he can be read as attempting to subvert the Enlightenment preoccupation with a certain model of science, and thus as incipiently postmodern.[1] This ambiguity appears most clearly in explicitly opposed interpretations of Vico's conception of the possibility of progress.

One of Vico's most famous doctrines is that of the corsi and ricorsi, the cyclical path charting the rise and fall of all nations or civilizations. According to Vico, a nation or civilization travels through three ages—of gods, heroes, and men—whose natures are, respectively, divine, heroic, and human;[2] following the development of rationality, what Vico calls the "barbarism of reflection" brings about a dissolution in the nation or civilization, resulting in a slide back to barbarism, after which the cycle begins anew. But what is the relationship of Vico's *New Science* to those corsi and ricorsi? Does the *New Science* merely describe this historical path, which Vico calls the "ideal eternal history" [349], as something external to its own working as a text, a diagnosis of a condition which it is *impossible* to cure? Or does the *New Science* serve to awaken us to impending dangers latent in, for instance, the present course of western civilization so that we may attempt to forestall or even prevent them; is it a diagnosis that is an indispensable part of a *possible* cure?

The issue, though seldom addressed in the literature, would seem to be a crucial one in Vichian scholarship. One reason is that it bears immediately and profoundly upon Vico's position on the idea of progress, and thus upon his ultimate role in eighteenth-century discussions of it by Fontenelle, Perrault, Turgot, Condorcet, Kant, and others. According to the traditional view, Vico has virtually no notion of continuous progress. Robert Nisbet, for instance, claims that Vico's interest in progress was restricted to the *problem* of progress, or "the conditions under which distinct intellectual advancement occurs in human history, assessed, however, against conditions under which decline and degeneration take place." Indeed, Nisbet sees possible Vichian influence on one of Turgot's few essays, "Researches into the Causes of the Progress and Decline of the Sciences and Arts," a discussion that does not claim universal and necessary progress for mankind. Vico, Nisbet finds, cannot be included in that "distinguished succession of minds in the modern West" enthralled and animated by the idea of progress, a succession which continued into the next century in the works of Comte, Hegel, Spencer and others.[3] A. Robert Caponigri and Alphons 't Hart, however, see Vico as pointing towards a radically new conception of progress, though one much different from his contemporaries. They thus view him as an eighteenth-century maverick, but one whose position essentially lies within the above-mentioned tradition of thinkers inspired by the idea of continuous progress.[4]

A second reason why this issue is a crucial one in Vichian scholarship is that it threatens to undermine the coherence of the doctrine of the *Scienza Nuova* itself. If, in accord with the views of those who deny an account of progress in Vico, the *New Science* is to be understood as merely describing a historical path, that would seem to violate Vico's insistence on the function of texts and their character as institutions. On the other hand, if the *New Science* is to be taken as a critical step towards forestalling the slide back to barbarism—the position of those who see Vico as an advocate of possible progress—that would seem to be in conflict with the doctrine of corsi and ricorsi.

To restate the issue: does the *New Science* provide a description of a deterministic process in such a way that the work is external to what it describes (thus resembling a "scientific" treatise), as some textual evidence suggests, or is the *New Science* fully and self-consciously a part of the process it describes and a tool leading to increasing synthesis rather than dissolution (as other textual evidence suggests, including the very existence of the *New Science* itself)? To put the matter still more sharply: if Vico believed that the *New Science* could help to avoid the dissolution of the age, this conflicts with his own theory of ricorsi; if he believed it could not, this conflicts with passages which suggest that this was his purpose in writing.

I do not claim to be able to make Vico's own intention any clearer. I do think, however, that examining the peculiar nature and function of narrative within the *New Science* sheds considerable light on this issue, and draws our attention to the fact that the work must be read in a different interpretive frame from the Cartesian one in which the issue of determinism or progress is posed as an "either-or" proposition. Vico's position, that is to say, is simply too rich to be adequately captured in that alternative. Moreover, I believe (though the topic is beyond the scope of this essay) that the issue of narrative in the *New Science* also bears centrally upon other important issues in Vichian scholarship besides that of his position on progress, such as the merging of philosophy and philology, the convertability of verum and factum, the critique of Cartesianism, and others.

* * * * * * * * *

The *New Science* begins with an allegorical picture for a frontispiece, followed by an introduction claiming to explain the allegorical picture, followed by five books and a conclusion. Book one begins with a chronological table schematizing the histories of seven civilizations, followed by one section explaining the table, and three more outlining Vico's elements, principles, and method. In them, Vico expresses his opposition, on the one hand, to the view that chance rules the course of human institutions, as per Epicurus, Hobbes, and Machiavelli, but also, on the other hand, to the view that fate rules human institutions, as per Zeno and Spinoza (130, 179). Rather, Vico argues, the similarities between the course of nations result from similarities in the course of the maturative process of what he calls "the indefinite nature of the human mind" (121). Though indefinite, this nature is articulated in human institutions; these institutions both shape human nature and are shaped by it in turn, via a process for which the ideal eternal history serves as a chart. The reciprocally maturing relation between institutions and human nature is one of the most fundamental and influential of Vichian insights.

The key point is that human motives provide the dynamism for this maturative process. Human choices, while by nature "most uncertain," become determined as human needs and utilities such as self-love, ferocity, avarice, lust, and ambition come to be expressed in a particular institutional context (141). In this way the maturative process is not a genetic unfolding or metaphysically determined or logically deducible on the one hand, nor arbitrary or chance-governed on the other. Rather, this maturative process is a self-creation, a self-unfolding. Human nature does not pass through time, but produces itself in time. "That which did all this was mind, for men did it with intelligence," Vico says; "it was not fate, for they did it by choice; not chance, for the results of their always so acting are perpetually the same" (1108). The ideal eternal history thus does not amount to a transcendent history, but rather an account of human self-development, for it shows that only in certain social conditions and contexts can human beings acquire certain capacities, such as rationality, and that such acquisition is a condition for further developments. Only by going through earlier stages can one get to the later stages.

The third of Vico's trio of stages—the human age, which follows the heroic and the divine ages—thus has a special stature. One must be careful with the adjective "human" here, which Vico uses in several senses. In one, it qualifies all three stages, as for instance when he says that his science begins at the beginning of the divine age when "these creatures began to think humanly" (338; also 447). Elsewhere, though, he qualifies the second and third stages as human as opposed to the first (629), while in still other sections he describes the third stage alone as properly human (1088). Here, he means that human nature is *tutta spiegata*, or fully unfolded; whatever capacities human beings have potentially have been realized. Moreover, he clearly views this stage as the most progressive; in government, for instance, it is marked by the breaking of the hegemony of patricians and the establishment of formal equality in the democratic or monarchical state.

But this stage also contains the seeds of its own dissolution. In reflection the mind detaches itself from its objects, putting them at a distance. Overreliance on reflection and the critical faculties leads human beings to withdraw from the prereflective level in which we live communally. We fancy ourselves able to live without this communal belonging—as Descartes, for instance, was able to do. The fabric of social life begins to pull apart, and human beings become increasingly isolated from each other and motivated by self-interest. This is what Vico calls the "barbarism of reflection," which he finds even more terrible than the barbarism of sense because the motive of self-interest is cloaked. The barbarism of reflection produces a bestialization of human beings, ultimately leading the cycle to start over again.

Here arises the issue with which I began: what is the role of the *New Science* in this stage? Is it merely an observation of this course in history, and as a product of reflection detached from its subject? Evidence that it is includes Vico's references to it as metaphysics, his insistence on the scientific methodology of his project, his view of human behavior as law-governed, and his insistence that the ideal eternal history is a necessary path. Consider:

> The decisive sort of proof in our Science is therefore this: that, since these institutions have been established by divine providence, the course of the institutions of the nations had to be, must now be, and will have to be such as our Science demonstrates, even if infinite worlds were born from time to time through eternity. . . . Our Science therefore comes to describe at the same time an ideal eternal history traversed in time by the history of every nation in its rise, development, maturity, decline, and fall. Indeed, we make bold to affirm that he who meditates this Science narrates to himself this ideal eternal history so far as he himself makes it for himself by that proof "it had, has, and will have to be." (348–49; 1096)

On the other hand, Vico also repeatedly argues, against Spinoza, that the path that civilizations traverse is not a determined one. In several previous works, including *On The Study Methods of Our Time,* Vico urges the practical value of philosophy for government and education. For one thing, as a philosophical text it belongs to the institutions of its age, which, Vico repeatedly stresses, are what shape human nature. Moreover, the *New Science* refers to institutions as serving the preservation of the human race or the highest good (344, 364), and occasionally promotes more directly the practical value of philosophy, even in a way seemingly addressed to precisely those things that cause the slide into barbarism. Consider: "To be useful to the human race, philosophy must raise and direct weak and fallen man, not rend his nature or abandon him in his corruption" (129). Later, in an account of Rome, philosophy is said to have inflamed people "to command good laws" (1101). And it seems perverse that the very work which claims for the first time to provide a true understanding of the real nature of humanity, written just at the time when humanity's powers are fully deployed, should by that act mark the moment of the onset of decadence and be in the service of social dissolution.

An additional, though mysterious piece to this puzzle is the *Pratica,* composed by Vico for the conclusion of the third edition of the *New Science,* but never included in that work.[5] Addressing the question of the practical value of the *New Science,* Vico says in the *Pratica* that, while the *New Science* seems purely contemplative and of no help to prudence or action in delaying if not preventing the ruin of nations, that is not the case. The properly educated young, along with "wise men and princes of our commonwealths," will be "instructed" by the contemplation of the course the nations run provided by the book, and, thanks to the way philosophy informs their practice, become able, "through good institutions, laws, and examples, to recall the peoples to their *acme* or perfect state" (1406). This presents a clear and plausible statement concerning the practical value of the *New Science*—yet Vico left it out. Why?

Various scholars have addressed the problem of the *Practica.* One partisan of the position that the attribution of a practical value to the *New Science* is inconsistent with the views expressed therein is Stephen Taylor Holmes. Noting Vico's characterization of thought in the early part of each *corso* as pre-reflective and in the later part as reflective, as well as Vico's own description of the *New Science* as scientific and reflective in nature, Holmes poses the following question: "In what way did Vico consider himself to have successfully *turned reflection against reflection,* and thus to have postponed (not to say prevented) the otherwise inevitable disintegration and decay of advanced society?" Holmes considers two possible strategies for handling such a question. One would view the *New Science* as part of a revival of poetic language and thought, the other would see the *New Science* as full of "noble lies" such as that of divine providence, which conceals from human beings that they themselves are the authors of their own actions and thus undermines reflective awareness of other possibilities. Holmes rejects both of these views as running contrary to Vico's repeated insistence on the scientific and reflective character of the *New Science*, leading him to conclude that the problem "remains yet unanswered."[6]

Another partisan of the view that the *Pratica* was suppressed because it ran counter to the deterministic principles of the *New Science* is Leon Pompa. Pompa, too, is puzzled by the apparent contradiction between the optimistic spirit of the *Pratica* as well as previous writings and the apparent pessimism and determinism of the *New Science*. But he finds indications in the *New Science* that could be cited in defense of such pessimism. One is that it is precisely at the time of the barbarism of reflection that institutions cease to appropriately reflect the social natures of the individuals in society and thus to promote cohesive social life. Another is Vico's assumption that the human capacity for reason and for imagination are mutually exclusive (185, 218–19). While human beings, then, lose the capacity for accepting false beliefs which nonetheless prevent social dissolution, they also seem prevented from accepting other socially supportive characteristics in their stead. In the light of these two views, Pompa says, one must conclude that the reason for Vico's failure to publish the *Pratica* is "his realization that its more optimistic prescriptions are incompatible with the basically deterministic character of the rest of the *Scienza Nuova*."[7] Pompa finds both of these assumptions, however, unnecessary and even mistaken, and claims they could be excised without affecting the remainder of the *New Science*.

A. Robert Caponigri, on the other hand, takes for granted that the practical ambitions expressed in the *Pratica* are in fact fulfilled by the *New Science* as it stands. Caponigri asserts, "It is the purpose of the 'New Science' to discover the law of the origin, growth, and decline of the social economy, that is, of the complex of institutions in which the social consciousness of humanity is incorporated and effected; even more, the 'New Science' seeks, through the determination of this law, to place in the hands of the nations, so to say, the power of recapturing the sources of their life and, even in the moment of decline of, initiating anew their movement toward ideality and vigorous life."[8] But this claim leaves unexplained the means of recapturing this power, especially given the antinomy of reason and imagination described by Pompa.

More persuasive is Alphonse 't Hart, who advances three reasons for thinking that the cyclical conception of history does not imply inevitability of repetition and incompatibility with progress. One is the progressive character of the succession of political systems, the second is the relative freedom within the "ideal eternal history" for diversified routes, and the third, once again, is the practical ambitions expressed in the first edition of the *New Science*. In countering the argument that the reason that Vico left the *Pratica* out of the *New Science* had to do with his recognition of its inconsistency with the position advanced by that text, 't Hart elaborates on the explanation given by Benedetto Croce and Max Fisch. The *Pratica*, 't Hart says, assumes an essentially Aristotelian view of the relation between contemplation, praxis, and production. But by the time the third edition was ready, 't Hart claims, Vico realized that the *New Science* could not be described in Aristotelian categories, since it was just as practical and productive as contemplative—the tripartate division is no longer applicable where knowing and making are convertible. Vico withheld the *Pratica*, neither because he had given up the practical ambitions of the *New Science* nor because such practical ambitions conflicted with the pessimistic doctrines of that work, but rather out of a deeper reflection on the nature of his science, and therewith on the inseparability of *verum* and *factum*.[9]

This suggestion contains implications for the role of narrative in the *New Science* and also bears on the question we have been considering concerning the work's status with respect to the corsi. By narrative I mean here simply the organization of material about a subject into a single descriptive episode following roughly chronological order. The raw material for the new scientist includes individual national histories considered as the large-scale metabolism of "notable men and most pertinent deeds . . . through whom and by which the decisive changes in human institutions have come about" (43). But the new scientist treats this metabolistic process as but one exemplar of a universal history and narrates *that* process in presenting the ideal eternal history. By narrating that process—or so runs the implication—the new scientist becomes part of the very historical process which is studied, effecting an identity between historian and historical agent, observing as well as producing and practicing history.[10]

Several questions should be considered at this point. Does it makes sense to claim that the *New Science* contains a narrative of the ideal eternal history? If so, what is the real subject of that narrative? Finally, what is entailed by the claim that a narrative is just as much practical and productive as contemplative?

Regarding the first question, the *New Science* does insist that it makes visible the ideal eternal history in the form of a single descriptive and complete episode whose structure unfolds over time. Indeed, meditation of "this Science," Vico writes, involves a reader in narrating the ideal eternal history to oneself. This narrative describes the naturalness of each institution's birth, its institutive order, and the good it winds up serving, even though that good is always different than what was intended (344). The process described by the narrative is often conflictive; see, for instance, Vico's marvelous metaphor about how certain institutions continue a long time into the next historical period, much like "great and rapid rivers continue far into the sea, keeping sweet the waters borne on by the force of their flow" (412), disintegrating into eddies and cross-currents far from land.

The narrative subject is human nature itself. For human nature by itself is "indefinite" (120), and only becomes definite by its belonging within an institutional context; outside of such, Vico says (echoing Aristotle), human beings "would live alone like wild beasts" (2). Human nature must then be sought through interpretation of the institutional context, and there is no *a priori* exteriority between human nature and any elements of human social life, which is why in reading the *New Science* one finds onself led into some rather peculiar subjects, such as numismatics, the "science of blazonry," etc. Yet even within institutional contexts human nature is unstable due to the perpetual lack of identity between human intentions and the consequences of their realization—precisely the dynamism which spurs the human mind to self-produce itself in history. The tale of the ideal eternal history thus involves an "uninterrupted order of causes and effects" (915) over the course the nations run, which is why Vico says that the one who meditates this science "narrates to himself" the ideal eternal history. To apprehend human nature, one must know, not an essence or definition, but a story. The narrative provided by the *New Science* is therefore the essential vehicle by which human nature comes to be recognized by human beings: narrative for Vico is the means—the *only* means—of human self-recognition.

The self-recognition that transpires in the *Scienza Nuova* thus bears certain similarities with Jacques Lacan's well-known "mirror stage" in which the child first recognizes its own image.[11] The insight achieved by the *Scienza Nuova*, that is, is not merely a situational apperception, an apprehension of identity between subject and image, but simultaneously also the apprehension of a continuous reciprocity and play between subject and image. There are, however, numerous differences between Lacan's *stade du miroir* and the self-apprehension achieved by the *Scienza Nuova*. In the Vichian specular moment, even the *speculum* or object thanks to which the self-recognition is achieved is not an other. It, too, is a human production—a human production disclosing the history of the reciprocity between human productions and the character of the human mind, a mirror mirroring the full story of the mirroring relation between institutions and human mind.

Another significant difference is that in the Vichian mirror stage there is no sense of the danger that Lacan sees looming in the specular moment— the alienation and captivation or self-absorption by the image, the deeper loss of self that accompanies its apparent achievement of self-apprehension.[12] Far from it; the self-apprehension achieved by the *Scienza Nuova* comes for Vico as the ultimate epistemological triumph. Oddly enough, precisely at this point appears an indebtedness to the Cartesian model of knowledge according to which the veracity of a thing is assured by a certainty achieved through clarity of apprehension in intuition. "Indeed, we make bold to affirm that he who meditates this Science narrates to himself this ideal eternal history so far as he himself makes it for himself by that proof 'it had, has, and will have to be' . . . And history cannot be more certain than when he who creates the things also narrates them" (349).

While Vico recognizes that Descartes' *cogito* has no significant epistemological status insofar as it has been marked by history and is thus but an "ordinary acquaintance" or "awareness" (and awareness, for Vico, "is had of things whose form or manner of becoming we are not able to demonstrate"),[13] the *Scienza Nuova*, in compiling the register of effects marking the mind and demonstrating their coherence in the form of a narrative, provides the possibility of a complete apprehension of mind in its evolving character, density, and diversity. The *New Science* thus ultimately appears to fulfill the Cartesian model of knowledge, though in new, historical terms, spanning the gap between *cogito* and what one might call "the Cogito."[14]

For Vico, therefore, narrative has a unique kind of power, for it can disclose something that neither philosophy nor history alone can. The human nature which appears thanks to the narrative provided by the ideal eternal history cannot appear in the historically or philologically complete tale of a single individual history. Nor could it be made to appear *a priori* via abstract logical or metaphysical considerations. For the *way* we acquire reason is as basic to our humanity as the capacity for reason itself. If a civilization of beings were able to traverse the cycle differently, and could take different routes or skip stages, this would not be a *human* civilization. To put it still another way, it is the mark of the humanity of a nation to have evolved in just this sort of way described by the ideal eternal history.[15]

This bears upon the third question I posed above concerning the sense it makes to claim that a narrative is just as much practical and productive as contemplative. For this disclosure is a production; it is not the result of an induction, deduction, or description. It involves not a catalogue or compendium of one detail after another, but is the outcome of a creative process involving judicious selection and interweaving of details in the service of the appearing of the phenomenon. In the *New Science*, assimilation is prized over explanation and description, and the work relies principally not on definition and deduction but on imagination and interpretation. The actualization of self achieved through the narration of the ideal eternal history is not described but *produced*.

Not only is this narrative a produced self-presence, but it is a *stage-dependent* one as well.[16] It could not have been produced in the age of gods or heroes. For both to produce as well as to narrate to oneself the ideal eternal history requires robust use of the faculties of each era, including imagination, *ingenium*, and reason. To produce and narrate to oneself a narrative, for instance, requires what D. P. Verene has called the "recollective imagination," or the faculty required "to visualize the drama of a mediated identity between an origin and an end."[17] *Ingenium*, or "the faculty of connecting separate and diverse elements," is also an essential tool of the new scientist in piecing together the narrative.[18] Also required is reflection, or the ability to detach the principle from the example and to reason from causes.

Inasmuch as the narrative which produces human self-presence requires reason, it is not possible outside of the third or "human" stage; inasmuch as it requires imagination and *ingenium*, it also requires capabilities developed during the other two ages. Vico's use of narrative, then, involves the union of sense and intellect, figure and fact, image and idea (in a way reminiscent of the frontispiece).

The role of narrative in the *New Science* exemplifies a kind of knowledge that unites the capabilities that Pompa pointed out were considered to be mutually exclusionary in the *New Science*, and which thus supports his contention that imagination need not be destroyed in order that reason may develop. Moreover, the narrative in question also overcomes the analytical detachment of reason toward its objects, for in narrating the ideal eternal history to oneself, the new scientist is forced to apprehend the barbarism of reflection as one's own possibility, for it is not contingent but rooted in human nature itself; one recognizes the humanity of the barbarism of reflection. But this analytical detachment is precisely what Vico claims is the origin of the slide back into barbarism. Vico's use of narrative in the *New Science*, then, exemplifies in deed, in *ergon*, the refutation of the two contentions used in defense of the claim of that work's commitment to pessimism; namely, the antinomy between reason and the imagination, and the analytical detachment of reflection.

Yet neither does Vico's use of narrative in the *New Science* support an optimistic reading of that text. If the *New Science* is not a theoretical and scientific work claiming to present an account of an object divorced from that object, neither is it a practical text that aims, or can be used, to apply a knowledge of its object in order to change that object. The *New Science* makes possible human self-recognition, but nothing guarantees that self-apprehension, even when it involves the prospect of self-destruction, will lead to self-transformation.

An analogy with a situation often described by Freud may help to elucidate this point. In *Studies in Hysteria, Beyond the Pleasure Principle*, and elsewhere, Freud remarks that a patient's recognition that s/he has been following a repetitive behavior is only the first step towards a cure, and that it is perfectly possible and indeed all too common for a patient to have insight into the existence and causes of his or her own destructive and repetitive behavior and still continue to repeat such behavior. Freud, of course, is often read as though he viewed insight as the end of analysis, and as though insight were the essential vehicle of change and by itself sufficient to resolve resistances. But that he is read in such a way is a reflection of how strongly the Enlightenment assumption of the priority of knowledge and insight in human behavior has a hold over us. Insight into the causes of one's own behavior, and recognition of one's repetition of that behavior, opens the possibility of change (without it, we continue to repeat, though without recognizing it), but by itself is insufficient to effect that change.

Freud's remarks concerning the relation between a patient, repetitive behavior, and insight may be considered as analogous to Vico's conception of the relation between human beings, the ideal eternal history, and the knowledge provided by the *New Science*. The self-recognition achieved in the *New Science* is not by itself sufficient to alter the slide of a nation or civilization back into barbarism. It may be that the self-recognition is achieved by almost everyone in the nation or civilization, or only by a few "new scientists"; in either case, it is not a logical incompatibility that, despite the existence of a narrative practice compatible with human self-presence such as is embodied in the *New Science*, Vico could still maintain that the dominance of a form of reason alienated from imagination and ingenuity doomed the nation or civilization to slide back into barbarism, repeating the ideal eternal history. This makes Vico's sensibility, as Sandra R. Luft has put it, "ultimately more tragic than Enlightenment."[19]

The existence of a narrative text revealing the existence of past repetitions, and the exposure of the causes of such repetitions as rooted directly in human nature, only creates the opening, the possibility of avoiding that repetition. To realize that possibility would involve *performing* differently, which is not a question of using theoretical knowledge to tinker with the operation of a whole, but of imaginatively altering a thousand little behaviors to affect the ensemble in different ways. What would have to happen to develop that possibility? Clearly, in Vico's view, were it to take place it would have to involve the imaginative creation of myriad new kinds of institutions. The *New Science* invites us to pose such questions as: If one such book as the *New Science* can be written, what other books could be written? What political structures, educational systems, and philosophies could be created? Each institution is connected with thousands of others: what would be the nature and effect of the ensemble of institutions? To these questions Vico provides no answers—as we should expect, given that in each case it would be a work of imagination whose ultimate impact on human nature would be different from what was intended.

Armed with the notion of narrative, therefore, we can see that the position of Vico's *New Science* with respect to the ideal eternal history is much richer than the simple dichotomy of pessimistically and deterministically following it or optimistically and progressively departing from it. Expressing the issue as an either/or proposition is itself the product of an Enlightenment view of knowledge as either theoretical and detached from its object, or practical and geared toward changing the object. But the *New Science*—an imaginative work—transcends this distinction, and points to a conception of reason no longer Enlightenment, in which the growth of knowledge of natural and social laws is neither guaranteed nor necessarily progressive. In so doing, Vico's work provides an entirely new meaning to the expression, "new science."

NOTES

I am grateful to Eugene T. Gendlin and Sandra R. Luft for helpful comments on a previous draft of this paper.

1. For a consideration of Vico's relation to modern and postmodern perspectives that attempts to distinguish his own more idiosyncratic stance, see Sandra R. Luft, "The Legitimacy of Hans Blumenberg's Conception of Originary Activity," *Annals of Scholarship* 5 (Fall 1987): 3–36; and "Derrida, Vico, Genesis, and the Originary Power of Language," *The Eighteenth Century: Theory and Interpretation* 34 (Spring, 1993): 65–84.
2. Giambattista Vico, *The New Science*, trans. T. G. Bergin and M. H. Fisch (Ithaca: Cornell University Press, 1968), section 916. The sections of subsequent references to this work will be identified in parentheses immediately following the quote.
3. Robert Nisbet, "Vico and the Idea of Progress," in *Social Research* 43 (Autumn 1976): 625–39, quotes on 626, 625. Gustavo Costa wrote an accompanying note to Nisbet's paper in support of the latter's conjecture of a Vichian influence on Turgot, "Vico's Influence on Eighteenth-Century European Culture: A Footnote to Professor Nisbet's Paper," 637–39.
4. A. Robert Caponigri, *Time & Idea: The Theory of History in Giambattista Vico* (Notre Dame: University of Notre Dame Press, 1968); Alphonse C. 't Hart, *Recht en Staat in het denken van Giambattista Vico* (Alphen aan den Rijn: H. D. Tjeenk Willink, 1979), esp. unit 5, part B, sec. 4: "Cyclische Periodisering en de Idee der Vooruitgang," 201–7.
5. See Giambattista Vico, "Practic of the *New Science*," trans. T. H. Bergin and Max H. Fisch, in G. Tagliacozzo and D. P. Verene, eds., *Giambattista Vico's Science of Humanity* (Baltimore: Johns Hopkins University Press, 1976): 451-54.
6. Stephen Taylor Holmes, "The Barbarism of Reflection," in G. Tagliacozzo, ed., *Vico: Past and Present* (Atlantic Highlands: Humanities Press, 1981): 213–22.
7. Leon Pompa, *Vico: A Study of the 'New Science,'* 2nd ed. (Cambridge: Cambridge University Press, 1990), 212.
8. Caponigri, *Time & Idea*, 132–33.
9. 't Hart, *Recht en Staat*, 201–7. See my review of this book in the *Review of Metaphysics* 1980, 806–7, and again in *Philosophy and Rhetoric* 1981, 133–35.
10. It is interesting to compare here Erik Erikson's comments on the role of psychoanalyst as historian in *Childhood and Society* (New York: Norton, 1963), 16.
11. Jacques Lacan, "The Mirror Stage as Formative of the Function of the I as Revealed in Psychoanalytic Experience," in *Écrits*, trans. Alan Sheridan (New York: Norton, 1977), 1–7.

12. These dangerous aspects of Lacan's mirror stage have recently been emphasized by Malcolm Bowie in *Lacan* (Cambridge: Harvard University Press, 1991), 21–26.
13. Giambattista Vico, *De antiquissima Italorum sapientia*, in *Opere filosofiche*, ed. P. Cristofolini (Florence: Cansoni, 1971), 139.
14. See Robert P. Crease, "Vico and the 'Cogito,'" in *Vico: Past and Present*, ed. G. Tagliacozzo (Atlantic Highlands, N.J.: Humanities Press, 1981), 171–81.
15. Leon Pompa makes this point in *Vico: A Study of the 'New Science,'* 184–85.
16. On stage-dependence and other features of recognition, see Robert P. Crease, *The Play of Nature: Experimentation as Performance* (Bloomington: Indiana University Press, 1993).
17. D. P. Verene, "Vico's Philosophy of Imagination," *Social Research* 43 (Autumn 1976): 418.
18. Giambattista Vico, *Selected Writings*, ed. and trans., Leon Pompa (Cambridge: Cambridge University Press, 1982), 70.
19. Personal communication with Sandra R. Luft.

Nature, Sodomy, and Semantics in Sade's
La Philosophie dans le boudoir

> Que la nature fût bonté, c'est ce que les philosophes crurent d'abord; ce fut aussi ce qu'ils cessèrent de croire, après y avoir mieux réfléchi.
> [Nature was goodness, that is what the *philosophes* believed at first; it is also what they ceased to believe, after having thought better of it.][1]

Many writers in the eighteenth century attempted to establish a normative concept of nature as a form of moral authority that might replace that of Scripture. As an ethical norm, nature was deployed to judge the merits of human institutions and social legislation. By the end of the century, it had become commonplace to say that nature was a legislative voice. But "nature" meant many different things to many writers. In the *Encyclopédie*, d'Alembert begins his article on the subject with disarming understatement: "Nature," he writes, "est un terme dont on fait différents usages" [Nature is a term for which one has different uses].[2] D'Alembert enumerates various of these uses, as articulated by individuals ranging from Aristotle to Newton and Boyle. His list includes the universe, being, essence, the laws of motion, the chain of causes and effects, and even God. Speaking of the term "nature" in his landmark *Essays in the History of Ideas*, Arthur O. Lovejoy explained that "the multiplicity of its meanings has made it easy, and common, to slip more or less insensibly from one connotation to another, and thus in the end to pass from one ethical or aesthetic standard to its very antithesis, while nominally professing the same principles."[3] It is precisely this slippage of referents that I would like to examine in the Marquis de Sade's *La Philosophie dans le boudoir*, a text in which slippage applies not only to the term "nature" but also to the related notions of "law," "crime," and "sodomy." I would like to look first at the way in which semantic shifting is incorporated into a rhetorical strategy used to promote Sade's propaganda, and then at certain destabilizing features of his text which seem to undermine its presumed message.

La Philosophie dans le boudoir is a philosophical dialogue published in 1795, perhaps largely written a decade earlier. The text has a definite pedagogic character. Its subtitle is "Les Instituteurs immoraux: Dialogues destinés à l'éducation des jeunes Demoiselles" [The Immoral Schoolteachers: Dialogues Devoted to the Education of Young Ladies]. Its title page announces that "la mère en prescrira la lecture à sa fille" [mothers will prescribe its reading to their daughters]. The content of the text is also an educational experience, in which two libertines, Dolmancé and Madame de Saint-Ange, assisted by the latter's brother, the Chevalier de Mirvel, spend several late-afternoon hours with a fifteen-year-old girl, Eugénie de Mistival, in order to educate her erotically and philosophically. Eugénie's initiation to the "most secret mysteries of Venus" includes nearly every sexual act except "la route ordinaire," the one act that can lead to pregnancy. The myriad sexual activities are interspersed with long discussions by the two "schoolteachers" about a philosophy of nature upon which all this eroticism is based. In the tradition of eighteenth-century philosophical literature, this text is didactic and propagandist, yet it departs from tradition in the relationship it attempts to establish between nature and moral conduct. Sade differs from his predecessors, not in his belief that nature should be the ethical model, nor even in his conception of nature, but especially in the radical conclusions he draws concerning nature as a basis for social behavior.[4]

There are at least two discourses of nature at work in the text, and these are grouped around two polarized concepts of nature: one stems from an empirical view of nature, encompassing everything that can be observed, and the other reveals a teleological view of nature as a force that prescribes laws designed to meet certain ends. The rhetorical strategy used by Sade's characters to integrate these discourses moves from one pole to the other through four logical (but not always sequential) stages. Stage one is based on an existential and descriptive view of nature. According to this first stage, natural law can be seen in everything that exists, and particularly in whatever gives pleasure. Sade's libertines appeal to descriptive laws of nature, an existential and non-hierarchical concept in which "law" seems to mean nothing more than "the way things are." Dolmancé instructs Eugénie as follows:

> Aucune [fantaisie] ne peut se qualifier ainsi [extraordinaire], ma chère; toutes sont dans la nature; elle s'est plu, en créant les hommes, à différencier leurs goûts comme leurs figures, et nous ne devons pas plus nous étonner de la diversité qu'elle a mise dans nos traits que de celle qu'elle a placée dans nos affections. [No notion may be qualified as

extraordinary, my dear; all are found in nature; when she created men, it pleased her to make their tastes as various as their faces, and we should no more be astonished by the diversity that she has placed in our features than by that which she has placed in our affections.][5]

In this empirical, non-teleological conception, which conforms to eighteenth-century materialist thinking, nature is matter, motion, and transformation. Nature is therefore amoral, oblivious to mankind, indifferent to the loss of sperm as well as to human suffering. The libertines speak of the diversity of human pleasures, all of which are natural, for man is not the master of his inclinations. What is in nature? All acts, everything that exists: specifically mentioned are adultery, illegitimacy, rape, incest, sodomy, masturbation, destruction, murder, infanticide, parricide, selfishness, cruelty, nakedness, homosexual desire, libertinage, as well as sensibility and—curiously—affectionate feelings toward fathers. When "law" means "the way things are," there can be no referent for "crime" or "infraction" or "transgression." Nothing is a crime because nature has no laws and no ends. Nature knows no restraints, not even those imposed by human laws, and there is no crime except that which is defined as such by society. By human standards, nature seems unjust because she treats criminals and victims with equality, and she is therefore at odds with the human invention of a just God. Pleasure is the principle that guides mankind to nature's design, that is, human happiness. No action is criminal and none is virtuous, for morality is relative, the product of human convention.[6]

The existential argument already contains markers of a teleological discourse. If pleasure is a guiding principle, then anything leading to pleasure is natural, while anything opposing pleasure is anti-natural. There is slippage from the descriptive toward the prescriptive, and the second stage of the text's rhetorical strategy becomes an attack on traditional Christian interdicts, especially those which oppose pleasure and therefore happiness. Such restraints are denounced as anti-natural. Geoff Bennington speaks of the superimposition of two discourses, that of "positive law" and that of a certain "law of nature" as defined by Sade: in one system "crime" has meaning, while in the other it is denied meaning.[7] Eugénie is quick to grasp the distinction between these two sets of laws:

Oh! mes divins instituteurs, je vois bien que, d'après vos principes, il est très peu de crimes sur la terre, et que nous pouvons nous livrer en paix à tous nos désirs, quelques singuliers qu'ils puissent paraître aux sots qui, s'offensant et s'alarmant de tout, prennent imbécilement les institutions sociales pour les divines lois de la nature. [Oh! my divine teachers, I see very well that, according to your principles, there are very few crimes on earth, and that we may peacefully surrender to all our desires, as strange as they may appear to fools who, shocked and alarmed by everything, stupidly confuse social institutions with the divine laws of nature.] (3:421)

Like many of his Enlightenment predecessors, Sade deploys this descriptive concept of nature to undermine the prescriptive moral imperatives of Christian tradition and of eighteenth-century French society. In the latter system, "crime" is defined as an infraction of a positive law, which usually bears no relation to nature. Such infractions are not crimes in the eyes of nature, and society has no rational excuse for carrying out punitive acts against those who commit them. Man is thus denied even the possibility of committing a crime. According to Dolmancé, the civil laws forbid what is in nature because the general interest is almost always in conflict with individual interests. While there is no conflict between nature and an individual's penchants, there is a tremendous struggle between the latter and the false principles of society.[8]

These "false principles of society" include not only Christian prohibitions that oppose pleasure and happiness, but also many traditional virtues (and here we see another slippage away from the empirical). The third stage of the rhetorical strategy moves farther toward the teleological pole, criticizing many acts and sentiments that not only exist in nature but which have usually been valorized in Western ethics, and which are summarily denounced as unnatural in this text. Whereas stage two attacks the traditional interdictions, stage three aims at the traditional positives. Christian virtues such as chastity and monogamous marriage, as well as the fear of pregnancy and concern for one's reputation, are based on the opinions of men and are viewed by the libertines as attempts to combat nature. The text mentions many acts and sentiments that nature does not counsel because they go against her laws, and the list may be reduced to three types of outrages: everything that bonds one human being to another, everything that prevents women from having indiscriminate sex, and everything that promotes population. These include not only the Christian values of chastity, marital fidelity, and filial obedience, but also many humanitarian values that even the materialists found to be natural, such as decency, charity, beneficence, altruism, fraternity, pity, love, friendship, family sentiment, and that holiest of *philosophe* holies, virtue (a term that often included all of the preceding). In short, Sade's libertines are bent on destroying a monolithic interpretation of natural law, which they decry as merely a fictional construct devised by writers who have misread nature or only half understood her.[9]

As we have seen, Sade's libertines do not confine themselves to defending the realm of the empirical. They slip frequently from the materialist, descriptive laws of nature to prescriptive laws dictating action in society.[10] In their hands, or rather in their speeches, a hierarchy is reimposed. Nature once again becomes a teleological concept, but one that replaces that of the *philosophes*. The libertines' substitute teleology is also a substitute theology. Sade's nature is substituted for God: she becomes the Creator, a goddess who has divine laws and ends. Once nature becomes teleological, she can be outraged. There *can* be infractions, and in a dizzying shift of reference "crime" once again assumes a significance. It signifies everything that inhibits or prohibits, as well as everything that society has permitted and encouraged. But just as the goddess can be outraged, she can also be served. In stage four, the discourse moves from attack on "virtues" to advocacy of so-called "crimes" which do not offend nature but indeed serve her. The "crimes" and "vices" of Christian discourse are stripped of their traditional negative meanings and are promoted as positive services to nature, homage to the goddess. The text spells out ways in which nature may be served: these include adultery, sodomy, enjoyment of women by men, women's giving in to sexual desire and offering themselves to men, incest, murder, and the extinction of the human race.

The structuring principle of Sade's argument is a systematic inversion of the age-old valorization of reproduction over pleasure, promoted by Christian theologians and Enlightenment thinkers alike. Echoing Diderot's *Pensées philosophiques* a half-century earlier, Sade explains in his preface that the passions are the means that nature uses to make men arrive at her designs for them, that is to say, their happiness.[11] The preface encourages women, whom Diderot had regarded as the safeguards of morality, to scorn anything that opposes the "divine laws of pleasure." If nature were offended by sodomy, incest, and masturbation, she would not permit us to find pleasure in them. From the materialist argument of nature's indifference toward the loss of sperm, Sade concludes that pleasure, rather than population, is the goal of human sexuality. Pleasure not only replaces population as *telos*, but population is rejected from the value system and becomes anathema. Whereas orgasm serves nature, pregnancy offends her. The libertines affirm that all sexual acts that do *not* lead to reproduction are a service to nature's laws, while those that *do* are an outrage. Since nature's goal is pleasure, she approves of what is selfish. Madame de Saint-Ange says that women must arrive at pleasure through pain—a happy convenience for men who enjoy inflicting pain on women—and that anal sex is therefore preferable to vaginal sex. The realm of the empirical is all but forgotten, as the libertines express disgust for what they call "the ordinary route," the one that leads to pregnancy. Because of their materialist belief in the necessity of destruction in nature, Sade's characters conclude that nature encourages selfishness, cruelty, and murder—another example of slippage from the existential to the teleological.

The four stages of the text's rhetorical strategy might be represented schematically as follows: (1) X is natural because *everything* is; (2) to forbid X is therefore anti-natural and wrong; (3) to refrain from performing X is anti-natural and wrong; and (4) X therefore serves nature and should be performed. One textual example among many is that of incest: (1) incest is natural because it exists; (2) prohibition of incest is anti-natural (even though such a prohibition may be deemed to have a social value); (3) voluntary avoidance of incest is anti-natural; and (4) therefore incest serves nature and it becomes a positive value in Sade's fictional world. In this text, Thomas Moore's statement—"If nature sanctions a certain human behavior in any society whatsoever, Sade implies, that is evidence of the necessity and value of that behavior"—is valid only in its existential and descriptive mode. In its teleological mode, the libertines condemn chastity, fidelity, and other behaviors that are sanctioned in many societies.[12]

The four stages are not always unfolded sequentially. Stage one is often implicit, while the teleological stages are presented in alternating positions. For example, exclusive love is posited as anti-natural. The fact that erotic desire for more than one person exists in nature is implicit, and the fact that exclusive love also exists is simply ignored. The conclusion is then drawn that indiscriminate sexual activity with anyone and everyone is a service rendered to nature. In other cases, advocacy of one value may precede the offensive attack on its opposite. Destruction serves nature, therefore procreation is anti-natural. The same tactic is used to advocate nakedness, selfishness, and adultery, which requires the denunciation of clothing, friendship, and marriage, respectively.

I would like to look a bit more closely at the representation of sodomy in this text because, outside of Sade's writings, sodomy, "that utterly confused category," as Michel Foucault has called it, was a loosely defined sexual category in eighteenth-century society, as it continues to be in our own.[13] For this reason I believe "sodomy," perhaps more than any other item in the Sadean lexicon, emblematizes the recurring semantic slippage that operates between one concept of "nature" and the other, and between two corresponding sets of ethical guidelines. Sodomy is first presented as a neutral act in an indifferent universe. The Chevalier de Mirvel, who admits to a decided sexual preference for women, defends nonetheless what he calls the "bizarre tastes" of Dolmancé by stating that man is not the master of his tastes, which are dictated by nature, and by asserting that a reasonable man will never speak harshly of those who have this inclination. On several occasions Dolmancé asks the rhetorical question: why would nature have created such pleasures, or created humans who are sensitive to them, if sodomy were forbidden by her? Nature, says Dolmancé, does not care how we use our bodily fluids, and would not care if the human race died out. Here we see the first slippage from stage one to stage two, and from the existential toward the teleological pole. If nature decrees an inclination toward sodomy in a man, if that man finds pleasure in sodomy, and if nature does not demand propagation of the species, then Christian prohibitions of this sexual act are anti-natural and wrong. Next (stage three), vaginal intercourse, an alternative (*the* alternative?) to sodomy, is unnatural and wrong. In stage four, sodomy becomes a means of serving nature by refusing reproduction. Nature, says Dolmancé, has inspired this taste in us, and we serve the goddess in the rectum as well as elsewhere, perhaps in a more holy way ("peut-être plus saintement encore" [3:414]). The anus is said to have a more convenient shape than the vagina, thus indicating nature's preference for the former. Further, reproduction is so anti-natural that the total extinction of the human race would be a service rendered to nature. Once again we see the juxtaposition and vacillation between the description of an aberrant act—which constitutes a plea for tolerance of such an act—and an imperative to perform it.

Similar juxtaposition and vacillation may be seen in the pamphlet entitled "Français, encore un effort si vous voulez être républicains" [Frenchmen, yet another effort if you wish to be republicans], which constitutes roughly one quarter of the text of *La Philosophie dans le boudoir*. In the context of the plot, the pamphlet is a recently published text that has been purchased by Dolmancé and that is read aloud by the Chevalier to the other characters. The pamphlet adds a new and anonymous narrative voice, one that lends a political dimension to the libertines' philosophical discussion. It appeals to a utilitarian social morality that is designed to form good citizens, husbands, and fathers for the Republic. Like the dialogue that surrounds it, it invokes both an existential and a teleological view of nature, defending murder as an observable natural phenomenon, for example, and also advocating it as part of nature's plan. This interpolated propagandist text generally supports the libertines' principles but in rather dubious ways. On one hand, Enlightenment ideals are brought to rest upon Sadean premises. The pamphlet's author is against officially-sanctioned violence, stating that murder is the atrocity of kings, not republicans. Republicans, s/he says, should be guided by virtue and justice, and on these grounds s/he is opposed to capital punishment. Unlike Voltaire and Beccaria, however, the author maintains that the death penalty is wrong because it punishes murder, which is prompted by nature. Once again, civil law is in conflict with natural law. Man is naturally inclined to kill his neighbor, and the State must not punish him for what amounts to merely a transgression of an absurd civil law. On the other hand, an Enlightenment ideal can be deployed to bolster a Sadean conclusion. For example, Nature brings family members together and enjoins them to love one another. Therefore, writes the author of the pamphlet, it is natural for mother to love son, father to love daughter, and brother to love sister. Nature thus encourages incest, which gives pleasure, and which only positive law and its Christian basis forbid. The pamphlet contains elements of an Enlightenment protest against political and religious oppression, yet most of its message is in line with the discourse of Dolmancé.[14]

It should be apparent that Sade's use of language is a major and deliberate destabilizing element of this text. Unlike the first-person narrator of *Justine*, who recounts her own story in an authorized and classical language, the characters of *La Philosophie dans le boudoir* respect no linguistic proprieties. Each transgressive act and idea is designated by its crudest name. The girl's initiation into sex is also an entry into language. As the libertines undress and point out to Eugénie various body parts and uses to which they may be put, the pupil repeatedly asks, "Comment cela se nomme-t-il?" and "Comment appelle-t-on ce que nous faisons là?" [What is that called? What do you call what we are doing now?] (3:388). She wants to know the words, and she is quickly corrupted by them. When Saint-Ange explains to her that rape, sodomy, incest, and even murder are found in nature and are therefore not really crimes, the girl exclaims: "Ah! cher amour, comme ces discours séducteurs enflamment ma tête et séduisent mon âme!" [Oh! my dear love, how these seductive speeches inflame my mind and seduce my soul!] (3:405). Lynn Hunt discusses the power of language in the education of Eugénie, who is corrupted by the sheer force of words and their "taboo-transgressing effect."[15] Forbidden language can be obscene and scatological, but also sacrilegious. Dolmancé is equally affected by the power of words. He confesses to achieving greater sexual pleasure when he blasphemes a god in whom he does not believe.[16] According to Roland Barthes, "we begin to recognize that the transgressions of language possess an offensive power at least as strong as that of moral transgressions."[17]

Sade's use of forbidden language is certainly intended to transgress linguistic propriety, but what about conventional terms like "crime" and "law?" Despite their repudiation of Christian morality, Dolmancé and Saint-Ange repeatedly use its terminology. As they seek to describe and valorize their tastes, acts, and pleasures, they use a negatively-charged moral vocabulary that is completely in keeping with traditional moral interdictions. Their attempted inversion of ethical values clings to a vocabulary that is semantically packed with traditional notions of right and wrong. Saint-Ange speaks of the "obscene" plans that they have laid, and of her own "criminal" pleasures. She admits to her brother that she will go to great lengths in order to pervert and degrade the false moral principles of Eugénie, "la rendre aussi scélérate que moi . . . aussi impie . . . aussi débauchée" [to make her as wicked as I . . . as impious . . . as debauched] (3:376). She enjoins Eugénie to atrocities, horrors, the most odious crimes, adding that the dirtiest, the most infamous, and the most forbidden acts provoke the most delicious orgasms. The Chevalier describes Dolmancé as corrupted and dangerous, and speaks of his "irreligion, impiety, and inhumanity." Dolmancé confesses that he has committed atrocious crimes and horrors, with delight. Saint-Ange urges her pupil to witness all the transgressions she is committing simultaneously with her brother and with Dolmancé: "Vois, mon amour, vois tout ce que je fais à la fois: scandale, séduction, mauvais exemple, inceste, adultère, sodomie!" [Look, my love, see all that I am doing at the same time: scandal, seduction, bad example, incest, adultery, sodomy!] (3:455). Saint-Ange, informing Eugénie about the pleasures of fellatio, rhapsodizes about "cette précieuse liqueur, méchamment dérobée à sa destination d'usage" [this precious liquid, wickedly diverted from its customary destination] (3:414). Why "wickedly," one wonders, if there are no acts that offend nature? Why is the seminal fluid "precious," if nature is indifferent or indeed hostile toward the creation of human life?

The negative terms imply that a law has been broken, a principle transgressed, while laws and principles are being emptied of their semantic content. The text at once denies the existence of crimes and prompts us to commit them. Small wonder that Eugénie gets confused. When Saint-Ange exhorts her to commit the blackest and most frightful of crimes, Eugénie replies "Mais tu dis qu'il n'en existe pas" [But you say there are no crimes] (3:419).[18] Nonetheless, Eugénie is quick to learn the game. When Dolmancé asks if she still believes that sodomy is a crime, she retorts: "Et quand elle en serait un, que m'importe? Ne m'avez-vous pas démontré le néant des crimes? Il est bien peu d'actions maintenant qui soient criminelles à mes yeux" [And even if it were, what do I care? Have you not demonstrated the non-existence of crimes? There are now very few acts that are criminal in my eyes] (3:465). One can only guess what these "very few acts" are, and what the term "criminal" means to Eugénie by the end of the afternoon. In any case, she has learned to break all the rules. While sodomizing her own mother with an artificial penis, she describes herself as "incestuous, adulterous, and a sodomite" (3:542). The plethora of conventional, negatively-charged terms is designed to make a direct contribution to the didactic project at hand. Beatrice Fink contends that the juxtaposition in Sadean texts of forbidden lexical items—the obscene, the scatological, the blasphemous—along with an authorized, conventional and classical language effects a "de-semantization" of the latter. Incongruity, ambiguity, and accumulation of forbidden lexical items can transform conventional language into a subversive ideological tool.[19] In similar fashion, the libertines' use of a negative moral vocabulary—"obscene," "criminal," "debauched," etc.—empties these terms of their semantic value and makes it more difficult to sort out the puzzle of their ambivalent message. As Scott Carpenter explains, the intent is the creation of a new set of signs:

> Sade desires to create an enclosed, self-contained language, one that does not point "away" or "outside" of itself, and the only way to achieve this is for him to rupture the hymen that marries the signifier to a conventional signified. Dolmancé's instruction works to methodically annihilate reference and signification, convincingly demonstrating to Eugénie that words such as God, law, right, and wrong point to nothing, and have no existence except in the materiality of the words themselves.[20]

When we remember that some words take on new meanings in the substitute teleology, we might say that Sade's intention was not to "de-semanticize" but rather to "re-semanticize," to reinvest certain lexical items—nature, law, crime—with new signifieds.

The semantic shifting and destabilizing language that occurs in this text recalls a definition of transgression discussed by Robert R. Wilson, from the perspective of post-structuralist textualism. Wilson explains that

transgression—and this is one of its more positive and literary meanings—
is used to describe "the inevitable play of language itself. All language may
be said to transgress itself: it always subverts, through its inherent abstract-
ness and arbitrariness, the conventions of its speaking, or its writing, even
if this is not readily perceived." This textualist meaning of transgression
indicates "a generalized linguistic condition, perhaps automatic and inescap-
able, in which utterances are stripped of their contextual meaning, depleted."
This kind of transgression, says Wilson, is no longer an act or a conscious
move that the writer makes.[21]   Following Wilson's thinking, then, if
language is forged into a subversive ideological tool in *La Philosophie dans
le boudoir*, it also might work to subvert the ideology. The dialogue seems
to (unconsciously?) invalidate some of its own premises, to reinforce the
older, conventional hierarchies and thus to undermine the author's inten-
tional transgressions.   The rhetorical stance of this text, designed to
destabilize conventional morality, is beset with inconsistencies that might
be viewed as weaknesses in its arguments.

The propagandist discourse of the principal libertines is somewhat
subverted by the protests of the Chevalier de Mirvel, who is given a voice
to contradict the prevailing message, and who does so at some length:
"Qu'il me soit permis, je vous en conjure, de reprendre en sous-oeuvre et
d'anéantir, si je peux, les principes de Dolmancé" [May I be permitted, I beg
you, to examine the foundations of, and to annihilate, if I can, the principles
of Dolmancé] (3:525). The Chevalier seems to represent a more or less conventional eighteenth-century attitude toward nature. He states, for example,
that nature commands a woman to care for her children. His position is
clearly teleological, yet his notions of law and crime are quite different from
those of his fellow libertines. Despite his active participation in the erotic
education of the girl, the Chevalier recommends beneficence and the laws of
humanity to Eugénie, and he is the only one in the text to do so:

> Eugénie, Eugénie, n'éteignez jamais dans votre âme la voix sacrée de la
> nature. . . . Laissons là les principes religieux, j'y consens; mais
> n'abandonnons pas les vertus que la sensibilité nous inspire. [Eugénie,
> Eugénie, never stifle the sacred voice of nature in your soul. . . . Let us
> abandon religious principles, I consent to that, but not the virtues
> inspired in us by sensitivity.] (3:526, my ellipsis)

The Chevalier is also the only character to affirm that vaginal intercourse is
the type indicated by nature (although it must be noted that neither the
Chevalier nor any other character in this text exhibits exclusively
heterosexual behavior). Finally, during the brutal punishment of Eugénie's
mother by the other characters, only the Chevalier cries out in protest,
telling the others that they are outraging the laws of nature. He is perhaps
intended to be a foil for the libertines' superior philosophy, a kind of
cautionary tale that fails to convince, since his attempts to influence
Eugénie are foiled. Yet the divergent voice of this character in the text

sounds a curiously discordant note in the didactic project by drawing attention to the polyvalent and often contradictory senses of the term "nature."

The ambivalence of the didactic message is further heightened by several contradictions in Dolmancé's position, revealing a tension between the existential and the teleological discourses. First, Dolmancé advises Eugénie never to listen to her heart, "le guide le plus faux que nous ayons reçu de la nature" [the falsest guide that we have received from nature] (3:524). Following logically from this remark, one must conclude that nature works against herself, providing counsel against her own designs, or perhaps providing two sets of laws that are in conflict with one another. We must choose between her true guides and her false ones. Second, Dolmancé states that nature has inculcated in man the irresistible desire to commit crimes, but has prudently deprived him of acts that might disturb her laws. The referent of the term "crime" here seems to be the infraction of man-made prohibitions, which humans naturally seek to transgress, yet since humans are incapable of disturbing nature's "laws," one wonders what these laws can mean. Any act committed by a human being seems to be within the laws of nature, except those—chastity, fidelity, charity—which are specifically promoted by Christian morality. It is obvious that humans are capable of committing these "crimes," and indeed sometimes do so. Finally, on several occasions Dolmancé advises Eugénie that in order to know nature one must consult the behavior of animals.[22] Such a statement, usually proffered by those who view sex teleologically and who consider childbirth as its ultimate goal, is surprising on the part of one who advocates sodomy between men and other "unproductive" sexual acts in the name of pleasure. All of this may lead us to wonder whether Sade is attempting to substitute a radically different view of nature for the contemporary prevailing one—to "re-semanticize" the term—or whether he is striving on the contrary to "de-semanticize" it, and to demonstrate the linguistic and conceptual futility of the entire enterprise.

Even the apology of sodomy is undermined by textual ambivalences. First, as we have seen, sodomy is at once a neutral act in an indifferent universe and an affirmative service that one provides to nature. Dolmancé is described as a "sodomite by conviction," and he affirms his preference for men over women. The text emphatically asserts that this sexual orientation, as we would call it today, cannot be criminal because it is inspired by nature. Yet it is referred to variously as an "error," a "bizarre taste," a "weakness," a "vice," a "depravity," and a "debauchery," that is, by the very negative terms eighteenth-century Christian moralists might have used to denounce it. Second, Dolmancé says he has never had vaginal sex because he cannot contradict his "dogmas." Is his preference for men and for sodomy a result of his *principles* or of his *tastes*? Is it merely inspired by nature or dictated by her? Finally, what is the semantic value of the term? Dolmancé is described as one who likes only men in his pleasures, which the following pages of the text reveal to be false, as the libertine willingly engages in sexual acts with both female characters (although he steadfastly avoids "the ordinary route"). Eugénie also describes herself as a sodomite, as we have seen, and Saint-Ange sodomizes Dolmancé with an artificial penis. The term "sodomy" slips from a specific act—anal copulation between males, an alternative to vaginal intercourse—to any sexual activity that precludes reproduction—*the* alternative to vaginal intercourse. As Jane Gallop points out, Dolmancé proves unfaithful to his own perversion, as the term "sodomy" is expanded from its primary sense to include the entire realm of countergenerality.[23] But if the category of perversion does not exist at all, then on what are we to base this notion of countergenerality, which the text at once promotes and undermines?[24] Likewise, if there are no crimes, then what language are Sade's characters to use in order to speak about acts that are regarded as crimes by others? Unconventional sexual acts are exalted, yet they must be described by the very terms they are striving to subvert. As language proves to be unstable, so do moral imperatives.

What conclusions may be drawn from this brief and summary analysis of *La Philosophie dans le boudoir*? The first is that there is a pervasive rhetorical strategy at work in this text, striving to invert and replace the prevailing teleological notion of nature. The strategy sets out from an all-encompassing, descriptive, existential, empirical view of nature, which is non-hierarchical and which follows a materialist intertextual tradition. As it moves through offensive attacks first on traditional prohibitions and then on traditionally positive values, it begins to erect new hierarchies, until finally it becomes a replacement, a substitute teleology, prescriptive of positive values and of services to be rendered to nature, but quite different from the one constructed by Sade's predecessors, whom he disdainfully lumps together and calls "philosophes." At the same time this propaganda, this doctrine-to-be-propagated, is subverted by certain rhetorical, logical, and lexical features of the text, and this is my second conclusion. The textual tensions, slippages, and ambivalences strive to destabilize received notions about morality, yet they run the risk of undermining the libertines' didactic message, perhaps because of a certain semantic "transgressiveness" of language that is beyond the author's control. The destabilization threatens to subvert the intended subversion. Or could that be, perhaps, the point—Sade's point—that the very attempt to define and conceptualize "nature" is a futile enterprise? Perhaps the author realized that language can never be possessive of absolute truth, since words can be used to mean anything an author wishes to say. Lovejoy points out that "since the term [nature] had dozens of different, often vague, and sometimes incompatible connotations, it could be invoked—as it still is—in support of almost any conclusion one desired to establish."[25] A third conclusion is that this text (and perhaps the entire work of Sade) represents a definitive turning point in eighteenth-century ideology. It dramatizes the failure of the ethical norm of nature, revealing as it does that nature and reason no longer lead down the same path. By radicalizing the thought of his predecessors and contemporaries, Sade has unpacked the cherished notion of natural law. In the words of A. E. Pilkington, Sade "calls attention to the fragility of the great value upon which so many different kinds of moral weight had been placed throughout the eighteenth century—the idea of nature."[26] Whether a conscious parody or not, Sade's text deals a mortal blow to natural law as a viable construct. Perhaps these conclusions can be related. Perhaps the concept of nature had proved to be an alluring ethical norm in the eighteenth century precisely because it was easily manipulated and because it meant so many things to so many writers.

N O T E S

1. Paul Hazard, *La Pensée européenne au XVIIIe siècle, de Montesquieu à Lessing* (Paris: Fayard, 1963), 304. Unless otherwise indicated, all English translations of French texts are my own.
2. Denis Diderot, ed., *Encyclopédie* (Paris: Briasson, 1751–65), s.v. "Nature."
3. Arthur O. Lovejoy, *Essays in the History of Ideas* (Baltimore: Johns Hopkins University Press, 1948), 69. There is a substantial literature on the problem of nature in eighteenth-century France. See, for example, Jean Ehrard, *L'Idée de nature en France dans la première moitié du XVIIIe siècle*, 2 vols. (Paris: Education Nationale, 1963); Lester G. Crocker, *Nature and Culture: Ethical Thought in the French Enlightenment* (Baltimore: Johns Hopkins University Press, 1963); and more recently, D. G. Charlton, *New Images of the Natural in France: A Study in European Cultural History 1750–1800* (Cambridge: Cambridge University Press, 1984).
4. Geoff Bennington states that there is nothing particularly original about Sade's statements on nature and points to an eighteenth-century materialist intertext: "What is perhaps new in Sade is the assertion that the laws of nature bear no relation to political or moral law, or are at least irrecuperably in excess of such law." "Sade: Laying Down the Law," *Oxford Literary Review* 6 (1984): 47.
5. *Oeuvres complètes du marquis de Sade*, ed. Gilbert Lely (Paris: Cercle du livre précieux, 1966–67), 3:411. All future references to Sade's writings are from this edition and will be noted in the text.
6. Diderot's view of nature was quite similar to this one. As he had stated in *Le Rêve de d'Alembert*—a text that Sade could not have known—nothing that exists can be contrary to nature or outside of nature, and it is not possible to sin against her. *Oeuvres philosophiques*, ed. Paul Vernière (Paris: Garnier, 1964), 380.
7. Bennington, "Sade: Laying Down the Law," 44.
8. Cf. Diderot's *Supplément au voyage de Bougainville*: "Parcourez l'histoire des siècles et des nations tant anciennes que modernes, et vous trouverez les hommes assujettis à trois codes, le code de la nature, le code civil, et le code religieux, et contraints d'enfreindre alternativement ces trois codes qui

n'ont jamais été d'accord" [Glance over the history of the ages and the nations both ancient and modern, and you will find men subjected to three codes, the code of nature, the civil code, and the religious code, and forced to transgress, one after the other, these three codes that have never been in harmony]. *Oeuvres philosophiques*, 504–5.

9. Nature, says the narrator of Sade's *Les 120 Journées de Sodome*, is "cette bête dont tu parles sans cesse sans la connaître . . ." [this beast that you discuss endlessly and ignorantly . . .]. *Oeuvres complètes*, 13:60–61. Despite Sade's dismissal of other philosophers, their belief in natural law, variously interpreted, may have been less a product of ignorance than, on the contrary, one of lucid understanding: the construct of natural morality was perhaps a protest against the brute reality of nature, against her indifference and her blindness. In other words, some theorists of natural law held convictions about nature similar to those of Sade, but from these convictions they drew quite different conclusions.

10. Bennington states that a similar slippage between prescriptive and descriptive senses of the word "law" is typical of eighteenth-century discourse. "Sade: Laying Down the Law," 48.

11. "On déclame sans fin contre les passions; on leur impute toutes les peines de l'homme, et l'on oublie qu'elles sont aussi la source de tous ses plaisirs" [Everyone inveighs endlessly against the passions; all the pains of man are attributed to them, and one forgets that they are also the source of all his pleasures]. Diderot, *Oeuvres philosophiques*, 9. But even Diderot, in his *Supplément*, created a Tahiti in which sexual relations are entirely subjected to the public interest, so that restrictions are applied to all sexual acts that cannot increase population.

12. Thomas Moore, *Dark Eros: The Imagination of Sadism* (Dallas: Spring Publications, 1990), 4. Michel Tort discusses the status of the norm in Sade's enterprise by using a spatial metaphor. In Tort's model of Sadean logic, the notion of sexual normality no longer has its usual organizing function at the center, from which deviation means distance, departure from the center. Instead, Sade substitutes a chain with no center, in which each link is absolutely homogeneous with every other. The norm is then re-integrated, says Tort, but only as an index of transgression. In this decentered model, it is merely one of many possibilities available to the pervert. Tort admits, however, that a hierarchy is maintained among the deviations. I am not convinced that the norm is allowed to retain a neutral status as one of many possibilities. In our text, at least, it is completely proscribed to Eugénie. Tort, "L'Effet Sade," *Oeuvres complètes du marquis de Sade* 16:587–95.

13. Michel Foucault, *The History of Sexuality,* vol. 1, *An Introduction,* trans. Robert Hurley (New York: Vintage, 1990), 101. Claude Courouve states that "sodomy," one of the most negatively-charged sexual terms, was used to denote variously masculine and feminine homosexual activity, anal penetration of males and females, and even bestiality. *Vocabulaire de l'homosexualité masculine* (Paris: Payot, 1985), 191–98. G. S. Rousseau points out that beyond the realm of sexuality there was a larger class of "sodomites" who may have committed any number of non-sexual crimes: "sodomite" was "an extreme and opprobrious form of condemnation

designating religious blasphemy, political sedition, and even satanic activities." "The Pursuit of Homosexuality in the Eighteenth Century: 'Utterly Confused Category' and/or Rich Repository?" *Eighteenth-Century Life* 9 (1985): 136.

14. This is not to say that there are no contradictions. The republican pamphlet affirms equal rights for men and women, for example, whereas Dolmancé denounces sexual equality as intolerable for libertines. Michel Delon points out the ideological heterogeneity in other texts by Sade, such as the coexistence of revolutionary discourse and long apologies of despotism. "Sade thermidorien," *Sade: Ecrire la crise*, ed. Michel Camus and Philippe Roger (Paris: Belfond, 1983), 113–14.

15. Lynn Hunt, *The Family Romance of the French Revolution* (Berkeley and Los Angeles: University of California Press, 1992), 132. My interest in this text owes a great deal to Lynn Hunt's cogent analysis, first presented to me in her seminar at the Folger Institute in 1991.

16. Josué V. Harari demonstrates the logical (but not metaphysical) necessity of God to Sade's atheistic libertines. If God does not exist, then blasphemy loses all meaning. So God is resurrected as a logical necessity to justify blasphemy, which acquires a transgressive value. Profanity becomes the quintessential antisocial act, the ultimate outrage to those who live in the superstition of belief. "D'une raison à l'autre: le dispositif Sade," *Studies on Voltaire and the Eighteenth Century* 230 (1985): 275–76.

17. Roland Barthes, *Sade, Fourier, Loyola*, trans. Richard Miller (Berkeley and Los Angeles: University of California Press, 1976), 34.

18. I find some evidence in this text (this last quotation is an example) of a playful attitude toward semantic instability, so that I am tempted to propose that Sade himself was very much aware of the slippery character of language.

19. Beatrice Fink, "La Langue de Sade," *Eroticism in French Literature,* French Literature Series 10 (1983): 110.

20. Scott Carpenter, "Sade and the Problem of Closure: Keeping Philosophy in the Bedroom," *Neophilologus* 75 (1991): 523.

21. Robert R. Wilson, "Play, Transgression and Carnival: Bakhtin and Derrida on *Scriptor Ludens*," *Mosaic* 19 (1986): 76–79. I wonder if "transgression" is the most felicitous name for a linguistic phenomenon that is inherent in language, inevitable, unconscious. If it does not involve a deliberate violation of laws or a moving across boundaries, then what exactly is being transgressed?

22. Dolmancé refers to animals to prove that cruelty is in nature (3:437) whereas filial love and obedience are not (3:537–38). Madame de Saint-Ange makes a similar statement (3:402).

23. Jane Gallop, *Intersections: A Reading of Sade with Bataille, Blanchot, and Klossowski* (Lincoln and London: University of Nebraska Press, 1981), 95–96.

24. My position is somewhat different from that of Annie Le Brun, who asks this question and concludes that there is no notion of countergenerality in Sade's vision. *Sade: A Sudden Abyss*, trans. Camille Naish (San Francisco: City Light Books, 1990), 94. I would argue that countergenerality in Sade's work means any sexual activity other than "the ordinary route." It is *any* alternative to male-female, penile-vaginal intercourse.

25. Lovejoy, *Essays in the History of Ideas*, 336.
26. A. E. Pilkington, "'Nature' as Ethical Norm in the Enlightenment," *Languages of Nature: Critical Essays on Science and Literature*, ed. L. J. Jordanova (New Brunswick: Rutgers University Press, 1986), 84.

Letters and Political Judgment:
John Adams and Cicero's Style

JAMES M. FARRELL

A number of eighteenth-century rhetoricians offered prescriptions on letter-writing as part of their treatment of rhetorical style. As it had been in previous ages, letter writing remained in the eighteenth century among the genres of composition commonly taught by rhetoricians. Moreover, as had earlier rhetoricians, the writers of the *belles lettres* movement turned to Cicero's epistles as the principal model for letter writing style. Charles Rollin, for example, found in Cicero's letters "the proper character of the epistolary style," while Hugh Blair called them "the most valuable collection of letters, extant, in any language."[1] These professional assessments of Cicero's letters, however, do not reveal much about the influence of the Roman's epistolary style on the practice of letter writing in the eighteenth century. Nor do these recommendations, concerned exclusively and narrowly with style, suggest the political advantages such a style might afford a letter writer involved, as Cicero was, in the day to day business of statecraft. In at least one case, however, Cicero's epistolary style was consciously adopted and imitated. As this study of certain political letters of John Adams will show, he turned to Cicero as the paradigm for his epistolary discourse.

Ciceronian Style and Political Judgment

There was wide agreement among eighteenth-century scholars about those attributes of Cicero's style which made his letters worthy of imitation. William Guthrie, whose translations of Cicero's letters was among the most popular in the eighteenth century, wrote about Cicero's "extremely free" style and his "epistolary familiarity." Blair believed Cicero's letters were "composed with purity and elegance, but without the least affectation," a point agreed to by Conyers Middleton who thought the Roman's epistles revealed "the genuine man, without disguise or affectation." Such revelation was possible, Middleton said, because the letters were written in "the language of conversation." Rollin noted "the easy, simple, and natural turn in these letters of Tully," and observed further their "beauty and delicacy of expression." John Ward also praised the "stile of Cicero's epistles, in which the plainness and simplicity of his diction, is accompanied with something so pleasant and ingaging [sic], that he keeps up the attention of his reader without suffering him to tire."[2]

The critical language used to describe Cicero's epistolary style suggests that the letters were widely admired because they answered the impulse toward a "natural language" in eighteenth-century theories of expression. As Jay Fliegelman has recently argued, communication culture in the eighteenth century recommended cultivation of a "living voice" and "conversational freedom" in both public and private discourse. "The conversational ideal," he writes, "would quickly be impressed into the service of the revolutionary project of defining the distinctiveness of American letters." Fliegelman's essay begins to show how "the conditions of speaking and writing operative in 1776: what was assumed, but not spoken, in the domain of action and speech," had a fundamental influence on how politics was perceived and practiced.[3] In the specific case of John Adams' letters from the Continental Congress, we see how adoption of the Ciceronian style of writing facilitated his practice of politics. Imitating Cicero's conversational style allowed Adams to use his own letters as a vital medium of political judgment.

In his study of John Dickinson's "Farmer's Letter," Stephen Browne shows how Dickinson's reliance on pastoral configurations creates "a model of rhetorical judgement." The pastoral sensibilities heightened by Dickinson's ethos and style, Browne explains, allow the author to "address current issues by redefining the terms of public action and rhetorical judgment." The "model of judgment implicit in pastoral," resulting from a "fusion of style and substance," creates a perspective which "requires distance but mandates action." The pastoral "can be heard only at a distance and emerges from the quiet haunts of the study, village, and farm." Dickinson's appropriation of the pastoral for rhetorical ends composes an essentially contemplative voice for his *Letter*, a persona which embodies "calm, wise judgment," rooted in the virtues of "distance, reflection, and disinterest."[4]

Browne's study of Dickinson discovers the model of political judgment implicit in the conventions of a particular literary genre. The pastoral invites a judgment of political events consistent with the vantage of the farmer who has "freely chosen the *vita contemplativa*, a world and perspective removed from the hectic, distorted scenes of city life." Although Dickinson's "Farmer" was a fiction, we can easily recognize the possibility of invoking the "cluster of values, most prominently the agrarian virtues of steady perspective and prudence" associated with the pastoral style for other rhetorical purposes. Yet it is also clear that, by definition, the pastoral is reserved for those who are removed, actually or artistically, from the "volatile demands of immediate action." It cannot answer the rhetorical needs of those immersed in the busy scenes of city politics. Another style and mode of rhetorical judgment must serve those who pursue the *vita activa*.[5]

Perhaps more than any other historical character known to the men of the eighteenth century, Cicero embodied the *vita activa*. Cicero's complete immersion in the stormy political life of the late Roman republic is immediately evident from his letters. In his study of Cicero's letters to Atticus, Robert Hariman identifies the epistles as part of the "literature of political thought." Cicero's letters, he explains, articulate the "republican style, which is the style designed to maximize the political opportunities inherent to republican government." As manifestations of the republican style, the letters become "a hermeneutical space," a "medium of understanding," by which Cicero discerns "the preferable from other courses of action." Hariman concludes that Cicero's letters are the chief means by which the Roman composes his public character. Cicero must constantly answer the question "how is he to comport himself—in all of his decisions, from selecting his place of residence to choosing his allies to concluding his next speech—in order to be the public figure he wishes to become?"[6] Cicero's "republican style," therefore, offers a counterweight to the pastoral configurations of John Dickinson. The Ciceronian voice speaks to the *vita activa*, it reveals a character seeking a medium for political judgment amidst the busy scenes of Roman politics.

John Adams reveled in the *vita activa*. "I swear I will renounce the Contemplative, and betake myself to an active roving Life," he remarked in an early diary entry. "I will push myself into Business. I will watch my Opportunity, to speak in Court, and will strike with surprize—surprize Bench, Bar, Jury, Auditors and all. Activity, Boldness, Forwardness, will draw attention. Ile not lean with my Elbows on the Table, forever like Read, Swift, Fitch, Skinner Story, &c." Later he confessed his desire to "move and stir from one scene of Action and Debate and Business, and Pleasure, and Conversation, to another and grow weary of all before I shall feel the strong Desire of retiring to contemplation."[7]

Yet when Adams learned he would represent Massachusetts in the Continental Congress, he was overwhelmed by the political burden he faced. At first, he did not even know what to think of the forthcoming assembly. Did it compare to "the Court of Ariopagus, the Council of the Amphyctions," or was it "a Conclave, a Sanhedrin, A Divan?" "It is to be a School of Political Prophets I Suppose," he concluded. "A Nursery of American Statesmen."[8] The many doubts he expressed about his inability to succeed in Congress were much more than conventional office-taking fare. "I wander alone, and ponder," he wrote in his diary. "I muse, I mope, I ruminate.—I am often In Reveries and Brown Studies." Adams thought the task of Congress was "Too grand, and multifarious" for his comprehension, and he regretted the lack of trained politicians in America. "We have not Men, fit for the Times," he complained. "We are deficient in Genius, in Education, in Travel, in Fortune—in every Thing. I feel unutterable Anxiety."[9]

John Adams and Cicero's Letters

Believing he and his colleagues lacked the capacity for competent political judgment, Adams gained some confidence by emulating Cicero, the Roman patriot who had excelled in oratory and statesmanship during the period of ancient history that was most familiar to Adams and his contemporaries. Increasingly as the events of the Revolution developed and engulfed him, Adams was inclined to view Anglo-American politics in Roman terms. Not only did he see broad historical parallels between the decline of Rome and the corruption in Great Britain, but he envisioned a specific role for himself in the repeating drama. Just before leaving Braintree to attend the First Continental Congress, for example, Adams recalled Cicero's first political mission away from Rome. He wrote to William Tudor about the virtue of "this great and excellent orator, and Statesman," telling him that Cicero "did not receive this office, as Persons do now a days, as a Gift," but rather as "a public Trust." Cicero considered his office to be "a Theatre, in which the Eyes of the World, were upon him," said Adams, and "he determined to devote himself to it, and deny himself every Pleasure, which could interfere with a laudable Discharge of it."[10] Chosen to attend the most important political meeting in colonial history, Adams must have questioned whether his own character and service would satisfy or even surpass the Ciceronian standard. During his service in Congress Adams thought of himself as an "American Senator" (a term not yet applied to American legislators but quite familiar to students of ancient Rome), and wondered in a letter to James Warren "what Plans would be adopted at the Congress if . . . a Demosthenes or a Cicero were there."[11]

But Adams did more than admire Cicero. There is ample evidence to show that this American patriot consciously imitated his Roman hero's letter writing style. Adams probably first encountered Cicero's letters as a young scholar preparing to enter Harvard, since the epistles were commonly assigned by Latin tutors to prepare students for college entrance examinations. Later Adams read the letters in Latin in the third volume of Cicero's *Opera Omnia*.[12] In 1758, as he prepared to take the attorney's oath in Boston, he told Jeremiah Gridley he had recently read "Cicero's Orations and Epistles."[13] Adams also read many of Cicero's letters in English in Conyers Middleton's *Life of M. Tullius Cicero*.[14] In the course of his biography, Middleton translated and reprinted, in whole or in part, more than

130 of Cicero's letters. He also included hundreds of additional epistolary excerpts in Latin in the footnotes of his work. Adams may also have read one or more of the English translations of Cicero's letters available in eighteenth-century America, the most popular of which were William Guthrie's 1752 edition of Cicero's letters to Atticus, and William Melmoth's 1755 collection of Cicero's epistles to his friends.[15] Given the importance of Cicero's letters in rhetorical tradition, their popularity in the eighteenth century, and Adams' easy access to them in both Latin and English, it is not surprising to find Adams selecting Cicero as his epistolary paradigm.

Adams, like other letter writers of his time, had many examples to emulate, and although he considered several models to be worthwhile, he left no doubt about that which guided his own correspondence. "Among the ancients," he told his wife, "there are two illustrious Examples of the Epistolary style, Cicero and Pliny." The letters of these two Romans, Adams thought, "present you with Modells of fine Writing, which has borne the Criticism of almost two thousand Years." Those ancient writers, he said, conveyed "the Sublime, the beautifull, the Novell, and the Pathetick," and did so with "as much Simplicity, Ease, Freedom, and familiarity, as Language is capable of."[16] Later, however, Adams revised his opinion of Pliny's productions and pared his list of great epistolary models to one. Pliny's letters, he finally decided, "are too studied and too elegant. Cicero's are the only ones of perfect simplicity, confidence, and familiarity."[17] This view of Cicero's letters echoes Adams' own philosophy of the epistolary art. Letter writing, he wrote, had "all the advantages of Conversation" and "was essentially different from the oratorical, and the Historical style." Letters, he thought, "like conversations, should be free, easy and familiar."[18]

Adams and the Ciceronian Style

Like Cicero, Adams wrote letters which comfortably blended private communication with public business. His epistolary style, like that of Cicero, was colloquial, exclamatory, metaphorical, interrogatory, and often elliptical. His letters echoed the passionate, often hurried, sometimes incomplete style of conversational discourse and, like those of Cicero, often contained an element of drama.

The dramatic character of Adams' epistolary style is especially evident in those letters in which he reconstructs a dialogue, such as that he composed to Abigail on June 29, 1774. "We had a curious Dialogue Yesterday, at Dinner, between our Justices Trowbridge and Hutchinson," Adams wrote.

> T. said he had seen a Letter, from England, in which it was said that the Conduct of the Chief Justice was highly approved, and that of the other Judges highly disapproved, at the Court End of the Town.—T. added, I dont know whether they impute it all to me or not.—Aye says H. but it

was all owing to you. You laid Brother Ropes, Cushing and me, under
the Necessity of refusing the Royal Grant, and accepting the Province
Salary.[19]

The dialogue continues in this fashion for several more paragraphs with
Adams both writing the lines and providing editorial comment.

Adams, of course, may have naturally resorted to dialogue to heighten the
dramatic effect of his composition. But we must note that Cicero, too,
often reported Roman events in dialogue form. In a letter to Atticus, for
example, Cicero relates an exchange between him and Clodius which
occurred in the Roman Senate:

> Our little Beauty gets on his feet and accuses me of having been at
> Baiae—not true, but anyhow, "Well," I reply, "is that like saying I
> intruded on the Mysteries?" "What business has an Arpinum man with
> the waters?" "Tell that to your counsel," I retorted; "He was keen
> enough to get certain of them that belonged to an Arpinum man" (you
> know Marius' place of course). "How long," cried he, "are we going to
> put up with the king?" "You talk about kings," I answered, "when Rex
> didn't have a word to say about you?" (he had hoped to have the
> squandering of Rex's money). "So you've bought a house," said he. I
> rejoined, "one might think he was saying that I had bought a jury."
> "They didn't credit you on oath." "On the contrary 25 jurymen gave me
> credit and 31 gave *you* none—they got their money in advance!" The
> roars of applause were too much for him and he collapsed into
> silence.[20]

Despite the gap in the centuries and the differences in content, there is little
stylistically to separate Adams' letter from that of Cicero.

At times of less leisure, Adams communicated the political atmosphere in
short bursts. On September 14, 1774, he wrote to Abigail from
Philadelphia: "My time is totally filled from the Moment I get out of Bed,
untill I return to it. Visits, Ceremonies, Company, Business, News Papers,
Pamphlets &c. &c. &c." He also assured her that "A Tory here is the most
despicable Animal in the Creation. Spiders, Toads, Snakes, are their only
proper Emblems."[21] Adams' hurried pace is evident in these excerpts. The
style, as much as the content, conveys the message clearly. Yet the letter is
written without apparent art or formal construction. Conjunctions are
missing and sentences rush to their completion. The thought and passion
are more important than the formalities of composition. Reading Adams'
letter is like having him present to lament his busy life or spout his venom
at the Tories.[22] And, it is much like the style used by Cicero in his busiest
moments. "He's jealous," Cicero wrote to Atticus about a political
flatterer, "Awkward, tortuous, politically paltry, shabby, timid,
disingenuous—but I shall go more into detail on another occasion." [23]

The sense of conversation and immediate presence is equally evident in
Adams' letter to Abigail of July 6, 1774:

Our Justice Hutchinson is eternally giving his Political Hints. In a Cause, this Morning, Somebody named Captn. Mackay as a Refferee [*sic*]. I said "an honest Man!"—"Yes" says Hutchinson, "he's an honest Man, only *misled*.—He he he," blinking and grinning.—At dinner, to day, Somebody mentioned Determinations in the Lords House (the Court sitts in the Meeting House).—"I've known many very bad Determinations in the Lords House of late" says he, meaning a Fling upon the Clergy.—He is perpetually flinging about the Fasts, and ironically talking about getting Home to the Fast. A Gentleman told me, that he had heard him say frequently, that the Fast was perfect Blasphemy.—"Why dont they pay for the Tea? Refuse to pay for the Tea! and go to fasting and praying for Direction! perfect Blasphemy!" This is the Moderation, Candor, Impartiality, Prudence, Patience, Forbearance, and Condescention of our Justice.[24]

Note here Adams' effort to reproduce the style of conversation. His construction of dialogue, his use of ellipsis, his grammatical license, and his sense of irony, all contribute to the familiarity of the composition.

The rich description, the conversational style, and the sense of immediate presence we experience in Adams' letters is very much like the style of Cicero's epistles, as we can see in the following excerpt from a communication to Atticus:

Pray, what's all this? What is going on? I am in the dark. "We hold Cingulum, we've lost Ancona, Labienus has deserted Caesar." Is it a Roman general or Hannibal we are talking of? Deluded wretch, with never in his life a glimpse of even the shadow of Good! And he says he is doing all this for his honour's sake! Where is honour without moral good? And is it good to have an army without public authority, to seize Roman towns by way of opening the road to the mother city, to plan debt cancellations, recall of exiles, and a hundred other villainies "all for that first of deities, Sole Power"? He is welcome to his greatness.[25]

This letter closes the distance between Cicero and his correspondent and communicates the spontaneous boiling of a mind in action. More than a report of ideas or events, it brings the writer to the reader with all the confusion, frustration, emotion, pace, and language of a personal interaction. Cicero uses questions, answers, exclamations, incomplete periods, and apparently random disposition to create his conversational tone. He seems unconcerned about the elegance or art of his epistles to Atticus. His goal, rather, is to communicate his message and personality in clear and colorful terms, relying on the resources of both his invention and style.

While the stylistic affinity between the letters of Cicero and Adams is somewhat difficult to demonstrate with only a few excerpts, there can be no doubt that Adams had Cicero in mind as he composed his letters home. Amidst the activity of the Continental Congress and in the martial atmosphere of wartime Philadelphia, Adams told Abigail he wished he could write letters to her which would lay open "the whole system of Politicks and War, and delineate all the Characters in Either Drama, as minutely, altho I could not do it, so elegantly, as Tully [Marcus Tullius Cicero] did in his Letters to Atticus."[26]

Adams' Letters and Political Judgment

While Adams' imitation of Cicero's epistolary style is itself significant as further evidence of classical influence on the thought and language of eighteenth-century Americans, to Adams it was the political advantages of Cicero's mode of letter writing that led him to imitate the Roman.

There is no doubt that questions of political judgment weighed heavily on Adams as he confronted the momentous issues facing the Continental Congress. "We have a delicate Course to steer," he wrote, "between too much Activity and too much Insensibility, in our critical situation." Charting that course was exceedingly difficult as he had to weigh the "Characters and Tempers, the Principles and Views of fifty Gentlemen total Strangers." Along with the opinion of the "Multitude of Pamphlets, News Papers, and private Letters," he lamented, "I have numberless Plans of policy and many Arguments to consider." He believed the Congress had "as great Questions to discuss as ever engaged the Attention of Men, and an infinite Multitude of them." The times demanded that "every Man, upon every Question must shew his oratory, his Criticism and his Political Abilities." He regularly lamented that "Such a vast Multitude of Objects, civil, political, commercial and military, press and crowd upon Us so fast," that he and his Congressional colleagues "know not what to do first."[27]

Adams' letter writing assisted his political judgment. The style he borrowed from Cicero is ideal for deliberating on political issues within the epistolary form. Its informal, conversational quality, provides an excellent medium for playing with political ideas and arriving at political judgments. Adams' letters, written in a Ciceronian style, become his means of discovering a course of action in the chaos of the Revolution. The letters are exceedingly practical texts, the very manifestation of Adams' politics. Without the burdens imposed by formal public speaking or didactic discourse, the epistolary style adopted by Adams permits the writer to explore issues in a preliminary fashion. The style encourages Adams to propose tentative principles, advance incomplete arguments, seek advice, ask questions, reveal doubts, measure his stance, test his wit, and explore his options. As an informal style it does not demand consistency, determination, or certainty. Adams is not burdened by the demands of proper grammar, structure, logic, or polite address. Such constraints would undoubtedly narrow the deliberative space within the discourse and consequently weaken its capacity to function as a medium of political judgment. The private epistle, unlike a public letter (such as Dickinson's) imposes no burden of ethos.[28] Like Cicero who often complained that he was "eaten up with anxiety," Adams, in the confidence of his private correspondence, is free to present a character with all its human frailties and inconsistencies.[29] Nor do such letters constrain the future discourse of the writer in the way a public statement might. In addition, regular correspondence with friends in Massachusetts enables Adams to secure part of that detached view so important for competent political judgment, but a view he cannot achieve "amidst the suffocating Heats of the City, and the wasting, exhausting Debates of the Congress."[30] Epistolary communication, as a medium of judgment, extends the political vista and permits him, through correspondents, to include the distant view in his deliberation. The letters become, then, a text of engagement between what Ronald Beiner called the judging actor who "deliberates *within* his actual situation," and the judging spectator who "reflects *on* the actual situation."[31]

Adams clamors for that distant view in his constant call for intelligence from home. His letters portray him at the center of political business, yet he was sometimes overwhelmed by the immediacy of this political burden. "I am engaged from 7 in the Morning till 11. at Night," he told Abigail. "How I find Time to write half the Letters I do," he wondered, "I know not, for my whole Time seems engrossed with Business."[32] Adams is trapped in the bustle of the moment. Suffering with his political obligations, he was like Cicero who told Atticus "I am afraid it's not in the best of taste to tell you how busy I am, but in fact I am so harassed that I have hardly found time even for these few lines, and stolen it at that from most pressing business."[33]

The escape from the pressure of political business comes from writing and receiving letters. In correspondence Adams is able to achieve the proper deliberative attitude. "Pray write to me," he told his wife, "and get all my Friends to write and let me be informed of every Thing that occurs." "I write at this time," he scolded James Warren, "only to remind you that I have received no Letters." Adams felt isolated when not engaged in political correspondence. "I have lost all my friends in the Massachusetts Bay," he complained to Abigail, "excepting my Wife, Coll. Warren and Coll. Palmer. From each of these I have received only two or three Letters and no more. Not a scratch of a Pen have I been able to obtain from any Body else."[34] In his isolation, Adams could find consolation in the letters of Cicero, which were filled with calls to Atticus for more information. "It is thirty whole days from the time of writing since I heard anything from you. . . . I beg you to write to me in the plainest possible terms of anything that comes within your purview, whatever way it tends."[35]

Adams' feelings of isolation were compounded by his inability to consult his closest advisors. Cicero had often expressed the desire to be with Atticus in person to deliberate on political matters. "Caesar wants to have me on his staff," he wrote on one occasion. "That would be a more respectable evasion of the danger, which however I do not decline. It comes to this, I would rather fight. But my mind is not made up. Again I say, 'If only you were here!'"[36] In a similar fashion, Adams told Warren, "I want to be with you, Tete a Tete, to canvass, and discuss the complicated subject of Trade."[37]

Unable or unwilling to face the political arena alone, Adams constantly sought the advice of his friends. "Shall We then give Permission for our Vessells to go to foreign Nations, if they can escape the Men of War?" Adams asked Warren. "This vast object is never out of my mind. Help me to grapple it."[38] Like Cicero, who consistently told Atticus "I am eagerly waiting your advice," Adams, before speaking or acting on important political questions, regularly asked his closest personal advisors "What shall We do?"[39]

In one letter to Warren, Adams launches a barrage of questions and answers. The style of the letter (which Adams himself describes as "unconnected Scraps and broken Hints") and the act of judging seem inseparable.

> Shall We hush the Trade of the whole Continent and not permit a Vessell to go out of our Harbours except from one Colony to another? How long will or can our People bear this? I Say they can bear it forever—if Parliament Should build a Wall of Brass, at low Water Mark, We might live and be happy. We must change our Habits, our Prejudices our palates, our Taste in Dress, Furniture, Equipage, Architecture &c. But We can live and be happy. But the Question is whether our People have Virtue enough to be mere Husbandmen, Mechaniks and Soldiers? That they have not Virtue enough to bear it always, I take for granted. How long then will their Virtue last? Till next Spring?[40]

On another occasion, Adams set out a long series of questions about trade during non-exportation:

> But a Question arises, whether, our Association against Exportations, can be observed, so as to have its full Effect, upon Britain, Ireland, and the West Indies, unless We extend it further? We have agreed not to export to B., I., and the W. Indies. Parliament has made an Act that We Shall not export to any other Place. So that Trade is entirely stopped. But will not a Smuggling Trade be opened? . . . In short may not our associations be wholly evaded and eluded, if we dont draw it closer? My own opinion upon these great Questions I may possibly give you sometime or other. But I must have yours.[41]

Adams used interrogatories as a deliberative tool. Asking such questions enabled him to discover the central issues connected with complex political problems, and bring into focus various policy options.

This manner of deliberating in letters by composing a series of questions and answers is something Cicero also often did. In the following letter to

Atticus, Cicero explores the alternatives and consequences for dealing with his enemy Clodius and securing his own restoration to Roman politics:

> For what in your view can be done and how? Through the Senate? But you yourself told me that Clodius posted in the doorway of the Senate House a clause in his law banning "any motion or mention." How then could Domitius say that he would make a motion? And how was it that Clodius sat mum while the persons you mention spoke on the subject and demanded that a motion be put to the House? And if it is to go through the Assembly, will that be possible without the unanimous approval of the Tribunes? What about my property, and my house? Can it be restored, and, if not, how can I be? Unless you see solutions to these problems, what sort of hope are you asking me to entertain?[42]

As these letters show, both Adams and Cicero used their letter writing as the medium for their political judgment. And, the style of the letter—the interrogatives, the condensed argumentative tone, the rapid introduction of new topics, the incomplete development of ideas, the flavor of natural conversation—affords each writer the widest latitude for deliberation.

Even after seeking advice, however, Adams could not rest without rehearsing his deliberations for his correspondents. In this practice, too, he emulated Cicero, who often reasoned out loud in his letters to Atticus. "It may help you to advise me if I set out briefly the points which occur to my mind in favour of either course," Cicero would write. Or, he would tell Atticus "Practising myself upon these questions and setting out the arguments on either side, now in Greek now in Latin, I take my mind for a while off my troubles and at the same time ponder matters of relevance." Cicero's deliberations would be composed in the style of political debate, confirming the importance of private letters as a vital medium of political judgment:

> No doubt you will say that he [Caesar] be persuaded to hand over his army and so become Consul. True, this would be a course against which, if he were to bring himself to it, nothing could be said, and I am surprised that he does not do so if his claim to stand while training his army is not allowed. From our standpoint, however, as certain persons think, no prospect is more formidable than Caesar as Consul. "Better thus" you will say, "than with an army at his back." Assuredly, but this very "thus" is, I know, considered a disaster by somebody; and yet there is no help for it. If that is what he wants we must let him have it. "You have put up with him as Consul before, put up with him again." "Ah but he was weak then" comes the answer, "and yet stronger than the entire state. What do you think he will be like now?" And if he is Consul, Pompey is resolved to stay in Spain. A wretched situation indeed if the worst of all contingencies is something which cannot be refused and which, should he accept it, would make all the honest men immediately and heartily grateful to him![43]

As Adams wrote his own letters in this Ciceronian style, they became like drafts of his Congressional orations, as he discovered and laid out the reasons for his proposed course of action. In a letter to James Warren on October 19, 1775, for example, Adams considered the merits of funding a Navy:

> The Expence would be very great—true. But the Expence might be born and perhaps the Profits and Benefits to be obtained by it, would be a Compensation. A naval Force might be created, which would do something. It would destroy Single Cutters and Cruizers—it might destroy small Concerts or Fleets of those like Wallaces at R. Island and Lord Dunmores at Virginia. . . . But, there is a great objection to this. All the Trade of Pensylvania, the Lower Counties, a great Part of Maryland and N. Jersey Sails in between the Capes of Delaware Bay— and if a strong Fleet should be posted in that Bay, Superiour to our Fleet it might obstruct all the Trade of this River.[44]

Although Adams admitted to Warren that he was "speculating now about Things at a Distance," he nevertheless was using his letter writing as an important deliberative tool. He may not have expected Warren to offer specific answers to his questions (as he did when he solicited advice directly), but by writing letters he could become more confident himself in the views he held.

Indeed, the continuous demand upon Adams' political judgment led him to dash off letters to Warren and others which seem to commence in mid-argument. It is as if Adams had been privately deliberating for some time. Then, seeking clarification or solidification of his ideas, he creates a deliberative space in a letter, ostensibly addressed to his correspondent, in which he can set out his ideas and test his judgment. On one occasion he begins a letter to Warren:

> Dear Sir
>   Can The Inhabitants of North America *live* without foreign Trade? There is Beef and Pork, and Poultry, and Mutton and Venison and Veal, milk, Butter, Cheese, Corn, Barley, Rye, Wheat, in short every Species of Eatables animal and Vegetable in a vast abundance, an immense Profusion. We raise about Eleven hundred Thousand Bushells of Corn, yearly more than We can possibly consume.

The letter goes on in this fashion for seven paragraphs and then ends as abruptly as it begins: "On the other Hand if We give Liberty Trade, will not most of our Vessells be Seized? Perhaps all but those of the Tories who may be privileged."[45] The letter, without any personal remarks at all, is a pure deliberative text. By presenting all the relevant arguments and questions in a letter to Warren, Adams focused his thinking, tuned his reasoning, and polished the presentation he might one day make in Congress. In this way his correspondence allowed him to gain a firm grasp on the issues he faced and to test his reasoning in a deliberative discourse free from the risks of public speaking. While the letter informs Warren, it nevertheless functions almost exclusively as a text of political judgment in which the writer deals with the contingencies and immediacy of revolutionary politics. As with his other political letters, the character of this epistle as a deliberative discourse is formed as much from its style as from its substance. Indeed, Adams seems acutely aware that it is his free style of writing that permits his epistolary deliberation. At one point he tells Warren, "You dont Expect Correctness nor Ceremony from me. When I have any Thing to write and one Moment to write it in I scratch it off to you, who dont expect that I should dissect these Things, or reduce them to correct Writing."[46]

Private Letters as Public Record

Reflecting on his correspondence as a record of political judgment, Adams advised his wife to save all his letters to her and "put them up safe, and preserve them." The letters, he thought, "may exhibit to our Posterity a kind of Picture of the Manners, Opinions, and Principles of these Times of Perplexity, Danger and Distress."[47] As the record of his own political judgment, Adams' letters would enable him to appear to future generations with distinction, just as Cicero's had done.

Adams always considered the letters of Cicero to constitute a remarkable historical record. "The period in the history of the world the best understood is that of Rome from the time of Marius to the death of Cicero," he told Benjamin Rush, "and this distinction is entirely owing to Cicero's letters and orations." In Cicero's letters, said Adams, "we see the true character of the times and the passions of all the actors on the stage."[48] Here Adams echoed Middleton, who wrote in his *Life of Cicero* that Cicero's letters were "the most authentic materials for the history of that age," because they laid open "the grounds and motives of all the great events that happened in it." Middleton told his readers to attend especially to Cicero's political letters, in which "all his maxims are drawn from an intimate knowledge of men and things" and in which "he always touches the point on which the whole affair turns."[49]

Conscious that his own time was also an age of extraordinary historical significance, and aiming to emulate the accomplishments of Cicero, Adams hoped his letters would become "the most authentic materials for the history of that age." For his letters, too, would lay open "the grounds and motives of all the great events that happened" and show Adams deliberating on "the point on which the whole affair turns." Adams hoped this informal conversational record of his political judgment would be as inspiring to posterity as Cicero's epistles had been to him.

Moses Coit Tyler encouraged later students of the Revolution to view the letters as Adams had hoped they would be viewed. Tyler believed the private correspondence of the revolutionary period "would set forth for us, in vivid contemporary colors, every passing phase of that time of mighty commotion." With their letters, the men and women of the Revolution "found one another out, informed one another, stimulated, guided, aided one another in the common struggle." As I have argued here, John Adams relied on Cicero's assistance in that struggle. He mastered Cicero's epistolary style; but in imitating Cicero, he not only wrote in a style praised by the literary-minded men of his day, he also discovered a medium of political expression, appropriate for his active life, which empowered him by facilitating his political judgment. Cicero's style was liberating. It allowed Adams to pursue freely the political questions which vexed him and his colleagues in the Continental Congress. Like Cicero before him, Adams relied on letters as a space for deliberation. In his letters, style and politics became inseparable. For this reason they remain for students of the eighteenth century, as they were for Tyler, among the best examples of "a vast, a fascinating, and a significant branch" of the literature of the American Revolution.[50]

NOTES

1. Charles Rollin, *The Method of Teaching and Studying the Belles Lettres*, 6th ed., 4 vols. (London: 1769), 1:107; Hugh Blair, *Lectures on Rhetoric and Belles Lettres*, 2 vols., ed. Harold F. Harding (Carbondale: Southern Illinois University Press, 1965), 2:300. On the tradition of letter writing as a rhetorical art, see James J. Murphy, *Rhetoric in the Middle Ages: A History of Rhetorical Theory from St. Augustine to the Renaissance* (Berkeley: University of California Press, 1974), 194–268; Jean Robertson, *The Art of Letter Writing: An Essay on the Handbooks Published in England During the Sixteenth and Seventeenth Centuries* (London: University Press of Liverpool, 1943); Katherine Gee Hornbeak, *The Complete Letter Writer in English, 1568–1800*, Smith College Studies in Modern Languages (Northampton, MA: Smith College Press, 1934); Harry B. Weiss, *American Letter Writers 1698–1943* (New York: New York Public Library, 1945). See also Raoul N. Smith, "A Bibliography of Books on Language and Languages Printed in the United States Through the Year 1800," *Historiographia Linguistica*, 4 (1977): 207–43.
2. William Guthrie, trans., *Cicero's Epistles to Atticus. With Notes Historical, Explanatory, and Critical*, new edition corrected and amended, 3 vols. (London: Lackington, Allen, and Co., et al., 1806), 2:74n, 70n; Blair, *Lectures* 2:300; Conyers Middleton, *Life of M. Tullius Cicero*, 2 vols. (London: Baynes and Son, 1823), 2:404–5; Rollin, *Method* 1:106–7; John Ward, *A System of Oratory, Delivered in a Course of Lectures Publicly Read at Gresham College London*, 2 vols. (London: 1759), 2:217.

3. Jay Fliegelman, *Declaring Independence: Jefferson, Natural Language, & the Culture of Performance* (Stanford: Stanford University Press, 1993), 59, 3.

4. Stephen H. Browne, "The Pastoral Voice in John Dickinson's First *Letter from a Farmer in Pennsylvania,*" *Quarterly Journal of Speech* 76 (1990): 46, 47, 52, 53, 52, 54, 53, 54.

5. Ibid., 49, 53, 48.

6. Robert Hariman, "Political Style in Cicero's Letters to Atticus," *Rhetorica* 7 (1989): 145–58. See also Lenore Kramp Geweke, "Notes on the Political Relationship of Cicero and Atticus from 63–59 B.C." *Classical Journal* 29 (1934): 269–83.

7. *Diary and Autobiography of John Adams,* ed. L. H. Butterfield, 4 vols. (Cambridge: Belknap Press of Harvard University Press, 1961), 1:73, 96. See also John Adams to Josiah Quincy, October 6, 1775, *Papers of John Adams,* ed. Robert J. Taylor, Mary-Jo Kline, and Gregg L. Lint, 8 vols. to date (Cambridge: Belknap Press of Harvard University Press, 1977–), 3:186. The virtues of the *Vita Activa* are most eloquently described by Hannah Arendt in *The Human Condition* (Chicago: University of Chicago Press, 1958).

8. John Adams to James Warren, June 25, 1774, *Papers* 2:99.

9. *Diary and Autobiography of John Adams* 2:97.

10. John Adams to William Tudor, August 4, 1774, *Papers* 2:126. On eighteenth-century American politics as "theatre" see Fliegelman, *Declaring Independence,* 79–94. Cicero boasted of the justice and temperance of his provincial administration in letters to Atticus. See for example Cicero to Atticus 109.3 and 110.2 in *Cicero's Letters to Atticus* ed. D. R. Shackelton Bailey, vol. 3 (Cambridge: Cambridge University Press, 1968). All references to Cicero's letters are taken from this edition. Letters will be identified in notes by the number from this collection.

11. John Adams to James Warren, July 17, 1774 and July 24, 1774, *Papers* 2:109, 117. On Adams at Congress see Richard A. Ryerson, "John Adams' First Diplomatic Mission: Philadelphia, 1774," *Proceedings of the Massachusetts Historical Society* 95 (1983): 17–28. On Adams' early emulation of Cicero see James M. Farrell, "Syren Tully and the Young John Adams," *Classical Journal* 87 (1992): 373–90.

12. *Opera Omnia cum Gruteri et Select variorum notis & inicibus locupletissimus,* ed. C. Schrevello (Amsterdam: 1661).

13. *Diary and Autobiography of John Adams* 3:271.

14. Adams owned the 5th edition (London: W. Innys and J. Richardson, and H. S. Cox, 1755).

15. On the importance and popularity of these translations in eighteenth-century America see Myer Reinhold, *The Classick Pages: Classical Reading of Eighteenth-Century Americans* (University Park, PA: American Philological Association, 1975), 51. See also James Beister, "Samuel Johnson on Letters," *Rhetorica* 5 (1988): 145–66.

16. John Adams to Abigail Adams, July 7, 1776, *Adams Family Correspondence,* ed. L. H. Butterfield, 4 vols. (Cambridge: Belknap Press of Harvard University Press, 1963), 2:39.

17 John Adams to Benjamin Rush, December 27, 1812, *The Spur of Fame: Dialogues of John Adams and Benjamin Rush, 1805–1813*, ed. John A. Shutz and Douglass Adair (San Marino: The Huntington Library, 1966), 263.

18. John Adams to Robert Treat Paine, December 6, 1756, *Papers* 1:31; John Adams to Abigail Adams, July 7, 1776, *Family Correspondence* 2:39.

19. John Adams to Abigail Adams, June 29, 1774, *Family Correspondence* 1:111–12. See also John Adams to Abigail Adams July 5, 1774, ibid. 124; John Adams to Abigail Adams, July 6, 1774, ibid. 129–30.

20. Cicero to Atticus 16.10. See also Cicero to Atticus 21.5, 30.2, 94.3, 195.9–10, 354, 389.1.

21. John Adams to Abigail Adams, September 14, 1774, *Family Correspondence* 1:155.

22. The rapid style here suggests how a figurative construction communicates at the formal, as well as the substantive level. See Michael Leff and Andrew Sachs, "Words the Most Like Things: Iconicity and the Rhetorical Text," *Western Journal of Speech Communication* 54 (1990): 252–73.

23. Cicero to Atticus 13.4. See also 55.2.

24. John Adams to Abigail Adams, September 14, 1774, *Family Correspondence* 1:128.

25. Cicero to Atticus 134.1

26. John Adams to Abigail Adams, March 31, 1777, *Family Correspondence* 2:192.

27. John Adams to Abigail Adams, September 16, 1774, ibid. 1:158; John Adams to Abigail Adams October 7, 1774, ibid. 164–65; John Adams to Abigail Adams, October 9, 1774, ibid. 166; John Adams to James Warren, May 21, 1775, *Papers* 3:11.

28. Insofar as letter writing is free from these various burdens of formality, it is even more of a "natural language" phenomenon than the "oratorical ideal" described by Fliegelman as dominant in the revolutionary period. As he explains, there was a "presumption that intimate conversation and correspondence were more frank than public utterance, that to tell the truth was to speak in private." He also notes that "Adams was a man who turned correspondents into confessors, audiences, and publicists," *Declaring Independence*, 44, 125.

29. Cicero to Atticus 214. See also 18.1, 39.1, 39.5, 44.5, 50, 53.2, 115.14, 133, 134.5.

30. John Adams to Abigail Adams, July 17, 1775, *Family Correspondence* 1:251.

31. Ronald Beiner, *Political Judgment* (Chicago: University of Chicago Press, 1983), 197.

32. John Adams to Abigail Adams, November 4, 1775, *Family Correspondence* 1:320; John Adams to Abigail Adams December 3, 1775, *Family Correspondence* 1:331.

33. Cicero to Atticus 14.1. See also 19.1, 43.1, 74.1.

34. John Adams to Abigail Adams, May 2, 1775, *Family Correspondence* 1:191; John Adams to James Warren, September 28, 1775, *Papers* 3:171; John Adams to Abigail Adams, July 4, 1775 *Family Correspondence* 1:238.

35. Cicero to Atticus 66. See also 55.3, 56.2, 61, 105.2, 106.3, 135.1.

36. Cicero to Atticus 39.5
37. John Adams to James Warren, October 19, 1775, *Papers* 3:215.
38. John Adams to James Warren, October 19, 1775, ibid. 215–16.
39. Cicero to Atticus 424.1; John Adams to James Warren, July 23, 1775, *Papers* 3:88. Adams must have considered Warren to be his "Atticus," someone like Cicero's confidant, with whom he "could share all that gives me any anxiety, a wise, affectionate friend to whom I could talk without pretence or evasion or concealment." Cicero to Atticus, 18.1.
40. John Adams to James Warren, October 19, 1775, *Papers* 3:215. Cicero once described the style of his letters to Atticus in similar fashion. "If you complain of my chopping and changing, I answer that I talk to you as to myself. In so great a matter must not any man argue with himself this way and that? Besides I want to draw your opinion—if it is still the same I shall be the steadier, if it has changed I shall agree with you." Cicero to Atticus 164.2–3.
41. John Adams to James Warren, October 28, 1775, *Papers* 254–55.
42. Cicero to Atticus 60.6; see also Cicero to Atticus 21.8, 25.2, 134.1, 169.1–2, 173.2–3, 199.3–4, 388.
43. Cicero to Atticus 153.1–7, 173.3, 132.3.
44. John Adams to James Warren, October 19, 1775, *Papers* 3:214–15. See also John Adams to Moses Gill, June 10, 1775, ibid. 20–21.
45. John Adams to James Warren, October 20, 1775, ibid. 216–17.
46. John Adams to James Warren, October 25, 1775, ibid. 244.
47. John Adams to Abigail Adams, July 2, 1774, *Family Correspondence* 1:121.
48. John Adams to Benjamin Rush, December 4, 1805, *Spur of Fame*, 44.
49. Middleton, *Life of Cicero* 2:405. Hugh Blair also read Middleton. Cicero's letters "contain the most authentic materials of the history of that age," he wrote. They are "the last monuments which remain of Rome in its free state; the greatest part of them being written during that important crisis, when the Republic was on the point of ruin; the most interesting situation, perhaps, which is to be found in the affairs of mankind." *Lectures on Rhetoric* 2:301.
50. Moses Coit Tyler, *The Literary History of the American Revolution, 1763–1783* (1897; reprint New York: Burt Franklin, 1970), 12–14.

Janet Little and Robert Burns:
An Alliance with Reservations

MOIRA FERGUSON

The late eighteenth-century Scottish poet, Janet Little, is an exceptional individual, articulating, in verse no less, the dynamic between the eighteenth-century Scottish laboring world and middle- and upper-class society. She voices a perspective rarely chronicled by a laboring class female, but one she shares with her more famous contemporary, Robert Burns. Her career intersects Burns' life and text, contextualizing Burns' poems in a special way. Little protects a complex class and cultural position by extending mandated politeness to patrons and employers from the middle class and gentry while commending Burns in verse. She understands at first hand that life is not experienced at a harmonious level by rich and poor alike. At the same time, as an upholder of the Kirk, Little questions Burns' relationship with women by obliquely critiquing power-based gender relations in seemingly benign conventional lyrics and poems. In so doing, she not only represents women of her economic class, but women of all social strata who breach the cultural arena despite embedded contempt for the talents of the sex. Little's personal attraction to Robert Burns further complicates her text. Put bluntly, Janet Little's quiet challenge to Burns is freighted with unstated feelings for the poet whose attentions to women she so vehemently deplores. Her politics of class, national and gendered identity, moreover, directly relate to her background.

* * * * * * * * *

Born in 1759, the same year as Robert Burns, Janet Little was the daughter of George Little, a hired farm laborer or cottar in Nether Bogside, near Ecclefechan in Dumfrieshire.[1] After a short time in service, she was hired by the Reverend Johnstone and remained in his household for several years as a family servant. She began writing poems during this time. Subsequently, as a chamber maid or "bairn's-woman" (dry nurse), she entered the service of Frances Dunlop, her patron-cum-employer, who was also a patron and correspondent of Robert Burns. Energetically encouraged by Mrs. Dunlop, Janet Little continued to write poems while at Dunlop House.[2] Dunlop remained her informal patron after Little left Dunlop's service sometime after 1786 to become a child's nurse and eventually superintendent of the dairy at Loudoun Castle in Ayrshire. The business was leased by Dunlop's daughter, Susan, following the suicide of the earl of Loudoun,[3] father of the young countess to whom Little dedicated her volume of poems. This position as dairy superintendent, highly valued for its financial security, was precious in a decade when death prompted substantial emigration "from the Lowlands . . . [of Scotland and] mainly from the Borders" where Little grew up.[4] Little's job led to her identification on the title page of her 1792 volume of poems as the Scottish milkmaid or "Scotch" milkmaid, a cognomen by which she became popularly known.[5]

At that time, Scottish laboring-class poets enjoyed a wide audience among working- and middle-class communities, as well as gentry like Frances Dunlop. Their poems were much in demand. Robert Burns, especially renowned in Scotland, was invariably called the ploughman poet.[6] The "poetical mania" of the period, as well as Burns' own fame after the Kilmarnock edition of his poems appeared in 1786, inspired "a host of shoddy imitators . . . much . . . in tribute to him." Burns even complained about the "servility of my plebeian brethren." Little's volume was the beneficiary of both this poetic fashion and aristocratic patronage.[7]

On the shrewd advice of James Boswell whom she initially asked to be her dedicatee, Janet Little dedicated her volume of poems to twelve-year-old Flora Mure Campbell, countess of Loudoun.[8] The power of the countess of Loudoun's name, Robert Burns' assistance in filling up the subscription bill, probably at Dunlop's request, and Frances Dunlop's vigorous drumming up of takers attracted about seven hundred subscriptions. The countess herself purchased twelve copies, Dunlop and her relatives twenty copies. Little opens her volume with a tribute "To the Countess of Londoun" that precedes the text proper. She delineates the aristocrat's superior class position and the conduciveness of Loudoun Castle to art and joy: "Will gentle Loudoun deign to lend an ear . . . Within your walls my happiness I found . . . Luxuriant flourish, like the plants around: / Blithe as birds . . . I pour'd the willing lay" (25). The speaker rejoices (she claims) in her situation at the castle, expressing appreciation for the charity and lessons in virtue accorded by aristocrats to the aged and the rural poor: "ev'ry comfort rural life affords" (26). She enjoys herself so much, she writes, "My life in careless ease might run, / My age supported by my master's son." Somewhat ambiguously, with a whisper of self-satisfaction, she contrasts the immortality of her humble lines with the lying low in the earth of "honor'd Patrons" (25). Sadness further reigns in the household because a child has died. Only the speaker's "sad verse" can "grant that shelter" which the "good and great" no longer can give (27). Although Little apologizes for the anguish her lines about mortality elicit, she intimates that her verse is, by contrast, eternal. In later poems Little also gracefully and sensibly acknowledges Frances Dunlop. One is entitled "To a Lady, A Patroness of the Muses, on Her Recovery from Sickness." The other—"Verses. Written on a foreigner's visiting the grave of a Swiss gentleman, buried among the descendants of Sir William Wallace, guardian of Scotland in the thirteenth century"—eulogizes Dunlop's ancestor, William Wallace, one of Scottland's national heroes.

Disguised as commendations to altruistic benefactors, Little's poems of praise amount to a standard appeal, addressed to useful patrons of the arts, who can easily facilitate the cultural ascent and modest economic advancement of a socially disadvantaged woman. But patronage cuts two ways, especially in these tumultuous revolutionary times. Not to put too fine a point on it, the patronage extended by the conservative bourgeoisie and the aristocracy is complicated by a collective fear of republican values that were popularly held among the Scottish peasantry and urban workers. Applauding Janet Little partially purchased social absolution at a time when the French Revolution was inspiring working people to assert themselves.

Little, in turn, is keenly sensitive to contradictions at work in her own life: employers and patrons treat her well and respect her needs, but she is permanently condescended to and patronized. She responds through social verse and cultural confrontations. Her poetry abounds with references to poverty, woe, the toughness of laboring women, and the reality of life at the castle, albeit obliquely rendered. Through this unspoken contrast, the customary trope of commendation that endears Janet Little to a highly desirable audience, for both economic and cultural reasons, speaks for itself. Her volume of poetry may constitute a cultural declaration, but it is also an economic proposition. Her poem on Janet Nicol, "A Poem on Content-ment" is a case in point. Its subtitle reads "Inscribed To Janet Nicol, A Poor Old Wandering Woman, Who Lives By the Wall At Loudoun and Used Sometimes To Be Visited By the Countess." Little congratulates Janet Nicol on not having the pain of being a writer or a person crossed in love. Instead she wishes that

> . . . blithly may ilk neighbour greet you;
> May cakes, and scones, and kibbocks meet you;
> And may they weel ilk pocket cram,
> And in your bottle slip a dram.
> May your wee glass, your pipe and specks,
> Be ay preserv'd frae doleful wrecks.
> May your wee house, baith snug and warm,
> Be safe frae ev'ry rude alarm.
>   (177)

Janet Nicol, asserts Janet Little, need not worry for the aristocrat will always provide for her, a statement that is more a hope than an assumption. Does Janet Little believe such protection is guaranteed? "For age and want, and wo provides / And over misery presides" (178). Although seemingly unalloyed tributes to aristocratic generosity and charity validate the general philosophical tenor of her poems, Little persistently, though subtly, problematizes the idea that patrons and employers foster happy lives among workers. In contrast to the dedicatory poem praising the countess, the first poem in the volume, "To Hope," emphatically denotes the world as an unmitigated "scene of dole and care." Life is a struggle in which hearts bleed. The narrator is severely divided against herself, as if she started off intending to placate and ingratiate herself with at least the conservative wing of the reading public and her Tory patron only to be consumed by repressed feelings of anger.

At a highly generalized level, Little discerns disappointment everywhere. Evidence of anguish saturates the poem, not least when the speaker announces that hope's favor "shall ever / alleviate my wo" (28). Hope illuminates our "dark and dreary way, . . . bend[s] our steps to heav'n, [and] stem[s] the trickling tear." Hope, too, "decorates the chain" of marriage. Though illusory, "we all thy flatt'ring tales believe, / Enamour'd of thy art" (30). Everyone hopes. She ends by focussing on hope's power to cancel the terror of death—almost as a cover-up—and an authentic view of an unhappy world.

* * * * * * * * *

Janet Little partly constructs her cultural and class identity through her interaction with Robert Burns, Scotland's national poet. The two share a knowledge of poverty that locates them in a similar relationship to middle- and upper-class people.[9] Little sides with Burns on democratic principles and the people's rights. As if to accentuate their class solidarity and locate herself in a Scottish cultural continuum, Janet Little wrote a cordial poem and letter of introduction to Robert Burns in 1789, exhorting him to peruse her poems. She appeals to him as a fellow laborer who should favor his own: "I felt a partiality for the author, which I should not have experienced had you been in a more dignified station. . . . I shall, in hope of your future friendship, take the liberty to transcribe them."[10] Someone like Janet Little, even lower in the class scale than Burns—her father was a hired laborer, his was a tenant farmer—would have appreciated the struggle Burns endured to become recognized as a poet. His life was one of "thwarted progress as well as of sturdy rooted vitality."[11] Robert Fizhugh notes that

> Burns' sympathy for the old Scots royal house which had won independence from England, his national pride, his hatred of tyranny, and his enthusiasm for the Rights of Man and for the Promise of

Liberty, Equality, and Fraternity offered by the French Revolution then developing—all form a persuasive sequence. *Scots Wha Hae* is its ringing statement, particularly stanzas Five and Six, and a noble prelude [in 1794] to the Jacobin cry, "A man's a man for a' that."[12]

Burns' venerated class-leveling song (1795) struck no common chord among those who sympathized with the old regime during the French revolutionary struggle after 1789 and deemed rank much more than "the guinea's stamp."[13] Although their friendship ultimately survived, Frances Dunlop stopped corresponding with Burns for eighteen months after he made light of the royal guillotinings in France.

In her poem of introduction to Burns, entitled "An Epistle to Mr. Robert Burns," Janet Little applauds and updates the distinguished lineage of Scottish culture that ran through Allan Ramsay, one of the recognized champions of vernacular poetry, to Burns, its new embodiment. Little extols Burns' ability to captivate an audience of different classes, and amply praises his surpassing nature poems: "To hear thy song, all ranks desire; / Sae well thou strik'st the dormant lyre" (161). She also singles out Burns' dedication to his friend and landlord, Gavin Hamilton, who had been censured by the Kirk for breaking the Sabbath and for contumacy.[14] "In unco' bonny, hamespun speech" (ibid.) in order to mock the lavish dedications of "servile bards wha fawn an' fleech, / Like beggar's messin." (ibid.) These lines contest her relatively lavish dedication to the countess. She acclaims Burns' nature poems, and adds, probably in reference to his poem in praise of "Scotch Drink" and his "Earnest Cry and Prayer": "An' weel ye praise the whiskey gill." No matter how blunt her own quill might become in complimenting him, that praise, she insists, will be accorded him "frae ilka hill" (162). All she can do, she humbly confesses, is "blot thy brilliant shine" with her "rude, unpolish'd strokes" (163).

With patriotic spirit, Little further lauds Burns by speculating how English men of letters passionately envy his poetic genius. She conjures up the English tradition, represented by Joseph Addison, Alexander Pope, and Samuel Johnson who are distraught with jealousy at "the plough-boy who sings, wi' throat sae clear, / They, in a rage, / Their works wad a' in pieces tear / An' Curse your page (162). She ends by asserting that she will stop venerating his talents. Instead she will pray for all mortals to dispense blessings "with an indulgent care / To Robert Burns" (163).

Extending her nationalist sentiment, Little foregrounds her gratitude at the honor Burns brings to Scotland in a poem entitled, "Given to a Lady Who Asked Me to Write a Poem." After discussing the difficulty of writing "in royal Anna's golden days, / Hard was the talk to gain the bays," she launches into those who "got near [Parnassus'] top: that little fellow Pope, Homer, Swift, Thomson, Addison, an' Young."

Almost immediately, she opts for Scots after stating that Samuel Johnson showed them all up:

> But Doctor Johnson, in a rage,
> Unto posterity did shew
> Their blunders great, their beauties few.
> But now he's dead, we weel may ken;
> For ilka dunce maun hae a pen,
> To write in hamely, uncouth rhymes;
> An' yet forsooth they please the times.
>
> $(114)^{15}$

Patriotically parodying and avenging Johnson's critique of Scottish society, she denotes Burns as an overreacher "sous[ing] his sonnets on the court." Here Little uses a concrete image for her activities as a domestic servant. In addition to its meaning of "pouring," souse also means sloshing from a pail or a bucket. It may also have forceful associations from the dialect sense of "souse," meaning to strike a blow. Then she rapidly reverses the initial negative reaction followed by a self-eulogy. If Johnson were still alive, she protests self-mockingly, he would have gleaned capital for another anti-Scottish diatribe:

> An' what is strange, they praise him for 'it.
> Even folks, wha're of the highest station,
> Ca' him the glory of our nation.
>
> But what is more surprising still,
> A milkmaid must tak up her quill;
> An' she will write, shame fa' the rabble!
> That think to please wi' ilka bawble.
> They may thank heav'n, auld Sam's asleep:
> For could he ance but get a peep,
> He, wi' a vengeance wad them sen'
> A' headlong to the dunces' den.
>
> (114)

Unlike Burns, she concludes, a "rustic country queen" like herself claims no such versatility, her self-parody not only intact to the last line but turning itself inside out. Indirectly, through her use of queen, a common word for girl in northeast Scots, Little refers to the debate over writing in Scots. She challenges any idea of the vernacular as inferior, pooh-poohing potential anxieties about measuring up to an ideal correct English usage, "pernicious Anglicizing."[16] Her stated detachment from Burns only serves to enhance her connection to him as her reference point, while her firm use of "wise" affirms a deep-rooted sense of female capacity: "Does she, poor silly thing, pretend / The manners of our age to mend? / Mad as we are, we're wise enough / Still to despise sic paultry stuff" (115). Burns' talent, she stresses, is to please "a' denominations," instruct people in love, set forth deft though pithy political commentary, and intimidate critics.

Burns is polite but unforthcoming about this poem. Writing to Dunlop, who had frequently commended the "rustic poetess" to Burns,[17] he uses his allegedly untutored social manners to excuse his lack of response to Little:

> I had some time ago an epistle, part poetic and part prosaic, from your poetess, Mrs. J. L——, a very ingenious but modest composition. I should have written her, as she requested, but for the hurry of this new business. I have heard of her and her compositions in this country; and, I am happy to add, always to the honour of her character. The fact is, I know not well how to write to her: I should sit down to a sheet of paper that I knew not how to stain. I am no dab at fine-drawn letter-writing.[18]

His subsequent harsh criticisms of Little's poems provoked a furious rejoinder from Frances Dunlop:

> How did I upbraid my own conceited folly at that instant that had ever subjected one of mine to so haughty an imperious critic! I never liked so little in my life as at that moment the man whom at all others I delighted to honour. . . . I then felt for Mrs. Richmond (Jenny Little), for you, [Burns] and for myself, and not one of the sensations were such as I would wish to cherish in remembrance.[19]

In a real sense, Little functions as a quasi (and partly unconscious) mediator in the class conflict between Dunlop and Burns whose friendship was tested by Burns' pro-revolutionary sympathies.

Little wrote a second poem about Burns entitled "On a Visit to Mr. Burns" occasioned by their meeting at Ellisland in Dumfriesshire, near where she was born. Negotiated through Dunlop's good offices, the encounter was one Little had long desired.[20] Unfortunately, Little arrived on an inauspicious day when Burns had fallen off his horse. Her response oscillates between delight in his presence and commiseration at his condition. Little's recollections of the event—her poem to Burns read unmediated, we assume, by a public enamored of Burns—expresses astonishment at her good fortune in meeting Scotland's—even, she hints in "isle," Britain's—foremost contemporary poet: "Is't true? or does some magic spell / My wond'ring eyes beguile? / Is this the place where deigns to dwell / The honour of our isle?" (111). Now she stands in his presence, she coyly asserts, he no longer "bequeath[s] her a poignant dart" (112). She deplores his present injured condition with a reminder that human life constantly meshes joy and sorrow. In token of her fascinated fervour and awe of his talents, Little dialogizes some dependence on Burns and perhaps some fear of his power and dominance.

In other poems, Little's references to Burns are more indirect and conflicted. In "To My Aunty," the speaker recalls a dream in which her poems are widely published and critics pounce on her alleged imperfections. Although nothing about the critics' debate centers specifically on a female poet, the speaker proclaims the vulnerability of all poets that would include Little herself. At a slant, the poem urges Burns to aid her career while descriptions of the critics resemble certain remarks made about Burns' "characteristic touchiness and pride."[21] In this poem, Tom Touchy emerges as the iconic figure whom all critics desire to please. If he wants a line scratched out, they do so. No one—Jack Tim'rous is the example given—wants to oppose this "foremost man": "So much he fear'd a brother's scorn, / The whole escap'd his claws untorn" (166). When James Easy barely whispers that he likes the poem, Touchy denounces him abusively—at which point the speaker awakes. In her always precarious position as a servant and a female poet, Little commends Burns indirectly, while echoing inequitable cultural relationships.

Little's need to contain her discontent when she applauds aristocratic generosity is matched by certain confrontational attitudes toward Robert Burns that she likewise has to suppress. Once again, a faint disdain for class superiors who are often associated with hard, irreverent, licentious living echoes throughout. But this time she combines her doubled theme of veiled contempt for class superiors with some apprehension about Robert Burns' interactions with women.

In her poem "On Happiness," Little sketches out her values, marshalling a discourse against the character of the libertine that intermittently informs the collection of her poems. A Burgher, Little was a respected member of a Dissenting congregation in Galston, a few miles from Mauchline where Burns attended an old light Calvinist Church. The minister, the Reverend Mr. Blackwood, considered her pious and intelligent, a woman of "excellent judgment" who: "appreciate[d] something more than mere declamation in a preacher."[22] In "On Happiness" Janet Little characterizes religion as that institution whose "force alone can soothe the anxious beast." Her wishes and desires, she confides, are "centre'd all on Him." She attacks those whose immoral way of life prevents happiness (35). The libertine, like the drunkard in the poem, seemingly fixed in his attitudes, never knows happiness and is left with "cruel disappointment's rage, / Remorse, despair, the inmates of his soul" (34). Toward the close of her litany about people whose lives preclude happiness, Little mentions lovers who feed on illusion and married couples beset by a "thousand ills . . . and . . . bitterness & wo" (35). This conglomeration of people seem to concur that: "Successless is the search; / to nobler objects henceforth bend your view" (35). Interjecting a personal viewpoint, the speaker (Little herself) observes that divine law alone brings "content and calm serenity" to her "humble station."

This poem and others allude to contemporary events in Ayrshire. Between June and August of 1786, following a time-honored practice in the Sunday church service, the Mauchline Kirk Session in Ayrshire to which Burns belonged rebuked him for fornication. Burns had persistently challenged Scottish religious practices with a "common-sense humani-tarianism that stressed salvation by good works.[23] He especially deplored the domination of the people by the Kirk.[24] After being censured for getting Elizabeth Paton pregnant, Burns composed a poem to celebrate the birth, defiantly entitled "Welcome to a Bastard Wean."[25]

Despite abhorring Burns' modus operandi toward women, Janet Little had to be wary about attacking Scotland's new standard bearer. While questioning Burns' way of life, Little confines her resentment to nuance and allusion. For one thing, she dialogizes Burns' making free with women—as Little would see it—by voicing women from another era denouncing men like Burns.[26] She intertextualizes Burns' actions through displaying the negative experiences of vulnerable women in pastoral verse; she pens direct addresses to Burns that subtly remind readers of his conduct toward women; she speaks through the early eighteenth-century religious poet, Elizabeth Rowe, not only about the efficacy of spiritual values but about the social significance—albeit muted—of Lady Mary Wortley Montagu. Echoing Little's deeply internalized conflict is her poem, "On Reading Lady Mary Montague and Mrs Rowe's Letters," that contrasts the pious Elizabeth Rowe with the outspoken Lady Mary: "As Venus by night, so Montague bright / Long in the gay circle did shine: / She tun'd well the lyre, mankind did admire; / They prais'd, and they call'd her divine" (153). So pure was Rowe, however, Little argues, that national morality altered:

> O excellent Rowe, much Britain does owe
>   To what you've ingen'ously penn'd:
> Of virtue and wit, the model you've hit;
>   Who reads must you ever commend.
> Would ladies pursue, the paths trod by you,
>   And jointly to learning aspire,
> The men soon would yield unto them the field,
>   And critics in silence admire.
>
>   (154)

By citing Rowe last and approbating her as the most significant model for women, Little downplays Lady Mary's association with a "gay circle" and energetic social activity. On the other hand, she still marks Lady Mary as a crucial figure. Her praise for Rowe's virtue at the expense of Lady Mary's raciness contains a compliment to Lady Mary, and possibly some recognition of a simple bipolarized middle- and upper-class femininity that excludes Janet Little.

In the cluster of neoclassical poems from Delia to Alonzo, Little tells of and warns against smiling, emotionally fraudulent seducers. Fashioned in a mode related to the *pastourelle*,[27] the poems unmask sexual practices openly. In a subtly feminized reworking of Burns' masculinist tropes, the Delia-Alonzo poems intertextualize disquiet about Burns through exposing male manipulation of women which Delia cannily rejects.

Little's Alonzo first addresses Delia in "From Alonzo to Delia" as the "empress of my heart" to whom "I'm urg'd to vent my pure untainted flame." In classical mythology, Delia is "a name for *Diana* [or Pallas Athene] from her birthplace, *Delos*."[28] Alonzo graphically confides that his "swelling sighs your kind attentions claim." Flattering her, with no mention of marriage, he begs her to "hasten" to his arms, and resign her "heart and hand," and render them in the eyes of all the muses, a "happy pair" (184–85).

In a second poem, "From Delia to Alonzo," Alonzo is then suggestively portrayed as a smooth-talking rake. Delia uses Alonzo's reference to Adam to denounce the evanescence of Adam and Eve's happiness as a consequence of Eve's actions. Ironically she recommends that he learn from Adam "lest some fond nymph your pleasures all expel." She ends with an encomium on celibacy that complements Little's attacks on marriage elsewhere in the volume: "A single life we find replete with joys. / The matrimonial chain I ever dread. / A state of celibacy is my choice; / Therefore Alonzo never can succeed" (187).

Then in a third poem, "From Delia to Alonzo. Who Had Sent Her a Slighting Epistle," she parodically beats the would-be cunning suitor at his own game while flattering his great wit and learning. She leaves his machinations and ribaldry to the reader's imagination. Alonzo sings more sweetly than Philomel, Delia avows, and flies on Pegasus, the description resonating with Burns' recent real life experience when he took a hard tumble on his horse. Then she cleverly softens her tribute, almost with a sense of eighteenth-century camp:

> That dire, deceitful creature man . . .
>   is fill'd with mazy wiles;
> His count'nance stor'd with fickle smiles:
> His flatt'ring speech too oft beguiles
>   Pure innocence; . . .
>   (189)

Pointedly invoking facts in Burns' life, Delia refers to Alonzo, "The laureate of our days," and goes on:

> 'Tis pity, sir, that such as you
> Should agriculture's paths pursue,
> Or destin'd to hold the plough
>   On the cold plain;
> More fit that laurels deck'd the brow
>   Of such a swain.
>   (190)

Delia plays with Alonzo, too, as he toyed with her, by speculating that he might turn out to be famous, a future age might be "Struck with the beauties of your page, / Old Scotia's chieftains may engage / Your name to raise" (190).

Lastly, Delia trivializes Alonzo's "weak attempts" at a "ponderous theme." Regretting that love never rests within her—a knock at his rakishness—she forthrightly stresses that she would think twice about entertaining a guest who would bring her pain (a possible sexual reference?) and the sexually freighted final statement: "I wish you, sir, so much distress'd, / Soon well again" (191).

Again indirectly but more in tune with the times, "The Month's Love," is addressed to "maidens" who should "attend to my tale" and avoid, "that sly archer" called love whose arrow kills contentment. The narrator then relates her experiences as a naive young female with an unnamed youth: "Who was the sole cause of my smart . . . / When absent from him I ador'd, One minute as ages did prove; / Though plenty replenish'd my board, / I fasted and feasted on love." (48). When she spies her suitor with Susan, she feels instant resentment and obliterates her fond memories with a warning: "But be not too forward, ye fair, / Nor take too much courage from me, / How many have fall'n in the snare / That got not so easily free?" (49).

Most telling of all, however, is a poem entitled "On Seeing Mr. —— Baking Cakes," the significant blank name in the title followed by an opening line that boasts an identifying signifier: Mr. Blank of the title turns out to bear the name Rab by which Robert Burns was and is known throughout Scotland: "As Rab, who ever frugal was, / Some oat-meal cakes was baking" (171). This baker crumbles before a young female poet who enters his bakery: "a crazy scribbling lass, / Which set his heart a-quaking. I fear, says he, she'll verses write, / An' to her neebors show it" (171). These words complicate Burns' earlier offhand attentions toward Little and his soon-to-be-delivered, post-publication critique of her poems that infuriate Frances Dunlop. By eliding the silent signifier verses and sexuality to cake, the baker implicitly blends Burns' talent with his personal designs on women. He affects not to care because everyone likes his wares.

Rather than have a customer simply glance down at his cakes, the baker prefers them to be physically touched and invites any female passer-by to: "Put out her han' an' pree them" (172). Polyvalent and suggestive, pree is a Scots word that ranges in meaning from experience or taste to partake of or kiss.[29] The sense of "to sample" is also relevant. The so-called cakes are eagerly received by the lasses. And although Mr. Blank runs away, he cries out that he has "cakes in plenty." Moreover, he can supplement the cakes with: "Baith ale and porter, when I please, / To treat the lasses slily" (172). The last stanza insinuatingly recalls the evolving legend of Burns as a man who periodically impregnates women:[30]

> Some ca' me wild an' roving youth;
> But sure they are mistaken:
> The maid wha gets me, of a truth,
> Her bread will ay be baken.
>
> (172)

The speaker's buried excoriation of Burns' carousing was a popularly held attitude, highlighted by Frances Dunlop in one of her letters to Burns: "A gentleman told me with a grave face the other day that you certainly were a sad wretch, that your works were immoral and infamous, that you lampooned the clergy and laughed at the ridiculous parts of religion, and he was told you were a scandalous free-liver in every sense of the word."[31] Burns retorts cavalierly, claiming the privilege of foregrounding male exploits in his poems, regardless of the reader's gender. Burns wants simultaneously to titillate and respect prescribed female delicacy.

Whereas Burns could openly inscribe versions of his personal adventures into his poetry, social prescription barred Little from fulminating directly against inequitable gender relations; nor could she use an idiom, as he does, close to her experience to express outrage at male-female relations. Instead, adopting English diction, she often employs rigid, restricting forms. Although he did not patronize her work in the formal sense, Burns helped to open Janet Little's eyes to the condition of her existence. His prestige and presence gave her a certain kind of permission to explore the contradictions she saw. Little recognized some of these difficulties because she had very little cultural mobility compared to Burns. Hence she attacks injustice much more opaquely.[32]

The complex task Janet Little sets herself—to be judicious in public and textually embed her opinions with some subtlety—curtails her options. In "Given to a Lady," for instance, her highly problematized commentary about the charity of the aristocracy intersects with veiled hints about Burns' fornication that pinpoint her equivocation regarding Scotland's republican hero. Little approvingly foregrounds Burns' genius and his egalitarian politics, his depiction of nature and reactionary critics, yet seems to dislike Burns' non-marital relations with women. Her reservations about Burns permeate her text, culminating in some thematic mockery. She inflects the poem attached to the letter that she first sent Burns with his persistent theme of the hurt and slighted male suitor, victim of "women's faithless vows." She parodies Burns. On a fluid sexual scale in Burns' poetry, the jilted and abused slide into each other.

Attuned to the sexual vulnerability of women, Little knows that a fallen woman was virtually unemployable and employment itself was difficult enough. In other words, rather than attacking "the masters" outright, through her discussion of Burns, Little might be articulating her apprehensions about the precarious position of women in her own class. As Bridget Hill notes, "many husbands looked rather to their female domestics than to their wives for sexual satisfaction. What has been called "the eroticism of inequality" may in part explain the frequency with which masters are found seducing their dependent menials. It may explain the instant dismissal of servants found pregnant; mistresses must always have suspected that their husbands were responsible."[33] Unable to expose sexual exploitation openly, and keenly aware of the vexed life that awaited laboring women who "fell," Little could mention such common practices only through the guise of neoclassical or carefully distanced discourse. Nonetheless, however subtly she couches her opposition, Little seems to use Burns as a target. She broaches subtextually, from a female point of view, what the Kirk elders were authorized to execute in front of the congregation: a public assault on Burns for fornication. Burns' public contempt for the values of the Kirk, an institution that dominated the life of the country, polarized discomfited contemporaries like Janet Little. As an ardent Burgher and active member of the church-going community, however unorthodox certain of her views, Little censures the "Breughel quality in Ayrshire peasant life"[34] personified by Burns. In doing so, she operated under certain cultural constraints.

More than that, her second poem to Burns, "On a Visit to Mr. Burns," suggests an attraction for the carousing poet that collides head-on with her opposition to his moral license. Her playful characterization of Burns as a charmer of women who has woven a magic spell over her precedes a sexually laden stanza in which an eroticized discourse of dreams unconsciously erupts: "Oft have my thoughts, at midnight hour, / To him excursions made; / This bliss in dreams was premature, / And with my slumbers fled" (111). Such reverie is juxtaposed against the reality of the poet's situation: the presence of Jean Armour, Burns' wife, his riding accident, and the pain he suffers from a broken arm directly confront the milkmaid poet who initially appears awestruck. It is not just Burns who has fallen and suffers pain; Janet Little has fallen. Hence her multivalenced sentiments about human fate comprising "alternate joy and wo" and, perhaps more to the point, her erotic, anguishing last stanza: "With beating breast I view'd the bard; / All trembling did him greet: / With sighs bewail'd his fate so hard, / Whose notes were ever sweet" (112). Her boldness and delight in watching this domestic scenario of pain and intimacy, with the implication of a cathected relationship with Burns, underscores the richness of Little's relationship with Burns, a relationship that manifests personal attraction, nationalist sentiment, and cultural attachments to an eminent compatriot.

* * * * * * * *

An early female cultural activist with an intricate public self-representation, Janet Little recognizes the frailty of her social position and takes pride in her gender. She voices herself into the public arena—in some senses—as representative: as a cottar's daughter, a laboring-class woman, a servant, a dairy supervisor, and a poet. But just as much to the point, as an upholder of the Kirk who privileges laboring class values, Janet Little seems to have tolerated a difficult relationship with her famed ploughman-compatriot, Robert Burns. Given Burns' popularity, however, even a fantasy of opposition to the local hero was scarcely permitted. Moreover, Little needed to sustain friendships with affluent people, her class antagonists—though not necessarily personal ones—to bolster her standing as an artist. She prides herself on her art and is prepared to fight for acceptance or a chance to display it. To negotiate these varying vantage points, Little employs a form of dialectical reasoning by expressing difference while forging several informal alliances. She creates a counter-discourse that allows for substantial slippage of meaning and a fluid political perspective. She subtly sides with Robert Burns against the aristocracy but rejects his free relations with women.

Thus, despite her Presbyterian frame of mind that took umbrage at Burns' high jinks and anti-Kirk machinations, Janet Little guarded her opinions; her praise of Burns' genius allowed her to move easily between the poles of conservatism and less conventional assertions of gender and class equality. As a laboring woman and a poet, her cultural solidarity with Burns challenged conservative values that were opposed to class interests that she had assimilated. The reservations she expressed about Burns enable her to attack class superiors indirectly.

Little's use of plural discourses, from pastoral to polemic, preserves social and political flexibility. While appearing to internalize her position as a servant underwriting orthodox opinions, she concurrently subverts domination by aristocrats through exposing their corruption in diverse ways and using conventional deference to her own advantage. She feels acutely a certain female exclusion on the part of Burns. But even Little's low-key scoffing has its limits. Inevitably, her poems betray traces of an elite culture's influence, for her class position denies her aesthetic freedom.

How did she feel, we wonder, soliciting help from Burns and Boswell, relying on Dunlop for diverse favors, and then petitioning a twelve-year-old countess to clear the ground for publication? Since this triumvirate represents quite antinomic sets of values, Janet Little is obliged to navigate through rather diverse ideological waters, the Scylla of arch conservatism on one side, the Charybdis of fornication (which Little deplores) and competition on the other. Individually, these supporters and patrons reflect a many-sided self that she can develop; collectively, they deny her rights and expropriate her freedom.

As a self-styled "crazy scribbling lass" fused with a "rustic damsel," notwithstanding her pragmatic use of passivity, Little cannot efface the textual influences of those she is obliged to placate and those she seeks to condemn.[35] But she is used to such complexity, even inured. Like Burns, she espouses unorthodox religious views; she is a dissenter in Presbyterian Scotland, a follower of the famed secessionist, the Reverend Ebenezer Erskine.[36] As a Burgher, liminality is part and parcel of her life. She always functions as a maid and a woman with limited resources at her disposal for dissolving certain vantage points. In several poems, she presents herself modestly to preserve the "correct" demeanour expected of her. In the final poem in the volume, "To A Lady Who Sent the Author Some Paper With a Reading of Sillar's Poems," again self-deprecatingly she denotes herself as untalented—like David Sillar, one of Burns' working-class imitators—while still rather disarmingly, and perhaps with a self-effacing wit, reaffirming the fact that this poem is the last in a two-hundred-plus-page volume. "But, madam, the Muses are fled far away, / They deem it disgrace with a milkmaid to stay." She proclaims, somewhat wryly, that she will cease being a poet: "And left with such dunces as these I number'd, / The task I will drop, nor with verse be incumber'd; / Tho' pen, ink and paper, are by me in store, / O madam excuse, for I ne'er shall write more" (207).

Gender, too, denies her the mobility of Burns, while Burns' bravado inspires and to some extent enables the possibility of her texts in the first place. Taking a stance against the abuse of women produces a sense of gendered class solidarity while facilitating a construction of self that cannot be denied.

Little thus saturates her poems with coiled messages and concerns, some overt, some submerged, due to her status as a woman from the laboring class who aims to enter the public arena of letters. She occupies multiple though conflicted and assailable positions that overlap, coalesce, and separate, concurrently closed and open-minded, at once involuntary and controlled. Little's matrix of values and her social conditioning, in other words, yield deep and understandable tensions and double-edged meanings. At another level, attuned to the economic and cultural precariousness of her life, Janet Little appears as an agent of traditional values, simultaneously dedicated to hierarchy and exclusion, complicitous in one way or another with those who socially dominate her.[37]

While allying herself with labor and against gender exploitation, she joins battle on both fronts, recognizing Burns as a class ally, as a male who psychosexually moves her. Besides, Janet Little desires standing as an artist and is prepared to struggle for acceptance and a chance to display her abilities. She marks her poems with the signs of a revolutionary era and a laboring woman in complex and ultimately irreconcilable cultural positions.

NOTES

1. James Patterson, *The Contemporaries of Burns and The More Recent Poets of Ayrshire* (Edinburgh: Adam Hugh Paton, 1840).
2. *Robert Burns and Mrs. Dunlop. Correspondence Now Published in Full for the First Time*, ed. William Wallace, 2 vols. (New York: Dodd, Mead, and Company, 1898), 1:190. It was probably not as easy for laboring women to be as literate as men in the eighteenth century, although the myth of Scottish poverty tied to literacy has long been laid to rest. See James Kinsley, ed., *The Poems and Songs of Robert Burns*, vol. 3, (Oxford: Clarendon Press, 1968), 973. For details of Scottish education at the time of Burns and Little, see Alexander Law, "Scottish Schoolbooks of the

Eighteenth and Nineteenth Centuries," *Studies in Scottish Literature*, ed. G. Ross Roy, vol. 28 (Columbia: University of South Carolina, 1983), 1–32.

3. In 1789, Susan Dunlop had married a French refugee and landed proprietor, James Henri, earl of Loudon. For the countess' lineage, see *The Complete Peerage of George Edward Cokayne*, revised and enlarged by Vicary Gibbs (London: St. Catherine Press, 1932), 8:163. Robert Burns and his brother Gilbert had an indirect connection with the earl of Loudon through their sublease of Mossgiel Farm.

4. J. D. Mackie, *A History of Scotland* (Middlesex: Penguin Books Ltd., 1964), 319. The cost of living in Ayrshire doubled between 1740 and 1790. With butter at 9d. a pound, Janet Little's job was invaluable. See Marjorie Plant, *The Domestic Life of Scotland in the Eighteenth Century* (Edinburgh: Edinburgh University Press, 1952), 109. See also John Strawhorn, *Ayrshire in the Time of Burns*, (Ayr, Scotland: Archaelogical Natural History Society, 1959); James Handley, *The Agricultural Revolution in Scotland* (London: Faber & Faber Limited, 1953); William Fullarton, *General View of the Agriculture of the County of Ayr, with Observations on the Means of Its Improvement* (Edinburgh: Printed by John Paterson, 1793); Ivy Pinchbeck, *Women Workers and the Industrial Revolution 1750–1850* (New York: F. S. Crofts & Co., 1930), 10–26.

5. Janet Little, *The Poetical Works of Janet Little. The Scotch Milkmaid* (Ayr, Scotland: John & Peter Wilson, 1792). All references will be to this edition. Please note this edition is mispaginated.

6. James Kinsley calls Burns' humble description of himself in the preface to his poems a "calculatèd appeal to critical orthodoxy," *The Poems and Songs*, 972; David Daiches notes his "deliberate public appearance." See *Robert Burns* (New York: Macmillan, 1966), 103; A. M. Kinghorn talks of Burns' striking a pose, "The Literary and Historical Origins of the Burns' Myth," *Dalhousie Review* 39 (1959): 76–85. On the other hand, James Currie quotes Dugald Steward on the range of Burns' early education. See Kinsley "Contemporary Impressions of Robert Burns" in *The Poems and Songs*, 1535. For an English standandization of Burns' cultural self-portrait, see Robert Southey, *The Lives and Works of the Uneducated Poets*, ed. J. S. Childers (London: 1925). For Burns' instant popularity with the cross-class British public, see Kinsley, *The Poems and Songs*, 975–76.

7. David Craig, *Scottish Literature and the Scottish People 1630–1830* (London: Chatto and Windus, 1961), 117; Patterson, *The Contemporaries of Burns*, 83; for further discussion of the contention that the popularity of vernacular poems is separate from quality, see Carol McGuirk, *Robert Burns and the Sentimental Era* (Athens: University of Georgia Press, 1985), 35–37.

8. Frank Brady, *James Boswell. The Later Years 1769–1795* (New York: McGraw-Hill Book Company, 1984), 464. Countess of Loudoun in *The Scots Peerage Founded on Wood's Edition of Sir Robert Douglas's Peerage of Scotland*, ed. Sir James Balfour Paul, LLD, Lord Lyon King of Arms (Edinburgh: D. Douglas, 1904–14). For details of the Loudoun family, see also Strawhorn, *Ayrshire*, 39–40 and passim.

9. Janet Little's identification with Robert Burns is always, at least, on the basis of their relatively similar class backgrounds. Donna Landry addresses

Little's concerns as a laboring-class woman in *The Muses Of Resistance. Laboring-Class Women's Poetry in Britain, 1739–1796* (Cambridge: Cambridge University Press, 1990), 220–57. For a general class context, see also E. P. Thompson, "Patrician Society, Plebian Culture," *Journal of Social History* (Summer 1974): 382–405. The poverty Burns experienced growing up and his consequent efforts to help class equals like Janet Little is well documented in John C. Weston "Robert Burns' Satire," in *The Art of Robert Burns*, ed. R. D. S. Jack and Andrew Noble (New York: Vision and Barnes and Noble, 1982), 53. Burns had one noble patron, the earl of Glencairn, but received no sinecure. See J. DeLancey Ferguson, *Pride and Passion: Robert Burns* (New York: Oxford University Press, 1939), 98–101. Before his marriage, Burns had a child with Elizabeth Paton whom he supported, the child being reared by his mother. He had at least three subsequent children with other women while he was married to Jean Armour. The two daughters who survived were reared in his own family. In "The Court of Equity," Burns discusses male responsibility in sexual matters outside marriage. Although there is abundant evidence to suggest that Burns' sexual relationships were consensual, Little seems to assume a very traditional view of Burns' relationships, not unlike the early view of Jean Armour's parents.

10. *Robert Burns and Mrs. Dunlop: Correspondence*, 1:80.
11. Craig, *Scottish Literature*, 110. See also T. C. Smout, *A History of the Scottish People 1560–1650* (London: Collins, 1969), 302–8.
12. Robert T. Fitzhugh, *Robert Burns: The Man and the Poet. A Round, Unvarnished Account* (Boston: Houghton Mifflin Company, 1970), 202. For public support for national leaders, see *Ancient Laws and Customs of the Burghs of Scotland* (Burgh Records Society), preface, xlix. For Burns' pro-working class sentiments, see also Thomas Johnston, *The History of the Working Class in Scotland* (Yorkshire: EP Publishing Ltd., Rowman & Littlefield, 1974), 61.
13. I am not suggesting that Little is responding to Burns' poem "For a' That," as it was written after her publication; rather, that his poem encapsulated the sentiments which struck fear in people following the French and San Domingan revolutions in 1789 and 1791. Burns himself recanted. See T. M. Devine, "The Failure of Radical Reformism in Scotland in the Late Eighteenth Century: The Social and Economic Context," *Conflict and Stability in Scottish Society*, Proceedings of the Scottish Historical Studies Seminar, University of Strathclyde 1988–89, ed. T. M. Devine (Edinburgh: John Donald Publishers, Ltd., 1990), 59. During the French Revolution, a "police atmosphere" pervaded Scotland. Craig, *Scottish Literature*, 90. For Burns' views on the French Revolution and reaction to them, see Johnson, *The History of the Working Class in Scotland*, 222.
14. See below, n. 25.
15. Given the popularity and wide circulation of Johnson's *Lives of the Poets* and the controversay over John Bell's multiple volumes of *The Poets of Great Britain*, printed in Edinburgh, Janet Little had easy access to Johnson's *Lives*, if only though Mrs. Dunlop's collection. See Thomas F. Bonnell, "John Bell's *Poets of Great Britain*: The "Little Trifling Edition," *Modern Philology* 85 (November 1987): 128–52.

16. Craig, *Scottish Literature*, 57, 62–63.

17. Frances Dunlop comments on Janet Little to Burns on several occasions with a view, it seems, of securing Burns' good opinion of Janet Little. She states that: "Jenny Little . . . has wrote some things of late that I would have sent you . . . She says ten guineas would make her as happy as worldly circumstances could do . . . were her rhymes properly put out, as . . . she might be made happy and indebted to none but herself, since her modest wishes are placed within humble bounds." Janet Little might well have been aware of Mrs. Dunlop's superciliousness mixed with concern. Dunlop goes on:

> She is industrious, and seems good-temper'd and discreet, but betrays no one indication that I could discover of ever having opened a book or tagged a rhyme; so that I hope she will not be less happy for having tryed it . . . . Tell me what you think of Jenny Little's "Looking Glass." The occasion on which she wrote it was to convince a young lady who doubted the authenticity of her having wrote something else she had shewed her, and asked her to write on a given subject. She said she had never done so, but, since she wished it, would try if she would give her one. She told me she had that forenoon broke a glass she was vext about, and bid her celebrate it. (*Robert Burns and Mrs. Dunlop: Correspondence* 1:102–3, 274)

DeLancey Ferguson suggests Dunlop saw "no *essential* difference between [Robert Burns] and Janet Little." *Pride and Passion*, 159.

18. J. DeLancey Ferguson, *The Letters of Robert Burns*, 2nd ed., ed. G. Ross Roy (Oxford: Clarendon Press, 1985) 1:438.

19. *Robert Burns and Mrs. Dunlop: Correspondence* 2:242. In critiquing her poems, Robert Burns may well have been trying to help her. He operated similarly toward male poet-friends, virtually rewriting John Lapraik's.

20. Ibid. 1:96, 274.

21. David Daiches, *Robert Burns*, 104.

22. Patterson, *The Contemporaries of Burns*, 88.

23. Daiches, *Robert Burns*, 75. John Ramsay records that Burns referred to himself as a "Jacobite, an Arminian, and a Socinian." John Ramsay, *Scotland and Scotsmen in Eighteenth Century* (Edinburgh and London: William Blackwood and Sons, 1888), 554. See also John C. Weston, "Robert Burns' Satire," in *The Art of Robert Burns*, ed. R. D. S. Jack and Andrew Noble (New York: Vision & Barnes and Noble, 1982), 53.

24. Craig, *Scottish Literature*, 125. In a letter to Mrs. Dunlop, Burns spoke about his "sentiments respecting the present two great Parties that divide our Scots Ecclesiastics.—I do not care three farthings for Commentators and authorities." Ferguson, *The Letters of Robert Burns*, 1:422. See also J. H. S. Burleigh, *A Church History of Scotland* (London: Oxford University Press, 1960), 323.

25. Fitzhugh, *Robert Burns*, 68. Previously the Kirk Session had denounced Gavin Hamilton, Burns' friend and landlord, for "breaking the Sabbath" and for "contumacy." Little mentions Gavin Hamilton somewhat ambiguously in her poem about the Scottish literary tradition, "Given to a Lady." In "Holy Willie's Prayer," Burns ridiculed this censure that Gavin Hamilton subsequently and successfully appealed. This title appears only in the Alloway Ms. The other title is "A Poet's Welcome to his love-begotten Daughter" (Glenriddell MS); "Address to an Illegitimate Child" (Stewart,

1801). Thomas Crawford discusses Burns' response in verse to religious controversies in Mauchline parish. Thomas Crawford, *Burns. A Study of the Poems and Songs* (Stanford: Stanford University Press, 1960), 67–69. Note also that negative narratives to Burns' public behavior are manufactured after his political opinions became controversial. See Donald Low, ed. *Robert Burns: The Critical Heritage* (London: Routledge & Kegan Hall, 1974).

26. I am indebted here and elsewhere in the article to David Morris' study of Burns' poems from a Bakhtinian point of view, especially the idea that conflict in diction bespeaks social conflict. David Morris, "Burns and Heteroglossia," in *The Eighteenth Century: Theory and Interpretation* (Winter, 1987): 3–27.

27. *Princeton Encyclopedia of Poetry and Poetics*, ed. Alex Preminger (Princeton: Princeton University Press, 1965), 606.

28. Eric Smith, *A Dictionary of Classical References in English Poetry* (Cambridge: D. S. Brewer, 1984), 76.

29. See Morris, "Burns and Heteroglossia"; see also Alexander Warrack, *Scots Dictionary serving as a glossary for Ramsay, Fergusson, Burns, Galt, minor poets, kailyard novelists, and a host of other writers of the Scottish tongue* (1911; reprint, University of Alabama Press, 1965), 427; and William Graham, *The Scots Word Book* (Edinburgh: The Ramsay Head Press, 1977), 165.

30. Burns' relationship to women has frequently been distorted due to inaccuracies in an earlier biography by James Currie. In 1793, Burns is said to have given verbal offense to Elizabeth Riddell, wife of Robert Riddell. Burns was rumored to be having an affair with her. The Riddell family coldshouldered Burns from then on, despite Burns' letter of apology sent the following day. See Ferguson, *The Letters of Robert Burns*, 2:473. For a reevaluation of Currie's biography, see Fitzhugh, *Robert Burns*, especially 91–111.

31. *Robert Burns and Mrs. Dunlop: Correspondence*, xiv–xv.

32. Landry, *Muses of Resistance*, 230–37. Janet Little, for example, had no access to the cultural society of freemasons, with its secret and comforting promotion of comradely feeling and tacit sympathy among like-minded members. See Douglas Knoop, *An Introduction to Freemasonry* (Manchester: Manchester University Press, 1937).

33. Bridget Hill, *Women, Work, and Sexual Politics in Eighteenth-Century England* (Oxford: Basil Blackwell, 1989), 146; Fitzhugh, *Robert Burns*, 70.

34. Strawhorn, *Ayrshire*, 142; Fitzhugh, *Robert Burns*, 75. For Burns' relationship with women, see also Hilton Brown, *There Was a Lad* (London: Hamish Hamilton, 1949), especially 103–65.

35. "On Seeing Mr. —— Baking Cakes," 170, and "To the Public," 29. If she were Janet Nicol, she would have no such dilemma. In her poem to Janet Nicol, rather ambiguously entitled "A Poem on Contentment. Inscribed to Janet Nicol, a Poor Old Wandering Woman, Who Lives by the Wall at Loudoun and Used Sometimes to Be Visited by the Countess" (173), Little addresses her namesake Janet Nicol and imbricates her dilemma as a woman and as a poet. Little informs Nicol how lucky she is to avoid snares set for

females. In particular, she congratulates her for never feeling the pain "we heedless scribbling fools sustain."

36. In 1737, Janet Little's Parish Kirk in Galston, south of the river Irvine, became part of a Scottish-style secession from the Church of Scotland, led by the Reverend Ebenezer Erskine. For historical and geographical details about Galston and Erskine, see Robert Chambers, *A Biographical Dictionary of Eminent Scotsman.*, new ed., edited Thomas Thomson (1855; reprint New York: Georg Olms Verlag, 1971).

37. Janet Little, for example, finds some alternative ways of relating to the men and women around her, most notably through tender friendships. Peppering her volume with poems to friends, she acknowledges that while happiness continually eludes us like disappearing "snows on Ailsa falling," love for a friend is incomparable. Hence separation is one of the sharpest pains:

> I have lost no valu'd charter,
> Nor lament a fickle swain;
> But, alas! a friend's departure,
> Fills my heart with piercing pain.
>
> Pond'ring sharpens ev'ry arrow,
> Sighing but augments my grief:
> Now I mourn, o'erwhelm'd with sorrow,
> But next hour May bring relief.
>   (105)

Smith's The Theory of Moral Sentiments: Sympathy, Women, and Emulation

MAUREEN HARKIN

Of the diverse questions engaged by the discourse on sympathy in eighteenth-century Britain, it is the function, or ambition, of sympathy to promote social cohesion and to provide a support to prevailing social conditions, which has dominated most recent critical attention to this discourse. Among critics attempting to link the works of theorists like Adam Smith and David Hume to both social practice and aesthetic (especially literary) production,[1] Smith's *The Theory of Moral Sentiments* (1759) occupies a position of eminence, a position which owes something to Smith's status as the author of the *Wealth of Nations*, as well as to the complexity of the *Theory*'s model of sympathy, and to its contemporary success.[2] Most of these recent discussions have tended to view Smith's concept of sympathy as essentially providing a principle of virtue adapted for a commercial society. In Nicholas Phillipson's representative account, for example, the propensity to sympathize with the joys and misfortunes of one's fellows provides a useful, even necessary counter to the atomizing tendencies of the society of self-interested traders and "higglers" of Smith's economic theory. The *Theory* is described as articulating "a system of social bonding based on sympathy," one which "would be of [more] use to . . . men of middling rank, living in a modern, commercial society . . . than the libertarian civic virtues of the classical republican."[3]

Absent from analyses such as Phillipson's is a consideration of the place of women in Smith's schema, an omission all the more surprising in that Smith makes frequent reference to their role. In opposition to readings which privilege the production of community through sympathy, feminist criticism of Smith has highlighted the restrictions and divisions effectively imposed by a notion of community based on sympathy between men. Here the emphasis has been on Smith's exclusion of women from the practice of this social virtue,[4] either because they are unable to compel a properly public acknowledgment of their efforts or fail to exercise the rigor and self-discipline necessary to virtue. Lucinda Cole, tracking the numerous instances in Smith's text of criticism and distaste for what passes for virtue among women, concludes that Smithian sympathy is confined to men, based on the "resemblance and mutual admiration of (upwardly mobile) men for each other," and that it underpins a "homosocial vision of community"[5] where women drop out entirely from the circuit of social exchange.

In raising questions about the nature of political community and the gendering of Smith's constructions, Phillipson, Cole, and others open paths for future work; yet, I would argue, they also make a fundamental miscalculation about Smith's position. Investing in the stereotype of Smith as zealous and unwavering prophet of a new moral order founded on commercialism and reading the *Theory*, in effect, as companion volume and groundwork for the more confident assessment of the benefits of commercialism in *The Wealth of Nations*, these accounts either ignore Smith's doubts about the pernicious aspects of sympathy, or attempt to resolve these doubts by dividing sympathy into a higher, masculine form and a feminine subvariant, designated "excessive sympathy."[6] It is my contention that neither of these readings allow for the complexity of Smith's early analysis of the mechanisms of social order, or acknowledge the unease pervading his study of sympathy, which for Smith is always at least potentially "excessive." Represented by Smith as simultaneously providing a socially useful, bonding force and as a feminine and disruptive response, sympathy is by no means a characteristically male phenomenon which helps maintain social order. Rather, drawing from eighteenth-century discourse on women and the novel, Smith repeatedly defines sympathy as an essentially feminine tendency to imaginatively recreate the experience of others, an impulse at work in all kinds of social exchange, that requires certain mechanisms of control.[7]

Smith's concept of sympathy, in short, should be read as an attempt to describe some of the forces animating a commercial and consumerist age, rather than as a putative solution to the problem of conflicting personal and class interests or a way of ex(or)cising women from social exchange. It is the recurrent image of a typically feminine compulsion to sympathetic emulation as the heart of social and commercial life that makes the *Theory* something quite other than a blueprint for "men in a commercial society." In this essay I will note some of the ways in which sympathy and the feminine intersect in the *Theory* to complicate readings of the *Theory* as a system of practical morality, demonstrating that both endorsements and critiques of the success of Smith as architect of community have relied on a too unproblematic notion of what, for Smith, constitutes that community.

* * * * * * * * *

Like Hume in *A Treatise of Human Nature,* Smith posits sympathy as the foundation of morality[8] in the system of ethics described in *The Theory of Moral Sentiments.* It motivates the concern for and behaviour toward others that Smith describes via the sense of "propriety," a "direct sympathy with the affections and motives of the person who acts," and of "merit," an "indirect sympathy with the gratitude of the person who . . . is acted upon" (*TMS,* 74). However, though it plays such an important part in Smith's scheme, the status of sympathy as a solution to fundamental epistemological and moral questions—how do we know what others feel? how should we act towards others?—is less assured than in Hume, who asserts that, "No quality of human nature is more remarkable . . . than that propensity we have to sympathize with others, and to receive by communication their inclinations and sentiments, however different from, or contrary to our own. . . . [B]y sympathy . . . the . . . idea [of another's passions] is presently converted into an impression, and acquires such a degree of force and vivacity, as to become the very passion itself" (*THN,* 316–17). Smith's account of the sympathetic recreation of the sentiments of others exhibits considerably less confidence than Hume's that the copy thus produced will be either a strong or faithful one. Sympathy, rather than transmitting an exact copy of the sentiments of another, is the more or less faulty means by which we solve the problem of our ignorance of these sentiments, by representing in our imagination copies of what we would feel in that person's place. In the opening lines of the *Treatise,* Smith provides a striking example of the workings of sympathy in the spectacle of the man on the rack:

> As we have no immediate experience of what other men feel, we can form no idea of the manner in which they are affected, but by conceiving what we ourselves should feel in the like situation. Though our brother is upon the rack, as long as we ourselves are at our ease, our senses will never inform us of what he suffers. They never did, and never can carry us beyond our own person, and it is by the imagination only that we can form any conception of what are his sensations. Neither can that faculty help us to this any other way, than by representing to us what would be our own, if we were in his case. It is by the impressions of our own senses only, not those of his, which our imaginations copy. By the imagination we place ourselves in his situation, we conceive ourselves enduring all the same torments, we enter as it were into his body, and become in some measure the same person with him, and thence form some idea of his sensations, and even feel something which, though weaker in degree, is not altogether unlike them. His agonies, when they are thus brought home to ourselves, when we have thus adopted and made them our own, begin at last to affect us, and we then tremble and shudder at the thought of what he feels. For as to be in pain or distress of any kind excites the most excessive sorrow, so to conceive or to imagine that we are in it, excites

some degree of the same emotion, in proportion to the vivacity or
dulness of the conception. (*TMS*, 9)

Hume's metaphor of the "mirror of sympathy"[9] is replaced in Smith by
the notion of the observing subject's imaginative representation of the
experiences of others: representations that have weaker, and far less certain
ties to the original, at least in the case of sympathy with misfortune.
Smith's concept of sympathy, it should be noted, is not limited to cases of
pity for victims. His account indeed emphasizes fellow-feeling with good
fortune (*TMS*, 50), here following Hume's long discussion in the *Treatise*,
"Of Our Esteem for the Rich and Powerful,"[10] a form of sympathy, which,
as will become clearer, is beset with far fewer obstacles. But in opening his
treatise with this arresting image of the beholder's response to a victim of
torture,[11] Smith evidently seeks to dramatize the discrepancies between the
sentiments of observer and observed in the scenes of distress.

The workings of sympathy, as derived from this tableau, have a further
dimension. Sympathy towards another is not limited to the observer; the
sufferer too, makes an effort to enter into, or recreate the sentiments of the
spectators: "To see the emotions of [the spectators'] hearts . . . beat time to
his own . . . constitutes [the sufferer's] sole consolation. But he can only
hope to obtain this by lowering his passion to that pitch, in which the
spectators are capable of going along with him" (*TMS*, 22). Both parties
endeavour to adjust their sentiments to those of the other, motivated by an
apparent need for sympathetic communion. Ideally a third, median point is
attained: "The propriety of every passion excited by objects peculiarly
related to ourselves, the pitch which the spectator can go along with, must
lie, it is evident, in a certain mediocrity" (*TMS*, 27).

The attempt, however, which observer and observed make to approximate
as closely as each can the sentiments of the other, is clearly unequal. This
results in two kinds of virtuous effort. The attempt made by the bystander
to enter into the sentiments of the sufferer require only that he or she
imagine the sentiments likely to be experienced by the other. This effort
produces "the soft, the gentle, the amiable virtues, the virtues of candid
condescension and indulgent humanity" (*TMS*, 23). The greater effort made
by the sufferer, to imagine the feelings of a witness and then, out of a kind
of consideration of the limits of the observer's sympathetic capacity, to
moderate the expression of his suffering, underlies "the great, the awful and
respectable, the virtues of self-denial, of self-government, of that command
of the passions which subjects all the movements of our nature to what our
own dignity and honour, and the propriety of our own conduct require"
(*TMS*, 23). Smith's distinction, apart from echoing Hume's distinction on
the amiable and awful characters of Caesar and Cato (*THN*, 607), also recalls
Edmund Burke's discussion of virtue in his *Philosophical Enquiry into the
Origin of Our Ideas of the Sublime and the Beautiful* published two years
earlier. Burke's sublime virtues, such as fortitude, justice and wisdom,
which "produce terror rather than love," are associated with "the authority of

a father," and contrast with the lesser, "softer," "amiable," or beautiful virtues, which include "easiness of temper, compassion, kindness and liberality," typified in a "mother's fondness and indulgence."[12] The parallel with Burke's division of virtues along such lines further underlines Smith's obvious gendering of these "amiable" and "great" virtues. The terms in which he describes the two kinds of virtues establish the observer's sentiments of compassion as feminine, while the "awful" sentiments of the sufferer, or object of her sympathetic gaze, are given masculine status.

Smith's argument, then, is that the ability or inclination to feel intense sympathy for others, especially in scenes of distress, is a feminine response, while the ability to combine this with great self-restraint, to be a sensitive spectator of the distresses of others even when the natural object of all spectatorial sympathy, is typically masculine. His representation of the greater effort required in such self-restraint and consideration for the feelings of the spectator, compared to mere sympathy, clearly undermines the claim for sympathy as a virtue.

This gendering of virtues is explicit in Smith's remarks on humanity and generosity:

> Humanity is the virtue of a woman, generosity of a man. The fair-sex, who have commonly much more tenderness than ours, have seldom so much generosity. That women rarely make considerable donations, is an observation of the civil law. Humanity consists merely in the exquisite fellow-feeling which the spectator entertains with the sentiments of the persons principally concerned, so as to grieve for their sufferings, to resent their injuries, and to rejoice at their good fortune. The most humane actions require no self-denial, no self-command, no great exertion of the sense of propriety. They consist only in doing what this exquisite sympathy would of its own accord prompt us to do. But it is otherwise with generosity. We never are generous except when in some respect we prefer some other person to ourselves, and sacrifice some great and important interest of our own to an equal interest of a friend or of a superior. The man who gives up his pretensions to an office that was the great object of his ambition, because he imagines that the services of another are better entitled to it; the man who exposes his life to defend that of his friend, which he judges to be of more importance; neither of them act from humanity, or because they feel more exquisitely what concerns that other person than what concerns themselves. They both consider those opposite interests, not in the light in which they naturally appear to themselves, but in that in which they apppear to others. . . . When to the interest of this other person, therefore, they sacrifice their own, they accommodate themselves to the sentiments of the spectator, and by an effort of magnanimity act according to those views of things which, they feel, must naturally occur to any third person. The soldier who throws away his life in order to defend that of his officer, would perhaps be but little affected by the death of that officer, if it should happen without any fault of his own. . . . But when he endeavours to act

so as to deserve applause, and to make the impartial spectator enter into the principles of his conduct, he feels, that to every body but himself, his own life is a trifle compared with that of his officer. (*TMS*, 190–91)

Humanity is nothing but the more or less effortless sympathetic recreation of the sentiments of another, while generosity is the result of a consideration of the situation from the perspective of an impartial spectator, and of the readiness to translate such an understanding into action, regardless of risk. Humanity or sympathy, therefore, is an inadequate basis for morality, too easily aroused and too cheaply indulged to be much respected. It is the virtue practised by niggardly women, who need make no gifts, no effort of self-restraint, nor risk any action. Masculine generosity accepts such duties, which the logic of the passage above transforms successively from charitable donations, into the sacrifice of ambition, and thence into martyrdom. Women's failure either to transform feelings into deeds, or to consider matters from the point of view of the impartial spectator marks sympathy as a lesser virtue. At this point, it may be added, any claim that sympathy forms the basis for a specifically homosocial bonding in Smith's schema is effectively undermined by the gendering of sympathy itself as feminine.[13]

Smith appears to believe that women's keen sympathy is divorced from action through a willed miserliness rather than incapacity. But his comments on the generous man who assumes the perspective of the impartial spectator, and acts acordingly, rather than following his own inclination or interest, suggest a second difference between male and female virtue, one based not on volition but on simple incapacity on the part of women. Smith's concept of the impartial spectator, which is given here as the second defining difference between feminine sympathy and masculine generosity, plays a crucial role in *The Theory of Moral Sentiments*. This figure constitutes a third, privileged spectator in the scene of sympathy, which, with its doubling of audience and spectacle is, as David Marshall has demonstrated, already a thoroughly theatrical one, criss-crossed with gazes.[14] Smith posits this figure as the ideal observer, who sees correctly how much distress, joy, indifference, and so forth, a given event actually warrants, because free of the immediate self-concern or partiality of either observed or observer. Moreover, it is the impartial spectator, rather than any prompting by sympathy, who dictates what appropriate, or moral action is to be taken. The impartial spectator acts as a judge of our actions towards others and reminds us of the relative insignificance of our own joys and woes (*TMS*, 83). It, or rather, he, is supposed to be "the ideal man within the breast," introjected by the moral subject (*TMS*, 148), the desire of pleasing whom inspires the most generous actions, the most severe self-restraint in spectator and object of the scene of sympathy alike.

> In order to defend ourselves from . . . partial judgments, we soon learn to set up in our own minds a judge between ourselves and those we live with. We conceive ourselves to be acting in the presence of a person quite candid and equitable, of one who has no particular relation either to ourselves, or to those whose interests are affected by our conduct, who is neither father, nor brother, nor friend either to them or to us, but is merely a man in general, an impartial spectator." (*TMS*, 129n)

This impartial spectator, this "judge" or "man within the breast" is a term of considerable complexity in Smith's text, though one which we cannot explore in detail here.[15] It is perhaps helpful to note, however, that, in distinguishing masculine virtue from feminine sympathy, the impartial spectator performs a function similar to the Freudian super-ego. Freud's conception of the super-ego as that part of the psyche which observes and judges the ego, taking the role which in earlier life was played by parental authority ("the installation of the super-ego can be described as a successful instance of identification with the parental agency"),[16] is also deployed to establish the essential deficiency of women as moral agents.[17]

In comparison with the self-denial and scrupulous adherence to the dictates of this impartial spectator in acts of generosity, sympathetic humanity appears as an easily and cheaply procured indulgence of inclination divorced from any consequences in action. The merely sympathetic spectator participates in an aesthetic rather than ethical practice, indulging her "exquisite fellow-feeling" as free from consequences or responsibility as if she were merely reading a fictitious account of suffering. Elsewhere in the *Theory* Smith tends to take a more benign view of the relation between aesthetics and ethics, seeing aesthetic pleasure in the possessions of the rich, for example, as a useful form of sympathy harnessing the energies of the less well-to-do which might otherwise find an outlet in critique or attack on social inequity (*TMS*, 179–83).[18] Here, however, Smith's formulations instead parallel the terms of contemporary debate about the response of readers, especially female readers, whose enjoyment of fictional representations of distress was the subject of voluminous, disapproving commentary: "[I]n these writings [picturing distress] our sensibility is strongly called forth without any possibility of exerting itself in virtuous action. . . . The being affected with a pathetic story is undoubtedly a sign of an amiable disposition, but perhaps no means of increasing it."[19]

Indeed, Smith's tendency to characterize feminine response to spectacles of suffering or pleasure as a simple two-term system of model and copy appears to owe a considerable debt to contemporary discourse on the novel. At the heart of the debate on the effects of novel- and romance-reading (the distinction between which was often seen as largely irrelevant to their common status as enticing fictions) by authors from Samuel Richardson to Hannah More is a claim about the tendency of the suggestible reader, characterized as the young of both sexes and women in general, to replicate the situations of figures from novels.[20] Some doubt has been cast on the evidence for the popular notion that women indeed constituted the majority of novel-readers, or that they preferred it to all other kinds of reading.[21] However, the supposed feminine affinity for fiction was proverbial, and in discussions of romances and especially novels, women were commonly described as all too inclined to construct imaginative simulacra of the fortunes of figures in novels, and worse, to act out the situations about which they had read. Johnson's discussion of the problem in the fourth number of the *Rambler* in 1750 lays out the familiar terms of the debate, stressing the novel's tendency to inspire imitation, and the force of such texts on the suggestible reader: "[Their] power of example is so great, as to take possession of the memory by a kind of violence, and produce effects almost without the intervention of the will."[22] Richardson's concern to create in Clarissa Harlowe an appropriate "Exemplar to her Sex"[23] for susceptible female readers, and the history of the attempts of Charlotte Lennox's naive heroine, Arabella, to re-enact episodes from romance in *The Female Quixote* (1752),[24] are further evidence that by the 1750s fears of a readerly "madness by romantic identification,"[25] so famously embodied in Cervantes' text, had come to be seen as a peculiarly feminine danger. The concern, repeatedly voiced in connection with women reading novels, as John Taylor observed in his study of early opposition to the novel, was that "a copy would produce an original":[26] a definition which clearly underlines the structural similarity of Smithian sympathy to well-established notions of the practice of susceptible female novel-readers.

This striking correspondence between Smith's conception of feminine "virtue" and the concerns of Richardson, Johnson, Lennox and others about women's tendencies to replicate fictional characters' experiences has been entirely overlooked in arguments about the appropriate context in which to view Smith's social theorizing about women and imitation.[27] The discourse on the novel, along with that on increasing consumerism in eighteenth-century Britain, repeatedly links compulsive imitation and women in mid-century literary and moral-philosophical debate, and indicates that the working of imaginative reconstruction and emulation was already a topic of general concern and investigation when Smith formulated his remarks.[28] Such anticipation of the structure of Smith's sympathy in these discourses should then signal that a practice as dependent on imaginative recreation of the situation of an other as sympathy is in the *Theory* is likely to generate unease as well as an interest in harnessing this emulative impulse for socially productive use.[29] Seen in this context, Smith's ambivalence about sympathetic emulation appears symptomatic of widespread anxieties about the effects of new forces and forms of interaction in a commercial society. It becomes even more difficult to see how recent studies of sympathy in Smith could ignore such fears in favor of an explanation of its function as a principle of (male) social bonding.

These new forces include developments in the sphere of commerce which produce noticeably greater anxiety than the effects of fiction, even in Smith.

For despite his reputation as a promoter of commercialization, a characterization based on *The Wealth of Nations*, Smith evidences considerable concern in the *Theory* about social mobility and other social changes associated with modernization. Here too sympathy functions as a force which, Smith allows, produces some social benefit, but which is not by nature necessarily useful or productive of social unity. This theme emerges in Smith's discussion of sympathy with the wealthy and influential, which, he argues, is a far more powerful force than sympathy with the distressed:

> [O]ur propensity to sympathize with joy is much stronger than our propensity to sympathize with sorrow; and . . . our fellow-feeling for the agreeable emotion approaches much more nearly to the vivacity of what is naturally felt by the persons principally concerned, than that which we conceive for the painful one. (*TMS*, 45)

> The spectator enters by sympathy into the sentiments of the master, and necessarily views [the master's possessions] under the same agreeable aspect. When we visit the palaces of the great, we cannot help conceiving the satisfaction we should enjoy if we ourselves were the masters, and were possessed of so much artful and ingeniously contrived accommodation. (*TMS*, 179)

Smith's argument evidently follows Hume, whose account of sympathy dwells on explaining the means of our satisfaction in the riches of others and only briefly remarks on sympathetic feeling for distress (*THN*, 362–71). Smith's assertion that the most likely trigger of sympathy is someone else's good fortune, wealth, or power echoes Hume's description of the vicarious pleasure the spectator is supposed to receive from surveying the possessions of the great.

This kind of sympathy with wealth, unlike the sentiments of passive humanity, or even of active generosity, drawn forth by the sight of distress, is described by Smith as the work of a wise Providence. Sympathy with the wealthy or powerful performs a socially useful task, first of all, by consolidating support for the social order: "The distinction of ranks, the peace and order of society, are, in a great measure, founded upon the respect which we naturally conceive for the [rich and powerful]. The relief and consolation of human misery depend altogether upon our compassion for the [poor and wretched]. The peace and order of society is of more importance than even the relief of the miserable" (*TMS*, 226). Thus sympathy with the great is a strong means for maintaining social hierarchy, allowing a vicarious enjoyment of the property and privileges of others (*TMS*, 179). Secondly, sympathy with the wealthy inspires an active response on the part of the spectator; not some act of generosity approved by the impartial spectator, but an emulation of the fortunate object of the subject's gaze. In order to attain such wealth and prominence, persons of low rank take on a share of labor and willingly endure hardships that benefit society as a whole. Their "patience, industry, fortitude, and application of thought" are highly useful to the state; especially as such qualities "are hardly ever to be met with in men who are born to . . . high stations. In all governments accordingly . . . the highest offices are generally possessed . . . by men who were educated in the middle and inferior ranks of of life, who have been carried forward by their own industry and abilities" (*TMS*, 56). Here Smith stresses the productive energies of individuals striving to better their lot in terms anticipating the *Wealth of Nations*.[30]

Yet Smith's account of this supposed sympathy with the wealthy, however useful in harnessing talent and industry, generates a number of serious problems for his account. Smith points out that the "fascination of greatness" may promote too much indulgence of the conduct of affairs by the prominent (*TMS*, 226). More importantly, his characterization of sympathetic emulation of the great suggests that its power far outstrips its social usefulness:

> It is from our disposition to admire, and consequently to imitate, the rich and the great, that they are enabled to set, or to lead what is called the fashion. Their dress is the fashionable dress; the language of their conversation, the fashionable style. . . . Even their vices and follies are fashionable; and the greater part of men are proud to resemble them in the very qualities which dishonour and degrade them. . . . [A vain man] . . . assumes the equipage and splendid way of living of his superiors, without considering that whatever may be praise-worthy in any of these, derives its whole merit and propriety from its suitableness to that situation and fortune which both require and can easily support the expence. . . . To attain to this envied situation [of the great], the candidates for fortune too frequently abandon the paths of virtue. (*TMS*, 64)

Sympathy with the great prompts a desire to imitate their enviable station that is quite independent of any necessary tie to larger social benefits. Smith's earlier account of the kind of emulation of the great practised by industrious men of low birth, pursuing greatness through diligent application, appears as a lengthy and unlikely detour compared to this imitation of upper-class fashions, profligacy, and vices. As described here, sympathetic emulation has an almost compulsive character: we admire, and consequently, we imitate the great. Smith's concern with such sympathetic imitation is clearly its operation independent of any regulating, moral force. It is indeed "apt to offend by its excess" (*TMS*, 226) and functions, as it were, without reference to an impartial spectator, one who would, among other things, presumably point out the qualifications to be met for maintaining an equipage. In fact, the major problem with the concept of sympathetic emulation of the wealthy in Smith is that, like the feminine virtue of "humanity," it is a two-term system, original and copy, lacking any mediating third term provided by the impartial spectator to limit or regulate its functioning. Hence its compulsive aspect. As with the model of humanity, the subject here merely reproduces, although this time through action rather than through imaginative recreation, the situation of the object of sympathy.

This two-term, feminine model for the workings of what Smith nominates as our strongest sympathetic response, that for the great, undermines Smith's moral schema and puts in question the basis of social cohesion, both disrupted by the more or less indiscriminate tendency toward duplication represented by sympathy. This tendency to emulation clearly troubles Smith, because of the blurring of social divisions and the mobility that it makes possible. In an apparent effort to neutralize the appeal of power and wealth that he elsewhere describes as such a powerful incentive to labor and display, Smith claims that between one permanent state and another there is generally very little difference, that the effort expended by the man of low birth to achieve eminence finally obtains for him a state little better than a tranquil acceptance of his own original station would have achieved, and that "wealth and greatness are mere trinkets of frivolous utility" (*TMS*, 180–81). Smith attempts to resolve the conflict apparent between this position and his other remarks on a generalized appetite for sympathy through his observation that it is less the actual experience of greatness than its appearance to spectators which attracts so strongly, continuing his theatrical or scopic metaphor: "we constantly pay more regard to the sentiments of the spectator, than to those of the person principally concerned, and consider rather how his situation will appear to other people, than how it will appear to himself" (*TMS*, 182). Smith's insistence, however, that the contentment to be found by accepting one's station in life is equal to anything to be earned by labor inspired by emulation, suggests, at this point in his argument, less conviction than a concern about the mobility that sympathetic emulation initiates. In his notable example, even a man with a wooden leg, will, by accepting his permanent situation be as happy as a man in any other condition (*TMS*, 148). In emphasizing the virtues and advantages of staying put, as it were, Smith highlights the very considerable movement across the barriers of class, or at least the signs of class, that accompanies sympathetic emulation.

Smith's account of the workings of sympathy, then, demonstrates a notable ambivalence about its value and power. While he indicates that it is insufficient to motivate acts of true (that is, self-restraining, self-sacrificing) virtue, it is evidently a formidable force motivating women and inspiring those of humble social rank to emulate the great. Given its force in these two groups, Smith's description of the limits of sympathy seems to be the product of his desire for such constraints, rather than an account of any evident boundaries. For Smith sympathy fails as a basis for virtuous action or community, and its role in maintaining social order is threatened by the very strength of the desires it generates.

To return to the critical issues raised at the beginning of this essay, studies of Smith's text and its account of an unstable, feminine principle of sympathy subtending social relations have heretofore overlooked the ambiguities and contradictions in the *Theory*, or attempted to resolve them by recourse to an oddly uncomplicated notion of homosociality.[31] Smith is credited with more success for a programmatic social statement than his own text claims. One reason for this is the tendency to read Smith's *Theory* as a complement to or basis for the economic theory of the *Wealth of Nations*. Without promoting a return to a reading of Smith which posits a complete break between the moral philosophy of the *Theory* and his writings on economics, it is helpful to pause at the assumption that Smith's early work must provide a consistent basis for (or counterforce to the self-interested independent agents of) the *Wealth of Nations*. In other words, sympathy does not underwrite a social contract in Smith.

Moreover, this notion of Smith ushering in a new age of confident commercialism, marking the rise, to borrow J. G. A. Pocock's terms, of "[nineteenth-century] economic man as masculine conquering hero," presents him as quelling (or at least confining within strict boundaries) every anticipated disturbance to social order, unlike his "feminised" eighteenth-century predecessor, "still wrestling with his own passions and hysterias."[32] As a careful reading of the *Theory* demonstrates, however, Smith, in the early phase of his social theorizing, was not only troubled by sympathetic emulation as a potentially explosive market and social force, and one only provisionally linked to productive labor, but at times expressed concerns very similar to the fears of earlier eighteenth-century commentators on economics—most famously exemplified in the vision of Credit as inconstant goddess in Addison's third *Spectator*. In showing how much sympathy in Smith depends on a notion of an excess coded as feminine and lower-class, I would suggest that a more satisfying account of Smith's work needs to take account of its contribution to the construction of notions of gender and class position beyond that of the prosperous male citizen. Smith's account of women as lacking in self-restraint and unable to govern their own passions clearly owes something to the anxieties projected onto women in earlier eighteenth-century literary and philosophical discourse;[33] but we need to further allow that Smith also incorporates these "passions and hysterias" as the engines of economic growth and the promoters of social rank in his *Theory*. Disturbing sympathies are not confined to the margins, but run all the way through Smith's system.

NOTES

1. See John Dwyer, *Virtuous Discourse: Sensibility and Community in Late Eighteenth-Century Scotland* (Edinburgh: John Donald, 1987), 168–85;

John Mullan, *Sentiment and Sociability: The Language of Feeling in the Eighteenth Century* (Oxford: Clarendon Press, 1988), 43–56, and "The Language of Sentiment: Hume, Smith and Henry Mackenzie," in Andrew Hook, ed., vol. 2 of *The History of Scottish Literature* (Aberdeen: Aberdeen University Press, 1987), 273–89; Nicholas Phillipson, "Adam Smith as Civic Moralist," in Istvan Hont and Michael Ignatieff, eds., *Wealth and Virtue: The Shaping of Political Economy in the Scottish Enlightenment* (Cambridge: Cambridge University Press, 1983), 179–202; Richard Teichgraeber, "Rethinking *Das Adam Smith Problem*," in John Dwyer et al., eds. *New Perspectives on the Politics and Culture of Early Modern Scotland* (Edinburgh: John Donald Publishers, 1982), 249–64. David Marshall's reading of the *Theory* represents a departure from this mode of approaching Smith and sympathy in its focus on the scope and theatrical aspects of Smith's "theater of sympathy," in *The Figure of Theater: Shaftesbury, Defoe, Adam Smith and George Eliot* (New York: Columbia University Press, 1986), 167–92.

2. Hume's exposition of sympathy in his notoriously neglected *A Treatise of Human Nature*, though reworked in his later writings, did not reach the same kind of audience as Smith's text, which went through six editions between 1759 and 1790. See Adam Smith, *The Theory of Moral Sentiments*, ed. D. D. Raphael and A. L. Macfie (Oxford: Clarendon Press, 1976), 1. All subsequent references are to this edition which will be cited in the text as *TMS*.

3. Adam Smith, *An Inquiry Into the Nature and Causes of the Wealth of Nations*, ed. R. H. Campbell, A. S. Skinner, and W. B. Todd, 2 vols. (Oxford: Oxford University Press, 1976), 1:26–27. Phillipson, "Adam Smith as Civic Moralist," 179, 188. See also Dwyer, *Virtuous Discourse*, 177–78. Teichgraeber's analysis of the old "Adam Smith problem," which posited a break between the assumptions of the *Theory* and those of his later *Wealth of Nations*, proposes a properly guided and controlled sympathy as supplying the partial basis for virtuous conduct in modern commercial life: "Rethinking *Das Adam Smith Problem*," 256–58. Mullan is the most attentive to certain obstacles to "sociability" presented by Smith's notion of sympathy. See *Sentiment and Sociability*, esp. 43–56.

4. Carol Kay, "Sympathy, Sex and Authority in Richardson and Hume," *Studies in Eighteenth-Century Culture*, vol. 12, ed. Harry C. Payne (Madison: University of Wisconsin Press, 1983), 86–87; Lucinda Cole, "(Anti)Feminist Sympathies: The Politics of Relationship in Smith, Wollstonecraft, and More," *ELH* 58 (1991): 107–40.

5. Cole, "(Anti)Feminist Sympathies," 109, 117.

6. Teichgraeber, "Rethinking *Das Adam Smith Problem*," 258.

7. This conception of women as given to sympathetic emotion was well established in contemporary discourse on women and the novel. See Geoffrey Day, *From Fiction to the Novel* (London: Routledge, 1987), esp. 111–55, and Ioan Williams, ed., *Novel and Romance 1700–1800: A Documentary Record* (New York: Barnes and Noble, 1970), 143, 279.

8. "[T]he principle of *sympathy* [is the means] by which we enter into the sentiments of the rich and poor, and partake of their pleasure and uneasiness. . . . [T]he soul or animating principle of [all passions] is

sympathy." David Hume, *A Treatise of Human Nature*, ed., L. A. Selby-
Bigge, 2d ed., revised P. H. Nidditch (Oxford: Oxford University Press,
1978), 362–63. All subsequent references to this edition will be citied in
the text as *THN*.

9. "In general we may remark, that the minds of men are mirrors to one
another, not only because they reflect each others [*sic*] emotions, but also
because those rays of passions, sentiments and opinions may be often
reverberated. . . . Thus [for example] the pleasure, which a rich man receives
from his possessions, being thrown upon the beholder, causes a pleasure
and esteem; which sentiments again, being perceiv'd and sympathiz'd with,
encrease the pleasure of the possessor." Ibid., 365. See also Annette
Baier's discussion of the strength of the principle of sympathy (compared
to other possible responses) in Hume's text, in *A Progress of Sentiments:
Reflections on Hume's "Treatise"* (Cambridge: Harvard University Press,
1991), 148–51.

10. See the discussion of the power of sympathy with the rich as opposed to the
weaker form activated in response to spectacles of poverty in Hume, *THN*,
357–65.

11. An earlier reader of this essay has pointed out the similarity between this
scene and the vision of a victim of the Inquisition in the second volume of
Tristram Shandy (published less than a year after Smith's text) which,
Sterne's annotators argue, shows a link between the discourse on sympathy
and Sterne's concerns as an author as early as 1759: "Behold this helpless
victim delivered up to his tormentors,—his body so wasted with sorrow and
confinement. . . . Consider the nature of the posture in which he now lies
stretched,—what exquisite tortures he endures by it!" *The Life and Opinions
of Tristram Shandy, Gentleman*, ed. Melvyn New et al., vols. 1–3 of *The
Florida Edition of the Works of Laurence Sterne* (Gainesville: University of
Florida, 1978–84), 1:162–63, 3:185.

12. Edmund Burke, *A Philosophical Enquiry into the Origin of our Ideas of the
Sublime and Beautiful*, ed. James T. Boulton (Notre Dame: University of
Notre Dame Press, 1968), 110–11.

13. See Cole, "(Anti)Feminist Sympathies," 110–17.

14. Marshall, *The Figure of Theater*, esp. 173–75.

15. See Vincent Hope's discussion in "Smith's Demigod," in Vincent Hope, ed.,
Philosophers of the Scottish Enlightenment (Edinburgh: Edinburgh University Press, 1984), 157–67. D. D. Raphael traces the development of the
concept in successive editions of the *Theory* in "The Impartial Spectator" in
Essays on Adam Smith, ed. Andrew Skinner (Oxford: Clarendon Press,
1975), 83–99.

16. Sigmund Freud, *New Introductory Lectures on Psycho-analysis*, trans. and
ed. James Strachey, vol. 22 of the *Standard Edition of the Complete
Psychological Works of Sigmund Freud*, (London: Hogarth Press, 1964),
63–64.

17. In Freud's schema women's lack of incentive and consequent failure to
surmount the Oedipus complex in the same way as men (whose fear of
castration causes them to lay the groundwork for the formation of the super-
ego) leaves their moral sense permanently underdeveloped and their
commitment to broader social ideals shaky: "[F]eminists are not pleased

when we point out to them the effects of this factor upon the average female character." Freud, *Standard Edition* 22:129.

18. See also editor's introduction to *The Theory of Moral Sentiments*, 13–14.

19. J. Aikin and A. L. Aikin (Mrs. Barbauld), excerpt from "An Enquiry into Those Kinds of Distress which excite Agreeable Sensations," quoted in Ioan Williams, *Novel and Romance*, 289.

20. See Day's survey of the main contributors to the debate in "Romances, Chocolate, Novels and the Like Inflamers," *From Fiction to the Novel*, esp. 121–32. Insofar as the novel was distinguished from the romance by such critics, it was seen as even more likely to promote emulation of the situation of fictional characters, because, picturing less fantastic personages and events, it was more likely to encourage sympathetic identification and imitation on the part of the reader: "In the romances formerly written, every transaction and sentiment was so remote from all that passes among men, that the reader was in very little danger of making any applications to himself; the virtues and crimes were equally beyond his scene of activity: and he amused himself with heroes . . . as with beings of another species. . . . But when an adventurer is levelled with the rest of the world, . . . young spectators fix their eyes upon him with closer attention, and hope, by observing his behavior and success, to regulate their own practices." Samuel Johnson, *Rambler* 4, March 31, 1750, in Williams, *Novel and Romance*, 144. James Fordyce echoes this argument in *Sermons to Young Women* (London, 1766), 144–56.

21. Paul Kaufman, *Libraries and Their Users: Collected Papers in Library History* (London: The Library Association, 1969), 223–27.

22. Samuel Johnson, *Rambler* 4, in Williams, *Novel and Romance*, 144. See also n. 21, above.

23. Samuel Richardson, preface to second edition of *Clarissa Harlowe* (1751), in Williams, *Novel and Romance*, 165. See also the discussion of Richardson's participation in the debate on the suggestible female reader, and the corresponding necessity he saw for novelists to provide moral exemplars in their texts in Day, *From Fiction to the Novel*, 131–36.

24. Charlotte Lennox, *The Female Quixote: or, The Adventures of Arabella*, ed. Margaret Dalziel (London: Oxford University Press, 1970).

25. Michel Foucault, *Madness and Civilization*, trans. Richard Howard (New York: Vintage Books, 1988), 28–29.

26. John Tinnon Taylor, *Early Opposition to the English Novel*, (New York: King's Crown Press in association with Columbia University Press, 1943), 69.

27. In particular, the attempt to establish Smith as continuing a tradition of humanist thought in Teichgraeber, "Rethinking Das Adam Smith Problem," 261–62; and the argument for Smith as inheritor of the voluntarist principles and civic morality of Addison in Phillipson, "Adam Smith as Civic Moralist," 188–90, 200–202.

28. The surveys of eighteenth-century concerns about the aping of various fashions by lower-class consumers provided by John Sekora and Neil McKendrick indicate the extent to which Smith's unease about the workings of sympathy intersect with a well-established conservative tradition of attacks on emulative consumerism. See John Sekora, *Luxury: The Concept in*

Western Thought, Eden to Smollett (Baltimore: Johns Hopkins University Press, 1977), 64–105; Neil McKendrick, J. H. Plumb, and John Brewer, *The Birth of a Consumer Society* (Bloomington: Indiana University Press, 1982), esp. 9–33.

29. Mullan correctly points out Smith's concern to regulate or limit the functioning of sympathy in "The Language of Sentiment," 286. His argument that "sympathy has to be controlled," however, makes no allowance for the manner in which sympathy tends to overrun such limits. See *Sentiment and Sociability*, 45–47.

30. Smith, *Wealth of Nations* 2:759-60.

31. Eve Kosofsky Sedgwick's original elaboration of homosociality, drawing on the work of René Girard and Claude Lévi-Strauss, notably emphasizes the instabilities and difficulties encompassed by this term, absent in Lucinda Cole's commentary. See Sedgewick, *Between Men: English Literature and Male Homosocial Desire* (New York: Columbia University Press, 1985), 1–5.

32. J. G. A. Pocock, *Virtue, Commerce and Industry* (Cambridge: Cambridge University Press, 1985), 114.

33. See Lennox, *The Female Quixote*, 380–81; and see Mary Poovey's discussion of the development, and continuing circulation of this notion of unrestrained female passions in later eighteenth-century discussions of women and literature, in *The Proper Lady and the Woman Writer* (Chicago: University of Chicago Press, 1984), 18–19.

The Pleasure of Business and the Business of Pleasure: Gender, Credit, and the South Sea Bubble

CATHERINE INGRASSIA

Defending his involvement in the South Sea Bubble before the House of Lords in 1721, Chancellor of the Exchequer John Aislabie denied that the preferential treatment he gave the South Sea Company was criminal. He said the decision to allow the company to assume the national debt (some 50 million pounds) and to repay lenders in stock rather than banknotes—a decision which contributed to the overselling of the stock and to its rapid rise and fall in value—had not been made deceptively. Rather, Aislabie claimed he was "visibly carried on with a Spirit very different from [his own] . . . suited to the Frenzy of the Times."[1] With the use of the term "frenzy," Aislabie attributed responsibility for his actions, and that of hundreds of speculators, to a moment of temporary insanity, an alternative state of mind. "Frenzy" associates speculative investment—financial ventures that depend on stocks, credit and the fluctuations of the marketplace—with hysteria, disorder and enthusiasm, distinctly transgressive impulses typically associated with females. In Aislabie's recounting of events, investors' excitement, indeed titillation, stemmed in part from a fascination with the mysterious possibilities of credit. The relatively new property, though intangible (for investors received only a symbolic representation of value in the form of stock certificates), laid the foundation for their willingness to believe in continuing, seemingly endless, future financial rewards. The untold possibilities of credit precipitated the formation of dozens of other joint-stock companies in early 1720, as well as the rapid rise in the value (and sale) of the South Sea Company stock. In January 1720, the stock stood at £178, and rose steadily until it peaked at £1100 in August.[2] But within less than a month the price of the stock plummeted to £190. Eager speculators who bought when the stock price was rising suddenly possessed nearly worthless pieces of paper.

The bursting of the South Sea Bubble confirmed the dire predictions of a variety of critics who, before and after the collapse, generated a discourse with constructions of gender and property that complicated the cultural implications of the South Sea Bubble and the activities of Exchange Alley. The verbal and visual representations of the South Sea Bubble portray participants either as "feminized" men, or as subversively empowered and sexually and financially rapacious women, all guided by fickle female goddesses who symbolically control the new economic world. The seepage of gendered oppositions into the world of stockjobbing and credit reveal the affinities between the cultural construction of fine ladies and the new economic man.

The apprehension created by the South Sea Bubble stemmed in part from the highly suspect nature of new types of increasingly dematerialized property. Investors had to construct imaginatively the relationship between sign, the stock certificate, and signified, its present and future monetary value; they essentially had to fantasize about the return on their investment. In *A Letter to a Conscientious Man* (1720), the author described speculative investment as "a Business founded upon nothing that is solid, rational, or honest, but meerly upon Artifice, Trick and Catch."[3] The symbolic and material role of women in the activities of Exchange Alley also fueled apprehension about the direction of the new financial world. Satiric representations emphasized the participation of "fine ladies" of the middling and upper classes who spent their pin money in the frenzied pursuit of a profitable investment and personal pleasure. Criticism of women's financial interests, like contemporaneous criticism of their fascination with popular fiction, confronted the spell these new imaginatively based pursuits cast over women's emotions and desires. While scholars have explored the role of women in the mercantile capitalist ideology, most recently Laura Brown with *Ends of Empire*, they have not addressed their equally important role in the representations of speculative investment and commercial capitalism.[4] The representations of the South Sea Bubble placed women symbolically and materially at the center of the crisis, as they warn of speculative investment's feminizing influence on culture as a whole.

* * * * * * * * *

J. G. A. Pocock has persuasively argued that in early eighteenth-century England, an "economic" man devoted to speculative financial activities was perceived as a feminized or even an "effeminate" being "still wrestling with his own passions and hysterias and with interior and exterior forces let loose by his fantasies and appetites." "Trading on expectations," economic man must rely on the imaginative forces necessary for financial investment in a fluctuating market, an environment where "production and exchange are regularly equated with the ascendancy of the passions and the female principle."[5] Unlike the essentially paternal and stable figure of the landed citizen, the economic man symbolically gives free rein to his passions and becomes susceptible to "frenzied" activities. By giving way to his appetites, the new economic man represented a stark departure from the Harringtonian model of civic humanism. Within the highly idealized and nostalgic discourse of civic humanism, the male citizen is "rendered independent by his property and permitted an autonomous engagement in public affairs."[6] By owning land, the citizen avoids a compromised or self-interested relationship with government, and contributes to the the moral economy and the political stability of the nation. In contrast to this idealized citizen motivated by virtue and rationality, the self-interested stockjobber abandons the land and the implicit tradition of civic humanism for a disordered and unstable world of paper credit and increasingly immaterial forms of property.

The author of *Some Considerations on the late Mismanagement of the South-Sea Stocks* (1721) condemns this disregard for tradition, honor, service and hospitality. He ponders what Britain's ancestors would think if they now saw

> their Descendants, instead of spending their Fortunes as they had done in the service of their Country, and instead of keeping up that antient Hospitality for which this Nation has been so famous; to see those, I say, who inherit their Honours and Estates, stockjobbing their estates in that Infamous Place called Exchange-Alley, and debasing the Honour of their Birth, in begging the Favour of a Subscription (to their own undoing) of such who were hardly company for their Footmen.[7]

The ancient laws of hospitality which strategically reassert the power and status of the landed citizen have been forsaken symbolically and literally. "Descendants" not only leave their traditional family estates but potentially gamble or "job" them away in the crowded confines of Exchange Alley. The geographic and ideological shift constricts and diminishes the male descendant by replacing the authority and identity of landed wealth with the anonymity of paper credit. The loss of status is compounded by the descendants' subordinate relationship to social inferiors to whom they debase themselves by "begging" favours. Such men, driven by the "itch of stockjobbing," abandon their traditional position to pursue a quick profit and the immediate pleasures of "sanctified gaming."

This "itch" not only diverts landed citizens from their traditional role, but it also distracts merchants from the stable values of trade, responsibility, and industry.[8] As described in *An Examination and Explanation of the South Sea Company's Scheme* (1720), stockjobbing constitutes a moral lapse

> that not only depraves, and debauches the Morals and Manners of Mankind, but turns them aside from pursuing their proper Business and Callings whereby they might maintain and enrich themselves and their families, as well as the Means of bringing Treasure into the Kingdom,

> and encouraging of the Manufactures of Great Britain, the Decay
> whereof is more owing to the Itch the People are fall into of
> Stockjobbing than to any other Cause whatsoever. [9]

In this representation, stockjobbing serves neither the kingdom's public nor the family's domestic good—it only satisfies the individual's "itch."

The shift from a world of tangible goods and property ("Treasures") to an invisible universe of paper credit, stock schemes, and intangible forces of the marketplace promotes the nation's decay. Stockjobbing also alters the terms of evaluative discourse; luxury goods, often regarded as the cause of moral lapse in their own right, gain new acceptance in the face of completely intangible kinds of property. Stockjobbing threatens to dissolve the social distinctions integral to society—footmen associate with landowners—and to divert individuals of all ranks from their appropriate and productive activities. The social and personal disorder created when specula-tors pursue passion, pleasure, and self-interest rather than the universal good threatens the social fabric and gender constructs. In *A Dissertation on Old Women* (1720), Thomas Gordon emphasizes the perception that traditional patriarchal values have been abandoned, and stockjobbing has turned Great Britain into a nation of "old women": "Let us, my Brethren and Countrymen, either properly and patiently put on Petticoats; or resume our Manhood, and shake off this shameful Delusion, this filthy yoke, put upon our Necks by dull Rogues from Jonathan's; plodding dunces!"[10] His language locates "manhood" in the past, prior to the feminizing "delusion" of a world of speculative investment. To wear the yoke—and presumably the petticoat—of involvement in an intangible financial system is to reject the past and to involve one's self in a "upside down world" populated by emasculated men and "plodding" economic dunces. The literary dunces of Grub Street "espoused the present and sought the values of the future," observes J. Paul Hunter, but the metaphor applies equally well in this economic environment.[11] Stockjobbers, like hack writers, frantically pursue future profit and power based almost exclusively on the proliferation and manipulation of paper.

In this environment, virtue becomes located in the past, and commerce, in Pocock's words, emerges as "the active form of culture itself."[12] The patriarchal virtues associated with civic humanism and the classic citizen—duty, hospitality, loyalty, heroism—give way to superficial values such as worth, opinion, and credit, so important to the new economic man; as Steele observes, credit is to the Trader "what Honour, . . . Fame or Glory is to other Sort of Men."[13] Significantly, the new qualities desirable for a stockjobber or a man of credit mirror those coveted by a woman of quality in the marriage market; both must rely on reputation (credit or virginity), assets (net worth or dowry), and potential for future gain (regular dividends or children). A stockjobber's success in the marketplace depends largely on public estimation of his value and credibility, for "credit is undone in whispers" just as a woman's reputation can be easily undone by gossip.

John Dennis, in *An Essay upon Public Spirit*, also claims that such increased participation in financial speculation has destabilized the characterizations of both genders, "transformed our sexes": "We have Men that are more soft, more languid, and more passive than women; Men, who like women, are come to use Red and White. . . . On the other side we have Women, who . . . in Revenge are Masculine in their Desires, and Masculine in their Practices."[14] Stockjobbing places men in a submissive, culturally feminine position, because it forces them to depend on opinion, reputation, and the approval of others.

Simultaneously, the economic man displays a willingness to be controlled by the allegorical female figures of disorder that similarly places him in a submissive, potentially emasculated position and makes him subject to the whims of unstable female figures like Credit, Fortune, and Luxury. These female goddesses continue a long misogynist tradition, and, in the words of Michael McKeon, "retain that association with the volatility of exchange which they possess under older, patrilineal assumptions."[15] For example, in a 1706 representation by Defoe in *The Review*, Credit appears as a vacillating young woman unduly influenced by the forces around her; she simultaneously reacts to and shapes the commercial world around her.[16] Addison continues this image when, in *Spectator* no. 3, he describes Credit as "a beautiful Virgin, seated on a Throne of Gold." An "infinitely timorous" young lady frequently "troubled with Vapours," Credit has a tendency to "change colour, and start at every thing" she hears. "In the twinkling of an Eye," Credit would

> fall away from the most florid Complexion, and the most healthful State of Body, and wither into a Skeleton. Her Recoveries were often as sudden as her Decays, insomuch that she would revive in a Moment out of wasting Distemper, into a Habit of the highest Health and Vigour.[17]

The physical and emotional vacillation of Credit suggests the delicacy and sensibility cultivated by ladies of quality to increase their sexual charms and desirability. Similarly Opinion, who does not have Credit's immediate financial influence, has a seductive quality and she appears to offer endless sexual pleasures: "Her Voice was pleasing . . . she seemed to have a tongue for every one; every one thought he heard of something that was valuable in himself, and expected a Paradise which she promised as the Reward of his Merit. Thus were we drawn to follow her, till she shou'd bring us where it was to be bestow'd."[18] Opinion is little more than popular perception of a speculator or stock's worth, an imaginary construction, which explains why she can distract and arouse everyone. Her ability to lead (perhaps mislead) and seduce speculators accounts for their willingness to invest, for Aislabie's "frenzy."

These allegorical female figures assume a much more specific form during the South Sea Crisis when James Milner illustrates the situation in *Three Letters, Relating to the South-Sea Company and The Bank* (1720).[19]

Milner represents the two most important financial institutions in England as women—the Lady of the South Sea and the Lady of the Bank. Milner's letters depict the changing fortunes of the two companies following the government's transfer of its debt from the Bank of England to the South Sea Company, rapidly increasing the stock price of the latter as a result. The first letter, written March 1719/20, portrays the Lady of the Bank "in deep mourning" (5) after the decision favoring the South Sea Company: "the object was too melancholy to be entertaining, when I consider'd her former glories, and how often I had seen her wallowing in her Millions. . . . It gave me a melancholy Idea of the Vicissitude of human affairs" (6). The Lady of the South Sea, "now worth as many Millions as the other would be thousands in a little time" (5), sits "on her throne in a most magnificent manner." Like an imperious ruler, she is surrounded by her sycophants and those wishing admission, "all paying her the utmost Adoration" (22), and she spurns them like a coquette rejecting pesky suitors:

> On her Right hand was, in Figures Capital, Twenty-seven Millions; on her left Hand was, A Million Three Hundred and Fifty Thousand a year Income; and over her Head, was, stock at Two Hundred per Cent. rising.
> At her Feet were the poor Annuitants in mourning, petitioning to be admitted Sharers in the glorious Harvest: But she spurned them from her with these words, No long Annuities! (5)

The image is part of a consistent pattern that portrays investors as suitors, suppliants before the unpredictable female figure of the South Sea Company.

Other representations increase the dangerous sexuality of that image. Aislabie characterizes the South Sea Company as a prostitute seducing men, as "a scheme more Voracious and destructive than a Lady that passes her Time in the Hundreds of Drury."[20] *The Battle of the Bubbles* (1720), by a "Stander-by," uses the female figure Oceana, daughter of "Avaritia, a Dutch woman," to illustrate the evil of the South Sea stock scheme.[21] An economic "Jezebel," Oceana bewitches men by casting a spell that puts them in an alternative state of mind. Her success in luring investors is compared to a sexually insatiable woman's success in seducing and unmanning male lovers:

> She bewitch'd thousands to fall in Love with her, and to spend their whole fortunes upon her: And what is monstrous in her, is, that tho' she has reduc'd 'em all to skin and Bone, yet her Lust is not one bit abated; and She runs a whoring after new Lovers every Day.

Another monstrous woman in Augustan satire, Oceana, completely devours her lovers to satisfy her own desire.[22] This description, like the previous ones, embodies many associations of stereotypically negative female

Plate 1. *A Monument dedicated to Posterity (Het Groote Tafereel der Dwaasheid* print collection). Photo courtesy of The Edward E. Ayer Collection, The Newberry Library.

qualities—avaricious sexuality, emotional instability, hysteria—used to characterize non-landed, intangible financial activities. The range of female types being depicted—coquettes, prostitutes, monstrous women—comprise a continuum of specifically female threats to masculinity and male control of financial structures.

The associations continue in the visual representations of Fortune and the Lady of the South Sea Company. A 1720 print titled *A Monument dedicated to Posterity* (figure 1), revises the iconic associations of Fortune to fit a world of speculative investment.[23] Fortune, traditionally depicted with a cornucopia scattering coins, here showers her followers with contracts, stocks and literally bubbles of air—she offers only paper credit to the group of men and women clamoring beneath her. The medieval image of the wheel of fortune is now a wagon wheel with the names of stock companies inscribed on it as their fortunes regularly rise and fall. The text describes how "books of Merchandise" are "crushed and turn beneath [the] Wheels of [the] Chariot, representing the destruction of Trade and Commerce." Folly drives that wagon and wears her distinct attire—a fool's cap and jester stick; she is "well known by her ordinary Attributes, and her Ample hoop petticoat, which is also a folly of the time." Folly and Fortune, like Credit and Opinion, contribute to the frenzy.

In the print entitled *The bedizened shareholders shown during their honour and influence* (figure 2), the South Sea Company sits on her high throne, viewing her adoring if somewhat unruly followers. Above her, Fortune, held aloft by clouds, puffs of air, scatters "cards of wind" or "delusions for the fellows of the mad South Sea Company." Credulity sits on the South Sea Company's lap, representing a successful stock scheme's need to generate credulity, a readiness—indeed over-readiness—to believe and thus invest. In the case of the South Sea Company, the initial description of the venture held the promised return on the monopoly of the South Seas, while the inflated rise of the stock's value sustained investors' belief. Credulity and Avarice also depend on each other. Credulity holds Avarice's chain as Avarice, with her breasts exposed, "tried to fill her bottomless stomach with a quantity of gold coins." Yet she holds only paper representing how an investor's tangible coin is replaced by mere paper.

The South Sea Company is also depicted as a woman in a state of recline. *The South Sea Company, having risen to the top by Wind, now laments her loss with a rueful aspect* (figure 3), depicts the South Sea Company as a woman reclining in a state of dishabille in a pose reminiscent of eighteenth-century pornography. She appears to be lamenting her devalued stock, expended resources, and absent investors—her 'loss' seems financial; yet her bare breast, unshod foot, and coy pose with her finger in her mouth also suggest she is a woman who is sexually spent (with all the economic force implicit in that image), and lamenting the loss of her lovers. The powers of attraction these women wield potentially erode the already precarious control men have over their finances and their impulses.

Plate 2. *The bedizened shareholders shown during their honour and influence* (*Het Groote Tafereel der Dwaasheid* print collection). Photo courtesy of The Edward E. Ayer Collection, The Newberry Library.

* * * * * * * * *

The allegorical representations of fickle goddesses guiding the new economic world draw upon traditional iconographic and philosophic config- urations of Credit and Fortune, and they reflect the emerging associations of speculative investment with "feminine" traits of passion, imagination, and fancy. These representations also exploit the role constructed for women in England's economic expansion and the mercantile capitalist ideology. The recurrent image of woman as "capricious consumer" underscores the culture's simultaneous dependence on and repudiation of female consump- tion of luxury goods. But texts surrounding the South Sea Bubble depict women as consumers of *stocks*, and as eager participants in the world of Exchange Alley. These texts suggestively represent women of the middling and upper classes as enthusiastic speculators who use stockjobbing as a means to gain funds to supplement or substitute for pin money.

While this area of scholarship remains incomplete, the striking pattern of representation indicates that women had a high level of actual participation—physically and financially—in Exchange Alley. Their level of participation, however, was controlled by the legal restraints placed on women. As Susan Staves explains in *Married Women's Separate Property in England*, early eighteenth-century judicial precedent determined that a married woman could be considered a *feme sole* with respect to her separate estate or personal property, which would include pin money, a possible source of investment funds. Personal property was to be used for mainten- ance, and for the purchase of paraphernalia—jewelry, clothes, personal items. Yet the attitude toward women's separate property and their limited control over it changed during the course of the century so that "by the end of the eighteenth century, allowing married women such powers of alien- ation with respect to their separate estates was found to be intolerable."[24] The amount of financial independence a woman possessed was also un- doubtedly limited by social constraints and a husband's undue influence. We cannot ascertain the discrepancy between the legal rules and their social applications, but, in theory, at the time of the South Sea Bubble a married woman could use her own funds to buy stock.

Peter Earle stresses "the enormous importance of women, particularly widows, in the London investment markets."[25] Women often had a great deal of stock in their jointure, because unlike land, stocks were not taxed and were, in James Carswell's words, "a form of property which a married woman could retain as a personal estate." Carswell estimates that by 1685, "20 percent of the holders of India and Africa bonds (what we should call preferred stock) were women; and between 1675 and 1691 the number of women holding the ordinary shares of the East India Company doubled."[26] Isaac Kramnick notes that the largest single holding in the Bank of England

Plate 3. *The South Sea Company, having risen to the top by Wind, now laments her loss with a rueful aspect* (*Het Groote Tafereel der Dwaasheid* print collection). Photo courtesy of The Edward E. Ayer Collection, The Newberry Library.

was that of Sarah, the Duchess of Marlborough at £166,855.[27] And, as Robert Halsband details, Lady Mary Wortley Montagu speculated in South Sea Company stock on behalf of her French admirer Nicolas-François Remond and her sister's mother-in-law Lady Gower.[28] Women could buy lottery tickets or take out insurance policies, both of which were another form of long-term speculative investment.

Discourse surrounding the South Sea Bubble exploits the fears this female involvement in finance aroused and consistently depicts women as part of the flurry of activity in Exchange Alley. Milner, in describing his imaginary visit to the Lady of the South Sea, notes that, in addition to the "Jews, Stock-jobbers, and Gamesters" paying their respects to the latest economic monarch, "Ladies were also there"; but "in respect to their sex," he refrains from making any reflections on such a scandalous activity (22). In William Rufus Chetwood's *South Sea; or, the Biters Bit* (1720) the exemplary heroine Marinda, demonstrates her "inclination for business" when she expresses her desire to "see the Bustle and Business of Change-Alley."[29] Thomas D'Urfey, in the "Prologue" to *The Two Queens of Brentford* (1720), describes how the price of stock has become a barometer for women's emotions:

> The Ladies too in Coach to Brokers run,
> The Fair, the Brown, the freckl'd, and the Dun;
> Fat Widows smile when dear Stock rises high;
> But if the vote comes that it falls—they cry.[30]

In the preface to the comedy *Exchange Alley: or, the Stockjobber turn'd Gentleman* (1720), the author complains that women's preoccupation with speculative investment distracts them from their normal pursuits: "If you wait upon a Lady of Quality, you'll find her hastening to her House of Intelligence in Exchange-Alley; and what is strange and wonderful, her every dress, Diamond shoe Buckles and Garters, neglected for the Stocks."[31] Just as men are abandoning their patriarchal duties to the land, women are ignoring their gender-defining activities and instead pursuing economic interests. The very consumer goods that make the "lady of quality" a scapegoat in the representations of luxury and its detrimental effects now become mementos of a romanticized past, when women could be lured by merely tangible luxury goods rather than enjoying for themselves the intangible allure of speculative investment.[32]

The texts also suggest that women use speculative investment to circumvent the financial restrictions placed on them by their husbands. Lady Pawn-Locket in William Rufus Chetwood's *The Stockjobbers* describes the dividends from stock as "better than Pin Money."[33] In *Exchange Alley*, Mrs. Cravemore pawns items often endowed with sentimental value—her "jewels, watch and tweezer case, and everything else" (21)—and commissions Cheatall to buy her some stock. "To tell you the Truth," she insists, "I should not venture to commence Stock-Jobber, were it not occasioned by my Mercenary Spouse, who at this time allows me nothing for Pin-money—and alas! I want it, at least, every Day" (20). Mrs. Cravemore's "mercenary" husband, whose own greed does not allow him to provide his wife with the stipend she desires, might in another context be praised for his frugality and money-making ability; or perhaps his obsession with stocks and his financial self-interest prevents him from sharing his income. The representation of women's desire for discretionary spending money suggests male apprehensions that increased financial independence could erode a husband's control over his wife and provide the material basis for equality between men and women. *Exchange Alley*'s author condemns such activities, advising that "when these extraordinary events are consider'd, and Women of the Town are become Dealers in the Stocks . . . it is high time to pronounce Exchange Alley truly a Farce" (ii).

Equal to the apprehension about the financial gains women will make is an apprehension about the dangerous attraction the pleasure of stockjobbing holds for women. A scene from Chetwood's *The Stock-Jobbers: or, the Humours of Exchange Alley* (1720) explores the benefits of stockjobbing for women and the different kinds of pleasures it affords. In a lengthy exchange, four women—wives of both merchants and aristocrats—discuss the material and emotional rewards of stockjobbing in terms that suggest it surpasses pleasures usually provided and sanctioned by men :

> *Lady Love-Pickett.* I declare I do not see why these wretches should monopolize the Pleasure of Business to themselves; it is only to keep us in Ignorance of all that's charming in Life: Like the Romish Priests, who refuse to let the Laity know anything, for fear of usurping upon their Authority.
> *Mrs. Figg.* I am sure my Neighbor, the Linen-draper's Wife, Mrs. Ghenting, had the vapours for a Gold-Watch two whole years, as she herself told me; and so she might still, poor soul, if her own Industry had not provided better for her. Oh ! this stock-jobbing, 'tis better than a Turn in the Park in a Hackney Coach.
> *Lady Pawn-Locket.* Better than Pin Money.
> *Lady Love-Pickett.* I was going to say better than an Evening at Cards with agreeable company.
> *Mrs. Subtle.* As for my Part, tho' I hardly ever saw the Inside of the City till within these three weeks, I am grown a perfect trader. (23)

Stockjobbing allows the women to transcend, however briefly, constraints on their activities and increase their knowledge, discretionary income, and perhaps power. Yet, Lady Love-Pickett observes that men monopolize finance and guard their knowledge of Exchange Alley, "all that's charming in life." She implies that women's ignorance is orchestrated by men who "fear [women] usurping upon their Authority." These women have all realized some profit through stockjobbing. Mrs. Subtle has gained an intimate knowledge of the City, a male domain with the vices and diversions that men such as Pinchwife in *The Country Wife* are represented as fearing. Mrs. Figg's story of her neighbor illustrates how stockjobbing gives a woman a rare opportunity to use her "own Industry" to her financial benefit. Her efforts in Exchange Alley transform her from a women beset with vapours to one able to acquire luxury goods by her own means. Mrs. Ghenting becomes empowered financially and physically as she transcends the private sphere to secure public economic success. At the same time, Mrs. Ghenting abandons the rational, thrifty, mercantile world of her husband to pursue her own interests; she retains the middle-class virtue of industry but she, in a sense, redirects it for her own purpose.

Similarly, Lady Love-Pickett no longer has to confine her gaming to only "an evening at cards with agreeable company," but can expand to the higher stakes and more public arena of stockjobbing. John Dennis, in *An Essay upon Public Spirit*, explains how any type of gaming—from cards to stockjobbing—robs women of their "natural" (and presumably appropriate) desires. Anticipating Pope's pronouncement that "love of pleasure" is one of women's two ruling passions ("Epistle to a Lady," line 210), Dennis expresses his concern that gaming will overcome women's "natural" pleasure with and passion for men, and redirect it to self-sufficient pursuits:[34]

> The Women lock themselves up at Cards whole Days and Nights successively, and forget their natural Pleasure of being seen, and of being admir'd; and Avarice gets the better of their Pride, as Luxury in some of them had done before; and gets the better of their Pleasure likewise, gets the better of that Pleasure which is so natural to them, and makes them shew a stronger Passion than that which they have for Men. (18)

Dennis' passage addresses both the concern about female pleasure generally, and female pleasure specifically in speculative activities and gambling. There is a lingering fear that women's pursuit of personal pleasure will determine their activity and that the pleasure women derive from stockjobbing will supplant the satisfaction they derive from men; they will find a vehicle for "self-pleasuring" as it were.

In fact, Lady Love-Pickett terms financial interests "the Pleasure of Business," and in many ways the pleasure of business can be a substitute for sexual pursuits, or the business of pleasure. Stockjobbing provides erotic and economic gratification. Mrs. Figg finds "this stockjobbing better than a Turn in the Park in a Hackney-Coach," a vehicle often the site of illicit sexual encounters. In other texts, stockjobbing and sexual pursuits are represented not just as substitutes but as supplements to each other—the business of pleasure enables the pleasure of business. As one anonymous 1720 poem explains, "our greatest ladies" pawn their jewels, possibly a gift from a husband or male admirer, "for a sum to venture in the Alley" just as "young harlots too from Drury Lane / Approach the 'Change in coaches / To fool away the gold they gain / by their impure debauches."[35] In a sense, these women take the fruits of their participation in a system of sexual exchange and use them to achieve greater power in a system of economic exchange.

In "An Excellent New Ballad upon the Masquerades," the poet explicitly compares "jobbing" for hearts at a masquerade with jobbing for stock in Exchange Alley, conflating sexual and financial economies. The text implicitly suggests that both activities involve women in a kind of prostitution—that there is perhaps too fine a line between the business of pleasure and the pleasure of business:

> O! a Masquerade's a fine Place
> For the young, the Old, the Witty:
> And Now's become a Rendezvous,
> For Ladies that are Pretty.
> At 'Change they job for money,
> But Traffic here for Hearts:
> The fairest Nymphs are willing
> To Show you their Best Parts.[36]

Locating the dual acts of "jobbing" at the masquerade heightens their already transgressive nature. More important, it intensifies the perceptions that women use stockjobbing as a vehicle for pleasure. The masquerade represented a site of sexual, political, and existential freedom enabled by the anonymity of the mask. Terry Castle suggests that "one might describe the masked assembly as a kind of machine for feminine pleasure . . . [where] a woman was free to circulate . . . according to her own pleasure."[37] Certainly these texts reflect the perception that women achieve a similar opportunity through stockjobbing and the anonymity of paper credit. Indeed, masquerade becomes a potent and accurate emblem for the South Sea Bubble and speculative investment; Exchange Alley can arguably be read as the primary site of "carnivalesque" activity in the early eighteenth century. Unbridled financial activities, like masquerade, disrupted traditional hierarchies of class and gender, and the signifying systems that dialectically organize eighteenth-century society. Perhaps as disturbing to Augustan conservatives as the categorical instabilities of gender, class, and property was the seeming ease with which an individual could gain or alter the existing signifiers of status and wealth. Paper credit in a sense became a form of disguise that extended the subversive power of masquerade from the ballroom to culture as a whole.

* * * * * * * * *

This pattern of provocative imagery underscores the profound mark the South Sea Bubble crisis left on eighteenth-century society. But the fears and animosities expressed stemmed from more than just anger about a society's ability to be financially duped. They were instead part of a larger cultural reaction to the frightening power of joint-stock companies, paper credit, and dematerialized property. The new objects of widespread cultural anxiety were "feminized" men led by their passions and emotions, empowered women diverted from their proscribed interests, and economies determined in part by the pursuit of pleasure.

Significantly, the nature of this discourse was not limited to the criticism of Exchange Alley and the participants in speculative investment. It was also used to depict expanding production and consumption of literary commodities. The fears expressed about new financial activities echo those expressed about the proliferation of primarily commercial writers, jobbing their own type of paper—writers who, at least in the *Dunciad*, are similarly represented as feminized. Just as much as a hawker of investment opportunities, the professional or hack writer of Grub Street depended on a text's reputation, notoriety or popularity for his or her livelihood—in other words, his or her credit on paper. Both booksellers and stockjobbers attracted clients seeking participation in an imaginatively constructed "future," desiring "future" returns on their initial investment, either in the form of stock dividends or an enjoyable reading experience. Like a stock scheme, fiction was based on nothing "real" or tangible; indeed it offered possibilities that may or may not be realized. Speculators in fiction or in finance must make an emotional and economic investment; they must exercise the power of fantasy in pursuit of immediate gratification; they must use their imagination to envisage the outcome of the narrative implicitly being offered.

As a result, the emergence of popular fiction was another cultural development that threatened to conflate the business of pleasure and the pleasure of business. Readers of popular genres such as the novel, primarily women, engaged in an imaginative displacement of self through participation in a narrative they helped construct. Women reading fiction exercised their fantasies and imagination, and developed emotional attachments with texts that, temporarily, removed them from immediate domestic concerns and restraints; in return, the text potentially provided a great deal of pleasure. Like women empowered, however briefly, by their forays into speculative investment, women reading (and writing) fiction were afforded the opportunity to transcend or surpass the pleasures potentially provided by men and gain knowledge not typically available to them. In the *Dunciad*, Pope, speaking specifically of Eliza Haywood, complains that "those shameless scriblers (for the most part of That sex, which ought least to be capable to such malice or impudence)" write novels that "reveal the faults and misfortunes of both sexes, to the ruin or disturbance, of publick fame or private happiness."[38] Pope argues that women are gaining from novels the knowledge and experience that Chetwood, in *The Stockjobbers*, suggests they are getting in Exchange Alley. One such novel, Haywood's *Love in Excess* (1719/20)—the most popular novel before *Pamela*—appeared just months before the frenzy over

South Sea Company stock.[39] *Love in Excess*, and amatory fiction like it, offers a "frenzy" that, though textual, nonetheless banks on its readers' continued willingness to be taken for a speculative ride, suggesting that financial and emotional investment in stocks and fiction are analogous cultural practices. Both activities, especially when practiced by women, arouse similar cultural resistance and anxiety and both stand as symptoms of an uneasy culture's simultaneous embrace of and resistance to the inevitable instabilities of social, literary and gendered categories appearing on the eighteenth-century landscape.

NOTES

The research for this paper was made possible by fellowships from the Newberry Library and the William Andrews Clark Memorial Library. I would also like to acknowledge the helpful suggestions from the members of the Folger Institute Colloquium 1992/93, "Women in the Eighteenth Century."

1. John Aislabie, *Mr. Aislabie's Second Speech on his Defence in the House of Lords*, on Thursday, July 20, 1721 (London, 1721), 12.
2. The South Sea Company was a joint-stock company that originated in 1710 as a means to help relieve the national debt. In exchange for monopoly rights to trade in the South Sea Islands, the company bought up £10 million of the government's debt. By 1719, however, under the guidance of John Blunt, the South Sea Company assumed the whole national debt. The self-perpetuating cycle of investment (speculators were often paid in company money and encouraged to buy more stock) caused the stock to be oversold and widely overvalued. On August 18, amid the collapse of other stock companies, a run on stock occurred, revealing the lack of real capital behind the scheme. Discussions of the South Sea Bubble can be found in John Carswell, *The South Sea Bubble* (Stanford: Stanford University Press, 1960); Virginia Spencer Cowles, *The Great Swindle: The Story of the South Sea Bubble* (London: Collins Press, 1960); P. G. M. Dickson, *The Financial Revolution in England: A Study in the Development of Public Credit* (New York: St. Martin Press, 1967); Isaac Kramnick, *Bolingbroke and His Circle: The Politics of Nostalgia in the Age of Walpole* (Cambridge: Harvard University Press, 1968).
3. *A Letter to a Conscientious Man: Concerning the Use and Abuse of Riches, and the Right and the wrong Ways of Acquiring them* (London, 1720), 22.
4. Laura Brown, *Ends of Empire: Women and Ideology in Early Eighteenth-Century English Literature* (Ithaca: Cornell University Press, 1993). See also Laura Brown, "Reading Race and Gender: Jonathan Swift," *Eighteenth-Century Studies* 23 (1990): 424–43; Felicity A. Nussbaum, *The Brink of All We Hate: English Satires on Women, 1660–1750* (Lexington: The University Press of Kentucky, 1984); J. G. A. Pocock, *The Machiavellian Moment: Florentine Political Thought and the Atlantic Republican*

Tradition (Princeton: Princeton University Press, 1975), especially chapters 5 and 6.

5. J. G. A. Pocock, "The Mobility of Property and the Rise of Eighteenth-Century Sociology," *Virtue, Commerce and History: Essays on Political Thought and History, Chiefly in the Eighteenth Century* (Cambridge: Cambridge University Press, 1985), 113, 114.

6. Ibid., 109.

7. *Some Considerations on the Late Mismanagement of the South-Sea Stock . . . in a Letter to a Friend* (1721), 4. In *A Poem on the South-Sea*, Alexander Ramsey similarly addresses the abandonment of the paternal heritage: "Waes me for him that sells paternal Land, / And buys shares the highest sumes demand: / He ne'er shall taste the sweets of rising Stock, / Which saws neist Day: Nae Help for it, he is broke." *A Poem on the South-Sea to which is Prefix'd a Familiar Epistle to Anthony Hammond, Esq* (London, 1720), 18–19.

8. Hogarth's 1721 engravings, "An Emblematic Print on the South Sea Bubble" and "The Lottery," both depict individuals who have forsaken their middle-class concerns to pursue new economic possibilities. Similarly, in *The Case of the Borrowers of the South-Sea Loans, Stated* (London, 1721), the author tells of the merchant "who thro' a long Diligence and great Variety of Hazard had gained a small Estate" only to grow "mad to see so many idle Fellows enrich themselves within a day or two" (6-7). As a result he "laid aside [his] Prudence," and at last became an "unhappy Convert to South-Sea" (7). But of course, the merchant is "undone" and ends up a beggar.

9. *An Examination and Explanation of the South Sea Company's Scheme for taking in the Publick Debts* (London, 1720), 16–17.

10. Thomas Gordon, *A Learned Dissertation Upon Old Women, Male and Female, Spiritual and Temporal, in all Ages; whether in Church, State, or Exchange-Alley* (London, 1720), 26. Jonathan's was a popular coffeehouse adjacent to Exchange Alley and was the site of both social and business gatherings for the growing number of stockjobbers.

11. J. Paul Hunter, *Before Novels: The Cultural Contexts of Eighteenth-Century English Fiction* (New York: W. W. Norton & Co., 1990), 99.

12. Pocock, *The Machiavellian Moment*, 431.

13. Richard Steele, *The Spectator* no. 509 (October 14, 1712), ed. Donald F. Bond, 5 vols. (Oxford: Clarendon Press, 1965), 4:309.

14. John Dennis, *An Essay Upon Publick Spirit; Being a Satyr on Prose upon the Manners and Luxury of the Times* (London, 1711), 15.

15. Michael McKeon, *The Origins of The English Novel 1600–1740* (Baltimore: Johns Hopkins University Press, 1987), 205. As Vincent Carretta writes of Pope's "Epistle to Bathurst," "The poet reminds Bathurst that the dangers inherent in the original South Sea Scheme will remain as long as men rely on Fortune's gifts. Those who put their faith in Fortune soon find with Turner that Riches can provide no more then 'Meat, Cloathes, and Fire' (82), and they become part of an incessant pattern that rises and falls, just as surely as does Hogarth's merry-go-round." *The Snarling Muse: Verbal and Visual Political Satire from Pope to Churchill* (Philadelphia: University of Pennsylvania Press, 1983), 76.

16. Pocock, *The Machiavellian Moment*, 453. For a discussion of Defoe and the South Sea Bubble, see Gary Hentzi, "'An Itch of Gaming': The South Sea Bubble and the Novels of Daniel Defoe," *Eighteenth-Century Life* 17 (February 1993): 32–45.

17. Joseph Addison, *Spectator* no. 3, 1:15–16. As Pocock observes, "like all these goddesses, Credit typifies the instability of secular things, brought out by the interaction of particular human wills, appetites and passions, . . . in which she is shown operating malignantly and irrationally." *Machiavellian Moment*, 453.

18. Steele, *Spectator* no. 460, 4:121–22.

19. James Milner, *Three Letters Relating to the South-Sea Company and the Bank. The First Written in March, 1719–20. The Second in April 1720. The Third in September, 1720.* (London, 1720), 6. As John Carswell explains, the Bank of England and the South Sea Company were essentially in competition over which would assume a larger portion of the nation debt and thus receive a larger annual payment from the government; Milner is illustrating the South Sea Company's victory. Carswell also describes how these companies capitalized on the euphoria or irrationality that marked the period: "No doubt the bank directors, like everyone else, were by now infected with the fashionable doctrine of infinitely expanding credit." *South Sea Bubble*, 111.

20. John Aislabie, *Mr. Aislabie's Two Speeches Considered* (London, 1721), 12.

21. *The Battle of the Bubbles. Shewing Their Several Constitutions, Alliances, Policies and Wars . . . By a Stander-By* (London, 1720), 10.

22. I am thinking here primarily of Pope's image of Dulness. For a discussion of this repeated image, see Susan Gubar, "The Female Monster in Augustan Satire," *Signs* 3 (1977): 380–94.

23. All the prints discussed here come from *The Great Mirror of Folly* [*Het Groote Tafereel der Dwaasheid*], a collection of Dutch, French and English prints depicting the South Sea Bubble crisis as well as the crises on the Continent. For further explication on the individual prints and the text as a whole see Arthur H. Cole, *The Great Mirror of Folly (Het Groote Tafereel der Dwaasheid): An Economic-Bibliographical Study* (Boston: Harvard University Press, 1949). See also *Catalogue of Prints and Drawings in the British Museum 1870–1954: Division I: Personal and Politic Satires*, vol. 2, June 1689–1733. (London, 1873), cf. 412, et. al. For a discussion of the iconography of the petticoat, see Erin Mackie, "Lady Credit and the Strange Case of the Hoop-Petticoat," *College Literature* 20 (June 1993): 27–43.

24. Susan Staves, *Married Women's Separate Property in England, 1660–1833* (Cambridge: Harvard University Press, 1990), 152. Staves is concerned with the legal positioning of women and property and explores "the crucial question of why the legal changes allowing women to become autonomous owners of property did not empower married women" (222). For married women, the possibility for their legal autonomy and financial independence caused them to be much more securely restricted. See also Patricia Okin's "Patriarchy and Married Women's Property in England: Questions on Some Current Views," *Eighteenth-Century Studies* 17 (Winter 83/84): 121–38.

25. Peter Earle, *The Making of the English Middle Class: Business, Society and Family Life in London, 1660–1730* (Berkeley and Los Angeles: University of California Press, 1989), 173.

26. Carswell, *South Sea Bubble*, 11.

27. Kramnick, *Bolingbroke and His Circle*, 42.

28. See Robert Halsband, *The Life of Lady Mary Wortley Montagu* (Oxford: Clarendon Press, 1956), 100–104, and *The Complete Letters of Lady Mary Wortley Montagu*, ed. Robert Halsband (Oxford: Clarendon Press, 1965–67), 1:450–53; 2:1–5, 14.

29. William Rufus Chetwood, *South Sea; or, the Biters Bit* (London 1720), 8.

30. Thomas D'Urfey, *The Two Queens of Brentford: or, Bayes no Poetaster: a Musical Farce, or Comical Opera. Being the sequel of the Famous Rehearsal. Written by the Late Duke of Buckingham. With a comical Prologue and Epilogue.* (London, 1721), 11.

31. *Exchange-Alley: or, the Stockjobber turn'd Gentleman; with the Humours of our Modern Projectors* (London, 1720), preface.

32. For a discussion of this scapegoating of women, particularly in Mandeville's *The Fable of the Bees*, see Laura Mandell, "Bawds and Merchants: Engendering Capitalist Desires, " *ELH* 59 (1992): 107–23.

33. William Rufus Chetwood, *The Stock-Jobbers: or the Humours of Exchange Alley. A Comedy in Three Acts* (London, 1720), 23.

34. Alexander Pope, "Epistle to a Lady," in *The Twickenham Edition of the Poems of Alexander Pope*, ed., John Butt et. al., 11 volumes (London: Methuen, 1938-68), 3.2: 67, line 210. Pope's idealized depiction of Martha Blount in this poem also specifically describes her as a woman who ignores gaming, the turns of fortune and the allure of lottery tickets which were really another form of speculative investment: "Lets Fops or Fortune fly which way they will; / [She] disdains all loss of Tickets or Codille" (265–66). For an interesting discussion of how the lottery worked in the early eighteenth century, see Richmond Bond, "The Lottery: A Note for the Year 1710," *The South Atlantic Quarterly* 70 (1971): 135–48.

35. Cited in Cowles, *Great Swindle*, 43.

36. "An Excellent New Ballad upon the Masquerades," in *Love's Invention: or, the recreation in Vogue* (London, 1718), 6.

37. Terry Castle, *Masquerade and Civilization: The Carnivalesque in Eighteenth-Century English Culture and Fiction* (Stanford: Stanford University Press, 1986), 254–55. Although Castle deals with many aspects of the carnivalesque, she never really does anything with this equation, or addresses the frequent appearance of masquerade and the carnivalesque in representations of financial activity.

38. Pope, *Twickenham Edition* 5:119.

39. Discussions on the significance of Haywood's early fiction can be found in Ros Ballaster, *Seductive Forms, Women's Amatory Fiction from 1684–1740* (Oxford: Clarendon Press, 1992); Jerry Beasley, *Novels of the 1740's* (Athens: University of Georgia Press, 1982); Christine Blouch, "Eliza Haywood and the Romance of Obscurity," *Studies in English Literature* 31 (1991): 225–52; John Richetti, *Popular Fiction Before Richardson* (Oxford: Oxford University Press, 1969).

In Search of Angélique:
The Dancourt Connection

PHILIP KOCH

In the 1992 issue of the *Revue Marivaux* (3:51–62), you will find an article of mine prompted by Marivaux's use of a female character type to which he normally gave the name Angélique. Briefly, the goal of "Onomastique marivaudienne: Angélique nubile" was to establish her as a rôle clearly, distinctly different from Silvia and other Marivaldian heroines. A final note stressed, however, that the playwright did not invent the name and that his exploitation of it might well represent more than a purely fortuitous or subliminal borrowing from theatrical predecessors, in particular Florent Carton Dancourt (1661–1725). The present reflections propose to explore the latter hypothesis.

Chronologically speaking, there is a curious continuity between Marivaux and Dancourt. In 1718, two years before the former's first Parisian stage productions (*L'Amour et la Vérité* and *Arlequin poli par l'amour*), Dancourt ended his thirty-three year association with the Théâtre-Français. Rather than a continuity one could more accurately speak of an overlapping, for, in Paris since 1710, the young Marivaux surely saw his predecessor's plays in performance. Even if he did not frequent the theater regularly, Dancourt's works were available to him in print, the first collected edition beginning to appear as early as 1706 (6 volumes, The Hague, E. Foulque).[1] And an impressive number they formed, especially in light of Dancourt's other activities as actor, designated orator of the French troupe, man about town, and womanizer.[2]

Between 1683 and 1718 Dancourt composed, adapted, collaborated on, or allowed his name to be affixed to sixty-five texts, only fifty-two of which have survived. Within the group of extant plays, by my count twenty-five contain a part for Angélique,[3] and Marivaux would have had to be uncharacteristically obtuse not to notice (and reflect on) the older writer's fascination, nay, obsession with the role. In turn, we might ponder two questions: (1) Why does Angélique appear only in some Dancourt plays (about fifty percent of them) and not others? (2) When she does participate, does Angélique display from plot to plot constant traits that give her a recognizable, unified character? The first is the easier question to answer.

Already in the eighteenth century, Dancourt's commentators were wont to note a recurrent feature of his theater: the use of peasant speech.

> Le talent singulier qu'il eut pour faire parler les paysans les lui fit souvent mettre en jeu. Il les peint toujours d'une manière agréable et naturelle; il les fait parler de même. Nul auteur avant lui n'avait osé composer une pièce tout en style villageois; Dancourt en a fait plusieurs et toutes ont réussi. La plupart même sont restées au théâtre.[4]

Given this skill, it is not surprising to see time and again peasants in supporting roles to back up Angélique. The appeal of that character type was apparently so strong that, on several occasions, Dancourt surrendered the entire play to it and created thereby, as the just quoted *Anecdotes dramatiques* suggests, a new theatrical sub-genre: the "paysannerie."[5] Never does Angélique dignify it with her presence, for she is a bourgeoise and therefore above the simple antics of "manants."[6]

Class distinctions thus constitute an exclusionary principle in the case of our "jeune première," but it is not the only one. There exists another but fairly heterogeneous group of plays that lack an Angélique. To begin with, we must mention a "féerie" appropriately titled *Les Fées* (1699) that takes place in an imaginary "Royaume des Asturies" replete with a shepherd king and fairy godmothers, or, rather, fairy wife/mother and aunts. Similar, by virtue of their unreality, are the mythologically oriented plays, *Céphale et Procris* (1711) and *La Métempsycose des amours* (1717), to which one could subjoin *L'Impromptu de Suresnes* (1713) and *Les Fêtes nocturnes du Cours* (1714) that, all the while taking place in or near Paris, do nevertheless introduce ancient divinities in what André Blanc calls a "badinage mythologique."[7]

If Angélique has nothing in common with the worlds of fairies and ancient gods, she is equally a stranger to tragedy and tragi-comedy, each genre represented by one Dancourt play: *La Mort d'Hercule* (1683) and *La Trahison punie* (1707), respectively. With the exception of the 1683 tragedy and *Les Fées*, these plays all come from Dancourt's late creative period when he obviously had high literary ambitions in which an Angélique clearly had no place. Such ambitions are further represented by *Sancho Pança gouverneur* (1712) set, like *La Trahison punie*, in Spain, and *Madame Artus* (1708), Dancourt's rather colorless attempt to provide Tartuffe with a female counterpart.

Though the preceding plays are disparate, they do have one quality in common. With respect to Angélique they are, in the broadest sense, "exotic," for they all seem geographically and/or spiritually "foreign" to the world in which she exists.[8] This world is adumbrated by two symbolic titles: *La Parisienne* (1691) and *Les Enfants de Paris* (1699). Both refer to Angélique, the former exclusively, the latter in partnership with a brother, Clitandre. Indeed, the symbiosis of Paris and Angélique is total, and she may well be considered the original Parigote. The latter observation does not mean, of course, that every Angélique comedy takes place within the still fortified walls of the capital. Since the events portrayed often occur during the summer, the daughter and her well-heeled middle-class family are inclined to vacation in the country. Although the locations may be distant (for example, Andrésy in *Colin-Maillard* [1701], Compiègne in *Les Curieux de Compiègne* [1698], an unspecified village of Brie in *Les Vacances* [1696]), they are nevertheless within a day's travel of the capital. Once this broad limit is exceeded, Angélique tends to be replaced—as in *Les Eaux de Bourbon* (1696), a spa André Blanc considers to be Bourbon-l'Archambault in the Allier,[9] or in *Le Retour des officiers* (1697), situated in Péronne near Amiens.[10]

Angélique's geographic confinement to Paris and its environs is paralleled by a clear civil status and general psychological traits attributed to our heroine. With one or two early exceptions (that suggest Dancourt had difficulty defining his character in the beginning), Angélique is unmarried.[11] Since only widowhood could provide a measure of independence for women of the time, *Mlle.* Angélique suffers perforce the authority of parent, relative, or guardian—again with some early exceptions.[12] Such absolute domination might gain begrudging acceptance even from the modern profeminist spectator, given the age and inexperience of the young lady in question, for it is occasionally specified that she "sort à peine du couvent."[13] We may conclude, then, this literally "cloistered" Angélique is about sixteen and has had little contact with the adult world into which she is ready to plunge, curious but unprepared. In short, Angélique is another name for the traditional ingénue about whom an old but understanding Mme. Brillard will say in scene 4 of *Colin-Maillard* (1701) by way of criticism of the unenlightened approach taken by her nephew M. Robinot in raising his young ward: "Le vieux fou qui pense amuser une fille de seize ans avec des ménétriers de village et des jeux d'enfant. Ce n'est ni l'esprit ni les oreilles, c'est le coeur qu'il faut amuser à cet âge-là." "Le coeur," or the initiation into love.

An already mentioned play, *Les Fées* (1699), is not only a "féerie," but also Dancourt's unexpected, labyrinthine manifesto on affairs of the heart. In the absence of their mother, the fairy queen Logistille, Cléonide, the first-born, and her sister Inégilde have been raised by their supernatural aunts according to the principles respectively of untrammeled pleasure and restrictive prudishness. When the play opens, the sisters are engaged, in order of age, to a handsome young prince and a doddering royal graybeard, an arrangement that displeases the less favored Inégilde.[14] In brief, the action of the comedy consists of the efforts to restructure the foursome. If the outcome is successful, it is largely due to the generosity of Cléonide who freely accepts a prince ancient in place of a prince charming on the principle that "quand il s'agit d'un attachement sérieux, les plaisirs ont moins de charmes que la sagesse" (act 3, sc. 7).

This surprisingly mature decision is the unexpected result of Cléonide's pampered upbringing, as she remarks to Inégilde: "Ah! ma soeur, que d'éternels plaisirs sont ennuyeux! . . . il faut un contraste plus sensible pour former le vrai bonheur de la vie, et les chagrins, les périls, les malheurs mêmes sont nécessaires pour mieux faire goûter l'avantage de les avoir évités" (act 1, sc. 7). Similarly, we must assume Inégilde's aggressive dissatisfaction stems from the constraints her aunt constantly imposed on her behavior. If we observe, finally, that Dancourt focuses his play preferably on the agitations of Inégilde, it is inevitable to conclude that the author found oppression and resistance to it a better representation of love than calm judgment and balance (Cléonide). In any case, the Inégilde situation is much more frequently found in Dancourt's theater—in all Western comedy, for that matter, since Greco-Roman antiquity. After all, what dramatic interest would love have if it were not thwarted?[15]

Like almost all other "jeunes premières" of Dancourt, then, Angélique is oppressed and opposed in her love; it is her reaction to this rather standard situation that distinguishes her from the rest of the young women in the Dancourt canon. On the one hand, the typical peasant girl appears dull-witted, gullible, passive. It is she who comes close in Dancourt to the Moliéresque Agnès, that is, the Agnès before love's enlightenment. And with some frequency our playwright will compare this simpler type to his Angélique. After several examples of resourcefulness on the part of her young mistress, Lisette, who in her traditional role of maid should be in a position to evaluate astute ploys, exclaims: "Ma foi, vive Paris. L'esprit ne vient point si vite aux filles de province" (*La Parisienne* [1691], sc. 11).

Lisette's statement is potentially ambiguous, because "filles de province" applies, without discrimination apparently, to all non-Parisian young ladies whatever their social class. Could not at least some of them acquire the same degree of "esprit" even if it were "moins vite"? Dancourt would probably answer in the negative, and unhesitatingly so if the "provinciale" were of peasant stock, as the following dialogue makes quite clear. It occurs between Claudine and Mme. Brillard who are commenting on clever defensive actions taken by the Angélique of their play, *Colin-Maillard* (1701):

> *Claudine.* Oh, ces demoiselles de Paris ont l'esprit bien plus joli que nous autres paysannes.
> *Mme Brillard.* Ha, merci de ma vie, vous paraissez une bonne pièce.
> *Claudine.* Oh! non, en vérité, je suis trop innocente.[16]

What seemed earlier an arbitrary distinction of Paris from the rest of France now reveals itself as the source of a mysterious (and precocious) blooming of personal strengths under the cultural stimulation, the environment, of "la Ville" supported by "la Cour." One of the first examples of the contrast "Paris et la province," as it were.

To the extent that the heroines of a heterogeneous grouping I have labeled "exotic" plays can be categorized, they too differ from Angélique in the intensity they bring to bear on their "problems" with passionate (*La Loterie* [1697]) or heroic (*Madame Artus* [1708]) resolve. When the father of Mariane unjustifiably breaks her engagement to Eraste after approving it, the Neapolitan (warm-blooded?) heroine explodes in anger against her father as she recalls her "passion toute légitime, autorisée par l'aveu de mon père, soutenue par tout le mérite d'Eraste et qui s'est augmentée de jour en jour par *un secret penchant que je ne puis vaincre.*"[17] Similarly frustrated in her love by a mother who has just arranged a new marriage for her, an indignant Célide exclaims to her brother (in struggling alexandrins):

> En un mot, comme en cent, Monsieur, mon pis-aller
> Sera de *résister à l'hymen qu'on m'apprête,*
> Et de ne faire rien qui ne soit à ma tête.
> *Je sais jusqu'où vont les droits qu'on a sur moi.*[18]

It is inconceivable that Angélique would have expressed herself in the lofty tone of the last two heroines or that she would have contented herself with the submissiveness of the "paysanne." Angélique's register lies somewhere between elevation and passivity. What characterizes the behavior of this quick-witted, perspicacious girl in the face of oppression is the need to act, to further her interests by doing something, *but* only if her action holds the promise of success. As she says in *Les Vacances* (1696): "Il n'y . . . aurait point [de résolutions] que je ne fusse capable de prendre *si je voyais jour à ne les pas prendre inutilement.*"[19] Perhaps this pragmatic spirit explains why Angélique's affection is always so moderate.[20] At any rate, she is forever involved, sometimes more, sometimes less, in the stratagems designed to overcome the obstacle. In *Le Tuteur* (1695), for example, where the oppressive guardian M. Bernard, disguised as a woman, is beaten mercilessly in the garden, it is Angélique who conceives this liberating scheme reminiscent of La Fontaine's *Cocu battu et content* (and, ultimately, of Boccaccio). In *La Gazette* (1692), likewise, in order to force a timid Clitandre to declare himself, our heroine inserts in the latest issue of the *Gazette de Hollande* a false announcement of her impending marriage with the hope (fully realized) that jealousy will provoke the bashful lover to speak up. Or again, in *Le Vert-Galant* (1714), having sent each other their portrait through the mail, Eraste and Angélique fall in love and promise to marry if a union can be arranged, all this without the knowledge and consent of her uncle-guardian. But the best example of Angélique's independence and revolt against tyrannical authority occurs in *Les Curieux de Compiègne*

(1698) where our ingénue and the go-between, Mme. Pinvin, discuss Angélique's potential interest in marrying Clitandre under the very nose of the girl's austere mother who fails to decipher their coded dialogue.

Without question this Angélique was Dancourt's favorite,[21] and his fascination was so constant that he must have had her in mind when he occasionally gave his young Parisian "amoureuse" another name, normally Mariane or Lucile.[22] But, more often still, these other names were used when the plot required the ingénue to be a slow-witted goose, an "exotically" intense heroine, or, for that matter, an unreconstructed coquette.[23] After all, to be born or to live in Paris does not automatically make one an Angélique.

Such was the legacy bequeathed by Dancourt, and that Marivaux was influenced by it is unquestionable. Even as late as 1734, Marivaux composed a play, *La Méprise*, that Frédéric Deloffre correctly identifies as inspired by Dancourt's general dramaturgy.[24] We note as well that Marivaux cultivated the same comic sub-genres as his predecessor: the "paysannerie" with *L'Héritier de village* (1725); the "féerie," perhaps in *L'Amour et la Vérité* (1720), of which there remains but a fragment, certainly in *Arlequin poli par l'amour* (1720); the "badinage mythologique" illustrated by *Le Triomphe de Plutus* (1728); and, finally, a purer if not more serious mythology represented by *La Réunion des Amours* (1731).[25] Most (but *not* all) of the remaining theatrical works by Marivaux take place in or near Paris and usually involve middle-class characters. Several even present plot details surprisingly similar to Dancourt's. Such is the case of *La Double Inconstance* (1723), inverse image of *La Métempsycose des amours* (1717), for, where the Marivaldian prince is successful in transferring Silvia's affections to himself, Dancourt's Jupiter fails miserably with the shepherdess Corine, though both "amoureux" have common recourse to force (a kidnapping) and false identity.[26]

The similarity is greater still between Marivaux's *La Fausse Suivante* (1724) and Dancourt's two plays, *La Folle Enchère* (1690) and *La Femme d'intrigues* (1692). All three include a woman masquerading in male dress, and, in two cases (Marivaux's play and *La Folle Enchère*), the disguise is a crucial element of the plot. If in Dancourt's other play the male impersonation occupies only one scene (act 2, sc. 6), the character justifies what she is doing as an attempt to see, unrecognized, how faithful her swain really is, a motive that comes close to that of Marivaux's heroine. It goes without saying that in both plays Dancourt calls his character Angélique. Although Marivaux leaves his equivalent role nameless, except for the false title of Le Chevalier, he does use Angélique as appellation six times (seven if we include *La Fausse Suivante*), a statistic that makes hers the most frequently used female name in all of Marivaux's theater.[27] This observation should become even more significant after a closer comparison of the character as drawn by the two authors.

In her extremely perspicacious article "Dancourt, Marivaux et l'éducation des filles," Lucette Desvignes has incontrovertibly proved Marivaux's debt in *L'Ecole des mères* (1732) and *La Mère confidente* (1735) to Dancourt's comedies *La Parisienne* (1691) and *Le Tuteur* (1695) in terms not only of plot but also of character portrayal, especially that of Angélique. Concerning the latter Mme. Desvignes writes: "C'est le type même de l'innocente qui s'éveille à l'amour et qui devient astucieuse pour défendre cet amour menacé."[28] Although the critic is referring here only to the Angélique of Marivaux's two plays, her remark applies equally well not only to the other Marivaldian Angéliques but also, as we have seen, to all the Angéliques of Dancourt—after his early hesitations. It is this actor-author who surely developed the model of the alert energetic girl on which Marivaux was to build.

If Marivaux's conceptualization of this ingénue recalls Dancourt's, the younger writer is not a slavish imitator of his precursor. For one thing, his Angéliques are not all Parisian, a *sine qua non* for Dancourt. In *L'Epreuve* (1740) and *Le Préjugé vaincu* (1746), Marivaux insists on their country upbringing, as though he were deliberately emancipating himself from his forerunner.[29] In addition, *La Mère confidente* and *L'Epreuve* introduce the question of congruent wealth in marriage partners, while *Le Préjugé vaincu* raises an even more delicate issue, that of class distinctions. Neither of these social problems, so dear to the "esprit philosophique," was of any apparent concern to Dancourt.[30] Further, the very concept of love seems to be at variance in the two writers: neither a deep nor durable feeling for Dancourt,[31] for Marivuax an emotion meant to last for life—if we may believe that the Silvia of *Le Jeu de l'amour et du hasard* (1730) is speaking for her creator.[32]

The most striking difference between the two playwrights is revealed, however, in the economy of a typical Dancourt play. It is not carefully crafted, as Blanc observes after admitting "la faiblesse habituelle de l'intrigue": "[La] conception habituelle de la comédie [chez Dancourt c'est] une intrigue apparemment compliquée, mais qui se dénoue sans aucune difficulté, tellement elle est dépourvue d'intérêt."[33] Harsh words, but in general true. These plays Dancourt hastily concocted for his companions[34] can be divided into two broad categories: the "obstacle" play, such as *Les Fonds perdus*[35] (1685), where clever servants overcome the roadblocks placed by those opposed to the union of the young lovers; the "revue" play, such as *La Femme d'intrigues* (1692), where, between a rather arbitrary exposition and a casual denouement, the audience is treated to a series of discrete sketches whose number depends on how many acts Dancourt had to fill. What is common to both manners is the clear preference for grotesque characters, whether domestics, peasants, foreigners, old people, or simple passers-by. Given the two formulaic patterns and the character types favored by Dancourt, it is obvious that Angélique will not be seen often—unless she becomes the driving force of the play, in a sense, its principal grotesque, as she does in *La Folle Enchère* (1690), *L'Eté des coquettes* (1690) and *La Parisienne* (1691). These early exceptions aside, *Colin-Maillard* (1701) is rather typical of the normal Angélique play. Here, although the other characters regularly raise the issue of her marriage to Eraste, despite the resistance of her guardian M. Robinot, and although they discuss in detail the progress made to date, the ingénue herself does not put in an appearance until scene sixteen of this twenty-three scene one-act play. Even then, the statistics are a bit deceptive, for she participates in only six of the last eight scenes.

Slightly more than one quarter of the total, as above (six scenes of twenty-three), is, in fact, an unusually generous proportion; Dancourt is in the habit of offering her less. Given her limited participation, it becomes difficult to discuss Angélique's character in any detail. Indeed, what I said previously about Dancourt's vision of the young lady is the result of generous extrapolations and interpretations whose accuracy cannot be guaranteed in all their ramifications. What a far cry from the depth, diversity, sympathy *and* extension of Marivaux's depiction! Angélique owes her initial "stardom," perhaps, to Dancourt, but Marivaux's claim to originality is in no danger. "En somme, tout était là et tout restait à faire."

NOTES

1. For this article I am using *Les Oeuvres de M. Dancourt*, 3rd ed., 9 vols. (Rouen & Paris: Veuve Ribou, 1729). Spelling and punctuation of all quotes from this edition will be modernized. Similar updating will be applied to the passages taken from the other eighteenth-century sources cited.
2. "On a dit de [Dancourt] qu'il jouait noblement la comédie et bourgeoisement la tragédie. Il fut longtemps l'orateur de la troupe, emploi dont il s'acquittait très bien. . . . Sa politesse et les agréments de sa conversation le firent rechercher des grands seigneurs," writes Léris in his *Dictionnaire portatif des théâtres* (Paris: Jombert, 1754), s. v. Dancourt (419). As for his amorous dalliances, see André Blanc, *F. C. Dancourt (1661–1725)*, Etudes littéraires françaises, 29 (Tübingen: Narr; Paris: Place, 1984), 43, 59–60.
3. The total would be twenty-six, should we include *Le Moulin de Javelle* (1696), where Angélique is named without playing any visible part in the action.
4. Abbé J.-B. de La Porte and J.-M.-B. Clément, *Anecdotes dramatiques*, vol. 3 (Paris: Veuve Duchesne, 1775), s. v. Dancourt, 135.
5. Dancourt's comedies "tout en style villageois" would include *L'Opéra de village* (1692), *Les Vendanges* (1694), *Le Mari retrouvé* (1698), *Les Trois Cousines* (1700), *Le Prix de l'arquebuse* (1717).
6. A clear insistence on social rank is explicitly made for this girl in *Le Diable boiteux* (1707), when Angélique's maidservant Marton exclaims spitefully: "Quel dommage que cela [c.-à-d., Angélique!] ne soit que bourgeoise et moi

soubrette! Nous avons bien les manières de qualité" (act 3, sc. 3); and in *La Déroute du pharaon* (1718) where her widowed mother Bélise is described as a "bourgeoise joueuse" in the "dramatis personae." To these examples one might add *Les Bourgeoises à la mode* (1692) in which one of the title characters is none other than our Angélique.

7. Blanc, *Dancourt*, 125.

8. The verse form used in many of the "exotic" plays offers further proof of their distance from the "prosaic" milieu that is Angélique's.

9. Blanc, *Dancourt*, 72.

10. The "Greater" Paris criterion is not observed in two early plays: *Les Nouvellistes de Lille* (1683), where Angélique appears in Lille, and *L'Impromptu de garnison* (1692), where she inhabits the Flemish city of Namur. Both exceptions can be easily explained. The former, Dancourt's first comedy, was written for performance in the title city while our actor-author was a member of a wandering theatrical troupe based in Rouen. As for the latter, Dancourt did no more than a quick touch-up job on a play mailed to the Théâtre-Français from Mons by its unknown author. By contrast, two other significant plays, *L'Opérateur Barry* (1702) and *La Loterie* (1697), are set in Paris without Angélique's participation, for evident reasons. In the first of these two plays, Dancourt was trying to recreate the atmosphere of the time, almost a century before, when the Italian charlatan Barry was selling his remedies not far from the 1702 emplacement of the Théâtre-Français (prologue, sc. 4). Although *La Loterie* takes place in contemporary Paris, the heroine Mariane is a Neapolitan girl who has been in the French capital for only two years (sc. 1). As well as geographic or social, the exclusionary principle can thus, if rarely, be chronological and national, although one would be hard pressed to explain why Dancourt considered Mariane a more appropriate "Italian" name than Angélique. After all, his opera parody *Angélique et Médor* (1685) establishes incontrovertibly that he was aware of his favorite heroine's filiation to Ariosto.

11. The major exception is *Les Bourgeoises à la mode* (1692) in which she plays the second and apparently much younger wife of M. Simon. Although she never comes on stage, another Angélique is mentioned as a new bride in *Le Moulin de Javelle* (1696). Other examples of this "flottement caractériel du début" follow in notes 12 and 20.

12. Had contemporary audiences given it any heed, they would surely have been uneasy about the freedom with which an unsupervised and unwed Angélique pranced about disguised as a man all through *La Folle Enchère* (1690) and briefly (act 1, sc. 6) in *La Femme d'intrigues* (1692). She displays more plausible emancipation in *L'Eté des coquettes* (1690), for, here, she merely (?) so manipulates a weak-willed mother that the latter is relegated nameless to a country estate during the play.

13. In *La Parisienne* (1691), *Les Vacances* (1696) and *Colin-Maillard* (1701). The same situation obtains for Angélique's occasional partial "Doppelgänger," Mariane (*La Foire de Bezons* [1695]) and Lucile (*Le Galant Jardinier* [1704]).

14. In describing Cléonide's initial fiancé, King Astur, the father, calls him "un jeune égrillard, beau, bien fait, de bonne mine, un peu étourdi, beaucoup

libertin, mais de fort bonne humeur en revanche. . . . c'est un prince qui vit prèsque aussi heureusement qu'un homme d'affaires" (act 1, sc. 9).

15. Only two other instances of young women willingly marrying older men (the Cléonide situation) come to mind: Lucile, second wife of M. Grichardin, the retired apothicary (*La Comédie des comédiens* [1710]), and the attractive second Mme. Jérôme (*Le Vert-Galant* [1714]). It is astonishing to see these three atypical Dancourt women accept their lot with tranquillity, even pleasure, thereby illustrating an attitude I am tempted to call the Elmire complex. After all, in the absence of an outlook implicitly similar to Cléonide's, how could this vibrant, appealing woman accept and remain faithful to an older husband as trying as Orgon?

16. Sc. 3. Consider further, if you will, this general, though somewhat tentative, belittling of "les provinciales" ("toutes classes confondues") on the part of Asmodée who is explaining to his heroines why he brought them non-stop to Paris from Madrid: "J'ai eu peur de vous laisser prendre un air de province dont les femmes ne se défont pas aisément. Il n'y a rien de plus ridicule que ces airs de province, à ce que l'on dit du moins. Il n'est rien tel que de se trouver d'abord dans le centre et de commencer . . . à se former sur ce modèle de la Cour et de Paris" (*Le Diable boiteux*, prologue).

17. *La Loterie*, sc. 1. Italics mine.

18. *Madame Artus*, act 2, sc, 2. Italics mine.

19. Sc. 6. Italics mine.

20. Further proof of Dancourt's early irresolution concerning Angélique's character can be found in *L'Eté des coquettes* (1690) and *Les Bourgeoises à la mode* (1692) where she plays both times a self-centered coquette. Instead of moderate affection, this Angélique displays total indifference toward the men in her life. Although the ingénue of *La Parisienne* (1691) initially presents the same traits, her flightiness seems more the result of inexperience than of commitment to a volatile mode of existence, for, as the play progresses, she becomes ever more inventive in her efforts to wed her dear Eraste. A coquettish Angélique does return in *Le Diable boiteux* (1707), but here Dancourt is surely trying to reproduce the cynical atmosphere of Lesage's recent best-seller.

21. It is likely that the Angélique rôle was written first with his wife Thérèse and later with his daughter Mimi in mind. See Blanc, *Dancourt*, 163.

22. The Mariane of *La Foire de Bezons* (1695) resembles Angélique closely, and they even appear together in *Les Vendanges de Suresnes* (1695) as well as in *Le Charivari* (1697) where they become almost indistinguishable. As for Lucile, her approximation of Angélique-like behavior is illustrated in *Le Galant Jardinier* (1704).

23. For example, Lucile is painfully simple, "innocente" in *Le Chevalier à la mode* (1687), Mariane excessively animated in an already quoted passage of *La Loterie* (1697), and another Lucile charmingly flirtatious in *Les Fêtes nocturnes du Cours* (1714).

24. Frédéric Deloffre, ed., *Théâtre complet de Marivaux*, Classiques Garnier, vol. 2 (Paris: Garnier, 1968), 109.

25. Marivaux composed other "exotic" plays, such as *Le Prince travesti* (1724) and *Le Triomphe de l'amour* (1732), hardly reminiscent of Dancourt. This

and similar illustrative lists were, furthermore, never intended to be exhaustive.

26. Neither of these plays is set in Paris, obviously.

27. The plays in question are: *La Seconde Surprise de l'amour* (1727), *L'Ecole des mères* (1732), *La Mère confidente* (1735), *L'Epreuve* (1740), *Le Préjugé vaincu* (1746), *Les Acteurs de bonne foi* (1757). For details on Marivaux's specific renditions of the character see my "Onomastique marivaudienne: Angélique nubile," *Revue Marivaux* 3 (1992): 51–62.

28. Lucette Desvignes, *RHLF* 63 (1963): 394–414; quote on 402. In her pursuit of sources for Marivaux's two "mother" plays in Dancourt, Mme. Desvignes could well have added the young girl of *Les Bourgeoises à la mode* (1692), as severely kept in check by her father as the heroine of *L'Ecole des mères* by her mother. It is true that the former is called Mariane, but this is a name Dancourt did on occasion substitute for Angélique. For that matter, it would seem that Marivaux at first called the Angélique of *L'Epreuve* Marianne! See Deloffre, ed., *Théâtre de Marivaux* 2:506, 508. *L'Epreuve* suggests a last "rapprochement de détail" with the theater of Dancourt, with his *Fête de village* (1700) and *Colin-Maillard* (1701), to be specific. All three Angéliques are tempted at least once to consider marriage to an unwanted suitor out of pique and frustration with their true loves.

29. The first of these two Angéliques is described as "une simple bourgeoise de campagne" (*L'Epreuve*, sc. 1), and about the second her father says: "[Voilà] six ans qu'elle est sortie de Paris" (*Le Préjugé vaincu*, sc. 5).

30. A certain degree of social permeability is implied in Dancourt's theater. If Angélique absents herself from the pure "paysanneries," she does so not out of disdainful snobbery but rather, one is tempted to think, from a recognition that the competition she represents would be unfair. In point of fact, Dancourt's characters not infrequently transgress official taboos. Bourgeois marry "petites fermières" (*Madame Artus* [1708]), nobles unite with bourgeoises (*Les Vacances* [1696], *La Fête de village* [1700]), perhaps even with untutored village girls (*L'Opéra de village* [1692]), and everyone is in pursuit of money, the great equalizer. When, in *La Fête de village*, the Count informs Naquart the lawyer that he is thinking of going into business, Naquart expresses incredulity: "Un homme de votre qualité dans les affaires?"—and he receives the following reply: "Pourquoi non? Les gens d'affaires achètent nos terres et nos noms même. Quel inconvénient de faire leur métier pour être quelque jour en état de rentrer dans nos maisons et dans nos charges?" (act 3, sc. 4). If one recalls King Astur's reference to a handsome young prince who is *almost* as happy as a business man (14n above), "la boucle est vraiment bouclée." In truth, class distinctions leave the playwright Dancourt politically indifferent, unconcerned.

31. In *Le Moulin de Javelle* (1696), to calm the fiery impetuosity of the Chevalier eager to know the new bride Angélique better, *much* better, his valet Lolive cynically advises patience: "De nouvelles mariées sont encore toutes sottes de leurs maris. Réservons cela [c.-à-d., les infidélités] pour le quartier d'hiver, au retour de la campagne" (sc. 24). The "campagne" to which he is referring is the present summer's military campaign by the conclusion of which the boredom of conjugal uniformity should have taken firm hold.

32. For example, when she exclaims excitedly to her father in anticipation of the happy denouement she believes she has arranged: "[S]i vous saviez combien tout ceci va rendre notre union aimable! Il [Dorante] ne pourra jamais se rappeler notre histoire sans m'aimer, je n'y songerai jamais que je ne l'aime, vous avez fondé notre bonheur *pour la vie*, en me laissant faire" (act 3, sc. 6). Italics mine.

33. Blanc, *Dancourt*, 78, 116.

34. Blanc calls Dancourt "l'homme d'octobre," for it was then that many of his "dancourades" were slapped together as a "planche de salut de la compagnie," or, rather, of that less sought-after part of the "compagnie" that remained in Paris while their happier colleagues annually entertained royalty at Fontainebleau. Ibid., 73.

35. Or *Le Notaire obligeant*, the original title.

"Beyond the Limits of a Vulgar Fate": The Renegotiation of Public and Private Concerns in the Careers of Gray and Other Mid-Eighteenth Century Poets

WILLIAM LEVINE

The essay that follows will argue against a prevailing interpretation of mid-eighteenth century poetry that emphasizes its forms of subjectivity and isolation at the expense of considering the social determinants of its seemingly private personae. Further, the argument will explain how this movement towards privacy constitutes a legitimate criticism of the limited professional conditions and opportunities for public responsibility that frustrated ambitious lyric poets of the 1740s, 1750s, and 1760s. In particular, the essay will discuss three related problems that "poets of sensibility" confronted: (1) The urge to uphold a purified notion of high poetic tradition that is not contaminated by the demands of commercial publishing, venality, or partisan politics: the isolated, sensitive poetic speaker attempts to preserve his artistic or ethical integrity in the face of these corrupting influences. (2) The search for a legitimate, socially responsive basis of poetic power: for example, odes about the powers of poetry or the heroics of King David reflect a desire for the convergence of aesthetic, moral, political, and cathartic aims in a reformed republic of letters; in addition, such poems idealize a state of public participation and civic responsibility for their writers, even as they assume an isolated stance to criticize political, commercial, and other forces that fragment the poet's traditional social purpose. (3) The correspondence of poetic form to social function: ironically, one of the most enduring verse forms of the mid- eighteenth century is Pindaric ode that points to a lack of public occasions to celebrate and to doubt about the poet's vocation; conversely, the solitary speaker of lyrics such as Thomas Gray's *Elegy* or Christopher Smart's "Song to David" is able to make broad, socially redeeming claims by distancing himself from public life. The ensuing interpretations will establish not only the validity of the social criticism in such lyrical gestures of isolation but also the poets' efforts, in the course of their careers, to renegotiate traditional public genres so as to accommodate their dramatized sense of exclusion. Owing to the greater extent of biographical information about Gray, the essay will concentrate upon the dilemmas of public obligation and private misgivings in his poetic career; to the extent that his concerns are typical, however, of a broader desire to reform the status of public verse, the discussion will also include comparable examples from Smart, William Collins, and John "Estimate" Brown.

In June of 1769 Gray offered the following observations on a collection of William Shenstone's letters: "poor Man! he was always wishing for money, for fame, & other distinctions, & his whole philosophy consisted in living against his will in retirement, & in a place, wch his taste had adorn'd; but wch he only enjoy'd, when People of note came to see & commend it."[1] These seemingly innocuous remarks suggest that Gray is struck by Shenstone's misguided efforts to promote his life and career. Shenstone's overadorned country estate, the Leasowes, recalls Alexander Pope's Twickenham, a neo-Horatian retreat that is both the visible sign of a poetic career in retirement as well as the locus of retirement poetry. Gray's comments point out the discrepancy between the ends and means of poetic "fame" in one model of a career. The author of "The Schoolmistress" has imitated Pope's well-known poetic lifestyle without reaping the expected social benefits—for example, the admiration of his more powerful neighbor, Lord Lyttelton, who scorned Shenstone's attempts to embellish his *petty State.*" Admittedly Shenstone lacked the capabilities or financial success of a Pope, and could not have warranted as much social recognition. But his example reflects the problems attendant upon the limited possibilities for a respectable poetic career in the 1740s, 1750s, and 1760s and the dissatisfaction with conventional channels of authorship that are fairly common to aspiring poets in these decades. If, as James Ralph declared in 1758, neither the booksellers nor the press nor political parties could be trusted as sources of support, then it is not surprising that writers sought openly unorthodox and seemingly anachronistic careers: Shenstone's impotent rural retirement is only an extreme case of this separation from literary London and the conditions of modern commercial authorship, which, as Alvin Kernan has claimed, Johnson embodies and dignifies.[2]

Thomas Gray chose another alternative to commercial forms of professional authorship: retirement at Cambridge as a fellow-commoner, and later, as Professor of Modern History, a sinecure that he obtained through his connections to the Grafton ministry. Gray rarely left the grounds of the college in his adult life, and when he did, he showed little interest in securing public power or recognition. Paradoxically, however, his *Elegy* (1751) and later his odes earned him more fame than he ever reckoned upon. Unlike Shenstone, who unsuccessfully adhered to one model of a poetic career, a form of publicized privacy in his retirement at the

Leasowes, Gray renounced most public channels of authorial life (limiting his involvement, for example, to overseeing the publication of his 1757 odes) but reluctantly won his reputation mainly on the basis of one poem, his *Elegy*, which succeeded in privatizing the public role of the poet, or uttering universal truths from the standpoint of a subjective, personally affected speaker.[3]

Accounts of the so-called "poets of sensibility" have traditionally emphasized this private character of their verse and the social isolation of poets like Gray who are not, to take one standard of public recognition, part of Johnson's circle. A glance at recent studies reveals such labels as "literary loneliness," a "flight from history," a "literature of ontology," an internalized "vocational doubt."[4] An unfortunate teleology also has sandwiched mid-eighteenth-century poetry between, and devalued it in comparison to, the public, didactic pronouncements of Dryden or Pope and the private yet expressive convictions of Wordsworth or Keats. Until very recently, however, the work of mid-century poets has not been vigorously interpreted in a public, political, or cultural context.[5] Admittedly, the odes and hymns of Gray, Smart, and Collins lack the qualities of "public lyrics" like Dryden's odes for St. Cecilia's Day, which even Gray's "Progress of Poesy" acknowledges are "heard no more."[6] Gray's 1757 Pindaric odes are routinely taken as exercises in a solitary figure's sublime visions, prospects that recount the glorified history of poetry for a brighter future, or the extended curse of the solitary Welsh bard upon a series of debased political leaders who are hostile to the free expression and moral purity of poetry. Even in Gray's own times, these odes were considered obscure, and he condescendingly inserted footnotes in his 1769 editions to explain his oblique allusions to mythology and English history. More cautious critical formulations point out, however, that this supposed movement away from public life is itself political, as it establishes a realm of purity that turns the solitary expressive poet against corrupt public customs and practices, even if the writer's particular state of affairs is allegorized as an event of past history, mythologized, or projected onto nature. One might remember William Empson's comments on the casuistry of Gray's *Elegy*: such topoi as the inevitability of wasted potential are disingenuous. What is perhaps the *Elegy*'s most memorable quatrain seems to naturalize the villagers' and, by implication, the sensibility-poet's unfulfilled lives:

> Full many a gem of purest ray serene
> The dark unfathomed caves of ocean bear:
> Full many a flower is born to blush unseen
> And waste its sweetness on the desert air.
>
> (53–56)

In Empson's view, this quatrain can be both an acceptance of inevitability as well as an implied critique of a government that does not have a system for conferring status and recognition upon scholars like Gray. The compensation that characterizes "sensibility" is to aestheticize, naturalize, and ultimately purify this loss of public acclaim, much as one of Gray's contemporaries had earlier depicted onanism: "To shed thy Blossoms thro' the desert air / And sow thy perished Off-spring in the winds."[7] In both cases, an object of humiliation or shame is projected onto a natural economy that can easily sustain such losses and preserve its virginal members for higher, purer duties, whether these consist of deferring coitus until maturity or foreskaing the corruptions of public life and fame while maintaining the bonds of human sympathy.

In this sublime moment of the *Elegy*, the poet-speaker's apparent disdain of fame and social empowerment should not prevent one from seeing that its recuperation of "wasted" private potential has tangible public implications. One of T. W. Adorno's formulations on the Kantian dynamical sublime pertains well to the mid-eighteenth-century oppositional aesthetics of sensibility: "the true substance of the idea of sublimity" is to "reverse" any form of "complicity with domination," and thus to foster the "resistance that spirit marshals against the prepotence of nature," where nature is figured as power.[8] Tropes like Gray's submerged gem and desert flower are measures of this resistance, because they legitimate a level of private experience that is all the more powerful for its aversion to public channels of power. Yet by overemphasizing the subjective tendencies of these lyrics, one loses sight of the ways poets such as Gray reconfigure their social position. The major lyrics of the mid-eighteenth century show a strong dissatisfaction with the social channels then available to writers. Their tropes of sublimity and sensibility demonstrate an awareness of the discrepancies between public roles and private expression and the social constraints on the poet's ability to address private experience and gain an adequate sense of public independence.

Although Gray's reclusive life seems to justify the typically ahistorical, formalist treatments of his poetry, his correspondence demonstrates how attentively he observed and responded to the literary climate of his time. As his allusion to Shenstone's estate indicates, Gray is especially alert to contradictions between the public forms of literary expression and their debased or meaningless content. Commenting upon Cibber's biography of Cicero in a 1747 letter to Horace Walpole, Gray recognizes that the sale of such works depends on style—particularly a degenerate, meretricious version of "sensibility"—rather than substance: he asks, for example, whether the commendatory verses in the preface were really written by the designated author, Mrs. Laetitia Pilkington, or whether "somebody [has] put on the Style of a scribbleing Woman's Panegyric to deceive & laugh at Colley" (1:264). Despite the apparent misogyny of this remark, Gray's criticism does not assume an ideal of male superiority, but rather imagines a virginal posture of sensibility for himself (albeit latched onto a Popean standard of satire, which maintains the continuity of Cibber as a butt of ridicule and upholds its force as the preserve of male rational judgment). The virginal man of sensibility, in a derisive satirical persona, criticizes the prostituted "market" version in Cibber.[9] Cibber and Mrs. Pilkington are commodities valued more for the types of product they signify (respectively, "flirty Saucy" observations on Cicero and "scribbleing Women's panegyric" [1:264]) than for their true selves; anyone could assume the name or type of their writing. Even if such debased writers were to chance upon "Reason & Truth," Gray claims, the degradations of popular style would obscure any potentially didactic effects. The personified "Reason and Truth," each given dual, mirror-like status as reader and text, would not "know their own Faces" if they "saw themselves so bedizen'd in tatter'd Fringe & tarnish'd Lace, in French Jewels, & dirty Furbelows, the Frippery of a Stroller's Wardrobe" (1:264–65). Cibber serves Gray's satirical purposes well because his persona conflates tawdry theatricality with popular literary style. But Gray's criticism of market conditions for writers encompasses larger targets than just the King of the Dunces: "Litterature [*sic*] . . . [taken] in its most comprehensive Sense, & includ[ing] every Thing, that requires Invention, or Judgement, or barely Application & Industry, seems indeed drawing apace to its Dissolution; & remarkably since the Beginning of the War [of Austrian Succession]" (1: 265).

Gray's satirical sallies mask an earnest criticism of an artificially produced, de-personalized network of public writing, in which the gaudy appearance and broad production of literature outweigh such concerns as the endurance, quality, or individual basis of a serious work. Gray's own small quantity of verse is an attempt to restore "Litterature" to its prelapsarian state. Often difficult, individualistic, and sporadically produced, his odes are ways of combatting the degenerative tendencies Gray has recognized in Cibber. The odes' consciously allusive style, tentative moral assertions, and cultivation of feeling (or "redeemed sensibility") as a manifestation of identity are efforts to make the style of a work speak the authentic voice of the socially marginal poet.

Gray's style deviates from the commercially successful writing of his time, but even more striking is his remoteness from the conventional forms of literary careers and his disdain for writing as a profession. Unlike Johnson, who accused Gray of relying upon "puerilities of obsolete mythology,"[10] or even Shenstone, Gray did little to gain professional recognition. The *Elegy* was the most popular poem of mid-century, but Gray had no desire to profit from this success, seeming to revert to a Renaissance idea of literature as a gentleman's profession. Gray's publisher, Robert Dodsley, earned £1000 from the *Elegy* and did not return the copyright to Gray, denying a common courtesy of the time. The Pindarics sold 1200–1300 copies in their first month. Gray received all of £40 for these; his only apparent gratification was to use Walpole's press at Strawberry-Hill for the first printing of the odes and thus "snatch . . . them out of Dodsley's hands," though the publisher still had the copyright (*Correspondence of Gray*, 2:512–13 n. 1; 2:513 n. 4). Characteristically insisting on the disparity between earning a reputation through the market place and earning it through the quality of literary work, Gray comments (in a 1746 letter to Dr. Thomas Wharton, one of his friends from Cambridge): "It is a foolish Thing, that one can't only not live as one pleases, but where & with whom one pleases, without Money. Swift somewhere says, that Money is Liberty; & I fear money is Friendship too & Society, & almost every external Blessing. it [*sic*] is a great tho' ill-natured, Comfort to see most of these, who have it in Plenty, without Pleasure, without Liberty, & without Friends" (1:255).

Scorning "The Great" in the name of individual Liberty typifies a Whig poetics common to the time and is consonant with Gray's personal sense of authorial freedom from publishers, patrons, and politicians.[11] But his apparent disdain of literary politics and the active public involvement such professionalism typically entailed did not preclude a socially responsible stance—however diffused, distanced, or displaced—on the part of Gray or like-minded friends, admirers, and writers outside the London literary community. And perhaps their mutual opposition to the established literary market and tastes provides a basis for the "lyric revival" that grew in mid-century. Donald Davie observes that the most significant literature of the period was didactic and often "out of sympathy" with the dominant Whig currents of eighteenth-century English society which emphasized "social mobility," "territorial and commercial expansion," and "conspicuous consumption." Davie asserts the importance, however, of an Augustan lyric tradition that never deserted these so-called "progressive" tendencies. But it is important to note that even the poems affiliated with "progress" did much to purify and idealize the individualistic or aggressive forces they celebrated—thereby underscoring the complexity of eighteenth-century Whiggery.[12] Moreover, while such lyric genres as songs, hymns, and ballads can be readily assimilated into Davie's thesis, extended, dialectical lyric forms present a more complicated stance towards the main currents of the age. A case in point is Christopher Smart's elaborate devotion on the Lord and His greatest Psalmist. "A Song to David" is neither simply celebratory nor plainly didactic. However much his verse displays a unique concern for praising God's creations, Smart absorbed qualities of both the "expansive" lyricism of his time and the "normative" literary modes that satirized aggressive individualism. As both a recorder of sacred history and the observer of festivals, David must "*keep* the days on Zion's mount" (10); he prays for all of God's work "With wish of infinite conceit," a transcendent, all-encompassing purifying imagination. Yet Smart contrasts this ideal office of a devotional poet with the less desirable mundane world of professional writing:

> O DAVID, highest in the list
> Of worthies, on God's ways insist,
>   The genuine word repeat:
> Vain are the documents of men,

> And vain the flourish of the pen
> That keeps the fool's conceit.
>
> (289-94)[13]

All other writers, who can only "keep" or own and persist in their profane wit, turn to hacks or dunces compared to David, a type for the highest aspirations of the sublime poet, even to the extent that devotion for the poetic calling converges with the act of worshiping the Lord and His creatures. Even if Smart's "Song" is not Whiggish in any secular sense, it is expansive, seeking accommodation of all nature to a larger pattern of devotion, and breaks down the boundaries between "high" and "low" objects of worship, as well as private and public expressions of faith. This private yet transcendent act of worship also deviates from the mundane, socially accepted idea of a poet's vocation, a "vain" exercise of wit and adherence to the fallen world of ordinary social intercourse. This stanza recontextualizes Proverbs 26.5, "Answer a fool according to his folly, lest he be wise in his own conceit," so as to satirize the mundane world of letters. In a sense, Smart relocates the Whiggish tendencies onto higher ground while maintaining the satiric force of Tory humanism, relying on his spiritual ambitions to justify his own pun on "conceit" against an overbearing, self-important tradition of secular wit.

In Gray's mid-century Pindarics, the cultural-political alliances appear even more complicated, and depend on the possibilities and limitations of the ode's form and literary tradition. Gray's Whig sentiments play a role in his 1757 Pindarics, but he only obliquely heeds such commonplaces as commercial expansion, peace by trade, individual aspiration or liberty, growing prosperity, and republican government. "Progress pieces" like Gray's history of poesy may embrace all these values, but one should mark the differences between extended panegyrics like James Thomson's *Liberty* or Richard Glover's *London* and the odes of Gray or Collins that lack explicit political statement. A thematic preoccupation with Liberty, especially in an allegorical, mythological, and oblique form, does not simply align the poet with unremitting Whig ideology, as in Thomson or Glover, but in fact assumes a broader, more problematic view of how poetry may restore the national conscience: for example, Collins' 1746 "Ode to Liberty," written in the midst of the controversial War of Austrian Succession and on the tail of the Highland uprisings, can conclude only an anxious anticipation that Liberty will arrive on "Britain's ravaged shore" (138). Undoubtedly such odes are the product of their times: though taking heed of the traditional Pindaric meditation upon athletic heroism, the strength of the state, and the powers of the heavens, they move inspired poetry, or its attendant powers, liberty, imagination, and musical feeling, into a position of prominence, a displacement of the odist's ideals in a state where the status of poetry and the writer in general has sunk, divorced not only from political power, but from an honorable view of authorship. As "Estimate" Brown pointed out, "The Laurel Wreath, once aspired after as the highest Object of Ambition, would now be rated at the Market-price of its Materials, and derided as a *Three-penny Crown.*"[14] Rather than, on the one hand, an aestheticized "flight" from history, or, on the other hand, a transparent acceptance, though allegorically depicted, of the expansionist Whig campaigns of the time, a different treatment of these odes could ground them in the circumstances of authorial status. As they concern themselves with the mythological origins of inspired poetry and trace the conditions that have led to its current, fallen state, the odes of Gray and Collins actually offer a substantially different account of history, an account that departs from both the progressivist celebrations of British nationalism and the culturally stabilizing transmission of learning and moral and aesthetic values, as in part three of Pope's *Essay on Criticism* (643–744).[15]

In one of the best known mid-century odes, "The Progress of Poesy," Gray concludes with a couplet that, because of its semantic indeterminacy, has drawn an amount of explication comparable to "Beauty is truth, truth beauty." After admitting that he lacks the capabilities or inspirations of Pindar, Shakespeare, Milton, or Dryden, the aspiring mid-eighteenth-century poet—presumably Gray himself—nonetheless resolves to draw on his modest, solitary visionary powers, to "mount and keep his distant way":

> Beyond the limits of a vulgar fate,
> Beneath the Good how far—but far above the Great.
>
> (122–23)

Interpretations of these lines vary widely. Virtually an index of recent critical schools, the couplet has been explained as a commentary upon Gray's own performance vis-à-vis literary history, an affirmation of the ode's ethical theme that poetry is enabled by political liberty, or even an heroic ideal of virtue and valor that Pitt's imperialism can legitimate.[16] Whether these final lines are about poetic tradition versus the present dearth of talent, the lack of contemporary occasions for public verse, or the self-imposed isolation of an ambitious modern poet who seeks to maintain moral and literary integrity, generally there is agreement that the couplet problematically addresses Gray's poetic vocation and transvaluates the meanings of "the Good" and "the Great."

Without adding unnecessary complications to an already cluttered history of explications, one may contextualize Gray's ending in some mid-century discussions of professional authorship. While Gray's disdain for "vulgar" writing like Cibber's has already been illustrated, the ethical stipulations that value "the Good" above "the Great" are typical of Whiggish writers such as Ralph and Brown, who oppose the notions of a "Commonwealth" of letters to a "tyranny." At various points in these writings, the terms pertain both literally to the actual form of government under which authors live, and metaphorically, to the community of writers and their professional practice. For example, in his survey of the rise, fall, and possible reunion of poetry and music, Brown notes that "the original *Dignity* of the *Bard's*

Character was always maintained longer in *Commonwealths* than under despotic or *kingly* Governments" because "the *Republican* Form subsists by an united Exertion of the Powers of every Rank: Under the *despotic* Rule, the Influence of these various Powers is swallowed up in the absolute Will of ONE."[17] In an ideal state of letters and politics, the poet instills moral virtues in all citizens; indeed, figures such as Orpheus, David, and Amphion combine the powers of lawmaker and poet as well as singer and versifier (*Dissertation*, 36–40). If this is the "Good" that a commonwealth of poets and a reinvigorated union of poetry and music can achieve, it stands in stark contrast to the present, overrefined, corrupt state of affairs, where not only have the characters of musician, poet, and legislator been separated but also the tyrannical principle of self-interest has pervaded all professions (ibid. 45–46). Gray's valuation of the "Good" over the "Great" is sorely needed to correct the contaminated world of "professional" ethics, where, according to James Ralph, "Money, however acquir'd, is at the Summit, and public Spirit [or Magnanimity] under foot" (*The Case of Authors*, 47). For an authorial state of "Liberty," a "Commonwealth" implies patriotism, virtue, disinterest, and public good as the ideal conditions of writing, whereas a "tyranny" can ensue not only under traditional forms of patronage (the aristocratic or Walpolean "Great"), but also under exploitative entrepreneurs in theatre, bookselling, or the political journalism; *The Case of Authors* sarcastically labels theatre-managers like Cibber as "the Great" for their tyrannical control of productions and arrogant, arbitrary patronage of aspiring authors (26–28).[18]

Although Brown's proposed reunion of poetry and music, as well as his implied example, "The Cure of Saul" (which could "make . . . the reader sick," according to one reviewer)[19] may seem to provide only illusionary therapy for a fallen society, Davie reminds us that much of eighteenth-century lyric poetry is composed to "*match an existing piece of music*,"[20] or with the possibility of a musical setting for it, and such traditional figurations of harmony are an available means for recovering the public force of lyric poetry. Considering that a number of the mid-century odes were performed, or intended to be performed, at ceremonies such as the installation of chancellors or the commemoration of a university's benefactors, the "solitary lyric voice" that exalts the public spirit can be taken as a key figure for the poet's wish to facilitate a self-governing, culturally pure, and commercially purged literary society that molds the nation's character. The odes for St. Cecilia's Day are especially representative, for the patron saint of music and reputed inventor of the organ is taken as a figure for the power of sublime poetry to morally and imaginatively transport its audience. Modeled upon Dryden's "Ode for St. Cecilia's Day" and "Alexander's Feast," which was placed in its most memorable setting by Handel in 1739, the odes for music celebrate a now-lost union of the arts and the acts of the state. In an ideally recovered union of poetry and music, a legislator-bard, such as David in Brown's "Cure of Saul," moderates the vicious passions of the ruler, eases distress, and controls dangerous anti-social energies as well as inspires valor and piety.

Although the Cecilia's Day tradition had lost some of its force by mid-century—Bonnell Thornton had written and published a parody of the typical ode in 1749, which was performed in 1763, requiring instruments such as a salt-box, a marrow-bone, a bladder, and a Jew's Harp—Gray, Collins, and Smart all wrote odes for public settings, and in some revealing instances assisted in arranging the performance. Virtually all ode-writers wrote testimonies to the powers of poetry—the original title of Gray's "Progress"—or music, as an analogue of lyric poetry.[21] The receptions of Dryden's "standard" neoclassical odes in the mid-century compositions can not only map social influences on a changing genre, but also articulate the poet's desired relation to the governors of society. For example, Brown criticized the manner in which the poet Timotheus manipulates the drunken, easily vindictive Alexander in Dryden's ode; this violent ending indicates an abuse of the powers of music.[22] To illustrate what he believes is a morally responsible palinode for a musical setting, Brown prefaces his 1763 dissertation on the origins of music with "The Cure of Saul," which focuses upon David as a more cathartic, healing figure who can implicitly correct the role of culture in sustaining virtuous civic government as well. In presenting scenes of David singing to the grief-stricken Saul about the creation, fall, and ultimate redemption of mankind, as well as acts of Divine wrath and a glimpse of a celestial afterlife, Brown combines elements from both of Dryden's major odes. "The Cure of Saul" maintains both the apocalyptic scale of Dryden's 1687 "Song for St. Cecilia's Day" and the dramatic effects of the poet's performance for the ruler in "Alexander's Feast." Yet Brown deliberately chooses a plot in which the poet needs to cure a fallen ruler, rather than arouse him into a state of fierce revenge and serve only as the instrument of his destructive appetite. Further, the apocalyptic pattern is not so much a Drydenesque celebration of music or poetry's powers, as a cathartic, internalized process for Saul to repent for his transgressions. The King must meditate on Divine retribution and grace in order to curb his errors, and the poet is of value to the state, yet possesses his own authority, when he enables this healing process. In an ode that tends to moralize rather heavy-handedly, Brown never leaves the reader in doubt as to whether Saul or David is in control:

> Thus while the frowning *Shepherd* pour'd along
> The deep impetuous Torrent of his Song;
>   SAUL, stung by dire Despair,
>   Gnash'd his Teeth, and tore his Hair;
>   From his Blood, by Horror chill'd,
> A cold and agonizing Sweat distill'd:
> Then, foaming with unutterable Smart,
>   He aim'd a Dagger at his Heart.
>   His watchful Train prevent the Blow;

> And call each lenient Balm to heal his frantic Woe:
> But pleas'd, the *Shepherd* now beheld
> His Pride by Heav'n's own Terrors quell'd:
> Then bade his potent Lyre controul
> The mighty Storm that rent his Soul.
> (*Dissertation*, 13–14)

Unlike the outwardly-directed anger of Alexander, Saul's nearly suicidal rage is directed inwardly, and this well orchestrated turn towards privacy ultimately serves David's cathartic purposes. The shepherd-musician-poet, and future king, is so attuned to God's creations that his song invokes "Heav'n's own Terrors," not merely their likeness. This ode, written for ceremonial recitation, describes a scene in which poetic mimesis assumes performative force, and the redeeming effect of poetry on public character is made legitimate.

In contrast to Brown's attempted rehabilitation of Dryden, Collins' ode, "The Passions," offers a less obvious and optimistic solution to the problems of reuniting poetry with politics. As a symptom of the absent public powers of poetry, "The Passions" is organized as a series of contiguous recitals by each passion with no cumulative effect on its specified audience, the personified yet isolated passions themselves, whose performances tend to interrupt or conflict with one another.[23] Offering some initially redeeming possibilities, the ode recounts a mythic contest among such passions as Fear, Anger, Despair, Hope, Revenge, Pity, Melancholy, Cheerfulness, and Joy. Although these personifications "snatch" the instruments from their teacher, Music (12), the relative enclosure of each performance and the broadly balancing array of passions suggest that any threat of usurpation or possible violence is contained and sublimated through artistic expression. Given the context of recent political violence affecting the English—the Young Pretender's 1745 uprising and the War of Austrian Succession—Collins' 1746 ode, the culminating work in his volume, could be interpreted as a comic resolution to the problems of excessive aggression and failed hopes, displaced from the ugly canvas of contemporary history onto an allegorical tableau. Yet the effects of such isolation can be disturbing as well. For example, Pity is able to check, if not overcome Revenge in the following passage:

> . . . but with a frown,
>   Revenge impatient rose;
> He threw his blood-stained sword in thunder down,
>   And with a withering look,
>   The war-denouncing trumpet took,
> And blew a blast so loud and dread,
> Were ne'er prophetic sounds so full of woe.
>   And ever and anon he beat
>   The doubling drum with furious heat;
> And though sometimes each dreary pause between,

> Dejected Pity at his side
> Her soul-subduing voice applied,
> Yet still he kept his wild unaltered mien,
> While each strained ball of sight seemed bursting from his
> head.
>
> (39–52)

Revenge may be kept "still" in being unable to act, or may persist in his desire to retaliate, but the lulling strains of Pity seem only to defer or temporarily immobilize the inevitable ruin prophesized by the trumpet or the call to arms of the drum. Rather than dramatic resolution and catharsis, what emerges is a series of separate voices shouting ineffectually, a less than idyllic golden age in which "madness ruled the hour" (15), despite a final concession to Music's "all-commanding power" (100).

The ode concludes with a self-consciously elegiac passage about the decline of poetic achievement since a mythic golden age, but in a more historicist view, a decline since the type of ode for music that Dryden established, in which the poet or musician is endowed with power to move worlds. Collins plaintively seeks for Music to revive this lost age:

> Thy wonders in that god-like age
> Fill thy recording Sister's page—
> 'Tis said, and I believe the tale,
> Thy humblest reed could more prevail,
> Had more of strength, diviner rage,
> Than all which charms this laggard age, ·
> Even all at once together found,
> Caecilia's mingled world of sound—
>
> (107–14)

Just as the allegorical portrayals of the individual passions seem to undermine Collins' wish for a harmonious union of lyric poetry and social power, this conclusion confirms that the arts are not progressive in "this laggard age." If classical Greece could record a simple, energetic Orphic power of Music in the pages of her Sister Muse, Clio, then the mid-eighteenth century, even with all its advantages of learning or supposed cultural sophistication, "Caecilia's mingled world of sound," has truly lost sight of music or lyric poetry's sources of empowerment—namely, the convergence of "virtue, fancy, art" (104) in a "Warm, energic, chaste, sublime" refrain (106). Where aesthetic qualities are allied to the audience's social graces, imaginative purification and ethical sense, the poet is most efficacious. But this unity is absent. Rather than arriving at the culminating apocalypses of Dryden's odes—cities burning or the heavens crumbling, owing to the unbounded powers of poetry or music—Collins can only envision a Brown-like unitary Greek ode (116), half in anticipation, half in elegiac regret. Even though the body of his own poem largely succeeds in dramatizing the separate lyrical powers, the lack of poetic and civic harmony remains.

Gray's efforts in this genre deserve special attention, for they offer the most revealing instance of an uneasy alliance between poetic and political powers. He wrote his "Ode for Music" (1769) under rather discomfiting circumstances, as a favor for the Duke of Grafton's assistance in attaining his Cambridge professorship. The ode was performed at a commencement ceremony, Grafton's Installation as Chancellor of Cambridge, and almost immediately parodied thereafter.[24] On the one hand, these circumstances suggest that Gray's "private" poetic voice was undercut by his venal attachments to an extremely unpopular government official. On the other hand, Gray's reluctance to write and supervise the performance of the ode indicates that he was frustrated with his inability to attain an ideal state of poetic liberty and independence from "the Great"—a freedom that was much less problematic for him in declining an offer in 1757 to become Poet Laureate, or "*Rat-Catcher* to his Majesty with a salary of 300£ a-year & two Butts of the best Malaga" (*Correspondence* 2:543–44). As if to maintain that such attachments undermine his autonomy over his art, Gray muses in one letter that the composer Randall could have written the words and he could have written the music without any noticeable effect on the performance (*Correspondence* 3:1065). Even Gray's attempts to "purify" the philandering, corrupt Grafton by extolling his lineage, "A Tudor's fire, a Beaufort's grace" (70), are counterproductive, at least in terms of warding off such critics as Junius, and point to the impossibility of reconciling venal political reality with the poetry of sublimity or sensibility.[25] One sign of Gray's discomfort may be a perverse intertextual allusion to his own *Elegy*, in which the poet absorbs the minister in imagery that he has previously used to describe his unfulfilled potential:

> Thy liberal heart, thy judging eye,
> The flower unheeded shall descry,
> And bid it round heaven's altars shed
> The fragrance of its blushing head
> Shall raise from earth the latent gem
> To glitter on the diadem.
>
> (71–76)

The gem, no longer submerged in the ocean, and the flower, no longer wasted on the desert air, have been appropriated for Grafton's heaven-blessed Installation, a public exploitation and distortion of what had seemed to be a private, but broadly redeeming pair of tropes about an inevitable seclusion from public life.[26] Such public settings for lyric poetry can illustrate the discrepancies between the private literary wish for greater jurisdiction over the realms of culture, taste, learning, and history, and the intrusions of the larger economy: signs of patronage, sponsorship, specialized audiences, and other forms of public support, to which the writer is ultimately bound.

While the "Ode for Music" desperately attempts to purify the corrupt Grafton and legitimize the poet's own feeble public role through the medium of the sublime ode, perhaps Gray most openly acknowledged the futility of aligning poetry with public power in an aborted didactic poem he began at least twenty years earlier, "The Alliance of Education and Government." Although the following passages, inspired by Montesquieu, are an open meditation on the national temperaments produced in different climates and the ways that racial or climatological differences may determine the outcomes of various wars, Gray's characteristic imagery of loss and compensation will later be displaced onto the victimized or remote, helpless poets of the Pindarics and the *Elegy*:

> As oft have issued, host impelling host,
> The blue-eyed myriads from the Baltic coast.
> The prostrate south to the destroyer yields
> Her boasted titles and her golden fields:
> With grim delight the brood of winter view
> A brighter day and heavens of azure hue,
> Scent the new fragrance of the breathing rose,
> And quaff the pendent vintage, as it grows.
> (50–57)
> . . . .
> Can opener skies and suns of fiercer flame
> O'erpower the fire that animates our frame,
> As lamps, that shed at even a cheerful ray,
> Fade and expire beneath the eye of day?
> (64–67)

In the first passage, the flower has not simply "waste[d] its sweetness on the desert air," but has been made to serve the stronger, conquering race, however much its feminine, civilizing virtues may contribute to a larger harmonizing purpose. Closer to Gray's immediate poetic aspirations, perhaps culture can only serve the ends of political expediency and inevitably must remain in a "prostrate" condition, if it is put to use at all. The second passage sets the stage for a denial that European Liberty can be extinguished by Turkish conquests, and that the will to freedom is dissipated in warmer climates, perhaps anticipating a never-completed celebration of the intrinsic moral strengths of the British climate. Even so, it allegorically verges upon surrendering any social significance for Gray's didactic verse and being resigned to the expiring light of individual freedom, which the eloquent bearers of inspired poesy carry to the end of Gray's two 1757 Pindarics.[27] Gray would later comment that he was unable to complete this Pope-like didactic "Essay" because he could not sustain the high degree of sublime imagery in its discursive couplet form:

> he had been used to write only Lyric poetry in which the poems being short, he had accustomed himself, & was able to polish every part; that

this having become habit, he could not write otherwise; & that the labor of this method in a long poem would be intolerable; besides which the poem would lose its effect for want of Chiaro-Oscuro; for that to produce effect it was absolutely necessary to have weak parts.[28]

Gray may have found a better vehicle for his imaginative flights in the irregular Pindarics and may have submitted with greater success to being "o'erpowered" or "expiring" in the evening mode of his *Elegy*, not in the didactic "eye of day," but can his admission of defeat to this moral-essay form be an early recognition of his incompatibility with the prevailing conventional and constraining forms of public poetry? The "opener skies and suns of fiercer flame," explicitly a synecdoche for those parts of southern Europe most vulnerable to the Turk's conquest, can be taken more broadly as the "climate" for mid-eighteenth century poets—an environment where their individual, rebellious strength could simply be extinguished and homogenized in an all too vulnerable, exposed, and powerless set of public roles: servitude to the commercial forces of publishing, political writing, or venal patronage. Gray's most apt persona, the retired twilight elegist or odist who "mounts and keeps his distant way," is a departure from the didactic writer he tried to become in the "Alliance," who, like Pope, might thrive upon bringing moral quandaries out into the "eye of day." Yet as the traditional objects and delineations of didactic verse become increasingly impersonal and systematized—even implicating the means of "public" literary production and the moral bases for poetic subjectivity—the poet becomes as helpless against this commercial climate as he would against an onslaught of Turks. To its credit, this passage does not suggest retirement or resignation so much as the forbearance of individualist, oppositional liberty that is nonetheless embedded in a set of contradictions between private expression and the public character that is demanded of this didactic genre; for example, Gray catches himself expressing an "Unmanly thought" of moral cowardice in harsh environments (72), even as he indulges in imagery of passive sensibility, and calls for imaginative transcendence of mortal conditions (83) despite an explicit theme of cultural determinism.

The opposition of public and private mid-century literary modes needs to be reconsidered, since Gray and his contemporaries write poetry that emanates from a solitary persona but nonetheless has the character of a public pronouncement. Even if such works assert the poet's exclusion from larger society, their criticism of the current channels of public life available to poets implies, if it does not always enact, a more viable set of alternatives. As the essay has argued, these alternatives do not indicate that the poet seeks privacy simply to renounce and divorce himself from the corruptions of public power, but rather suggest some tentative paths by which poetry can better recuperate its traditional lyric powers and purify moral or civic life. Such postures of isolation are products of a poetic tradition, especially the view of society from the elect, the retired, or the imaginatively transported speakers in, respectively, Milton, Horace, and Pindar. But these traditions are reinterpreted so as to resist the limiting conditions of commercial writing and public disenfranchisement for lyric poets. At its best, this renegotiated tradition redefines the role of private participation in public genres and searches for new configurations of poetry and social power, rather than remove the persona from the commerce of the world. Although the tropes of sensibility depict the plight of solitary, privileged but distant figures (or personifications, like the fleeing Liberty or Poesy), these should be regarded as strategies to establish and elevate a self-governing, though socially efficacious realm, for a reinvigorated tradition of sublime poetry.

NOTES

1. *Correspondence of Thomas Gray*, ed. Paget Toynbee and Leonard Whibley, with corrections and additions by H. W. Starr, 3 vols. (Oxford: Oxford University Press, 1971), 3:1067; hereafter cited parenthetically in text. On the ideology of country retirement, see Maynard Mack, *The Garden and the City: Retirement and Politics in the Later Poetry of Pope, 1731–43* (Toronto: University of Toronto Press, 1969). Shenstone's misfortunes at the Leasowes are recounted by Samuel Johnson in his *Lives of the English Poets*, ed. G. Birkbeck Hill, 3 vols. (Oxford: Clarendon, 1905), 3:350–52.
2. James Ralph, *The Case of Authors by Profession or Trade (1758) together with The Champion (1739–40)*, intro. Philip Stevick (Gainesville, FL: Scholars' Facsimiles and Reprints, 1966), hereafter cited parenthetically in text; Alvin Kernan, *Samuel Johnson and the Impact of Print* (originally published as *Printing Technology, Letters, and Samuel Johnson* [Princeton: Princeton University Press, 1987]).
3. Biographical information is taken from A. L. Lytton Sells, *Thomas Gray: His Life and Works* (London: George Allen and Unwin, 1980).
4. These labels are gathered from John Sitter, *Literary Loneliness in Mid-Eighteenth Century England* (Ithaca: Cornell University Press, 1982); Fredric V. Bogel, *Literature and Insubstantiality in Later Eighteenth-Century England* (Princeton: Princeton University Press, 1984); Paul Fry, *The Poet's Calling in the English Ode* (New Haven and London: Yale University Press, 1980).
5. Some of the recent studies that have provided historicist interpretations of Gray's career are as follows: Linda Zionkowski, "Bridging the Gulf Between: The Poet and the Audience in the Work of Gray," *ELH* 58 (1991): 331–50, which traces the poet's growing alienation from debasing conditions of commercial writing; Suvir Kaul, *Thomas Gray and Literary Authority: A Study in Ideology and Poetics* (Stanford: Stanford University Press, 1992), which places the poet's career in the context of an emergent nationalist literary ideology; and William H. Epstein, in "Counter-Intelligence: Cold-War Criticism and Eighteenth-Century Studies," *ELH* 57 (1990): 63-99, and "Assumed Identities: Gray's Correspondence and the 'Intelligence Communities' of Eighteenth-Century Studies," *The Eighteenth*

Century 32 (1991): 274–88. Epstein points to Gray's privacy and friend-ship with Horace Walpole as evidence of his complicity in a "counter-intelligence" network of high gossip about government and public figures.

6. The text for Gray and Collins is *The Poems of Gray, Collins, and Goldsmith*, ed. Roger Lonsdale (New York: Longman, 1969), 111.

7. William Empson, *Some Versions of Pastoral* (1950; repr. New York: New Directions, 1968), 4–5; the contemporary of Gray is physician John Armstrong, whose poem, "The Oeconomy of Love" (London: 1736), is a eulogistic, Latinate account of puberty, adolescence, and sexual maturation; quoted are lines 120-21. The first recorded observation of this possible source for the *Elegy* is J. D. Short, *Notes and Queries* 210 (1965): 454.

8. T. W. Adorno, *Aesthetic Theory*, ed. Gretel Adorno and Rolf Tiedermann, trans. C. Lenhardt (New York: Routlege, 1984), 284.

9. For an intriguing discussion of the strategies whereby male writers of sensibility dissociate themselves from weak "womanly" traits such as passivity or sensual indulgence, see G. J. Barker-Benfield, *The Culture of Sensibility: Sex and Society in Eighteenth-Century Britain* (Chicago: University of Chicago Press, 1992), esp. chap. 3, "The Question of Effeminacy," 104–53.

10. Johnson, *Lives of the English Poets* 3:439. In *Samuel Johnson and the Impact of Print*, Kernan explicitly argues with an inherited view of Johnson as "the last defender of the old neoclassic literary values" and the "pre-romantic poets, whom Johnson generally disliked" (22) as the avatars of a new age heralding authorial independence. By contrast, Kernan regards authors such as Gray, Walpole, and Gibbon as "gentleman-amateurs, congenial to the mores of aristocratic society, seemingly careless of fame and money" (16) and Johnson as the truly progressive first "romantic" professional writer (22). Yet at least one polemical respondent to Johnson's "Life of Gray," Robert Potter, took great pains to argue against its oddly reclusive portrait of Gray at Cambridge; see *An Inquiry into Some of the Passages in Dr. Johnson's Lives of the Poets: Particularly his Observations on Lyric Poetry, and the Odes of Gray* (London,1783), which emphasizes the poet's sociability while sequestered at Cambridge (16), as well as his intercourse with great minds, mannerliness, urbanity, taste, and piety. Potter even turns the plot of Gray's "Bard" into an allegory of authorial politics: Kings should fear to be tyrants, a possible lesson to literary tyrants like Johnson (38).

11. A. S. Collins, *Authorship in the Days of Johnson: Being a Study of the Relation between Author, Patron, Publisher, and Public, 1726–1780* (London: Robert Holden, 1927), 33, 37. For a thorough account of Whig aesthetics, see Michael Meehan, *Liberty and Poetics in Eighteenth Century England* (London: Croom Helm, 1986).

12. Donald Davie, ed., *Augustan Lyric* (London: Heinemann, 1974), 3.

13. I cite from *The Poetical Works of Christopher Smart*, ed. Marcus Walsh and Karina Williamson, vol. 3 (Oxford: Clarendon Press, 1983); on the dual sense of "keep," see 430 n. 10. In *A Form of Sound Words: The Religious Poetry of Christopher Smart* (Oxford: Clarendon Press, 1989), Harriet Guest addresses the poet's conflicts between public and private expressions of faith, noting the mixture of "retired devotion" and "congregational praise"

in his lyrics (67). She explains the "infinite conceit" of the psalmist's prayers as "their ability to . . . express the private circumstances both of the life of David and of every worshipper, and to describe prophetically the progress of the Church and of Christ in the universal drama of Salvation" (272–73).

14. John Brown, *An Estimate of the Manners and Principles of the Times*, 2 vols. (London: 1757–58), 1:59.

15. On the continuities of the mid-eighteenth-century ode with classical models, see Steven Shankman, "The Pindaric Tradition and the Quest for Pure Poetry," *Comparative Literature* 40 (1988): 219–44; e.g., "Pindar's odes were originally designed to perform the encomiastic function of praising an athlete who had been successful in the games; these Pindarics of Collins and Gray now praise the poetic imagination itself, which the failed modern poet attempts . . . to embody in a poem that is . . . purely the cry of its own failed occasion" (236–37). For an extensive treatment of Gray's "whiggish, imperialistic bourgeois" ideology, see James Steele, "Thomas Gray and the Season for Triumph," in *Fearful Joy: Papers from the Thomas Gray Bicentenary Conference at Carleton University*, ed. James Downey and Ben Jones (Montreal: McGill-Queen's University Press, 1974), 198–240; Steele claims that Gray was unable to conclude the "Progress of Poesy" because there were no causes of glory to celebrate until Pitt's advocacy of a war with France for British imperialist interests in 1754 (220–21).

16. Respectively, I take these capsule interpretations from Fry, *The Poet's Calling*, 88, Shankman, "Pindaric Tradition," 235–36, and Steele, "Thomas Gray," 220. See also Roger Lonsdale, "The Poetry of Thomas Gray: Versions of the Self," *Proceedings of the British Academy* 59 (1973): 119–20.

17. John Brown, *A Dissertation on the Rise, Union, and Power, the Progressions, Separations, and Corruptions, of Poetry and Music* (London, 1763; repr. New York: Garland, 1971), 100; hereafter cited parenthetically in text. On the relevance of the *Dissertation* to the mid-century genre, the "Ode for Music," see Richard Wendorf, *William Collins and Eighteenth-Century English Poetry* (Minneapolis: University of Minneapolis Press, 1981), 158–60. Dustin Griffin has recently contested such literary-historical assumptions as "the republic of letters," "literature's corruption by politics and commerce," the "Whig myth of the author's liberation," and "the public sphere" in "Fictions of Eighteenth-Century Authorship," *Essays in Criticism* 43 (1993): 181–92. Limiting his evidence to the ways that these terms conceal class biases and restrict democratic participation in authorship, Griffin effectively dismantles the self-interested and hypocritical functions of these "enduring fictions" (181).

18. Ralph quotes Fielding on the venality and self-interested basis of contemporary professional writers: "'why . . . is an Author, (in a Country where there is no public Provision for Men of Genius) obliged to be a more disinterested Patriot than any other? And why is he, whose Livelihood is in his Pen, a greater Monster in using it to serve himself, than he who uses his Tongue [i.e., a political orator] for the same Purpose?'" *Case of Authors*, 11. Brown also saw a threat to the established social hierarchy in an emergent professional class that financially manipulated the aristocracy, and thus gained its prominence by parasitical means that vitiated "the Great":

"Managers, Agents, and Burrough-Jobbers, which hang like Leeches upon the Great, nor ever quit their Hold till they are full gorged." *Estimate* 1:133.

19. From the *Critical Review* 15 (1763): 311, quoted in Meehan, *Liberty and Poetics*, 100.

20. Davie, *Augustan Lyric*, 4; Davie's italics.

21. Bonnell Thornton, "An Ode on Saint Cecilia's Day, adapted to the Ancient British Music" (London,1749); on the Wilkesite, populist implications of this burlesque, see Lance Bertelsen, *The Nonsense Club: Literature and Popular Culture, 1749–63* (New York: Oxford University Press, 1986), 155–60. On the genesis of titles for the "Progress," an ode that is a progress piece only in its second half, and more of a "Powers of Poetry" in its first half (lines 1–65), see Lonsdale, *Poems of Gray*, 157.

22. Brown, *Dissertation*, 236. Authors desiring independence from commercial pressure also make rhetorical pleas for literary academies to support talented writers or sponsor the best "Odes for Music," and offer another figure of possible alliance between government and poet. See [William Warburton], "A Letter from an Author to a Member of Parliament, concerning Literary Property" (London: 1747); Brown, *Dissertation*, 238–42, who proposes an academy for the reunion of poetry and music, a "wholesome Institution" (241) that would nurture and reward pure ethical values in new productions, thus warding off the corruption of art and manners; Ralph, *Case of Authors*, 62–63, who calls for the one remaining academy, the Society for Encouraging Arts and Sciences, to make disinterested awards to authors and playwrights based solely on merit. As Ralph must have realized, such academies as the "departed Society for the *Incouragement* of *Learning*" (ibid., 62), an independent Richmond co-operative from 1736–48, were powerless against well regulated networks of booksellers, and thus driven out of operation. See J. W. Saunders, *The Profession of English Letters* (London: Routledge and Kegan Paul, 1964), 123.

23. On the "Ode for Music" as a background to "The Passions," see Wendorf, *William Collins*, 135–65; on Collins' use of music as a trope for subjective response and anti-pictorialism, in addition to being a vehicle for doubting that any of the passions have a "settled public signification," see Kevin Barry, *Language, Music, and the Sign: A Study in Aesthetics, Poetics, and Poetic Practice from Collins to Coleridge* (Cambridge: Cambridge University Press, 1987), 27–55, citation on 38. Steven Knapp pursues the connections between Collins' allegorical representation of violence and poetic invention in *Personification and the Sublime: Milton to Coleridge* (Cambridge: Harvard University Press, 1985), 87–97. In my forthcoming essay, "Collins, Thomson, and the Whig Progress of Liberty," *Studies in English Literature* (Summer 1994), I further examine the ways in which Collins addresses the political crises of his times in the 1746 *Odes*, especially the "Ode to Liberty."

24. E.g., the first line, "Hence, Avaunt, ('tis Holy Ground)" was deflated as "venal ground." Lonsdale, *Poems of Gray*, 267.

25. Steele also notes that in line 84 Grafton is linked to Queen Elizabeth's Lord Treasurer Cecil, "an architect of British imperialism" and that this affiliation would be consistent with Gray's attachment to the expansionist policies of Pitt, Grafton's political ally. "Thomas Gray," 234.

26. On the allusion to the "Elegy" in the "Ode for Music," see Lonsdale, "Poetry of Thomas Gray," 121: this "disconcerting reappearance" attempts to "confirm that . . . [Gray's] problematic self had now been exorcised."

27. For a discussion of the "Alliance" as a record of Gray's early ambivalence towards an imperialist British poetry, see Kaul, *Thomas Gray and Literary Authority*, 185–89.

28. Norton Nicholls's *Reminiscences of Gray*, in *Correspondence* 3:1291.

Men Imagining Women Imagining Men: *Swift's* Cadenus and Vanessa

THOMAS E. MARESCA

> Consciousness awakens to independent ideological life precisely in a world of alien discourses surrounding it, and from which it cannot initially separate itself; the process of distinguishing between one's own and another's discourse, between one's own and another's thought, is activated rather late in development.[1]

I begin with this quotation, or rather epigraph, from Mikhail Bakhtin which I propose to use for rather unBakhtinian purposes. In the essay that follows, I propose to consider the ways in which Jonathan Swift's practice of parodic duplication and reduplication within the authoritative framework of classical precedent, within the precincts of Bakhtin's putatively monophonic poetry, floods *Cadenus and Vanessa* with "a world of alien discourses" that in turn open the poem to the voice of the Other.[2] The quasi-biographical roots of the poem shape this Other into a creation essentially more radical than the philosophic or imagistic "others" of Swift's prose works: no Houyhnhnm or Yahoo, but a being *other* than Swift himself, a woman conceived not as a man-manqué but as a person integrated and whole, an achieved polyphony in a world of monologues.[3]

In his best works, Swift writes *counter*, against the grain of convention, reader expectation, and literary tradition. His finest works always have behind them and sustaining them a model or paradigm against which they play out their internalized and textualized psychodramas. These foils are not so often explicitly invoked and parodied as they are implicitly reversed, inverted, turned inside-out. So, for example, *Gulliver's Travels* toys with *The Odyssey*; *A Tale of a Tub* plays with Lucretius and Petronius and classical Epicureanism; "A Description of a City Shower" counters classical pastoral and georgic; and "A Description of the Morning" plays against the pastoral and the aubade. In just that way, the narrative of *Cadenus and Vanessa* plays squarely against one of the paradigm anti-feminist fables, Hesiod's story of Pandora and her dangerous gifts. *Cadenus and Vanessa* enlarges from the story of Pandora's creation as an instrument of the gods' revenge to a comic narrative of education and character formation, involving both heavenly creators (Venus and company) and earthly (Cadenus the beloved tutor, who also distantly figures Hermes Psychopompos). In an explicit reversal of Hesiod's narrative, these ancestral Doctor Frankensteins are frustrated in their plans for their creature, Vanessa. Because they have wrought too well, because they have created her too successfully in their own images, their Pandora has a mind and most definite plans of her own. The central dilemma of the poem is the pansexual human tendency to see the self mirrored in the other, who, disquietingly, turns out not to be so *other* after all. Appropriately, even this confounding runs counter to the Hesiodic fable, whose central impulse is a stark differentiation and separation along strict sexual lines.

The Pandora myth enters *Cadenus and Vanessa* as the third of the poem's major framing devices, after a quasi-Ovidian court of love and a set of allusions to the Dido-Aeneas affair in Virgil.[4] Each different perspective that Swift sets up offers a divergent point of view on the events of the poem, another voice in the babel of conflicting authorities that complicate the single authorial voice of the poem—which is itself undercut and rendered richly complex by its own ironies and incomprehensions.[5] Swift's adaptation of the Pandora story sits at the center of this polylogy, both structurally (it is the inmost, and the most sustained, of the "mythic" or literary allusions that frame the action of the poem) and ideologically. The Pandora myth is the archetypal anti-feminist text, even more overtly misogynist than the Genesis story of Eve's role in the Fall. In it, woman is created separate from man, much later than man, and specifically as a curse for man. The works of Hesiod are the *loci classici* for the story: the account in *Theogony* 570–612 dilates more feelingly on Pandora's dangerous beauty, but that in the *Works and Days* is fuller and more detailed, even though briefer.

Here is the core of it:

> And [Zeus] bade famous Hephaestus make haste and mix earth and water and to put in it the voice and strength of human kind, and fashion a sweet, lovely maiden-shape, like to the immortal goddesses in face; and Athene to teach her needlework and the weaving of the varied web; and golden Aphrodite to shed grace upon her head and cruel longing and cares that weary the limbs. And he charged Hermes the guide, the Slayer of Argus, to put in her a shameless mind and a deceitful nature.
>
> So he ordered. And they obeyed the lord Zeus the son of Cronos. Forthwith the famous Lame God moulded clay in the likeness of a

modest maid, as the son of Cronos proposed. And the goddess bright-eyed Athene girded and clothed her, and the divine Graces and queenly Persuasion put necklaces of gold upon her, and the rich-haired Hours crowned her head with spring flowers. And Pallas Athene bedecked her form with all manner of finery. Also the Guide, the Slayer of Argus, contrived within her lies and crafty words and a deceitful nature at the will of loud thundering Zeus, and the Herald of the gods put speech in her. And he called this woman Pandora, because all they who dwelt on Olympus gave each a gift, a plague to men who eat bread.[6]

In the Greek, the passage is devastingly sexist: until Pandora's name is conferred, the creature is referred to in the neuter, and after the appearance of Pandora-as-feminine gender, the word by which the poet designates "men" switches from *anthropoi*, which means mankind, to *andres*, which indicates men as opposed to women. In the cycle of genesis myths Hesiod is recounting, the creation of woman is the ultimate consequence of the separation of men and gods, and the creation of woman is itself an action of further differentiation and privation. Deprived first of effortless life and separated from the companionship of the gods, men—*andres*—are now reduced even further, to a mere incomplete half of mankind, and this privation is brought about by an unreal thing, a made creature, a mannequin, woman, who is not just another sex but of separate creation, almost of utterly different nature.[7]

Swift's description of the heavenly origin of Vanessa emphasizes her separate creation and roughly parallels Pandora's beginnings as a tool of Zeus' revenge.[8] Vanessa, a surrogate Venus, a Venus diminutive, will avenge Venus' wrongs on sinning mankind. Swift's verses veer erratically between the lightest of comedy and the heaviest of irony in their redistribution of Hesiod's agents and emphases in the creation of this girl golem, the embodiment of the Other. As with Pandora, many gods contribute to the creation of Vanessa, and most of Hesiod's personnel are present either in person or in their effects and attributes. Venus, Pallas Athena, and the Graces all bestow gifts of intellectual, spiritual, and moral excellence rather than physical beauty (though that is not lacking either). The gift of the Hours is embodied in Vanessa's youth, that of Persuasion—and perhaps Hermes—in her verbal skills. Lucina replaces Hephaestus as the creator of Vanessa's physical being, and the shameless mind and deceitful nature with which Hesiod's Hermes endows Pandora are transformed into "The Seeds of Knowledge, Judgment, Wit" (205) with which Swift's Pallas blesses Vanessa. In a similar vein, Hesiod's Pallas gives "all manner of finery"; Swift's Pallas confers "some small Regard for State and Wealth" (216) and an estate that amounts to "just Five Thousand Pound" (227). Like Hesiod's account, Swift's narrative includes the conferring of a name on the divine creature, who—again like Hesiod's maiden—is designed by a god as the agent of his/her revenge and reassertion of power over men. If, to borrow a phrase from Joseph Conrad, all of Europe went into the making of Kurtz, all of Olympus goes into the making of Vanessa, with similarly disappointing results.

In effect compounding Hesiod's separation of the sexes, Swift makes the creation of Vanessa a project of goddesses only, converting all the male contributors to the making of Pandora into female equivalents (Lucina for Hephaistos, etc.). Swift's only conspicuous omission from Hesiod's cast of characters is Hermes, part of whose function is taken over in the English poem by Pallas and her intellectual gifts. The remainder of Hermes' role is supplied later in the poem by Cadenus, who completes the education and the shaping of the creature who was designed as a lure for mankind and who becomes a trap for him. The name Cadenus is not only an anagram for *decanus*, the dean, and thus a reference to Swift; it also recalls *caduceus*, the herald's staff that is Hermes' badge of office and distinctive attribute as messenger from gods to men, herder of dead souls, and patron of rhetoric, merchants, thieves, and liars. Hermes is the most ambiguous of all the gods, a go-between, a mediator, a god of limits and their violation. *Decanus* twisted into *Cadenus* not only distantly echoes *caduceus*, it linguistically intimates as well the ambiguity or ambivalence of the poem's embodiments of sexual and gender roles. I would suggest that in Swift's text it counterpoints and replaces the sexually charged box (*pithos*, literally a large jar) whose opening completes the separation of men and gods and the differentiation of men and women. The phallic staff of the divine messenger (you can see its Christian avatar in the hands of the angel of the Annunciation, in dozens of medieval and Renaissance paintings) externalizes and objectifies the most obvious attribute of the phallic herms that mark the edges of roads and fields, representations of Hermes as god of borders and limits. Ironically but richly for Swift's purposes, in Latin the root *cad-* means fall, decline, as in "cadenza," or "decadence." Just as Vanessa is made the uneasy synthesis of the opposite female archetypes of Venus and Athena, seductress and warrior virgin, motherless fruit of Cronos' genitals and motherless fruit of Zeus' mind, so Cadenus, from his name to his conduct, simultaneously embodies and enacts teacher and pupil, guide and misdirector, tumescence and detumescence, masculine dominance and feminine weakness. He crosses the borders of gender and role as readily as Hermes moves between realms. Remember always that in Hesiod's story, it is Hermes who gives Pandora "lies and crafty words," a role and function that are ironically fulfilled in Swift's redaction of the myth in Cadenus' simultaneously successful and disastrous literary education of Vanessa.[9]

The outcome of Swift's fable also runs counter to Hesiod's, wherein the hapless Epimetheus accepts Zeus' gift and thereby enables Pandora to let loose plagues and sorrows and death on humanity. Swift's Venus is hoist on her own petard when "fashionable Fops" (317) and "glittering Dames" (364) alike are repelled rather than attracted by Vanessa's superiority, and not a little of Swift's comedy consists precisely in the juxtaposition of the inevitability of Pandora and the easy avoidability of Vanessa, in the ironic parallel of Epimetheus trapped by his foolishness and moderns "saved" by theirs. The Pandora myth is steeped in sexual and gender differences construed as generic differences, so there is a wealth of comedy and irony in what doesn't happen in Swift's poem and in that poem's reticence about the openness or closedness of its Pandora's box. The basic pattern, however, is a mock epic one: the creator, Venus, is frustrated by her own creation and surrogate, Vanessa, who, far from extending the kingdom of love, neither inspires love in others nor, as the first movement of Swift's poem ends, feels love herself.[10]

> Thus, to the World's perpetual Shame,
> The *Queen of Beauty* lost her Aim.
> Too late with Grief she understood,
> *Pallas* had done more harm than good;
> For great Examples are but vain,
> Where Ignorance begets Disdain.
> Both Sexes, arm'd with Guilt and Spite,
> Against *Vanessa*'s Power unite;
> To copy her, few Nymphs aspir'd;
> Her Virtues fewer Swains admir'd:
> So Stars beyond a certain Height
> Give Mortals neither Heat nor Light.
> (432–37)

This climax occurs at almost the exact midpoint of the poem: immediately after, Cadenus enters the poem and ushers in a second redaction of the Pandora story, pushed this time one step further away from Hesiod and Olympus. Surrogates for the two principal creators of Vanessa now take over the action and direction of Vanessa's life: for Venus, her son Cupid now stands in, and for Athena, Cadenus,

> A Gownman of a diff'rent Make,
> Whom *Pallas*, once *Vanessa*'s Tutor,
> Had fix'd on for her Coadjutor.
> (463–65)

Cadenus completes on earth the creation begun in myth, shaping Vanessa's mind and taste to his own model. Unwittingly, he too becomes a classic mock-epic miscreator.

> She thought he had himself describ'd,
> His Doctrines when she first imbib'd;
> What he had planted, now was grown;
> His virtues she might call her own;
> As he approves, as he dislikes,
> Love or Contempt, her Fancy strikes.
> Self-Love, in Nature rooted fast,
> Attends us first, and leaves us last:

> Why she likes him, admire not at her,
> She loves herself, and that's the Matter.
>   (678–87)

That is the matter—or *mater*—indeed. Cadenus has re-created himself in Vanessa and his creature has turned on him in self-love. Vanessa duplicates Cadenus and embodies the feminine image of Cadenus. She sees in Cadenus the Other who is also herself, an Other who is both a man and, in a manner of speaking, the mother who brought her forth. That is a twist in the plot that satisfies neither Venus nor Pallas, neither Cadenus nor Vanessa—and, for that matter neither Bakhtin nor Jacques Lacan nor Julia Kristeva. According to Cadenus' and Pallas' plan, Vanessa is not supposed to love at all. According to Venus' plan and Vanessa's hopes, she ought to inspire love in others. She fulfills neither design. What she does accomplish, in a comic *reductio*, is to re-enact or re-create the love "those antient Poets sing" (28), a love that obliterates Otherness, whose absence in modern women had been the Shepherds' defense in the court of love and the motive for Venus' creation of Vanessa in the first place:

> A Fire celestial, chaste, refin'd,
> Conceiv'd and kindled in the Mind,
> Which having found an equal Flame,
> Unites, and both become the same,
> In different Breasts together burn,
> Together both to Ashes turn.
>   (29–34)

"Ev'ry Being loves its *Like*" (879), Venus tells us near the close of the poem, and this is exactly the plight of Cadenus and Vanessa. Vanessa, made in Cadenus' image, inevitably loves him, but do they both "together burn"? Do "both become the same"? Despite the poem's silence, the evidence suggests they do. Cadenus is governed by the same rules of self-love as Vanessa:

> *Cadenus*, who cou'd ne'er suspect
> His Lessons wou'd have such Effect,
> Or be so artfully apply'd
> Insensibly came on her Side . . .
>   (726–29)

In other words, Epimetheus accepts the gods' gift, and the result is precisely the role-reversal one would expect from the basic motif: Vanessa becomes the tutor, Cadenus the pupil, and a none-too-promising one at that:

> The Nymph will have her Turn, to be
> The Tutor; and the Pupil, he:
> Tho' she already can discern,

> Her Scholar is not apt to learn;
> Or wants Capacity to reach
> The Science she designs to teach . . .
> (806–11)

The master becomes the student in the lore of the heart. Only in the created, externalized image of him- or herself can mock-epic heroes discern the mysteries of their own hearts, so the texts that Vanessa sets for Cadenus are very familiar indeed—so much so, that the reversal of tutor and pupil roles even extends to a reversal of gender roles. Vanessa becomes the aggressive, masculine suitor, pressing Cadenus for love, commitment, and sex. What she desires is not "Friendship in its greatest Height" (780) but explicitly "less Seraphick Ends" (823). Cadenus, on the other hand, demurs like the conventional shy maiden, protesting affection and esteem, but not love, offering conventionally feminine "exalted Strains" (791) to forestall Vanessa's conventionally masculine "sober Words" (792) and straightforward desires. They become language, and each other's language at that.

The mock-epic creature has won her own autonomy: Cadenus "fairly abdicates his Throne, / The Government is now her own" (800–801). This reversal and the steps that have led up to it have been conceived and presented in resolutely literary terms. The frames and allusional systems provided by Ovid, Virgil, and Hesiod convey this most directly, of course, but it is certainly no less evident and important in the opening and closing conceit of the plea argued in the court of love by "The *Shepherds* and the *Nymphs*" (1)—a typically Swiftian literalization of the idea of courtship. The basic impetus behind Venus' decision to create Vanessa stems from literature, from a conception of love such "As . . . those antient Poets sing" (28). And her paradigm, the model for Vanessa's excellence, is not merely literary but even points forward to Cadenus:

> What Preachers talk, or Sages write,
> These I will gather and unite,
> And represent them to Mankind
> Collected in that Infant's Mind.
> (150–53)

That is to say that Vanessa is, *ab ovo*, conceived as other peoples' language, as heteroglossia. She exists in the poem, if you will, in the same intertextual manner as the poem itself exists, as a locus for multiple voices and multiple roles. By the time Cadenus enters the poem, Swift's emphasis has become relentlessly literary. Cadenus protects Vanessa from Cupid's arrows by "placing still some Book betwixt" (480), while Cupid in turn entraps Vanessa into love literally through Cadenus' book: a particularly suggestive arrow—

> A Dart of such prodigious Length,
> It pierc'd the feeble Volume thro',
> And deep transfix'd her Bosom too.
> Some Lines, more moving than the rest,
> Stuck to the Point that pierc'd her Breast;
> And, born directly to the Heart,
> With Pains unknown increas'd her Smart.
>
> (517–23)

From this point on, implications and imagery of literariness, of bookish-ness, of the power of different modes of discourse, develop apace. As gender roles elide into one another, so the means by which those roles are inculcated—books and language—begin to merge with the people who act the roles. The poem begins to blur differentiations of all sorts.[11] Writing, literature, discourse move out of the background of the poem, out of the frames as it were, and into the foreground. Swift has begun to foreground the usually concealed forces of social and cultural determination; he is in the process of converting a comic, quasi-erotic, semi-biographical poem into a psychomachia of gender roles and cultural coercions. In *Cadenus and Vanessa*, writings of all sorts begin to grow autonomous, while human beings subside into texts. Vanessa explicitly so describes her love for Cadenus:

> If one short Volume cou'd comprise
> All that was witty, learn'd, and wise,
> How wou'd it be esteem'd, and read,
> Altho' the Writer long were dead?
> If such an Author were alive,
> How all wou'd for his Friendship strive;
> And come in Crowds to see his Face:
> And this she takes to be her Case.
> *Cadenus* answers every End,
> The Book, the Author, and the Friend.
>
> (696–705)

The flustered Cadenus responds to all this by in his turn adopting other voices: he makes of himself a bad book, a second-rate romance packed with trite language, with "exalted Strains" and "sublime Conceits" (791,793), which elicits from the now-role-reversed Vanessa the following caustic literary-critical rebuke: "For why such Raptures, Flights, and Fancies, / To her, who durst not read Romances?" (794–95).

Once Vanessa has become Cadenus' tutor, "the Science she designs to teach" (811) him is the reading of a textualized universe,

> Wherein his Genius was below
> The Skill of ev'ry common Beau;
> Who, tho' he cannot spell, is wise

Enough to read a Lady's Eyes;
And will each accidental Glance
Interpret for a kind Advance.
(812–17)

However gendered those reading lessons are,[12] it is clear that Vanessa too has become a book that Cadenus must learn to read, as he had been a book that she has mastered. The merging of life and letters—the textualizing of self and sex and love—is virtually complete. The text of Swift's poem, like the texts that are Cadenus and Vanessa, has been flooded with "alien discourses." In such a context of systematic undifferentiation and categoric gene- and genre-splitting, Swift's final presentation of alternatives for Cadenus and Vanessa strongly implies which one they have chosen:

Whether the Nymph, to please her Swain,
Talks in a high Romantick Strain;
Or whether he at last descends
To like with less Seraphick Ends;
Or, to compound the Business, whether
They temper Love and Books together;
Must never to Mankind be told,
Nor shall the conscious Muse unfold.
(820–27)

"Since ev'ry Being loves its *Like*" (879), the odds are good that they "temper Love and Books together" as the whole of *Cadenus and Vanessa* has been doing from its opening lines.

The problem of the poem and the poem's world has been that of "distinguishing between one's own and another's discourse" in a world flooded with competing authoritative discourses (I have not even discussed here the other authorial voices—especially Ovid and Virgil—that echo in the poem, nor the obvious social voices of Belles and Beaux, nor the "educational" or "institutional" voices of morality and "good sense" that oppose the language and expectations of romance). Corollary to that concern are the tasks of tempering or uniting the physical and imaginative aspects of love, and the physical and intellectual aspects of human beings, as these have been segregated into differing gender roles, and further of reconciling the "high Romantick Strains" of literary versions of love with the "less Seraphick Ends" of "ev'ry common Beau" and Belle. Cadenus errs in a Hesiodic manner by over-differentiating, by separating the mental and the physical:

His Thoughts had wholly been confin'd
To form and cultivate her Mind.
He hardly knew, 'till he was told,
Whether the Nymph were Young or Old. . . .
(630–33)

But Cadenus has the rare good fortune, for a mock-epic hero, not to be destroyed by his creation but, perhaps, to be saved by her—if Vanessa has not become utterly Other, if she can in fact teach Cadenus to read people as well as he writes books. She will first have to teach him his common humanity and persuade him to abandon his Gulliverian schemes for "constant, rational Delight" (781). The gods are clearly not optimistic: it is a more than slightly disgruntled Venus who ends the poem, like Astrea in yet another myth, by withdrawing to the heavens and abandoning the earth to simple—or simpler—appetites.

Swift himself does not seem optimistic either: he holds Cadenus at more than arm's length, isolating him within a regressive series of narrative frames and reducing him still further by the more-in-sorrow-than-in-anger tone of his verse. The raillery that Swift here directs at a version of himself contrasts sharply with the aggressive prose that concludes *Gulliver's Travels* or with the violence of outward-directed satires such as *The Legion Club*. Cadenus may commit Gulliver's sin by simultaneously serving an unrealistically exalted notion of humanity's capabilities and an unnaturally narrow notion of men's and women's, but he does not compound it as Gulliver does by retreating from the empyrean to the stables. And it is not totally accurate to say that Cadenus is torn between the competing claims of mind and body; rather, he is trapped by his own mind-set, confined to a bloodless, authoritative discourse, restricted to the love of books—in both senses. *Inter feces et urinam nascimur*, St. Augustine says: "We are born between feces and urine"—and from the crudeness of that reality, from the vision of Celia shitting, Swift's protagonists have always sought refuge in the printed word. Vanessa counterpoints not just Hesiod's Pandora; she runs counter, too, to the mass of Swift's protagonists. Unlike them, she embraces the Other: she engages the frailties of the flesh directly, by the fact of falling in love with a man "declin'd in Health, advanc'd in Years" (529), "a Gown of forty-four" (525) "with Reading almost blind" (527). Vanessa transcends the limitations of the "normal" Swiftian protagonist and the limitations of conventional moral discourse by loving her Struldbrug, by learning the man and the book simultaneously, by reading the book in the man and the man in the book. She manages to circumvent Hesiodic separation, to erase gender differentiation, to combine the opposites whose polarity immobilizes Cadenus and so many other of Swift's protagonists and butts. More: Vanessa reverses the pervasive "grammophobia" of the Swiftian text and replaces it with a selective grammophilia. If, to borrow the language of Terry Castle's adaptation to Swift's particular case of Jacques Derrida's pervasive argument, "speech preserves a pure relation between Nature and Word," while writing "breaches Nature and Word" and "takes on the status of a tragic fatality come to prey upon natural innocence,"[13] then Vanessa heals that rift, rewrites Word into Nature and/or re-inscribes Nature into Word. Vanessa mimics—at a distance to be sure—the world-generating goddess whose name she diminutively bears. She incarnates the word: in her, the word becomes flesh, the flesh word, while Cadenus remains circumscribed, only a man of letters.[14] She enunciates—or she is—the voice of the Other. She is also the rarest of Swift's fictions, a whole being, integrated and unmocked.[15]

But the poem's name is *Cadenus and Vanessa*, and it contains not one but two duplications of Swift, two creatures made in his own image. Their relative success vis-a-vis each other—and what that success might be—is one of the poem's key problems. Swift gives us clues in the poem's extension to itself of the process of textualizing reality. The detailed literalization of the antique metaphors of the court of love and the lover's suit that frames the entire poem not only gives women the first and last word on the matter: it casts the entire action of the poem in the light of a peculiarly, pervasively, literalized version of "courtship," a version that translates that action into an archetypically Swiftian double-edged and paradoxical discourse. The act, or acts, of love culminate in coming to judgment—seemingly, the very subjection of passion to the process of reason that the narrative of the poem renders so intensely problematical.

What has been lacking in the world of *Cadenus and Vanessa*, however, has not been judgment—there has been rather too much of that—but wit: the wit to perceive Vanessa's perfections, as Venus charges (864–69), and, more importantly for Cadenus, the wit to see one's own folly. For the reader, this latter wit translates into the acuity to spot the key counterpoise in Swift's reconstruction or deconstruction of Hesiod's narrative, the countering of the Hesiodic drama of stark sexual differentiation with a Swiftian comedy of sameness. The gulf that keeps Cadenus from Vanessa and that which separates the litigating *"Shepherds"* and *"Nymphs"* is the same, the gulf of shared obtuseness: "ev'ry Being loves its *Like*" (879), folly for folly. That whimsical "judgment" (the word by now deserves its quotation marks) is ratified by Venus' abandoning the world of the poem to that noted master of judgment, her son, Cupid (880–83).

Before she does that, however, Venus passes "judgment" on the suit and countersuit that opened the poem, the Nymphs' charge that men love only for "Intrigue" (13) or money (14), and the Shepherds' countercharge that women have debased "modern Love" (27) from "A Fire celestial" (29) to "gross Desire" (36). Here is Venus' summation of the case:

> "She saw her Favour was misplac'd;
> "The Fellows had a wretched Taste;
> "She needs must tell them to their Face,
> "They were a senseless, stupid Race:
> "And were she to begin agen,
> "She'd study to reform the *Men* . . ."
>   (868–71)

That, of course, is a project of such dimensions that, rather than begin it, even Venus takes a vacation.

NOTES

1. Mikhail Bakhtin, "Discourse in the Novel," in *The Dialogic Imagination: Four Essays by M. M. Bakhtin,* edited by Michael Holquist, translated by Caryl Emerson and Michael Holquist (Austin: University of Texas Press, 1981), 345. Bakhtin of course confines his arguments about heteroglossia and its concommitant intertextuality to the prose novel, and seems indeed quite explicitly to deny the relevance of those concepts to poetry, which is one of the main points in which this paper will part company from him. I can only suggest that his idea of poetry was dominated by the nineteenth- and early twentieth-century subjective lyric, to which indeed his charge of "monophony" largely applies. Narrative poetry and satiric poetry, earlier and later, have never been so confined; one could make a very persuasive case, for instance, that Dante's *Commedia* is the single greatest extant example of heteroglossia.

2. The Other is the peculiar province of feminist criticism, and *Cadenus and Vanessa* has recently gotten a lot of favorable attention from feminist critics, and deservedly so, since the poem is unequivocally a woman-centered text, and a sympathetic one at that—at least on the surface. Opinion is hardly uniform, however: Ellen Pollak calls it "one of the finest and most neglected love poems of the eighteenth century," in *The Poetics of Sexual Myth: Gender and Ideology in the Verse of Swift and Pope* (Chicago and London: The University of Chicago Press, 1985), 128. Pollak's chapter on *Cadenus and Vanessa* (128–58) argues that Swift employs multiple linguistic strategies in the poem in order to escape or devalue conventional moral norms and/or gender roles and relationships, a position that I substantially agree with and in some particulars build upon. Claude Rawson, on the other hand, thinks it "one of Swift's most disingenuous and overrated achievements." In a paper read at the 1991 ASECS Conference (Pittsburgh, April 1991), Rawson argued that *Cadenus and Vanessa* is evasive and self-exculpatory and far more centered on Cadenus as a stand-in for Swift than on Vanessa as an ideal of womanhood. Though I don't share Rawson's dislike of the poem (and I tend to take Cadenus' excuses as more indicative of his failures of self-knowledge than what Rawson labels "an uneasy solipsistic coyness"), I strongly agree with the distinctions he makes among the kinds of "raillery" Swift directs at Cadenus and the sorts of raillery and rage aimed at the protagonists and butts of other works: see above, 252.

3. That *Cadenus and Vanessa* is in itself a complex poem, rendered yet more difficult by its undeniable biographical roots, is abundantly clear, but that is just about all that is clear about the poem. Recent studies have proposed numerous approaches and hypotheses about it. Louise K. Barnett's *Swift's Poetic Worlds* (Newark: University of Delaware Press, 1981) finds the poem unconvincing and marked by irresolution. Terry Castle in "Why the Houyhnhnms Don't Write: Swift, Satire, and the Fear of the Text," *Essays in Literature* 7 (1980): 31–44, argues that the bulk of Swift's satires are pervaded by "grammophobia," a kind of Derridean mythos of writing as

corruption, in itself a kind Fall of language, a suggestion that is certainly pertinent to the text-and-author haunted world of *Cadenus and Vanessa*. Margaret Anne Doody's "Swift among the Women," *Yearbook of English Studies* (1988), 75–77, sees the poem as inconclusive (because Swift's society would not allow an intelligent woman to choose her man) though sympathetic to women. Doody remarks pertinently on the mixing of gender traits in the two title characters, an aspect of the poem that is quite central to my own arguments. Anthony B. England argues for a running tension in the poem between its energy and emotion and the forms that are meant to contain them: "the prevailing tendency of the poem is to undermine the notion that its many neat structures and systems are adequate means of defining and thus, in a sense, containing the experience to which they allude." *Energy and Order in the Poetry of Swift* (1980), 175. See also England's "Rhetorical Order and Emotional Turbulence in 'Cadenus and Vanessa,'" *Contemporary Studies of Swift's Poetry*, ed. John Irwin Fischer and Donald C. Mell, Jr. (Newark: University of Delaware Press, 1981), 69–78. In "Swift's *Cadenus and Vanessa*: A Question of 'Positives,'" *Essays in Criticism*, 20 (1970), 424–40; reprinted in *Essential Articles for the Study of Jonathan Swift's Poetry*, ed. David M. Vieth [Hamden, CT: Archon Books, 1984], 155–71), Gareth Jones stresses Swift's ironies about the limits of reason vis-a-vis love as well as Swift's ambiguities about Cadenus, who is often portrayed as comically complacent. Ellen Pollak's above-quoted *Politics of Sexual Myth*, and Peter J. Schakel's *The Poetry of Jonathan Swift: Allusion and the Development of a Poetic Style* (Madison: University of Wisconsin Press, 1979) have also been useful to me; the latter will be cited below.

4. Almost twenty years ago, Peter Schakel delineated the mock epic dimensions of *Cadenus and Vanessa*, in particular its comic exploitation of Venus and Juno's sparring over Dido and Aeneas in the *Aeneid*, as frame and foil for its own romantic matrix. See "Swift's Dapper Clerk and the Matrix of Allusions in Cadenus and Vanessa," *Criticism* 17 (1975): 246–61. It is worth pointing out, as a succinct example of the way *Cadenus and Vanessa* sports with perspectives, frames, and their associated "discourses," that the first two couplets of the poem swiftly and deftly move the reader from pastoral to mythological to legal areas of reference without discarding or devaluing any of the three: all remain active and important for the duration of the poem.

5. See Gareth Jones' accurate observations about Cadenus' comic complacency, his "self-deceptions" and the ways he has "reasoned himself into a position which denies reason." "Swift's *Cadenus and Vanessa*," 163, 162.

6. The translation is quoted from *Hesiod: The Homeric Hymns and Homerica*, with an English translation by Hugh G. Evelyn-White (Cambridge, MA, and London: Harvard University Press and William Heinemann Ltd., 1977). The passage cited corresponds to *Works and Days* 60–82. It is relevant to the context of *Cadenus and Vanessa* to point out that what leads up to the tale of Pandora in Hesiod's poem is an opening warning of Zeus' judgments, the significant mention of a lawsuit and judgment (apparently involving the poet and his brother Perses), and the vengeance of Zeus on human cheats (in

this case, Prometheus' theft of fire), all of which answer somewhat loosely *Cadenus and Vanessa*'s court of love and vengeance-of-Venus opening.

7. See *Mythologies*, comp. Yves Bonnfoy, trans. under the direction of Wendy Doniger (Chicago and London: The University of Chicago Press, 1991), 1:390–93. See also Jean-Pierre Vernant, *Myth and Society in Ancient Greece*, trans. Janet Lloyd (Zone Books: New York, 1990), 183–201.

8. All quotations from *Cadenus and Vanessa* will be taken from *The Poems of Jonathan Swift*, ed. Harold Williams, 3 vols. (Oxford: Clarendon Press, 2nd ed., 1966), 2:683–713. Citations in the text are to lines in the poem. Vanessa's creation is described in lines 136–227.

9. See Bonnfoy, *Mythologies*, 1:485–89.

10. For an extended treatment of the pattern and consequences of the mock epic hero's miscreation in his/her own image, see my *Epic to Novel* (Columbus: Ohio State University Press, 1974).

11. Very pertinent in this regard are A. B. England's remarks in "Rhetorical Order and Emotional Turbulence" on the incommensurateness of *Cadenus and Vanessa*'s structures with the experience they are supposed to contain. Cadenus continues to have faith in those structures, while Vanessa recognizes that the available forms can't contain all reality. In a poem drawing as heavily on the Pandora story as this one does, all mentions of inadequate containers inescapably allude to Pandora's infamous *pithos* and thus raise disturbing questions as to what, exactly, Swift is analogizing with it. I intend much more than I have space to discuss here when I suggest that, in this poem at least, Swift positions his text and its consciousness in relation to the body of classical literature as a Lacanian ego in relation to the Other.

12. For important work on the gendering of the act of reading in the eighteenth century, see Ellen Gardiner's forthcoming *Writing Women Reading*, expanded from her 1989 Stony Brook dissertation of the same name.

13. I take the word and idea "grammophobia" from Terry Castle's provocative but I think finally wrong "Why the Houyhnhnms Don't Write," from which the next quotation is also taken. The final quotation in this paragraph is from Jacques Derrida, *Of Grammatology*, trans. Gayatri Chakravorty Spivak (Baltimore: The Johns Hopkins University Press, 1976), 168; cited in Castle, op. cit., 32.

14. That the notion of the Incarnation, with all its rich theological concommitants, stands at the center of "conservative" late-seventeenth- and early-eighteenth-century poetics can be quickly verified by the satiric uses and inversions of it loosed in poems such as Dryden's *MacFlecknoe* and Pope's *Dunciad*: cf my own *Epic to Novel* and "Language and Body in Augustan Poetic," *ELH* 37 (1970): 375–88.

15. Cf. Castle, "Why the Houyhnhnms Don't Write," 32: "The operation of this myth of writing in Lévi-Strauss is patent: a pure (oral) society is disrupted by the intervention of writing, a writing, moreover, that points up, pathetically, its own radical shoddiness, its inauthenticity as signifier. I would like to claim that a similar myth may be seen working in Swift. Book 4 of *Gulliver's Travels* is, in one reading, a complex meditation on the problematic nature of writing and the possible corruption implied by the text. But the theme reappears often in Swift's work. At these moments his

obsessive apprehension of the philosophical and sociological dilemmas posed by writing suggests that he is influenced by a mythic structure of the kind Derrida describes. Swift, as we will see, confronts the Fallen Text in a number of works, and this text itself becomes, with varying degrees of explicitness, a satiric subject par excellence." But not merely a satiric subject: the saving or the healing of the Fallen Text is also at the heart of Swift's concerns, and the core paradox of the book-begotten *Cadenus and Vanessa* is that Vanessa transcends the texts that form her. The bits and pieces of literature that shape her yield, in her, a meaning greater than the sum of its parts.

The Gendering of Divinity in Tom Jones

BETTY RIZZO

The machinery of *Tom Jones*, consisting of what appear to the unenlightened to be the comic antics of Fortune but are recognized by the enlightened as the well-ordered if slowly evolving adjudications of Providence, is useful dialectically, expressing and representing, as it does, illusion and reality, actual and ideal justice, bad and good government, false and true philosophy and theology, and—the aspect I want to consider here— raising the question of the natural attributes of both men and women and the proper relationship of the genders according to Fielding.[1]

Fortune and Providence are gender differentiated: while the silly, capricious, and inconstant Fortune deviates from the patriarchal norm in every way, Providence represents that norm. If the feckless Fortune is "she," what then is the responsible Providence? Fortune is always "she"; Providence, undesignated by pronoun, represents every value that is traditionally reliable and masculine, is a projection as well as instrument of the paternalistic God, is just, temperate, rational, benevolent, all good, all knowing, all wise, and all providing. Providence is the hand of God, divine power as manifested on earth. Fortune is delusory power and deformed other. Like the Holy Spirit that causes Mary to conceive, Providence is essentially if not designatedly male. Finally—a point to be more thoroughly explored below—the dynamics of the novel demand that both exemplary and non-exemplary characters be held up to gender-differentiated models, the males to the providential model only, while the females have to meet the standards of the providential model radically adapted by the superimposition of what I have here called the Halifax prescription, the requirement that women also be modest, submissive, non-judgmental, and silent. That is, the providential model is too masculine, too *empowered*, to be appropriate for a woman until adapted by the addition of special strictures.

Without deformity there would be no comedy, as Fielding knew, and Fortune presides lustily over the unstable comic world of *Tom Jones*. Hers is one of the most thorough characterizations in the book; but she can be summed up as lacking all of the virtues inherent in Providence: she is unjust, deceptive, intemperate, irrational, sometimes incontinently kind, but frequently malevolent. She is the principle not of evil—the devil is an important presence in the book—but of accident and disorder. She is a rash and reckless agent. She can be ruthless in her ministrations: she assists the wretchedness of that miserable couple the Partridges by "putting a final end to" the wife[2] and renders Captain Blifil once again agreeable to his wife by killing him (1:108). She is capricious and perverse, "fearing she had acted out of Character" when inclining too long to the same side, "especially as it was the right Side," and hastily turning about (1:181), changing the advantage from Tom to Blifil in a fight (1:254), customarily reversing the face of affairs (2:703). Whether unfairly fond and kind or unfairly harsh and cruel, she is always unfair, inconsistent, never moral or rational: *Fortuna numquam perpetuo est bona* (2:676).

Fielding distinguishes other particular effects of her light character, frequently underscoring, however ironically, her malice (1:109, 248; 2:642) and her cruelty (1:256). She is immoderate, seldom doing things by halves: "there is no End to her Freaks whenever she is disposed to gratify or displease" (1:258). She is "a tender Parent, and often doth more for her favourite Offspring than either they deserve or wish" (1:67). She is capricious, customarily diverting herself with "two or three Frolicks" before making any final disposition of matters (1:358). She "loves to play Tricks with those Gentlemen who put themselves entirely under her Conduct" (2:550). She is a coquette and tease, toying with her subjects, leading them to expect happiness, then disappointing them at the last moment: "These kind of hair-breadth Missings of Happiness look like the Insults of Fortune, who may be considered as thus playing Tricks with us, and wantonly diverting herself at our Expence" (2:691). She favors the unworthy and "seldom greatly relishes such Sparks as . . . *Tom*, perhaps because they do not pay more ardent Addresses to her" (1:170). But irrational, ruled by caprice and impulse, she can suddenly take pity (1:479; 2:622) and now and then "shows Compassion in her wantonest Tricks" (2:622). When "apprehensive lest *Jones* should sink under the Weight of his Adversity, and that she might thus lose any future Opportunity of tormenting him," or perhaps really abating "somewhat of her Severity towards him," she a little relaxes her persecution (2:892), if only to prolong her game.

She is a respecter of persons, distinguishing widely between "those Persons [of the lower orders] who are to be corrected for their Faults, and those who are not" (1:192). Apparently it is she who arranges that while Molly Seagrim, Jenny Jones, and Partridge are called to account for producing children out of wedlock (or seeming to), Bridget Allworthy escapes detection and censure; while Molly and Mrs. Waters are denigrated for their promiscuity, Bridget Allworthy, Harriet Fitzpatrick, and Lady Bellaston can indulge as they like; and while Black George may not poach and shoot a partridge, Partridge is fair game for Bridget. She carefully segregates the habitations of the rich in the "Regions of the Great" from those of the vulgar (2:689). One can neither earn nor predict the bestowal of her favors nor under her sway enjoy the dignity of participation in one's own fate. She is the manifestation of female as opposed to male government. Fortune, whom the improvident, those who are governed by chance, are condemned to follow, is insolent, punitive, power-mad, licentious, and immoderate.

In pre-Christian times she had a better reputation. Originally the powerful goddess Fortuna, she operated from a principle of fairness, moving prizes around, distributing and redistributing the good things of this world.[3] In Horace's ode to her, fate precedes her in her progress and Hope and Faith attend her (*Odes*, 1.35). Her name for an unattractive fickleness of character is the endowment of the Christian era. Fielding may have given her notoriously unstable character a final fillip by modelling it on the characters of the great tyrant-termagants of the Restoration stage, like Nourmahal in Dryden's *Aurenge-Zebe*. She is like Delariviere Manley's portrait of the Duchess of Cleveland: "Hilaria was *Querilous*, *Fierce*, *Loquacious*, excessively fond, or infamously rude. . . . The Extreams of Prodigality and Covetousness; of Love and Hatred; of Dotage and Aversion, were joyn'd together in Hilaria's Soul."[4] Fortune is an unreconstructed pagan, a type of the woman who, suspected of having great and dangerous powers uncontrollable by men, represents for them the anarchic principle. And, though Fielding almost invariably converts her antics into comedy, it is sometimes evident that he regards seriously the moral disorder and inconsistency which she represents. She can be safely comic only when she is recognized to be, in Fielding's own version of the divine comedy, and probably unbeknownst to herself, securely under the direction and control of the rational and moral Providence.[5]

On rare occasions the history's narrator suggests that after all she is not autonomous, once hesitating as to "whether it was that Fortune relented, or whether it was no longer in her Power to disappoint" Tom (2:689). Once he lightly calls her divinity into question (2:770–71), and once he is "very far from believing in any such Heathen Goddess [as Nemesis], or from encouraging any Superstition" and beseeches some philosopher to find out the real cause of sudden transitions from good to bad fortune (1:86). For the enlightened, then, Fortune is not really substantial. She is an illusion, an instrument of benevolent Providence, as Tom must learn at the climax of his education: "But why do I blame Fortune? I am myself the Cause of all my Misery. All the dreadful Mischiefs which have befallen me are the Consequences only of my own Folly and Vice."[6] Once Tom has abandoned the feckless path of Fortune and recognized the orderly and moral plan of Providence, he can look forward to earning his own just deserts and thus of collaborating, to some extent at least, in the directing of his life course. To do so, he must forsake the inconsistent, irrational, and immoral female principle and commit himself to Providence, the ideal patriarch, superior, worthy of reposed power, just, and careful of charges.

If Fortune represents all the worst aspects of the unenlightened folk who roil the surface of the novel's comic universe, there appears to be a difference according to gender in the manner in which the comic and satiric effects of the characters' failings are elicited, and the difference pertains even though Fielding elicits his comic effects in two discrete ways. A distinction between comedy and satire in Fielding's novels may be drawn. Strictly applied, Fielding's own definition of the comedic in the preface to *Joseph Andrews* excludes some of what strikes us as funny in the book. Comedy, he tells us, depends upon the exposure of vanity and hypocrisy, for "as Vanity puts us on affecting false Characters, in order to purchase Applause; so Hypocrisy sets us on an Endeavour to avoid Censure by concealing our Vices under an Appearance of their opposite Virtues." For Fielding vanity and hypocrisy are the only human failings at which we may properly laugh, for neither humiliation nor wickedness are funny. And in his books he tests the reader in regard to this definition—in *Tom Jones* toppling Sophia from her horse and exposing her to the grins of the onlookers—who are, we realize, mistaken in finding humor in the situation (2:574). Emblematically comic, however, is the sudden dropping of the curtain to expose the philosopher Square in Molly Seagrim's closet in an excretory posture "among other female Utensils" (1:229).

Fielding's "comedy" is therefore satiric in nature, involving the exposure of the gap between the satiric norm or ideal to which the characters pretend to conform and their actual failings or true natures. But some of the more fallible characters are neither vain nor hypocritical, but instead unashamedly what they are: Mrs. Partridge, the landlady at Upton, the willing maid Grace at the alehouse, the Merry Andrew and the puppet master, for instance—and yet they fall far beneath the norm already established in the book by the virtues of the exemplary figures as well as by the pretensions of the others. In their case, as in the case of the characters aware enough of their departure from the norm to pretend to be better than they are, the identical norms are invoked and in both cases the reader must do the work of discerning the gap between the characters' real natures and the satiric norms.

What are these norms, accepted by most in the world of Tom Jones, and from which most of the characters fall far short? I think there are two quite different norms in operation, for on the comic plane of the novel, the plane which in appearance is governed by Fortune and which is inhabited principally by people who recognize only her governance, male and female characters often are held up to different ideals, and satire is produced by the manner in which they fail to live up to two very different models. While in the world of Tom Jones both men and women are made comic because of their similarities to Fortune, men, supposed to be both rational and responsible, are held up only to the providential model, while women are confronted, as indeed they were in life, with two often conflicting or contradictory models to which to conform: the providential model and what can here be called the Halifax prescription. Angela Smallwood's conclusions that Fielding believed women not inferior by nature but by education, that moral ideals should be the same for both sexes, seem valid.[7] Thus far he grants women a most important equality. But as Fielding's apologist, Smallwood overstates her case in failing to recognize his approval of the instructions to women of George Savile, Lord Halifax, in his *The Lady's New-Year's Gift: Or, Advice to a Daughter* (1688). As Smallwood notes, Halifax recommends to women the qualities of modesty, discretion, silence, submissiveness, and gentleness.[8] This important model for women also lives in *Tom Jones*, providing much of the satiric humor produced by the female characters. Certainly Fielding exploited the situation that prescribed an additional ideal model for women. The comedy or satire derived from the gap between the assumed attributes of men and their actual characters rests on their comparison to Providence, whose characteristics represent the patriarchal ideal. The women, however, draw much of their comic character from displaying the opposite of the qualities prescribed for women by Lord Halifax: they outdo the men in immodesty, indiscretion, volubility and noisiness, overbearingness, and roughness. Comic women thus contrast sharply with both the providential model and the Halifax prescription, comic men with the attributes of Providence only.

But despite the presence of Providence as a norm, most characters of both genders follow Fortune. Without having considered every supernumerary who crosses the stage, I have identified approximately thirty-four men and twenty-three women who play parts sufficiently signicant to make feasible an analysis of their virtues and failings. For both sexes, among those who follow Fortune two classes can be distinguished. One class includes those who fail in moral responsibility and suffer from perversions of reason only, schemers and liars who use their reasoning powers for selfish and devious ends. These are typically working or professional people, brought onstage in their professional capacities, who use their professional expertise to further ambition, greed, or spite. A second class includes those (usually more fully developed) characters who also exhibit reason overcome by passion or total irrationality, violence, and sexual misconduct. The fallible male characters of the book are comparatively evenly divided between these two classes, nineteen and fifteen, with the balance tilted toward the first group, but of the female characters only two confine themselves to perversions of the reason, while sixteen indulge in sexual irregularity and violence. In other words, if there *were* one providential norm only for both genders, women in the book are falling from it differently from men, and are falling from it in a way that accentuates their distance from the Halifax norm.

While there are valid socio-historical reasons for the predominance in the book of men over women and the difference in distribution of their failings, the effect is also clear and important. True, of the working and professional people in the book, the doctors, lawyers, clerics, and men of business are male, and Fielding is here importantly employed in illustrating the methods by which members of the professions impose upon others. The sergeant who attempts to sell a sword to Tom for twenty guineas while he imagines him out of his senses (1:386) and the sentinel who for a bribe lets Northerton escape (1:388–90) fall into the same category. When he can, Fielding makes the same point with the female keepers of the inns and with servants of both genders. The male professionals include the three doctors who attend Allworthy, Tom, and Fitzpatrick, all of whom overstate the danger of their patients in order to protect and enhance their own reputations;[9] the lawyers Dowling and the pettifogger at the Bell Inn (1:432–33), who consistently deceive and cheat; the landlord at Meriden, known as "a very sagacious Fellow," who concludes that Sophia is the Pretender's mistress, Jenny Cameron (2:576–78); and the two senior Nightingales, both of whom consider young Nightingale's marriage a business venture without regard to the compatibility of the partners or the honor of either (2:773–74, 778–80). To them may be added the elder two calculating Blifils; Thwackum; those two corrupters of the Man of the Hill, Sir George Gresham and Mr. Watson (1:453–55, 462–79); the gypsy who attempts to sell his wife (2:669–71); and, it is probably fair to say, those misguided novelists Samuel Richardson and Tobias Smollett—a total by these calculations of eighteen. By contrast, only two women characters seem to fit this category—both, not coincidentally, working women: Deborah Wilkins[10] and the landlady at Cambridge who has stripped her family in behalf of one favorite daughter (1:408–14). The satire produced by these characters is a result of their *falling-away* from right reason; but the effect of the numerical distribution is to suggest that the norm for men, but not for women, is one of *right* rationality as the falling-away is characterized by *wrong*.

The better-developed flawed male characters typically display, like most of the women, not only crooked reasoning, but also lapses from rational control into unseemly passion. (In fact, it may be assumed that in this universe perversions of the passions will attend on perversions of the reason.) These include Squire Western; young Blifil, who engages in fisticuffs with Tom on more than one occasion (1:129, 254, 260–63); Black George (1:186); Square (1:229); Daniel Pearce or Dowdy, who terrifies inn guests for amusement (1:361); Ensign Northerton (1:375–76, 496); Henry Fisher, who robs and murders his friend and benefactor (1:402–3); the landlord at Upton who indulges in a physical melée (1:502–4); Fitzpatrick, who causes scenes and brawls (2:529–31, 872); Partridge, who brawls at Upton, excoriates and begins to beat a cripple, and attempts sex with the gypsy wife (2:502–4; 2:634, 670); the puppet master, guilty of the projected robbery of Sophia, and the Merry Andrew, guilty of fornication (2:640–42, 649); young Nightingale, who seduces a respectable young woman; and Lord Fellamar, willing to rape Sophia and have Tom kidnapped and pressed into sea service (2:794–98, 863–64, 873)—a total of fourteen. The Man of the Hill, a special case, adds one to either side by appearing in two aspects, in his younger days exhibiting perversions of both reason and passion, in his latter days exhibiting a serious perversion of reason.

Many of the women characters of *Tom Jones* correspond in selected aspects—none completely—to Fortune. These comic characters are universally incapable of making moral judgments or acting on them, and comedy is generated by the exposure of the selfish and unworthy motives for their opinions, attitudes, and actions. Though all of the comic female figures of the book display a failure of rationality, all but two also display inadequately controlled passions. The uncontrolled include the sexually unregulated Bridget Allworthy, Molly Seagrim, Jenny Jones, Goody Brown (1:181), Harriet Fitzpatrick, the alehouse maid Grace (2:641), the gypsy wife (2:670), and Lady Bellaston; the viragos Mrs. Partridge, Mrs. Western, who descends to violent verbal attack in defense of her opinions, and the Meriden landlady (2:606); the physical combatants Mrs. Western's maid (1:354–55), the thirteen female churchyard battlers (1:178–83), Honour, who indulges in two physical brawls (1:354–55; 2:603–4) and gets drunk (2:606–7), the alehouse landlady (also a virago) (2:641), the landlady at Upton and her maid Susan (1:501–4); and the tippler Harriet Fitzpatrick's maid (2:607)—a total, excluding the churchyard crew, of sixteen. They present quite a different profile from the preponderance of bent reasoners of the male gender.

Of these women, Mrs. Western is the best representative of the goddess because, unmarried and economically independent, she is autonomous and powerful, willful, impetuous and imperative, unreflective and without self-doubt, wrong-headed, violent, cruel and crude in choice of expedient, and yet always capable of an unregulated fondness expressed only when she is gratified. Mrs. Partridge, Fortune's second representative, is autonomous and tyrannous, quick to decide, wrong-headed and irrational, violent, and changeable. In her sudden reversals from furious to kind to furious she is like Fortune for "her Passions were, indeed, equally violent, which ever Way they inclined: for, as she could be extremely angry, so could she be altogether as fond" (1:86). Lady Bellaston, like Fortune and like Mrs. Western, is selfish, exclusively self-gratifying, and self-willed, liberal to temporary favorites but incapable of fidelity or "commitment." Very unnaturally, but like Fortune, she resists male government, and her refusal of Tom's offer of marriage has the comic effect invariably provided when his female characters act against the Halifax stereotype. Molly Seagrim is another of Fortune's daughters, seductive, deceptive, fickle, and undiscriminating in the distribution of her favors.

By contrast Jenny Jones/Mrs. Waters, never a great source of comedy, becomes faintly funny only after she too has become promiscuous with her favors. Mrs. Fitzpatrick is comic only in her hypocrisy, her pretense that she has not departed from virtue. But any woman who does not proceed by making moral judgments and cleaving to them, is in some way reflective of Fortune. For instance, Bridget Allworthy and the landlady at Hambrook (1:362–63), like Fortune, choose favorite children and deprive others of their just due. The Man of the Hill's irregular courses were precipitated by a mother who made his unworthy elder brother her favorite (1:451–52). In *Tom Jones* choosing unworthy favorites is a failing of Fortune and of women. By contrast, the narrator of *Tom Jones* confesses Sophia is a favorite child, "but sure a Parent can hardly be blamed, when . . . Superiority determines his Preference" (2:857); nor does he treat his other children unfairly. Women, however, like Fortune, choose their favorites foolishly. "What is the Reason, my Dear," Harriet Fitzpatrick asks Sophia, "that we who have Understandings equal to the wisest and greatest of the other Sex so often make Choice of the silliest Fellows for Companions and Favourites?" (2:586).

The book's female characters, in following Fortune, tend to be sexually promiscuous, stridently vociferous, physically violent, and unruly, or the opposite of modest, discreet, silent, submissive, and gentle. Ideology, which endorses the providential model as primarily a male model, interposes itself here, not unbeknownst to Fielding, to make the comedy and satire depend upon a comparison of the women's actual behavior to the Halifax stereotype.

Fielding was utilizing other resonances: his more libidinous and scolding viragos, like Fortune, seem modelled in part on the Restoration heroines of Manley and Aphra Behn. The domineering and willful women of the *New Atalantis* had in 1749 not yet quite been displaced as exemplars of the natural predispositions of women despite concerted Establishment efforts, and the Halifax prescription for women, written in such women's despite, had not yet been fully accepted as a description of woman's actual and true nature. But the pretence that the prescription was in fact in accordance with woman's true passive nature (a pretence paradoxically combined with vigorous efforts to impress this postulation on women as fact) had still to be popularized, most notably in John Gregory's *A Father's Legacy to his Daughters* (1774).[11] Fielding, in his emphasis and satire on Mrs. Western, vociferous landladies, and sexually active and physically combative women, in his approval of the decorous Sophia and Mrs. Miller, is making his contribution in support of the new prescription for women, but like other mid-century males, himself inclines more to the Restoration than the Gregory view of their nature.

In the case of the male characters, however, the satire must be generated by the comparison between the characters' failings and the male stereotype for the ruling class, which was in fact the providential model of justice, truth, temperateness, rationality, benevolence, and goodness. Of the male characters, only one, Squire Western, is, like Mrs. Western, Mrs. Partridge, Lady Bellaston, and Molly Seagrim, closely correspondent to Fortune in character. Of him the narrator significantly says, "Men over-violent in their Dispositions, are, for the most Part, as changeable in them" (2:957). In assuming more of the attributes of Fortune, perhaps, than any other character, Squire Western is comic because, in his resemblance to Fortune, he contradicts the stereotype for the male ruling class. That is, he is not, like Allworthy, an earthly representative of Providence, as his position and privileges require and assume he is. Similarly, in pretending to both reason and education, which as a schoolmaster he should have, but both of which to a considerable degree he lacks, Partridge is also comic.

No question but Fielding capitalized on the two different norms for much of the comedy of the book, and the different norms have the effect of associating women more firmly with Fortune and Halifax's prescription, of men more firmly with Providence and reason. More men than women exhibit perversions of reason, which suggests both that they are falling from the norm and that they think more; almost all the women exhibit unregulated passions, which suggests they are devoid of self-control. More women are sexually unrepressed perhaps because more of them—like Jenny Jones, Molly Seagrim, Harriet Fitzpatrick, and even the gypsy wife—have to use their bodies, rather than the professions to which they cannot aspire, to empower themselves, even to survive. Of male characters, Tom, Square, Black George, who impregnated and then married a clergyman's daughter, and the Merry Andrew are libidinous. None, however, are portrayed so crookedly and consistently prurient as the libidinous women, in whom the failing is apparently (with reference to the Halifax model) considerably more serious, as perhaps Fielding intends to convey by naming the guilty Square a female utensil. Other men use sex not for pleasure but for advancement: both Captain Blifil and Fitzpatrick have used their sexuality to marry fortunes and Partridge too has married Allworthy's kitchen maid for her twenty pounds (1:82) and was, in his one sexual lapse, inveigled by the gypsy wife and husband (2:669–71). Surprisingly, women are *more* likely than males *to be known* to indulge consistently in sex for gratification— vide Bridget Allworthy, Molly Seagrim, the alehouse's maid Grace (2:640–41) and Lady Bellaston; and Deborah Wilkins and Mrs. Partridge are signified not averse to sexual attentions.

In respect to violence and gender, the churchyard melée resulting from Molly's having appeared in Sophia's sack gown, in which nine men and thirteen women engage, is emblematic (1:178–83), suggesting that unregenerate women are at least as violent, if not more so, than men. Otherwise violent men and women are almost proportionately balanced, with the proportion of women slightly higher. Males who succumb to violence include twelve of those afflicted by perversions of the passions. Eight violent females include Mrs. Partridge; Molly Seagrim in the churchyard; Mrs. Weston's maid, who battles with Honour (1:354–56), who herself later attacks a landlord's face with her nails (2:606); Goody Brown, the churchyard combatant, who regularly both cuckolds and scores the face of her husband (1:181); and Mrs. Waters, the landlady at Upton and her maid Grace, who indulge in an epic battle. Probably male violence is too threatening to be comic or is an acceptable masculine, possibly even providential (since Providence often effects results through violence) prerogative. Male violence may constitute a strategy such as Black George's method for producing "a total Calm" (1:186), while female violence is a comic negation of submission and silence. A wife assaulting her husband may be funny (1:89); a battle royal between women in a churchyard is funny (1:177–84); a battle between two rival maids is funny (1:354–56); a battle in which men and women combat one another, the women employing tongues and nails, is funny (1:89–90, 178–83, 502–4); but an assault, like Northerton's on Tom (1:376) or Fellamar's on Sophia (2:796–98) can be useful only to advance the plot. Male attacks are funny only when conceivably great injuries are then trivialized, as in the case of the fisticuffs between Tom, Blifil, Thwackum, and Western (1:261–63), where the combat is also distanced by the mock-epic description and the chapter heading which "introduces as bloody a Battle as can possibly be fought, without the Assistance of Steel or cold Iron."

If men are elevated above women by a firmer identification with Providence, they are elevated by other means as well. There are simply more of them in the book, suggesting what is the truth, that it is a man's world. And, ultimately, as it is recognized, Providence and Fortune set up the proper order of the universe—rational male over irrational female—a powerful paradigm.

Fielding's own beliefs need to be queried here. What, in fact, *is* Fielding's idea of the true nature of women? Is it defined by Halifax, who attempted to enforce a stereotype against their true irrational and sexually unrestrained nature, or by latter eighteenth-century conduct books which claimed the Halifax prescription was woman's nature, or by some standard of Fielding's own? Is it his intention to suggest that men and women tend toward different vices, or is it only that violent women and scheming men were often funnier than the other way round? The irrational and misreasoning women of *Tom Jones* appear to endorse the notion that women are usually irrational. The misreasoning men do endorse one of Fielding's most important messages—that men ought to be living up to their high responsibilities instead of self-indulgently battening on their privileges.

An examination of those regenerate women of *Tom Jones*, Mrs. Miller and Sophia, will help elucidate the problem inherent in Fielding's position.

The comic universe of the morally deformed is left behind on the plane where Fielding's few regenerate characters exist. And an examination of those men and women in *Tom Jones* who reflect the character of Providence actually suggests that Fielding endorsed the single prescription for men, the double prescription for women. He believed that both men and women should live up to the providential model of justice, truth, temperateness, rationality, benevolence, and goodness. But Providence also regulates the universe, and ideology dictated an enormous difference between the powers of the two sexes. Here the Halifax prescription came into play, and Fielding endorsed the dictum that women should *also* be modest, discreet, silent, submissive, gentle. The difference between the male and the female exemplary figures is therefore significant.

The female exemplary characters are four: two of them major, Sophia and Mrs. Miller, and two of them minor, Mrs. Whitefield of the Bell Inn[12] and Mrs. Enderson, the would-be highwayman's wife (2:718–21). The male exemplary characters are also four: Allworthy, Parson Supple (perhaps so named only because he puts up with Squire Weston and marries Mrs. Waters), the poor lieutenant (1:370–71), the gypsy king (2:667–73). To these one may perhaps add Tom, who though no fully exemplary character, has much in his character to admire, and in the end arrives on Allworthy's plane. He is distinguishable from other *redeemable* characters because they—Nightingale, Enderson, and Nancy Miller—are saved by the efforts of others of the exemplary, while Tom is saved chiefly by his own efforts and the interposition of Providence.

The male and female exemplary characters in many ways are similar: they are charitable, benevolent, truthful, clear-thinking, self-controlled, and just. The reaction of the exemplary characters to the dispositions of Providence represents a model for others. Allworthy has been *given* only one gift by Fortune—a very large estate. His wife and three children have been *taken* from him. "This Loss, however great, he bore like a Man of Sense and Constancy" and looked on himself as a man whose wife has only gone a little before him on a journey he would take after her, and that he would meet with her again to part no more (1:34–35). Meanwhile he manages the estate for the benefit of everyone on it and in fact all whom he encounters; for instance, he accepts the charge of Tom which Fortune assigns him.[13] Sophia, when ordered by her father to marry Blifil, uses her reason rather than her passions to determine her course, discarding as not proper the temptation of the passion vanity to play the martyr to his whim (1:360), and, when she leaves her father's house, unlike Clarissa, she takes her "Honour" with her.[14] When she has lost her pocketbook and her bank note, she "immediately got the better of her Concern, and with her wonted Serenity and Cheerfulness of Countenance, returned to her Company" (2:610). The exemplary characters accept what Providence ordains and take full responsibility for their responses.

Fielding's providential community is, in numbers of the redeemed, only a little tilted toward a male majority, which means a larger proportion of the women are included. In any case the characters of Sophia and Mrs. Miller indicate Fielding's serious expectation for women: both are superior to all other women and both make discriminating moral judgments and act on them. It may be concluded that the moral pyramid of this universe, at the apex of which the exemplary characters stand, is an elongated one with a narrow pinnacle, but that even as some other characters were saved by the efforts of the worthy, so also Fielding did not despair of educating readers of both genders to more exemplary performance, and that the exemplary performance for both genders was to be in certain respects the same—after the education of the moral judgment and acquisition of the willingness to act only on its dictates. However, as we shall see, the acting out socially of the dictates of the moral judgment was to differ considerably for women.

Fielding, then, did not believe that the essential moral and spiritual nature of women was different from the essential moral and spiritual nature of men; he also believed that most women and men failed in a common obligation to live up to the ideals embodied by Providence. His eight or nine exemplary characters rest on a base of about sixty morally frailer persons who fail in this respect. But he did believe in a very significant difference between the capacities of the genders.

There is every indication that Fielding never questioned the assumption that men should retain their superior responsibilities and privileges. His Providence/Fortune dichotomy reflects this implication. Fielding endorses the powerful image of Providence standing over Fortune and manipulating her zany proceedings for moral ends; as the morally mature man or woman comes to see this image clearly, the image of wanton Fortune grows transparent and fades. Providence works slowly through the screen, Fortune: the mills of God grind slowly, as the name of Mrs. Miller may be intended to suggest. Then, while Providence is evident only to the morally elite but hidden to the majority, the power of Fortune seems "real" to the masses and her illusoriness is apparent only to the elite. Those who mature morally must give up their belief in Fortune and transfer their faith to Providence. The gender difference between the two divinities, the real one and the false one, must now have a powerful impact, and it is difficult to believe that the image fails to accord with Fielding's idea of the relative positions of the genders.

That Mrs. Miller is at all able to discuss with Allworthy the subject of his seriously mistaken opinions of Blifil and Tom is perhaps owing to Allworthy's being "too good a Man to be really offended with the Effects of so noble a Principle as now actuated" her (2:900); but we have here an example of the trepidation and tears with which a dependent woman attempts to correct a most egregious mistake of the most virtuous of men, who actually threatens to ruin her if she proceeds with a word against Blifil: "If you ever say a Word more of that Kind, I will depart from your House that

Instant" (2:899). Mrs. Miller has a moral obligation to try to put Allworthy right but the social injunction, even from Allworthy, is silence rather than contradiction of the patriarch who controls the well-being of herself and her daughters. The scene is emblematic of the contradictory charges laid on virtuous women. When the subject arises again, Mrs. Miller believes she may not contribute to it: "'Well, I must not speak, and yet it is certainly very hard to hold one's Tongue when one hears—.'" Allworthy, whose mind is now altering, replies, "Madam, . . . you may say whatever you please, you know me too well to think I have a Prejudice against any one" (2:922). She knows him well enough to know he has been very wrongly prejudiced against Tom, and his permission to her to speak is dependent merely upon his state of mind at the moment; had Providence withheld from him the clues that Mrs. Miller was right, he might with equal equanimity have bid her hold her tongue and she would have had to do so, as when at the moment of the discovery of Blifil's malevolence, she cries out "Guilty, upon my Honour! Guilty, upon my Soul!" and Allworthy "sharply rebuked her for this Impetuousity" (2:932); it is not for women to render judgment. It is hard for her to see truth and remain silent. Significantly, in such a situation, though a man may see that a woman believes she has a moral obligation to remonstrate with him, he feels no obligation himself to accommodate her. And Mrs. Miller ends in the same relationship to Allworthy in which she began, more than ever his—and Tom's—humble servant.

Sophia, like Mrs. Miller, is already, at the start of the book, firmly committed to the providential model, and she has the same difficulty: her moral judgments are not considered by the powers who rule her life. It would appear that Tom's education cannot be paralleled by Sophia's, since she already has the prudence which he must acquire. Tom must be educated into subjecting his behavior to his moral judgment. Sophia, more lacking in experience of the world, never fails, even as she acquires experience, to subject her behavior to her moral judgment. She is thus superior at the start, a beacon for Tom. Tom learns to act morally and to avoid the urgings of self-indulgent impulse. But in fact Sophia also has lessons to learn and also changes.

Open and ingenuous from the start, Sophia's initial troubles seem to have derived from her inexperience with the world and her inability to manipulate her father and her aunt. But out in the world she learns some of its lessons. After Harriet Fitzpatrick plainly edits *her* story, leaving out the role of her lover in her adventures, Sophia in exactly the same manner edits her own (2:601–2). "Indeed, if this may be called a Kind of Dishonesty," notes the narrator, "it seems the more inexcusable, from the apparent Openness and explicit Sincerity of the other Lady." That is, from the example of her cousin Sophia learns how not to be utterly candid, and for the first time (that we know) practices "a Kind of Dishonesty." Telling truth is an important touchstone of the providential characters, while the more fallible

ones lie persistently (and comically). We catch Sophia in an outright lie at
the end of the book (and, significantly, the end of her education), when she
quite easily, and without apparent distress, tells Lady Bellaston she does not
remember having seen the face of Tom Jones before (2:737). Yet after that
lie, she inquires of her father "Have I ever been found guilty of a Falshood
from my Cradle?" (2:840), tells her aunt, "I hope, Madam, you have too
good an Opinion of me, to imagine me capable of telling an Untruth"
(2:890), and later informs her, "I scorn a lie" (2:905). A close examination
of these statements suggests her language may even be somewhat jesuitical,
for she never directly denies that she has lied. Arguably, Fielding believed
that women, often barred from expressing their wants and beliefs openly,
had need of learning such art.

For Sophia also learns, however belatedly, to cajole and flatter her aunt by
referring to (what she could not herself have believed to be) the world's
awareness of the many lovers she has refused (2:890–91). "Thus *Sophia* by
a little well directed Flattery, for which surely none will blame her, obtained
a little Ease for herself" (2:891). To an extent Fielding palliates Sophia's
felix culpa by allowing Tom too to buy himself out of his relationship with
Lady Bellaston through the judicious application of an insincere proposal of
marriage (2:818–21). Perhaps the crafty manipulation of one's less rational
acquaintance is a necessary social art? But the reader does not hear Tom
lying and virtually professing always to speak truth, and cannot be blamed if
she assumes that the moral standard for women does after all vary a little
from that for men. Earlier Sophia has been repaid for having made peace
between her father and her aunt by having them turn in unity against her:
"Poor *Sophia*, who had first set on Foot this Reconciliation, was now made
the Sacrifice to it" (1:343). Instead of reconciling the pair, the narrator
remarks, "women who . . . know the World . . . would have immediately
availed themselves of the present Disposition of Mr. *Western*'s Mind; by
throwing in a few artful Compliments to his Understanding at the Expence
of his absent Adversary." But simple Sophia "wanted all that useful Art
which Females convert to so many good Purposes in Life, and which, as it
rather arises from the Heart, than from the Head, is often the Property of the
silliest of Women" (1:337–38).

Precisely what Fielding means by this last is elucidated a few pages later
when Blifil assures Allworthy "I would not myself, for any Consideration
. . . consent to marry this young Lady, if I was not persuaded she had all the
Passion for me which I desire she should have" (3:347). He has no desire
for any passion at all from Sophia, and "this excellent Method of conveying
a Falshood with the Heart only, without making the Tongue guilty of an
Untruth, by the Means of Equivocation and Imposture, hath quieted the
Conscience of many a notable Deceiver." In no time at all, after colluding
with Honour's deceitful method of being dismissed, Sophia is found
misleading her father in the same manner: about to run away, she convinces
him she intends to obey him and marry Blifil by saying, "You know, Sir, I

must not, nor can refuse to obey any absolute Command of yours" (1:359). Her reward is a large bank bill. The effect of this correspondence between Blifil and Sophia is not to be ignored, and it continues. At the end of her adventures, having learned not to strengthen her adversaries by making peace between them, by taking her father's part against her aunt she helps to set them against one another when each advocates a different husband for her: "This was the first Time of her so doing, and it was in the highest Degree acceptable to the Squire," and as a result he gives up his violent measures to force her to marry Blifil (2:919). Here is a Fortune-like action which would much have benefitted her cause at the start of her troubles—had she then been capable of it. It appears that simple Sophia has now learned that useful womanly art of deviously achieving her end through imperfect means, an art that helps a little (but not too much) to right the balance of power between the genders and that also usefully establishes women as less morally responsible than men and therefore needing to be ruled. Of course it was necessary so to reduce Sophia.

At Sophia's independent best she had declared that she would rather give up her understanding then see defects in her husband's judgment after marriage (2:595), which means that in marriage she *will* give up both understanding and moral judgment rather than judge him wrong in any important matter. Her judgment may be impeccable, but Allworthy commends her for having once refused to offer an opinion about a disagreement between Thwackum and Square: "I must absolutely be excused; for I will affront neither so much, as to give my Judgment on his Side" (2:883). Sophia is capable of sound judgment but knows better than to offer it in the company of men. Allworthy praises her modesty at length: "no dictatorial Sentiments, no judicial Opinions, no profound Criticisms. Whenever I have seen her in the Company of Men, she hath been all Attention, with the Modesty of a Learner, not the Forwardness of a Teacher. . . . Indeed, she always shewed the highest Deference to the Understandings of Men; a Quality, absolutely essential to the making a good Wife" (2:882–83). Like Mrs. Miller, she must eschew "judicial Opinions."[15]

At the end of the book, Sophia has apparently customarily adopted the flattering insincerity with which she has addressed her aunt on the subject of her lovers, and when her father finally orders her to marry Tom, she responds, "I will obey you. . . . Tomorrow Morning shall be the Day, Papa, since you will have it so. . . . Such are your Commands, Sir, and I dare not be guilty of Disobedience" (2:975). The high comedy of her complaisant acquiescence when her father's judgment and wishes at last accord with her own may mask her moral lapse, but Sophia has fallen—as the fact that one may laugh at her here demonstrates.[16] So while Tom becomes perfectly developed morally, and, as always, unabashedly self-expressive, Sophia has apparently learned habitually to lie, flatter, and manipulate.

In her independent apprenticeship, a brief interregnum, Sophia has been making her own moral judgments and acting on them as directly as possible in a manner superior to Tom's. But it is impossible for two people in a hierarchical arrangement each always to act from inner moral conviction. In marriage Sophia must be a wife, which apparently means that she may make moral judgments but may then, as the situation requires, have to conceal them, equivocate about them, or, in order to see them implemented, manipulate others. This is the female code of behavior, requiring that a woman have good moral judgment but not the right, granted only to men, to express or enforce it. I suggest that Fielding saw repression, equivocation, and manipulation as desirable womanly arts, arts which then in their expression conveniently helped to distinguish between moral virtue in men and in women, to privilege male moral virtue over female, and incidentally to identify even Sophia a little more closely with Fortuna.

Paradoxically, all Sophia needed to become perfect as a wife was to become detectably inferior to her husband. Women must be educated as moralists, Fielding's final admirable judgment may be—but they must also learn to be silent, manipulative moralists. That is, they must follow *both* providential and Halifax models, which it is, in fact, often impossible to do. While Fielding believed in the moral maturity of women, he held no brief for their social autonomy. Sophia's role was, it appears, educative and instrumental, her mission completed when Tom had surpassed her and become worthy to wield the domestic and social power with her support. As the arrangement in which Sophia dwindled into a wife and its ramifications were tendentious, Fielding failed to underscore them. But of course we knew already that in 1749, while the time for the ideal of friendship in marriage had arrived, the time for the ideal of equal partnership had not.

And of course Fielding cannot really be faulted for his position, since women writers decades later had only the same prescription to offer: that women ought to have autonomous and mature moral judgment which in the company of men, and particularly in marriage, they were often not permitted even to voice: "I shall never marry a Man in whose Understanding I see any Defects before Marriage; and I promise you I would rather give up my own, than see any such afterwards" (2:595). Torn between the ideology of full moral responsibility for every man and woman and the ideology of marriage, no one knew of any other solution than to put women in this constrained position—to be able to judge right for themselves and to be unable to do anything about it—even to argue for it. Elizabeth Cutts, an important member of the Bath community of women gathered around Sarah Fielding and Sarah Scott in the 1740s and 1750s, a woman who had thought about women's plight all her adult life, in 1775 published *Almeria: or, Parental Advice: A Didactic Poem. Addressed to the Daughters of Great Britain and Ireland, By a Friend to the Sex.*[17] In it a male authority figure preaches advice to daughters and insists, "Judge for *thyself*; nor idly rest thy faith / On what *another*, tho' a *parent*, saith. . . . / Nor leave thy *principles* the work of Chance" (15). Then he argues that women should display female modesty and female graces only—"The steady look would *then* be left to man: / To man the bold reply, th'intrepid mien" (30). Women are to let the husband rule, and, unluckily, the weaker the husband's reason, the more tenacious and determined will be his will to rule.

> Nor draw conclusions from his want of skill.
> Is Reason weak?—The stronger then the will;
> The more tenacious of the high-flown claim,
> And still more sacred held a Husband's name:
> While to preserve the dignity he loves,
> He spurns at counsels which his heart approves.
> Then keep thy distance, tho' well-qualify'd
> To *share* at least the sceptre, if not *guide*:
> Strive in thy humbler province to excel:
> Indifferent what the part, if acted well.
>
> (41)

Moreover

> The talents veil whose lustre may offend;
> Or better—throw that lustre round thy Friend;
> And with the ray reflected *safely* shine,
> Content to borrow what is fairly thine:
> With dex'trous hand deficiencies supply;
> And well repaid thy liberality;
> The Title *his*, but *thine* true Royalty.
>
> (42)

If such is the advice of a woman who herself abjured marriage because of all that it implied, but who honestly gave her best opinion as to how married women might fare best in a hostile institution, it would be unfair to fault Fielding for a like opinion.

One suspects, however, there was a substantial difference between Fielding and Cutts: she did not believe in man's superiority or his intrinsic right to dominance, and he apparently did. She gave directions for survival (of a sort) in an unfair situation. But she suggested women were actually well qualified to share the rule if not to guide alone, granted them talents and "a dex'trous hand." He showed the inability to rule wisely of Mrs. Partridge, Mrs. Western, and Lady Bellaston, and portrayed Sophia and even Mrs. Miller in their wisdom eschewing such ambition. He constructed a universe of which the deity itself provided a blueprint for male-female relations and justified masculine privilege. He provided a cast of characters of which the men exhibited more misdirected reason and the women more violence and irrationality. It must have been an entirely different novel—an eventuality we would all regret—had the machinery been comprised of Providence and Wisdom or Providence and Justice (even blindfolded) ruling together, side by side.

NOTES

1. This paper is in some respects a response to the conclusions of Angela Smallwood in *Fielding and the Woman Question: the Novels of Henry Fielding and Feminist Debate, 1700–1750* (New York: St. Martin's Press, 1989) that Fielding had enlightened and liberal views on the woman question, but that further examination needed to be made of his "blind side." I agree with both her statements.

2. Henry Fielding, *The History of Tom Jones, A Foundling*, 2 vols. (Oxford: Wesleyan University Press, 1975), 1:103. Subsequent references to this work will be by volume and page number in the text.

3. For a review of Fortune's career as a deity see Howard Rollin Patch, *The Goddess Fortuna in Medieval Literature* (Cambridge: Harvard University Press, 1927).

4. Delariviere Manley, *The Adventures of Rivella*, in *The Novels of Mary Delariviere Manley*, ed. Patricia Koster, 2 vols. (Gainesville, FL: Scholars' Facsimiles and Reprints, 1971), 34–35.

5. For discussions of Fortune's position, see Fielding, *Tom Jones*, 2:770–71 nn. 1–3 and 771 n. 1, and cited sources. See also *Tom Jones*, ed. Sheridan Baker (New York: W. W. Norton & Co., Inc., 1973), 591 n. 1 on the same text, with citations from Juvenal and Cicero on the non-divinity of Fortune.

6. Fielding, *Tom Jones* 2:915–16. Martin Battestin notes on this issue, "Without a proper understanding . . . that the trials of adversity are occasioned, not by blind Chance or Fortune, but by the benevolent and corrective Providence of God, affliction will end in despair, not wisdom." *The Moral Basis of Fielding's Art: A Study of Joseph Andrews* (Middletown, CT: Wesleyan University Press, 1959), 51. Immediately following Tom's enlightenment, Providence intervenes in his behalf (2:920).

7. Smallwood, *Fielding and the Woman Question*, 46, 52.

8. Ibid., 115.

9. Fielding, *Tom Jones* 1:241; 380–81, 411; 2:873, 893. The roughness of this artificial division should be apparent; some of these persons pursue their wrong-headed or crooked notions with a veritable passion, as does Tom's doctor, put into a rage when he learns his gentleman patient is only a poor bastard (1:412–13). Only a very rough division into errors of reason only and errors of violence or sexual misconduct is intended here.

10. Deborah Wilkins confines herself to insulting and tyrannizing over Allworthy's parish, but her failure to exhibit sexual irregularity is apparently less the result of firm principle than of lack of opportunity, as her response to her night-time summons by Allworthy makes plain. Ibid. 1:39–40.

11. See, for example, James Thomson's "Autumn" (1730), lines 570–609, in which he prescribes as appealing to men all the weakness, "winning softness," blushes, "tender limbs," trivial accomplishments, "submissive wisdom," and "modest skill" that Gregory endorses in 1774. Again Thomson: "In them 'tis graceful to dissolve at wo; / With every motion, every word, to wave / Quick o'er the kindling cheek the ready blush; / And

from the smallest violence to shrink / Unequal, then the loveliest in their fears; / And by this silent adulation soft, / To their protection more engaging man" (lines 579–85); but these lines are at least as much a prescription as an analysis of woman's natural character. The rake in Mary Davys' *The Accomplished Rake* (1727) proclaims "Women are naturally modest, men naturally impudent"—an early indication of things to come—but it remains for Gregory and his own contemporaries confidently to claim such prescribed behavior as "natural" to, rather than simply attractive in, women.

12. Fielding, *Tom Jones* 1:431. Fielding never faults exemplary characters, like Allworthy and Mrs. Whitefield, who arrive at wrong conclusions on sufficient and seemingly-accurate evidence, but he does like to show how the good can be misled by the crooked-minded.

13. "I have considered him as a Child sent by Fortune to my Care" (ibid. 2:923). One of Fielding's problems in the writing of the book is that he has chosen to make Tom's discovery that Providence, not Fortune, is the ruling principle of the world (2:916) the first such discovery. Accordingly both the narrator and the other exemplary characters repeatedly attribute the power to Fortune, which often, logically, knowing better, they would not have done.

14. This would appear to be the only reason for Honour's otherwise ironically-bestowed name. In contrast to Sophia, Honour makes her own decision about leaving after coolly weighing the advantages of either course to herself.

15. Smallwood argues that Sophia refuses to proffer an opinion because in the disagreement between Thwackum and Square she knows both speak nonsense. *Fielding and the Woman Question*, 132. The argument is ingenious, but nevertheless Allworthy praises Sophia for her silence—and Fielding does not allow her to offer her opinions in another forum where men are speaking good sense.

16. Sophia has, in her vanity, made us smile before—as when she changes her ribbons and thus fails to meet Tom (1:293); but here is an instance of hypocrisy displayed just at the crucial moment when Tom is made morally sound.

17. Elizabeth Cutts, *Almeria: or, Parental Advice: A Didactic Poem. Addressed to the Daughters of Great Britain and Ireland, By a Friend to the Sex* (London: E. and J. Rodwell, 1775).

The Politics of Literary Production:
The Reaction to the French Revolution and
the Transformation of the English Literary
Periodical

ZEYNEP TENGER and PAUL TROLANDER

It has long been noted that there was a significant change in the format of English literary reviews and magazines between the years 1780 and 1830. Recent scholars, whose efforts have focused largely on changes in literary reviewing, including Derek Roper, John Haydon, Jon Klancher and Joanne Shattock, have argued for the importance of the shift from the more comprehensive formats of eighteenth-century reviews and magazines that had attempted to account for the entire "republic of letters" to the more selective and critical formats of later Romantic and Victorian literary periodicals.[1] Derek Roper, investigating the causes of this shift in his study *Reviewing Before the Edinburgh*, maintains that a selective format emerged among literary reviews because the number of books published increased significantly after 1780. He cites statements by both reviewers and editors that suggest they could no longer cope with the rising tide of works needing to be reviewed, and he reasons as well that readers had grown weary of a format necessitating the consideration of the flood of mediocre works that choked the literary market.[2] These factors no doubt had an effect on the shift in the formats of reviews, but, as Roper himself points out, these conditions had existed long before any real editorial shift occurred. References to the low quality of works published for the literary market had been prevalent at least since the 1720s when Alexander Pope prophesied that London would be overwhelmed by the rule of literary dunces, and as early as 1772 the *Critical Review* had noted that its efforts to survey all book-length works necessitated that it vary the length of its reviews according to "the regard [to] which [each work was] justly entitled." Throughout the closing two decades of the eighteenth century, there was a growing interest on the part of editors in reducing the number of works they reviewed in an effort to contain the size and price of their periodicals.[3]

It is our contention that, although there was a desire to adjust editorial practices and to find a justification for a more selective approach, it was effectually impossible for literary periodicals (magazines as well as reviews) to shift their emphases away from the comprehensive coverage of all modes of writing until there were changes in the discourse formations that shaped and validated critical, literary, and editorial practices. These changes could emerge only after the political reaction to the discourse of philosophical reform—which conservatives argued had caused the French Revolution—had gained popular favor in England.

Before 1790 many periodicals and magazines, proclaiming their efforts to act as "repositories" of the arts and sciences and as impartial and unprejudiced records of the progress of learning, aligned themselves with the British variant of philosophical reform which was rooted in Commonwealthman ideology and the Scottish Enlightenment.[4] Regardless of their political affiliations, such publications frequently affirmed that their task was to explore all areas of knowledge and make such knowledge accessible and entertaining to the reader. In doing so, they believed that they were serving the common good by reforming the public's morals and creating rational individuals. Publications that "attempted to cater to all persuasions,"[5] such as the *Gentleman's Magazine* and *London Magazine*, as well as those that were considered partisan, such as the *Monthly Review* and the *Critical Review*, equally identified with this program. They declared that their goal was to provide complete coverage of "the productions of the press," and established editorial policies, including anonymous reviewing, to ensure impartiality. The *Critical Reviews*'s subtitle, the "Annals of Literature," was indicative of the aims and intentions of many periodical publications of the period.

But as the political reaction to the French Revolution gained favor after 1792, there was a tendency to shift the genealogy of the reform movement from a British provenance to an alleged French one and to characterize reform as "jacobinical" and predicated on "French principles."[6] The wholesale negation of the language and aims of philosophical reform politicized and greatly diminished the social prestige of this discourse which had validated perodicals' comprehensive coverage of all areas of knowledge. In the process, conservatives inverted previous assumptions about the nature and aims of literary and critical discourse, often valuing prejudice, partiality, and personality at the expense of reason, universality, general nature, and the strictures of benevolence. Discursive and epistemological practices that reformist ideology had marginalized were now priviledged and gave impetus to the push to constitute and justify editorial and writing practices that were at once more selective, critical, and personal. But more important than these changes, this volte face on the part of literary reviews and magazines both directly challenged and undermined neoclassical assumptions concerning a unified reading public, and it reconstituted the literary field as a public spectacle (rather than a public sphere), the chief work of which was to deploy and celebrate discursive representations of literary personality, rather than constitute domains of moral and social knowledge.[7]

* * * * * * * * *

The aspiration to provide comprehensive coverage of all areas of learning and thereby aid in the intellectual and moral education of the British nation was popular before and throughout the 1780s. Established periodicals, as well as newer ones, defined their goals by employing the language of philosophical reform. In the *London Magazine*'s 1781 dedication to King George III, the editor expressed hope that the publication "afforded . . . rational entertainment," claiming that it was a "repository for the labours of the learned, a fund of historical information, and a faithful register of public and private events of the current time."[8] Its book-reviewing department was titled "An Impartial Account of New Publications." In 1783, the editors of the *English Review* justified the review's inauguration by asserting that it would "ascertain the progressive improvements, as well as the reigning follies of mankind" by providing a "faithful report of every new Publication," and claimed that because they were "free and independent of any influence" their reviewers were capable of "exercis[ing] that candour and impartiality . . . so often professed, and so seldom practiced."[9] Similarly, in the 1788 preface to the *Universal Magazine* (1788), which not coincidentally had a frontispiece entitled "The Contemplative Philosopher," it was claimed that magazines in general had a beneficial effect on the English public by improving morals and manners.[10] And in the preface to its sixtieth volume (1790), the editors of the *Gentleman's Magazine* commended themselves for fulfilling their duty as a "Chronicle of the Times" and for contributing to the "general Fund of public Entertainment and Instruction." Their aim was to act as an unbiased "record" or "Picture" of "Object[s] of Research," a national warehouse of "copious Stores of information" and of "valuable Materials."[11]

Most literary periodicals, including those just cited, changed their editorial policies once the conservative reaction to the French Revolution began to dominate the English political scene after 1792. Before the reaction to the French Revolution had hardened attitudes toward reform in England, literary periodicals, including both reviews and magazines, persisted in advocating the philosophical ideals of impartiality, moral reform, and the progressive improvement of humanity and society. But after 1792, as the reformist agenda of philosophical discourse increasingly came to be associated with the violence of the French Revolution, there was a gradual decline in such assertions. Especially in the late 1790s, as announcements proliferated trumpeting partiality to all things British—including nation, temperament, constitution, and political regime—statements linking literary magazines and periodicals to philosophical reform tapered off.

As can be expected, these changes in editorial policy did not occur overnight. Indeed, right after the French Revolution, literary magazines and reviews correlated their reformist function with that of the Revolution. Hence, for instance, in the prefatory statements to the first volume of the *Monthly Review*'s new series (1790), the editor Ralph Griffiths celebrated, albeit indirectly, the contributions of the republic of letters to political events of the time, alluding without reservation to the nascent French Revolution:

> Amid the fluctuations of empires and of states, it was not to be expected, that the sciences and the arts should stop at any given stage of improvement: nor has this been the case. On the contrary, it is obvious that, in their wide and rapid progress, they have taken the lead in all those grand events which have distinguished the present century; and that the diffusion of knowledge, and the progress of mental improvement, are always the certain forerunners of great and happy revolutions, in the civil as well as in the moral world.[12]

Griffiths asserted that "THE AUTHORS OF THE LITERARY JOURNALS may be allowed to claim no inconsiderable portion" of this "praise." The editors of the *Gentleman's Magazine*, as well, commenting on the events of 1790, claimed that "the present Year has been pregnant with Events of the highest Importance both to Church and State; and those it has been our Study to detail with the strictest Impartiality." After this veiled reference to events in France, the editor approvingly called attention to their "Narrative of the Proceedings of the National Assembly in France . . . which an elegant Female Writer [radical Helen Maria Williams] . . . calls 'the most sublime Spectacle that ever was represented on the Theatre of the Earth.'"[13]

Following the September massacres in 1792 and Louis XVI's execution the following January, magazines and individuals associated with reform were no longer praised for "great and happy revolutions," but blamed for a bloody one. English reaction to these events in France prompted many periodicals to switch their positions in respect to philosophical reform and the French Revolution. They began to point to the dangers of reform and defined their duty to act as a check to radical innovation.

* * * * * * * * *

It was not an accident that the language adopted to criticize enlightened reform at this time echoed Edmund Burke's indictment of rationalism in the *Reflections on the Revolution in France* (1790). Burke's argument against reform and revolution challenged reformist assumptions that philosophical discourse could constitute a model of general nature, as well as the conviction that the goal of writers should be the reform of its nation's readers and the furthering of progress. In a passage whose ideas would be echoed by Tory publications throughout the decade, Burke not only questioned the efficacy of reason in effectuating reform, he subordinated it to liberal reform's nemesis, "prejudice." By that simple reversal, he signaled his aim to sever all writing about politics from philosophical discourse:

> In this enlightened age I am bold enough to confess, that we are generally men of untaught feelings; that instead of casting away all our old prejudices, we cherish them to a very considerable degree, and, to take more shame to ourselves, we cherish them because they are prejudices; and the longer they have lasted, and the more generally they have prevailed, the more we cherish them. We are afraid to put men to live and trade on his own private stock of reason; because we suspect that this stock in each man is small, and that individuals would do better to avail themselves of the general bank and capital of nations, and of ages.[14]

With a rhetorical flourish, Burke reversed the usual associations of reason with virtue and morality, and prejudice with narrow views and unethical acts. Rather, Burke asserted that prejudice was reasonable and rendered virtuous actions habitual:

> Prejudice, with its reason, has a motive to give action to that reason, and an affection which will give it permanence. Prejudice is of ready application in the emergency; it previously engages the mind in a steady course of wisdom and virtue, and does not leave the man hesitating in the moment of decision, sceptical, puzzled, and unresolved. Prejudice renders a man's virtue his habit.[15]

Prejudice insured that an individual acted according to his "untaught feelings." Where reason urged him to consider and reflect, prejudice helped him to act. Philosophical discourse viewed reason's impact upon the will as one step toward moral reform, but Burke implied that unaided reason, if it led anywhere, led to indecision. While those who subscribed to the principles of philosophical reform considered reason's interference with an individual's habits, prejudices, and feelings laudable, Burke argued that such interference was pernicious.

Following the Royal Proclamation against seditious writings and publications in May 1792, when the increasing violence of the French Revolution seemed to justify Burke's characterization of philosophical reform as the work of dangerous innovators and intriguers, literary periodicals began to employ his reasoning to counter such reform. Hence in 1793, the *Gentleman's Magazine* blamed this "strange and heterogeneous philosophy" for having caused the French Revolution without of course stating that this "strange" philosophy was very similar to that which it had advocated as late as 1790. Because the French had endeavored to spread this enlightened philosophy in England, the *Gentleman's Magazine* would do all it could "to resist and counteract these machinations." The magazine promised to provide "indefatigable support" for England's "Political and Religious Constitution" and do nothing that would tend "to subvert the principles of our Government." But while the magazine waged its war with French philosophy on this front, yet "in all other respects, our Publication will continue to exhibit a field for manly and impartial criticism."[16] The message was clear. Strict impartiality was inconsistent with patriotism and might actually help to foster the philosophical principles that inspired the French Revolution.

Conservative publications such as the *British Critic, Anti-Jacobin* and *Satirist* were more explicit in their denunciation of reform principles. In the preface to the first volume of the *British Critic* (1793), its editors claimed, much like their predecessors, that the magazine would provide "a repository of the most accurate knowledge this distinguished country can produce." But in fulfilling their mission to represent and promote the progress of knowledge in Britain, the editors of the *British Critic* suggested that impartiality was not the best policy if it led to positions opposing "the favourite opinions of our countrymen." They were representing not an impartial, general man but the "genuine sentiments" and "feelings of true Britons" who supported their state religion and "the unperverted form of their political constitution."[17] The editors denied that such a stance indicated a partiality for any one position or party. No one who loved Britain, they implied, would portray their support of its institutions and sentiments as issuing from an interested point of view.

The *Anti-Jacobin Review* (1798), in the prospectus to its first volume, was even more blatant in linking the philosophical principles of the other reviews and their avowed attempts at impartiality to "French Economists and other Philosophists of modern times . . . [who] have facilitated the propagation of principles, subversive of social order, and, consequently, destructive of social happiness."[18] The editor of the *Anti-Jacobin Review*, "John Gifford," declared the *Monthly, Critical*, and *Analytical* reviews vehicles for diffusing "over our country, and, circulating through secret channels, disguised in various ways" the "FRENCH PRINCIPLES" which could "ultimately undermine that fabric which can never be destroyed by an open attack."[19] The editor claimed that these liberal publications had become "the mere instruments of faction" and their reviewers "sinking the critic in the partisan, favour[ed] the designs of those writers who labour to undermine our civil and religious establishments."[20] Ironically, while "Gifford" charged more liberal reviews with prejudice, he did not promise impartiality to combat their wrongful partisanship. He proudly proclaimed that the *Anti-Jacobin*, too, would "sink the critic in the partisan":

> To *purity of intention* we boldly assert our claim. But to the charge of *prejudice* and *partiality* we plead guilty—For we are deeply prejudiced in favour of our country; and are highly partial to her constitution and laws, to her religion and government. These we shall defend to the

utmost of our ability. Indeed, their defence is our principle inducement for obtruding our work upon the public.[21]

The announcement echoed the thesis of Burke's *Reflections*: prejudice was preferable to impartiality. It was far better to rely on and defend national traditions and institutions long established than to create new systems based on rationalist presumptions.[22]

Ten years later the editors of the Tory-aligned *Satirist, or Monthly Meteor* reiterated the conservative rejection of the aims of philosophical reform. They boasted they had never "derived any light from the new school of philosophy" and were not "converts to the ethics of France." In a swipe at the principles of the universal amelioration of mankind, they claimed they "were so old-fashioned as to love our *kindred* better than our *kind*." They proudly proclaimed that they had "strong *partialities*" and clung "stubbornly to our inveterate *prejudices*." Those without such "prejudices" for the British constitution and Church of England "may be . . . *philosopher*[s]" but they "cannot be . . . patriot[s]."[23]

That attacks on impartiality in reviewing, especially in matters of philosophy and politics, were also attacks on the foundations of philosophical reform was not lost on the editors of the radical/dissenter-aligned *Analytical Review*. Apparently a victim of the vicious propaganda of the *Anti-Jacobin Review* and Pitt's program of political repression and censorship, the *Analytical Review* was forced to cease publication in 1799. In the preface to its last volume, the editors denounced conservative claims that partialities for the British Constitution and Church were philosophically sound, and insisted instead on the exercise of impartial judgment in political matters. They had thought at the outset of their undertaking that the "public mind" was prepared to support their "firm and ardent attachment to the abstract interests of truth," but they discovered that "the human intellect" was "in that state of degradation, in which its feeble struggles . . . serve but to irritate, oppression, and to render more galling the fetters which it cannot sunder." Philosophical principles could not yet counteract prejudice. Given these circumstances, the editors concluded it was senseless to continue their project for reform:

> Whilst the only mode which is left to us of influencing the sentiments of men is by leading them to sacrifice one prejudice in favour of another, and by engaging their passions in support of principles of which their reason is not allowed the examination,—whilst we are denied to enter into a rational and full discussion of the subjects in which the interests of man are most intimately involved, and are permitted only to guide him either by the more refined delusions of sophistry, or by the grosser ones of selfish interest,—we feel no hesitation in renouncing at once both expedients.[24]

The *Analytical Review*'s demise was certainly not the end of advocacy for liberal reform in England.[25] But even as literary periodicals espousing such principles emerged after 1796, they were forced to redefine their editorial policies in light of charges of Jacobinism, disloyalty, and outright treason. They no longer assumed that most educated readers would subscribe to principles of universalism and impartiality and were forced to use the language of resistance, opposition, and retreat. The new tone was evident in editorial statements made in the recently formed *Monthly Magazine*. In the preface to its fifth volume (1798), its editors inscribed the reactionary rhetoric along with their own as they claimed that "the success [the *Monthly Magazine*] has met with is a pleasing proof, that the cause of liberty is not in so deserted a state as some of its desponding friends have imagined." Their success was partial, for rather than being able to reclaim the souls lost to the reaction to the principles of reform, their work

> could not be relished by those who think, that the best way of preventing the dangers of innovation, is to check all spirit of improvement, to stifle all research, and to preclude all information concerning foreign institutions which might possibly suggest unfavourable comparisons with our own.[26]

Much like the conservative statements that defined "anti-jacobinical" ideology as the mere opposite of liberal ideology, the editors of the *Monthly Magazine* carved out of the general body of readers a target audience through the use of negatives.

The breadth of the audience for liberal periodicals was limited by the successful politicization of the language of philosophical reform by conservatives. Claims by the editors that the *Monthly Magazine* was "impartially conducted according to our best judgment . . . to deserve the approbation of liberal and enlightened Readers" directly signalled their political interests. The terms "impartial," "liberal," and "enlightened" marked their undertaking and their target audience as decidedly partial to the Revolution.[27] Readers of the *Monthly* were very aware of this sea-change in the prestige of philosophical reform and of their new status as a type of reader rather than as a part of a unified general will. A correspondent reflected in February 1805 that, whereas "notions of universal philanthropy, general amelioration, and emancipation from prejudices of every kind, [were] . . . so prevalent in the early period of the French Revolution," at present the nation (and presumably "other" kinds of readers) had yielded to "narrow maxims and coercive policy."[28] The editors of the more liberal *Universal Magazine*, too, announced the failure of the reform movement in their preface in 1807 with great disappointment: "[The philosopher] looks in vain, too, for the increasing perfection of human reason, and the establishment of human tranquillity! . . . the men of this day, unadmonished and unameliorated . . . are . . . still eager in the pursuit of objects wholly incompatible with the repose and prosperity of mankind."[29] According to the editors of the *Universal*, the desire to reform was being countered by a desire on the part of the public to resist reform.

During the first decade of the nineteenth century, liberal vehicles such as the *Edinburgh Review* recognized that progressivist rhetoric had been dealt a blow by the conservative reaction. Like their antagonists they adopted the editorial practices of partiality and selectivity and abandoned their support of the French Revolution. In the advertisement to the first volume of the *Edinburgh Review* (1802), the editor announced contemptuously that it was not the "object [of this publication] to take notice of every production that issues from the Press." The staff "wish[ed] their Journal to be distinguished, rather for the selection, than for the number of its articles." The definition of their aims provides a stark contrast to statements in previous liberal/radical literary reviews we have examined. Claims of comprehensiveness and impartiality were gone, along with aspirations to act as a judge of public taste. The editors, giving up any claims to neutrality, promised "to confine their notice, in a great degree, to works that either have attained, or deserve, a certain portion of celebrity." Far from directing public taste, they would be "guided in their choice by the tendencies of public opinion."[30] Yet the review's very buff and blue cover, the colors of the liberal Whig Foxite party, tacitly proclaimed the editors' attachment to "party" principles, suggesting the kind of "public opinion" it would be guided by and which works would be "deserving of notice."[31] The fact that the first article in this new Whig vehicle was a review of J. J. Mounier's *De L'Influence attribuée aux Philosophes, aux Francs-Maçons, et aux Illuminés, sur la Revolution de France* was not coincidental. Mounier had argued that the political and economic instability of France, not the influence of the writings of the philosophes, had caused the French Revolution. The reviewer for the *Edinburgh*, quietly placing the periodical on the conservative side of the debate and tacitly aligning it against the old principles of philosophical reform, commented that the author had "mistaken the cataracts that broke the stream, for the fountain from which it rose; and contented himself with referring the fruit to the blossom, without taking any account of the germination of the seed, or the subterraneous windings of the root."[32] In so many words, the reviewer was suggesting that reform was the root of that French political evil, the Revolution, and that English liberalism was severing itself from any connection with it.

Even the more radical *Examiner* (1808) was forced to subscribe to the new code of prejudiced impartiality and to disconnect the aims of reform from those of the French Revolution. Editor Leigh Hunt commented that "the abuses of the French Revolution threw back many lovers of reform upon prejudices, that were merely good as far as they were opposed to worse." Prejudices may be "bad," but Hunt was unwilling to side his weekly with "mere impartiality" because that did not "teach us to be patriots." Hunt attempted to side-step the political polarization expressed in the dispute over the terms impartiality and prejudice by reconciling their differences in a patriotic "freedom from party spirit." This new "freedom" consisted of what liberal ideologues just two decades before would have seen as contradictory aims, "universality, which is the great study of philosophy . . . and the love of one's country." Philosophy, at least as represented in literary magazines and reviews, would no longer organize and direct the general progress of knowledge or act to reform the public mind. The *Examiner* would not pose as a general repository of the arts and sciences. Hunt's claim that philosophy was akin to good or clear thinking, "the cultivation of common reason," conceded much to an audience made wary of reformist demands that they reshape their opinions and ethics. The *Examiner* would make no such demands on its readers' prejudices; it would simply undertake "an humble attempt, exclusive of mere impartiality in great matters, . . . to revive . . . philosophy."[33]

The advocacy of reform would no longer serve as a sign of a periodical's commitment to general principles or to universal progress. Such advocacy was now perceived to be politically interested and meant to cater to a particular segment of the reading public. Liberal periodicals such as the *Examiner* were, therefore, forced to represent their undertakings as that of one voice among many. Yet in claiming difference from the rest of society by virtue of their special unprejudiced point of view, they found themselves on the outside of society looking in. The irony of Hunt's position, when we consider the claims of earlier publications, was clearly apparent. While previous periodicals nearly equated their pages with the history of human progress and learning, Hunt, using similar rhetoric, represented his undertaking as countering the spirit of his age. In the prospectus to the *Examiner*, Hunt commented that while other individuals and literary journals went about their business, the unprejudiced observer of the *Examiner* "escape[d]" from their "bustle." The only safe haven from faction and party spirit was clearly on society's fringes. From that vantage point the *Examiner* would assume the role of advisor to a small number of "rational" readers:

> Yet in the present day . . . every man, as well as every journal, must belong to some class of politicians; he is either a Pittite or Foxite, Windamite, Wilberforcite, or Burdettite. . . .
>
> A crowd is no place for steady observation. THE EXAMINER has escaped from the throng and bustle, but he will seat himself by the wayside, and contemplate the moving multitude as they wrangle and wrestle along. He does not mean to be as noisy as the objects of his contemplation, or to abuse them for a bustle which resistance merely increases, or even to take any notice of those mischievous wags who might kick mud towards him . . . but the more rational part of the multitude will be obliged to him, when he warns them of an approaching shower, or invites them to sit down with him and rest themselves, or advises them to take care of their pockets.[34]

By the end of the first decade of the nineteenth century, there would be no going back to the philosophical discourse that had once justified a magazine or review's claim of all-inclusiveness and impartiality. This change stemmed from the growing conviction that espousals of benevolence, general nature, reason, and impartiality were signs of a magazine's attempt to regulate the opinions of its readers rather than sincere expressions of an intention to act as an unbiased repository of the general progress of knowledge. As a writer for the *London Magazine* commented, "Man's perfectibility [was] limited," no matter what "certain philosophers have pretended." The general progress of the human race was thwarted by "peculiar circumstances" that made every individual's and every nation's development different.[35] In a political climate where the literary magazine or review could no longer act as a repository of general principles of human and social advancement, they could no longer credit themselves with effecting general social, political, or moral reforms. If they did any work in the public sphere at all now, that work was local, within their own ideological backyards. They were forced to cultivate an image that was peculiar and attractive to some segment of the reading public. The "world" that they represented had closed in on itself—it was no longer "out there," but inside their own pages where it could be preserved against or for the prejudices of a particular political, religious, or social point of view.[36]

In a word, the literary magazine and review had become the site for the dissemination of a special or particular point of view that could be watched as an unfolding drama. Far from being a public sphere that invited the public to identify with its discourse, it was a literary stage that was not to be broached by the reading subject. *Blackwood's* and its look-a-like competitor *Fraser's*, for instance, made discursive representation into a kind of perverse "anti-world" of the general reading public. In their "worlds," where personality defined the practice of writing, it did not matter who was speaking, so long as what was said had the force of a particular personality. Literary celebrity need not be the result of a "real" individual actually disseminating his or her particular style through literary channels; it could be constituted through the dissemination of a particular style or mode of discursive representation as a peculiar personality through mass-market vehicles.[37]

In the preface to the eleventh volume of *Blackwood's*, for instance, "Christopher North," its fictional editor, is represented as occupying the same discursive space as the "real" Francis Jeffrey, editor of the *Edinburgh Review*, Thomas Moore, the writer of *Irish Melodies*, and Lord Byron. "Christopher North" deploys a textual world with a past, present, and future, as well as a tangible literary topography. The world of *Blackwood's* would soon host a veritable clash of literary titans which the reader is invited to watch if not participate in. Daring Thomas Moore to publish a satire on *Blackwood's*, "North" details his plans for reprisal: "It will amuse—

probably instruct, the public—to see two such great wits as Tom Moore and Kit North fairly *set-to*. A clear stage, and fair play, is all that either of us can desire."[38] In a battle purely literary and discursive, what did it matter whether personalities had real minds or bodies, so long as personalities could defend themselves? When a discursive "world" constituted writers, body and soul, it did not matter if a physical encounter between "North" and "Lord Byron" were possible, so long as that encounter could be recorded in the pages of *Blackwood's*: "We think we can fit him with the gloves, and that is pretty light play for one at our time of life. But we have still a blow or two left in us; and if a turn-up with the naked mauleys there must be, a hit on the jugular may peradventure do his Lordship's business."[39] The boundaries of the periodical defined the limits of a particular being, rather than the limits of the knowledge or interests of a community or society. It bodied forth a set of ideas, personalities, activities that had legitimacy insofar as they remained within the framework of a particular mode of discursive representation or within the margins of a particular periodical.

This new conceptualization of the periodicals' place and function in society can be seen in several of the opening addresses and prefaces of the newly formed and popular *Fraser's Magazine* (1830), where its editors attempted, by their own estimation at least, to make a spectacle of themselves by reversing the assumptions that had made literary magazines a public sphere. Whereas the editors of late-eighteenth-century periodicals had identified their undertaking with the goals of general human progress, *Fraser's* represented its writers as individuals, and therefore valuable—as ironic, petulant, difficult to pin down in their reasoning, and free-thinking enough to judge without reference to "principles" (read "system" or "party"). They snidely dismissed the necessity for stating their principles to their prospective readers. Although they made it clear that they held on to old Tory principles at a time when, in their estimation, "the Whigs have been un-whigged, the Tories un-toried," they refused to promise their readers "anything at all."[40] By setting themselves off from the general reader and from usual modes of acting and thinking, they suggested they were a world to themselves, free from the jibes, complaints, and threats of booksellers and writers who hoped to influence their reviews of books and of political parties that hoped to engage their services in their cause. They later claimed that their singularity elevated them above the pack of periodicals and above most people: "We fairly allow, that the occasional *bizarreries* of our conduct would be altogether preposterous, if practiced by ordinary individuals."[41] But they were not ordinary; the "standard" applied to judge the conduct of the "vulgar mass of humanity" would not do in measuring theirs.

Fraser's celebration of personality, peculiarity, and particularity is also evident in the opening article for 1835. In this narration of a supposed New Year's dinner for the writers associated with the magazine, gone were the impartial, or even "prejudiced" editors who pronounced in their prefaces the magazine's policies. Instead, the editorial persona "Oliver Yorke" mediated between his readers and the actions and conversations of the writers he depicted, acting as the line of division between the world of writers and the readers' public sphere. Here was their world which the readers "watched." As Crofton Croker, Tory politician and antiquarian, was made to say at one point, "We literary folk are always thinking that we are the finest fellows in the world, and have therefore a right to look down on the rest of mankind." By representing this distinction of writer from reader in the magazine, its producers seemed to endorse their separation from the "rest of mankind" and to see themselves as Croker later remarked as a kind of "writing-people." But while the "Fraserians" may have considered themselves in a sphere separated and higher than that of their readers, they were also aware, as Croker continued, that "if the truth was known, all the rest of mankind look down most damnably upon us." By taking the position that writing ought not to reform or promote social progress but to re-establish and preserve prejudices, to hold on to singularity and personality, literary magazines and reviews, only too successful, were left without a group to transform at all. As "Yorke" commented on the speech that Dr. Maginn (co-proprietor and editor of *Fraser's*) gave on the virtues of Tory principles and government, "If what he speaks is wisdom, it is like the wisdom which cries out and is not regarded."[42] With the reaction to philosophical reform, the literary magazine's only refuge became its own principles and personality, while its readers, aloof to both, judged it solely on its ability to entertain.

NOTES

An earlier form of this study, "Reinterpreting the English Enlightenment: Periodical Literature and the Reaction to the French Revolution," was delivered as a conference paper at the 1993 Southeastern American Society for Eighteenth-Century Studies regional conference.

1. Derek. Roper, *Reviewing Before the Edinburgh* (Newark: University of Delaware Press, 1978); John Haydon, *The Romantic Reviewers, 1802–24* (Chicago: Chicago University Press, 1969); Jon Klancher, *The Making of English Reading Audiences: 1790–1832* (Madison: University of Wisconsin Press, 1987); Joanne Shattock, *Politics and the Reviewers: The Edinburgh Review and The Quarterly in the Early Victorian Age* (London: Leicester University Press, 1989). Of these four, only Jon Klancher has examined the formats of literary magazines during this period.
2. Roper comments that "the reviewers' complaint was . . . against their obligation to deal with masses of mediocre books. . . . [U]ntil the ideal of comprehensive reviewing had been abandoned, large numbers of bad books had to be dealt with somehow. . . . The only practicable means of easing the burden for reviewers . . . was for editors to adopt a much more selective approach to the works chosen for review." *Reviewing Before the Edinburgh*, 40.

3. Preface to *The Critical Review* 34 (1772). See also the prospectus to *The English Review* 23 (1794): 1–2, as well as "To the Public," *Analytical Review* 1 (1788): iii–iv. The desire to contract the number of works reviewed is also evident in literary magazines such as the *London Magazine* (1732–1785). By 1776 the latter's "Impartial Account of New Publications" had greatly reduced the number of works that it reviewed from fifty or more per issue to fifteen or twenty.

4. See Caroline Robbins, *The Eighteenth-Century Commonwealthman* (Cambridge: Harvard University Press, 1959). There was significant confluence between the ideas of the Commonwealthmen and the agenda of Lord Bolingbroke's circle. See Isaac Kramnick, *Bolingbroke and his Circle; the Politics of Nostalgia in the Age of Walpole* (Cambridge: Harvard University Press, 1968).

5. This is how the *London Magazine* is described by Alvin Sullivan, ed., *British Literary Magazines: The Augustan Age and the Age of Johnson, 1698–1788*, (Westport, CT: Greenwood Press, 1983), 205. But the phrase applies equally well to *The Gentleman's Magazine*. Information on dates of publication and editorial tenure for individual periodicals has been borrowed freely from Sullivan's work, cited above, and from its companion, *British Literary Magazines: The Romantic Age, 1789*–1836, ed. Alvin Sullivan (Westport, CT: Greenwood Press, 1983).

6. See L. G. Mitchell's *Charles James Fox and the Disintegration of the Whig Party, 1782–1794* (Oxford: Oxford University Press, 1971), 153–238. As contemporary R. Dinsmore Jr., member of the Norwich Patriotic Society, later claimed in his *Exposition of the Principles of the English Jacobins* (1797), while the English "jacobins" took on the slur as a nickname, yet their "political principles were of pure English growth, derived from Locke, Sidney, Marvell and Milton." Quoted from Albert Goodwin's *The Friends of Liberty: The English Democratic Movement in the Age of the French Revolution* (Cambridge: Harvard University Press, 1979), 470–71. Elie Halévy points out that the liberal Lord Landsdowne had declared in the House of Lords in 1793 "that it was the actual ideas of [Josiah] Tucker and Adam Smith, and their criticisms of the feudal regime, which were so much detested under the misleading name of 'French Principles.'" *The Growth of Philosophic Radicalism*, trans. Mary Morris (1928; reprint, Boston: The Beacon Press, 1955), 165.

7. The first four chapters of Jon Klancher's *The Making of English Reading Audiences* studies the representation of the reading public in English periodicals, covering roughly the same period of time as that examined in our article. Klancher's thesis, that there was an increasing segmentation of the reading audience after 1790 that was largely the result of changing editorial practices and a growing class consciousness is not unsimilar to ours, but Klancher does not link this self-conscious segmentation to the reaction to the discourse of Enlightenment reform. The conclusions of his study are based on a survey of periodicals broader than our own. We have limited our remarks almost entirely to editorial statements made in literary reviews and magazines.

8. "To His Royal Highness," *London Magazine* 50 (January 1781).

9. Preface to *The English Review, or an Abstract of English and Foreign Literature* 1 (1783): 3–4.

10. Preface to *The Universal Magazine of Knowledge and Pleasure* 82 (1788): 4.

11. Preface to *The Gentleman's Magazine* 60 (December 1790): iii.

12. "To the Literary World," *The Monthly Review; or Literary Journal, Enlarged* 1 (1790): i.

13. *Gentleman's Magazine* 60: iii.

14. Edmund Burke, *Reflections on the Revolution in France*, 3rd ed. (London, 1790), 129–30.

15. Ibid., 130. For further discussion of Burke's attitude toward "scientific rationalism" see Peter Stanlis' essay "Edmund Burke and the Scientific Rationalism of the Enlightenment," in *Edmund Burke: The Enlightenment and the Modern World*, ed. Peter J. Stanlis (Detroit: University of Detroit Press, 1967), 81–116.

16. Preface to *The Gentleman's Magazine* 63 (December 1793): iii–iv.

17. Preface to *The British Critic; A New Review* 1 (1793): i–iii.

18. Prospectus to *The Anti-Jacobin Review and Magazine* 1 (July, 1798): 4.

19. Ibid., 4–5. "John Gifford" is a pseudonym for John Richards Greene.

20. Ibid., 2.

21. Ibid., 5.

22. In the "Prefatory Address to the Reader" appended to the first volume (July 1798) of the *Anti-Jacobin Review,* the reliance on Burke's arguments is even more clear. The editors suggest that innate prejudices are natural, while the attempt to reform the "public mind" debilitated the individual's "mental energy" at its source. The existence of the "body politic" depended upon fostering the public's prejudices in favor of its country's religious and political principles (ii–iii).

23. "Introduction to Politics," *The Satirist, or Monthly Meteor* 1 (October 1807): 4.

24. Preface to *The Analytical Review*, n.s. 1 (1799): iii, v. For a fuller treatment of the political context of the *Analytical Review*'s commitment to impartiality, comprehensiveness, and rational progress, see Brian Rigby's essay, "Radical Spectator of the Revolution: the Case of the Analytical Review," in *The French Revolution and British Culture*, ed. C. Crossley and I. Small (Oxford: Oxford University Press, 1989), 63–83. Rigby's contention that the reaction to the French Revolution helped to reveal a dissonance between the *Analytical*'s adherence to "rationalist ideology" on the one hand and its support for liberal and dissenting interests on the other, making its "dedication to reason" appear (ironically) "narrow-minded" (79), is certainly in line with our argument here.

25. J. E. Cookson, in disagreement with E. P. Thompson's contention that the liberal press waned in influence after the Wakefield Trials of 1799, argues that the prosperity of the publishing houses of the dissenters Joseph Johnson and George Robinson guaranteed liberal dominance over the literary market even in the face of loyalist suppression. But even the optimistic Cookson draws a distinction between the sense of fear, isolation and intimidation liberals felt and their successful (literary) business ventures. He also notes the collapse after 1799 of liberal influence over the older literary periodicals, the *Monthly Review, Critical Review,* and

Analytical Review. See *The Friends of Peace: Anti-War Liberalism in England, 1793–1815* (Cambridge: Cambridge University Press, 1982), especially 84–114.

26. Preface to *The Monthly Magazine and British Register* 5 (January to June 1798).

27. Ibid. Jon Klancher, certainly correct in his estimate, argues that *The Monthly Magazine* was one of the first literary magazines to appeal to a particular kind of reader aware of its "special" character. Klancher argues that this special character revolved around a growing class-consciousness, temporarily linking the interests of "middle-class intellectuals" with those of the emerging working class. This "alliance" was later severed by the "apostasy" of the middle-class, the greater part of *The Monthly*'s reading audience. *English Reading Audiences*, 41. However, if we assume that the language adopted by the editors of *The Monthly Magazine* was not entirely new but derived in large part from the agenda of old philosophical reform, then *The Monthly Magazine*'s appeal to a smaller segment of a larger readership represented not just the consolidation of "liberal" middle-class with more "radical" interests but also the recognition that other readers— either tòo critical (conservative) or too uncritical (the nascent working class) of the Revolution—no longer identified with its aims of moderate parliamentary and social reform. As J. E. Cookson remarks, "Discredited, victimized and terrorized by loyalism, the liberal intelligentsia made a counter-reply through [the press], . . . where their strength was greatest." Their efforts to extend their waning influence through such vehicles as *The Monthly Magazine* "fully reflected their anxiety that they should not be converted into an isolated and impotent group." *The Friends of Peace*, 85.

28. *The Monthly Magazine and British Register* 19 (February 1805): 1.

29. Preface to *The Universal Magazine*, n.s. 7 (1807): iii–iv.

30. Advertisement to *The Edinburgh Review* 1 (October 1802): A3. For a detailed discussion of the founding of the *Edinburgh*, see John Clives' *Scotch Reviewers: The Edinburgh Review, 1802–1815* (Cambridge: Harvard University Press, 1957), 186–97. A more recent treatment of the *Edinburgh Review* in Joanne Shattock's *Politics and Reviewers* suggests that the reason the review sent shock waves through the intellectual community in Britain was partly because it was "unashamedly partisan in politics," and because it was "determinedly free of any connections with booksellers, one of the major criticisms of the old Reviews" (4). However both of these factors seem questionable. It had been common to declare one's freedom from booksellers and authors at least as early as Edmund Cave's founding of *The Gentleman's Magazine.* See Roper, *Reviewing Before the Edinburgh*, 30–33. Both the *Anti-Jacobin* and *British Critic* had declared their political and religious biases in their prefaces and prospectuses in the decade before the founding of *The Edinburgh*. The shock value of the review probably lay in its open connection to the liberal (still perceived at this time as "radical") Foxite branch of the Whigs at a time when it was all but banished from the political scene for its open support of the French Revolution. See Mitchell, *Charles James Fox*, 260–69.

31. Clive, *Scotch Reviewers*, 36.

32. *Edinburgh Review* 1: 7.

33. Leigh Hunt, *Prefaces by Leigh Hunt Mainly to His Periodicals*, ed. R. Brimley Johnson (Chicago: Chicago University Press, 1927), 33–35.

34. Ibid., 29.

35. *The London Magazine* 1 (March 1820): 269, 271.

36. The sense that readers wanted partial or particular points of view after the first decade of the nineteenth century rather than "objective" or "impartial" points of view is also suggested by Joanne Shattock's *Politics and the Reviewers*. She argues that even while there was a sense among contemporary writers and readers alike that literary reviews and magazines were partisan and appealed to particular social or political interests, nonetheless, "the general sense, derived from letters, diaries, memoirs, and the perspective of editors and contributors, is that rather than being highly compartmentalized and segmented . . . into Whigs, Tories, Nonconformists, and High Churchmen, the readership of the quarterlies was a relatively unified group, intelligent, educated, middle-class and serious-minded, which read widely . . . sampling more than one Review" (13).

37. Peter Murphy's "Impersonation and Authorship in Romantic Britain," *ELH* 59 (1992): 625–49, treats this "mixing" of the "the bodily world" and "the writing world" and the difficult epistemological issues that it created for both contributors to and readers of *Blackwood's*. Murphy comments that "many of the magazine's pseudonyms developed into characters, with a recognizable style, who wrote often for the magazine and often had pet topics and favorite interests. Anonymity was the rule for all nineteenth-century periodicals, but *Blackwood's* turned this anonymity to account, producing a richly detailed if mostly fictional world" (630).

38. Preface to *Blackwood's Edinburgh Magazine* 11 (June 20, 1822): vii.

39. Ibid. viii.

40. "Our 'Confession of Faith,'" *Fraser's Magazine of Town and Country* 1 (1830): 2.

41. *Fraser's Magazine of Town and Country* 7 (1833): 12.

42. *Fraser's Magazine of Town and Country* 11 (1835): 17, 3.

The Whores Rhetorick: *Narrative, Pornography, and the Origins of the Novel*

JAMES GRANTHAM TURNER

In the last decade we have witnessed a surge of interest in the "discourse of sexuality" and its poor relation "pornography"—once dismissed by historians of the Enlightenment as an insignificant bore. This interest is shared by social historians seeking light on the family and the sexual underworld, by feminists exposing the politics of masculinity, by theorists trying to confirm or deny Foucault's "history of sexuality," and by literary scholars wanting to put "the body" back into their reading. In a parallel development of recent years, historians of the novel have explored its seventeenth-century origins, not in a single kind of predecessor, but in a complex web of high and low genres, scandal and philosophy, news and romance. This essay will map one small valley between these twin peaks: the possible contribution of earlier pornography—here exemplified by two seventeenth-century writings on prostitution—to the realism later associated with the novel.

Most definitions of "pornography," however, are too crude and too anachronistic to serve the needs of the eighteenth-century literary historian. "Pornography" is a fighting word, its goals local and polemic. Across the political spectrum, each camp has evolved its own criteria of definition, effective as tactical weapons but pitifully inadequate to anyone aware of the complex operation of texts in culture. Conservatives object to the sexual content *per se*, not to how it is presented. Liberals define the genre too narrowly, using conceptual models long since discarded by literary theorists. Most of these liberal definitions depend on a simple dichotomy between pornography (assumed to be evil and worthless) and some more acceptable way of representing sexuality ("Art," "Science," or "Erotica") that is never properly analyzed; many of them characterize the text in terms of a single intention or effect—something literary critics find unbearably naive. Meanwhile, radical anti-pornography feminists, still arguing from a single-effect model, define the genre too broadly, equating all male representations of women with the most violent and extreme form of commercial pornography: "Pornography is the theory, rape is the practice."

These twentieth-century controversies, which inevitably color any attempt to understand the relation of eighteenth-century "pornography" to its literary and social culture, replicate contemporary concerns that raged throughout the period. Astute feminists such as Sarah Fyge recognized that lewd representations of women were intended to violate them, not just in the imaginary text but in the real world: as she remarks to the obscene satirist Robert Gould,

> You would adulterate all Womankind,
> Not only with your Pen.[1]

In one sense the English novel grows out of the anti-pornography and anti-libertine campaign of Samuel Richardson, who insisted that the mono-maniac erotic fantasies of Lovelace inflicted real and irreversibly physical damage on women; rape *was* the practice of his libertine theory, and minor indecencies or soft-core "freedoms" *were* calculated to lead inexorably to the worst outrage. This essay will not, however, attempt to trace the porno-graphic in canonical fiction. Instead, it poses the question of "pornography and narrative" in more restricted terms—derived from the original etymology in *porne*, or prostitute—by concentrating on certain conjunctions of sexual and narrative effects in early modern writings about, or purportedly by, what John Cleland calls "women of pleasure." Narrow as this sample of *pornographia* may be, it still raises important questions. What connections can be traced between clandestine sexually explicit fiction and the "rise of the novel"? Could the libertine proclamation and display of taboo sexuality enjoy an affinity, guilty and secret, with the bourgeois constitution of "real life" and subjectivity in a detailed narrative?

Libertine discourse itself seems divided on this point. In a famous passage, Fanny Hill worries that with "a subject of this sort, whose bottom or groundwork [is], in the nature of things, eternally one and the same," words will "flatten, and lose much of their due spirit and energy, by the frequency they indispensably recur with, in a narrative of which that *practise* professedly composes the whole basis."[2] Sexuality and discourse are assumed to be at odds. Direct representation in gutter-language revolts the reader with its vulgarity, while the genteel vocabulary of Ardors, Transports, and Ecstasies lacks energy and requires the "supplements" of the reader's imagination, beyond discourse altogether. Cleland here anticipates one strand of the liberal objection to pornography, which distinguishes it from true art because it is monotonous, fixated on a single organ in a featureless *pornotopia*.[3] Fanny's narrative defines communicable language itself as a supplement to the sexual "subject," superadded (quite literally) by her "rational pleasurist" lover, who teaches her stylistic "cultivation" and bequeaths her an independent fortune, making her at once marriagable and expressive—in short, *novelizable*.

A contrary model, however, appears in a precisely contemporary libertine text, the Marquis d'Argens' *Thérèse philosophe*. Here the heroine's narrative seems to proceed directly from her sexual fulfilment. Thérèse lives quite content with masturbation and voyeuristic pleasure until the Count seduces her, appropriately enough in a book-lined picture gallery that sums up the whole history of erotic representation. This double "consummation" provides both the end and the beginning of the libertine fiction: it closes the book, since perfect pleasure leaves nothing more to be said, but it also provokes the act of writing itself. In the opening paragraph, Thérèse responds to the Count's challenge to transform her experiences into "a painting where the scenes in which we have been actors lose none of their lasciviousness, and metaphysical reasonings preserve all of their energy."[4] Writing her story becomes a seduction, an invitation to mutual pleasure ("écrivons!"), a promise to reveal "tous les replis de son coeur," all the folds of her heart (1:3)—just as the reader literally unfolds the pages and the fold-out prints of the book, engravings of the very images that seduced Thérèse in the first place. Indeed, she will be not only re-plicated but *created* by her narrative: "son ame toute entiere va se développer dans les détails" (1:2–3). Ian Watt's paradigm of English formal realism—the "bourgeois" constitution of reality and subjectivity in a detailed narrative—shows up where one would least expect it, in French libertine fiction. In this model, sexual fulfilment supposedly leads to a mutually-generating cycle of representation and action, an "unfolding" of novelistic realism by a complicity of narrator and reader exactly homologous to the unfolding of the body in arousal.

Yet even within this paradigmatic text the model does not hold. The other main narrative embedded in *Thérèse philosophe*, that of the heroine's friend Mme Bois-Laurier, puts this idyllic arrangement into question, suggesting a quite different relation between erotic wholeness and narrative authority; Bois-Laurier, the procuress and organizer of erotic tableaux, is a sexual mutant, "neither man nor woman" (2:3), born with her vagina permanently sealed. Narrative is generated by the *mutation* or *abolition* of sexuality. Moreover the *Ursprung* of the novel, the Count's desire to be recounted, occurs not immediately but only after a ten-year interval—as if the narrative impulse springs naturally, not from female sexual florescence, but from male aging.

* * * * * * * * *

Our examples so far come from a high point in the development both of the novel and of pornography, when Fanny Hill and Clarissa, Thérèse and Tom Jones, appeared within a few months of one another. Ambitious *philosophes* like Diderot and La Mettrie wrote erotica in the late 1740s, while ambitious novelists like Richardson found their work denounced as pornography—precisely because it gave central importance to sexuality and "unfolded" its meaning in the most intimate details. (As Richardson explained of his own fiction, "in the minutiae lie often the unfoldings of the Story, as well as of the heart.")[5] As we have seen, even a brief sampling from this efflorescence of clandestine writing reveals a highly self-conscious and complex sense of the relation between sexuality and fiction. But can this self-awareness be traced in those seventeenth-century texts that might constitute an "origin" for the novel of sexual experience? We should now begin to answer this large question with a small test-case, tracing the contradictory relation of narrative, sexual representation, and the "Novel" in a pair of texts that fall into the narrowest and most literal definition of *pornographia*: an anonymous treatise called *The Whores Rhetorick, Calculated to the Meridian of London, and Conformed to the Rules of Art* (London, 1683), and its prototype *La Retorica delle Puttane* by Ferrante Pallavicino, first published in 1642 but reissued in his complete works in 1671. Pallavicino had no hand in the later adaptation—he fell foul of the papal authorities and was burnt at the stake in his mid-twenties—but he contributed to literary history in several genres. Another work reissued in 1671, *Il Corriere Svaligiato*, influenced epistolary fiction in early eighteenth-century England; Charles Gildon adapted this collection of supposedly stolen letters under the suggestive title *The Post-Boy Rob'd of His Mail, or The Pacquet Broke Open*.

Pallavicino provides a good starting-point for this enquiry since he gives us not only a praxis of sexual narrative but a theory: his scandalous parody of the rhetorical treatise spells out exactly how *Narratio*, one of the main categories of rhetorical method, relates to the prostitute's art. Rhetorical invention allows her to capture any customer, and to prompt extra gifts on any occasion, by "folding herself into all the forms, and adjusting herself to all the pleasures," that might increase her profit; *piegarsi in tutte le forme*—compare Thérèse's promise to unfold the "replis de son coeur." But the sex worker must be totally aware of her fictionality, must "make a chimaera" of herself to create the impression that her caresses spring from love alone. This methodical self-production, going through all the subdivisions of rhetoric such as *Dispositio*, *Elocutio*, and so on, requires narrative at several levels. In the "exordio" the courtesan snares lovers by demure glances in public, "turning herself into a display apparatus or projection screen [*un'apparato, uno strato*]." Then in the "narratione" itself she invents an intriguing and affecting home life to involve the client more deeply and render her yielding more plausible; the whore becomes not a coarse trickster but a Thérèse-like novelist, "sweetening her narrative by weaving in fascinating incidents figured in her own person," by "distinct induction of particular accidents of her own life."[6] Pallavicino's language explicitly equates the "artificiosa tessitura" of sexual captivation, the "ben intessuto discorso" of the whore's narrative, and the "weaving" or *tessitura* of his own discourse ("this small contexture," as the English version puts it).[7] Admittedly this "narratione" is end-directed, a pretext to the "confirmatione" when the lovers actually go to bed. But the sexual act becomes a micronarrative in its own right, as the courtesan positions "her Members" like the elements of a well-structured sentence, for the "migliore effetto." Indeed, she arranges copulation like a "Comedy," "unfolding the amorous scene" and ending with a kind of reverse dénouement, "redoubling the knots of hands and feet"; correspondingly the customer's desire, which *he* believes "authenticated" by his experience, becomes merely an urge to "shew his skill in the imitation."[8] Even after the event, the prostitute is told to expel male post-coital nausea and reincite "il desiderio di gioire" with erotic discourse and song (*RP* 62). The English version increases this Chinese-box effect—aphrodisiac narrative within aphrodisiac narrative—by adding the "facetious Novel" (*WR* 44).

Our theories of what we used to call the Rise of the Novel would be fruitfully complicated by embedding them in this seventeenth-century context, which links narrative fiction simultaneously to two arts that make the private public: prostitution and rhetoric. Rhetoric enjoyed the highest artistic status, and yet its persuasive goal made it unashamedly "promotional," instrumental, and stimulative—precisely the criteria that are now used to distinguish art from pornography. Most recent condemnations of pornography (with the exception of the radical feminist critique, which allows no mitigation by artistic quality) depend on a Romantic ideology of art removed from "interest" and "arousal," free from goal-oriented persuasion and palpable designs upon the reader. But rhetoric—and arguably all art in the early modern period—was *supposed* to arouse. It placed narrative at the service of public causes in public places, even while recognizing that the act of persuasion itself was intensely private. According to a typical manual such as Cypriano Soarez's *De Arte Rhetorica*, the explicit target of Pallavicino's parody, the inner core of the listener must respond to the dynamism of an orator skilled in disposing language and bodily gesture for "maximum force," so as to be "in affectibus potentissimus." Every physical "*motus*" thus excited in the listener must also be felt by the speaker: Cicero and Horace are brought in to prove that "if you want to make me weep, you first must grieve yourself."[9] It seems, then, that the prestigious arts of persuasion were quite compatible with the scandalous arts of sexual arousal.

One obvious objection to this equation of rhetoric, proto-novel, and *pornographia* is that, according to official theories of rhetoric, persuasion must serve a moral end. Pallavicino and his English adapter sidestep this neatly. Out of one side of their mouths they claim to be warning young men against the evils of whoredom, announcing a didactic and dissuasive purpose for their *pornographia* (as Defoe would later do). But in the same breath they envisage a proto-Flaubertian role for the artist, whose responsibility is not to discriminate against abject and scandalous materials but to render them with supreme aesthetic power. The guiding principle *"in medio sita est virtus"* comes to mean that the virtuous man is "indifferent," distanced from good as well as evil, applying himself with equal spirit to both "as the designs in hand may seem to require"; *disegno* and *virtuoso* clearly imply aesthetic rather than moral criteria. Here again the writer identifies himself with the courtesan, whom he instructs to disregard "fas e nefas" and to transform the most bestial (anal) body-functions into the highest art—"con spirito elevato."[10]

The author at times claims to be exposing fraud, but his theory of moral indifference undermines this stance and his authorial practice suggests an affinity, even a complicity, with the art of prostitution. Pallavicino laments that he cannot "chimerizare tante fintioni e furberie," chimerize such fictions and fourberies as the courtesan produces daily, for their "talento" is "molto superiore alla debolezza del mio ingegno" (*RP* 3). As we saw with the *tessitura* of narration, the very "fictions" and "colors" he denounces in the prostitute define his own achievement. (Fanny Hill will fall into the same trap when she asks the sensitive reader to "give life to the colours where they are dull, or worn with too frequent handling," a double-entendre that ironically collapses the distinction between body and language that it purports to maintain.)[11] *The Whores Rhetorick* adds a public dimension to this parallel of sex and art: the prostitute tries "to satisfie all men according to their several exigences"; the author "would pretend with his Pen, to gratifie all Mankind."[12] Even the ostensible exposé communicates a furtive erotic pleasure, the pleasure of revealing secrets, sharing female space behind the scenes, stealing language that belongs to someone else, burying one's face in her most private things. It is no accident, I think, that Pallavicino also invents an important device for epistolary fiction in his *Corriere Svaligiato*—the transgressive meta-narrative of "the Post-boy robbed of his mail, or the packet broke open."

In both *La Retorica delle Puttane* and *The Whores Rhetorick* an older procuress gives advice to a young acolyte, adapting (and in the English version plagiarizing) Aretino's dialogues of 1535. But these seventeenth-century texts go much further than Aretino in laying bare the *apparato* of illusion and the psychological basis of deception: early modern pornography in effect *rehearses* novelistic realism by showing how to construct a new form of subjectivity, a consistent and close-woven character "unfolded" (*piegata, repliée*) in all its particularizing "details." Gesture, voice, motion, interior decoration and reading-matter should form an "authentic" model of affective individualism that the gullible client takes as a real person feeling "all the effects of a profound and sincere love," for him and him alone; the courtesan should "manage" her persona (*maneggiare*), should "finga di singolarizare," use fiction to create the illusion of a "singular" desire.[13] The Italian text does this entirely through the master-trope of rhetoric, but the English version—eager to satisfy McKeon's as well as Watt's account of the origins of the novel—adds a fragmentary mix of epistemology, theatre, "Novel," and "Romance," an unstable constellation of genres. Questions of (simulated) virtue merge into questions of (narrative) truth. The philosophical bawd cites "Mr. *Hobbs*" as her authority for the doctrine "that Wisdom is nothing but experience," which in turn leads her to an almost post-modern theory of the simulacrum: "the whole series of carnal satisfaction does purely consist in fancy." Following this logic, the genres of prose fiction are assumed to correspond exactly to modes of sexual behavior and belief. So for example the sexual shenanigans of Charles II and his son Monmouth might "afford matter for a Novel" and obviate the need for "translating daily such numbers of *French* ones, that are in my mind fitter for the necessary House than the Closet."[14] (Aphra Behn realized this possibility when she wove *Love-Letters between a Nobleman and His Sister* out of the scandals of Monmouth and his co-conspirator Lord Grey.) The openly sexual and aphrodisiac "Novel" can be used in private to repair sagging male desire, but would be too dangerous for public display; the bawd-preceptor Mrs. Cresswell, already raided by the police, fears an action of *scandalum magnatum*. "Modern Comedies" (especially those of Wycherley) are the best model for the *narratio* that shuttles between public and private. And the enemy is Romance: "I am against your reading Romances, where constancy in love is cryed up as a vertue" (*WR* 150). Thus *pornographia* rehearses what would become a key element in English fiction, articulated most obviously in the preface to Fielding's *Joseph Andrews*—the grafting of the ethos and actions of comedy onto a prose narrative derived from, but opposed to, Romance.

It is essential, then, to recognize the mutually-constitutive relation between narrative genres and sexual ideologies and practices. The notoriously Protean dichotomy of "Romance" and "Novel" can often refer, not to form or probability, but to sexual morality, whether libertine or marital. Pallavicino's "packet broke open" provides a lead here: after reading a particularly high-flown letter of adoration, one of the mail-thieves wonders "what Pen this Man had between his Fingers, when he wrote this Letter"— reducing Romance to a fit of adolescent autoeroticism.[15] Jane Barker would later try to revive Romance as a way to reverse the "Deluge of Libertinism" destroying society; she assumes that "unhappy Marriages and unkind Separations" stem directly from a change of taste in the reading public, preferring narratives of "Interest and loose Gallantry" to those of "Heroick Love." Romance is the theory, constancy is the practice—and the same relation holds between the Novel and promiscuity. Romance irritates the libertines because it "confin[es] the Subject to such strict Rules of Virtue and Honour," "Subject" here signifying both the literary topic and the actual person.[16] *The Whores Rhetorick* articulates the same assumption, but from the other side. When the courtesan needs to construct affective subjectivity in the throes of what she wants to be taken as an overwhelming and constant love, she naturally draws on the resources of "Romance." The ultimate goal is to marry the customer, combining the trickery of Shamela with the reclaimed sensuality of Fanny Hill; this requires the expert simulation, not just of intense passion, but of moral crisis. Several long and emotional speeches (in the English version) rehearse the outpouring of a lover pleading for a more legitimate relationship, "torn in pieces" by the conflict of love, shame, and religious guilt, and these high-flown effusions are inevitably linked to "the old Romantick Heathens," to "Romantick Ladies," or to "*Cleopatra, Cassandra, Pharamond*, and others of that nature" (*WR* 65–66, 106). We might conclude, then, that one of the most central and enduring narrative devices of the novel—the particularized character who develops through a wrenching crisis in the course of a "profound and sincere" emotional relationship—appears first as a whore's trick. Literary history stages its effects first as farce, and only later as tragedy.

Finally, if novel and romance "confine the Subject" according to opposing sexual ideologies, what kind of subject does pornography constitute? What lies behind the apparatus, the screen? What is replicated in the unfolding of the details? The old bawd's philosophy points to the answer: nothing. "A Whore is a Whore, but a Whore is not a Woman" (*WR* 221–22). Gendered subjectivity (as opposed to economic self-interest) is *purely* a product of trickery. Since "the World, and so all men in it, are governed by fancy and opinion[,] good and evil are therefore little understood as they are in themselves, but rather as they come represented to Mens various and often vitiated palates." If things and feelings are only true "as they come represented," then the sex worker must direct the representation. If "Men are oft of opinion, that Women were made only for their enjoyment," if they "force their Mistresses to dissolve in pleasure . . . believing these amorous pangs created by themselves," then she must retain control of the script by fashioning herself according to the lascivious image that men think *they* have fashioned.[17] Pornographic theory here undermines rather than endorses the conjunction of male "force" and biological essentialism, the usual ideology of later pornography. Like Eliza Haywood's *Fantomina* (1725), *The Whores Rhetorick* posits a free female agency behind, and made possible by, a controlled sequence of masks. But Fantomina, however much freedom and pleasure she finds by adopting a string of false identities, is brought down in the end by her biological femaleness, shattered and exposed when she becomes pregnant. In the seventeenth-century fabrication, ironically, mastery of erotic narrative depends on an austerely willed asexuality. In the whore's embodiments of male desire we encounter a strikingly early, and scandalous, exemplification of Catherine Gallagher's thesis that modern fiction—as distinct from the heroic Romance or the gossipy *roman à clef*—begins with stories about Nobody.[18]

NOTES

1. *The Female Advocate, or an Answer to a Late Satyr against the Pride, Lust and Inconstancy of Woman* (London, 1687), 4 (orig. "adult'rate").
2. John Cleland, *Memoirs of a Woman of Pleasure* (1748–49), ed. Peter Sabor (Oxford: Oxford University Press, 1985), 91; this passage is well analyzed in Robert Markley, "Language, Power, and Sexuality in Cleland's *Fanny Hill*," *Philological Quarterly* 62 (1984): 343–56.
3. For the term, and the argument, see Steven Marcus, *The Other Victorians: A Study of Sexuality and Pornography in Mid-Nineteenth-Century England* (New York: Basic Books, 1966). The idea that singleness of focus precludes artistic quality seems not to have been used against other one-theme genres like Petrarchan lyric or pastoral elegy.
4. Jean-Baptiste de Boyer, Marquis d'Argens, presumed author (also attributed to Xavier d'Arles de Montigny), *Thérèse philosophe, ou Mémoires pour servir à l'histoire de D. Dirrag et de Mademoiselle Eradice* (The Hague, [1748?]), 1:2. Further parenthetical references will be from this edition (British Library P.C. 30.f.24).
5. *Selected Letters of Samuel Richardson*, ed. John Carroll (Oxford: Clarendon Press, 1964), 289.
6. Ferrante Pallavicino, *La Retorica delle Puttane* (henceforth *RP*), 2nd ed. ("Villafranca," 1671), 24, 27, 29, 43 ("Renda soave la sua narrativa con tessitura di curiosi accidenti figurati nella propria persona"), 46 ("una induttione distinta de'particolari accidenti della sua vita"). The devices of "narratione" listed on 41–43 include adopting a Petrarchan disdain, displaying signs of religious devotion, and pretending to be an orphan or the abandoned victim of a treacherous and cruel lover. I would like to thank Giovanni Ugolini for drawing my attention to a new edition of *RP* by Laura Coci for the Fondazione Bembo (Florence: Guanda, 1993), which appeared too late to be used in this essay.
7. For example, Pallavicino refers to the "tessitura" of his own treatise *and* to the "artificiosa tessitura" with which the whore ensnares the young man (8); see also 43, 60, 82. Some of these passages survive in the English *Whores Rhetorick* (henceforth *WR*), f. B1v and 42 ("weaving fraudulent webs"). For the association of expert prostitution with high-quality fabric, cf. also Pallavicino's *Continuazione del Corriere Svaligiato* ("Villafranca," 1671), 149–50 (a fictional letter on Venetian prostitutes who "Possedono la vera arte per fabricare le dolcezze amorose"): the most expensive courtesans in Venice are like fine cloth whose nap may be enjoyed from both sides. This was one of the only references to buggery in Pallavicino to survive translation into English; see Charles Gildon, *The Post-Boy Rob'd of His Mail*, 2nd ed. (London, 1706), 1:185.
8. *WR* 108 (based on *RP* 72 ["porre i membri in quelle parte del periodo, in cui faranno migliore effetto"], but changing "effect" to "pleasure" and adding "in his particular fancy"); for "authentication" and "imitation" see *RP* 62, 80, 87, 92, for "Comedy" *WR* 44, 45, 175. The point of this "exquisite" performance is the "mutation of sex to find Variety, Mother of Pleasures"

(*RP* 84); like Fanny Hill later, Pallavicino's elderly speaker assumes that sex is fundamentally monotonous, and that sexual discourse must constantly strive to permutate "li termini medesmi," the same terms (*RP* 61, which *WP* 43 changes to the conventional culinary metaphor "always coming to feed on the same dish").

9. Cypriano Soarez, *De Arte Rhetorica Libri Tres, ex Aristotele, Cicerone, et Quinctiliano Praecipue Deprompti* (Cologne, 1591), 35 ("maxima vis") and 83, citing Cicero, *De Oratore* 2, Quintilian 6.ii, and Horace, *Ars Poetica*, 102–3: "si vis me flere, dolendum est / primum ipsi tibi."

10. *RP* 5 ("*in medio sita est virtus*: significa esser virtuoso quell'huomo, che indifferamente distante dalli estremi del bene e del male, sà applicarsi, o all'uno, o all'altro con eguale spirito, e con felicita conforme a'disegni" [my translation is based on *WR* f. A10, which changes the plural *disegni* to the singular "design"]), 6 ("Sono gloriosi que'pittori, che colpiscono nell'ammirabile dipingendo oggetti diformi. La brutezza è colpa dell'originale, bon della effigie"), 21, 55.

11. Cleland, *Memoirs*, 91.

12. *WR* 62, f. A8v; the English preface elaborates the parallels between pen and penis into a surreal fantasy on virgin quills, coloured sheets, and venereal ink flowing with all the hues of the rainbow.

13. *RP* 60, 70; for the art of "maneggiare la lingua," which turns out to mean not "Rhetoric" but the physical use of the tongue in kissing, see *RP* 84–85, *WR* 200.

14. *WR* 85, 167, 182–83. Concrete topical references also serve as generic markers: the renaming of the old bawd as Mrs Cresswell aligns *The Whores Rhetorick* with "news" pamphlets and Tory satires, the best-known being the sneers at "railing Rabsheka" in the second part of *Absalom and Achitophel*—inspired by the supposed discovery, in a police raid, of senior opposition politicians among Mrs. Cresswell's clientele (Sir Thomas Player, Whig City official, allegedly owed her £300); see *WR* 28–29, 61–62 (she should not be associated with sedition since in fact she "quell[s] all insurrections"), 190. Ironically, much of the up-to-date urban texture of the English version derives from massive plagiarism of Aretino, making up perhaps half the work—a fact that no scholar writing on *WR* has noticed.

15. Gildon, *Post-Boy Rob'd of His Mail*, 1:200, an accurate translation of Pallavicino, *Continuazione del Corriere Svaligiato*, 110. The letter itself had ended thus: "Nor can I any longer hold my Pen, which desires to be held by a Hand, where near the Purity of your Snowy whiteness, it might better be able to express the Sincerity of my Affection; I must therefore follow the Impulses of my Pen, of a suddain quite besides my self, as being entranc'd in the Contemplation of your Beauty, which makes me conclude with a thousand Kisses and Embraces" (1:199).

16. Introduction to *Exilius, or the Banish'd Roman* (London, 1725), ff. A2–v.

17. *WR* 45–46, 113, 167 (orig. "himself"), 168.

18. Plenary address, ASECS Annual Meeting, Seattle 1992.

Education and Ideology in Sarah Fielding's
The Governess

ARLENE FISH WILNER

Sarah Fielding, author of nine works of fiction and a translation of Xenophon's *Memoirs of Socrates*, has been characterized by several critics in recent years as a proto-feminist. One interpreter of her first novel, *The Adventures of David Simple* (1744), points to her "radical questioning of basic values" at mid-century and views that novel as a critique of the "feminine virtues" of innocence, passivity, and privacy, suggesting that Fielding ultimately sees these virtues as "crippling weaknesses" and that "in her vision of women together, where woman can be Self, not other, Sarah Fielding is revolutionary."[1] Another critic, similarly viewing Fielding's fictions as subversive of prevailing mores, details a number of narrative strategies that allow her to portray the culture of the "proper lady" while providing subtexts that undermine this culture.[2] Mary Anne Schofield, who shares the opinion that Fielding seeks radical change in gender relations, asserts in her introduction to *The Cry* (1754, attributed to Fielding and Jane Collier) that Fielding's novels "attack 'conventional' ideas generated by men, ideas that need revision for [Fielding's] female-oriented world."[3] Most recently, Fielding has been described as a "mid-century link" between the feminist tracts of Mary Astell in the beginning of the period and those of Mary Wollstonecraft at the end.[4] The sort of serious analysis to which Fielding's works have been subjected in the last decade is penetrating, important, and long overdue. A keenly intelligent, intellectually accomplished, and productive writer, who by virtue of her gender was denied the educational and professional opportunities available to her celebrated brother Henry, Sarah Fielding composed narratives that have much to tell us about mid-eighteenth-century manners and morals, particularly as viewed from a female perspective.

Nonetheless, to characterize Fielding as a potent voice for gender equality and a proponent of social reform is to risk distorting some of the evidence. Indeed, the contention that Sarah Fielding is not, after all, so radical in her views as some recent critics have argued is supported by the commentaries of Dale Spender and Jane Spencer in their respective studies of early female novelists. These literary historians see in Fielding's fiction not a bold and provocative feminist statement, but rather an interesting tension between, on the one hand, a recognition of the unfair limitations imposed on women in a male-dominated society and, on the other, an acceptance of partriarchy and the consequent inevitable repression of women.[5] Although both Spender and Spencer regard *The Adventures of David Simple* as Fielding's sharpest social critique and most spirited portrayal of female oppression, neither wants to claim that even this, her best-received novel, was intended as subversive. Spender, while praising Fielding's "ability to depict the world as it impinges on women," does not contend that such a depiction is a clear call for change. Spencer is more explicit in defining the boundaries of Fielding's feminist position, grouping her with other "women novelists of the mid-century [who] sought to keep masculine approval by disclaiming any intention to overturn the sexual hierarchy."[6]

None of these critics, however, whether they see in Fielding's fictions an agenda for female liberation or a tentative exploration of the effects of gender inequality, has offered a detailed interpretation of *The Governess or, Little Female Academy* (1749), the short fiction for girls that has been called Fielding's most original and most influential work.[7] And those who elaborate what are, in their view, the compelling feminist themes in Fielding's oeuvre tend to overlook or minimize aspects of a text in which the voice of protest, if present at all, is heard only dimly. My contention here is that Fielding's only piece of juvenile fiction, considered to be the first novel written for children, is primarily conservative in purpose and in effect.[8] Overtly didactic, *The Governess* teaches the old paradox that although female virtue resides in feeling rather than in thinking or in doing, feelings unchecked or uncultivated by social norms must be repressed at all costs. Furthermore, the book conserves the values of middle-class society and portrays powerfully the specifically defined role of women within that growing class. In this way, I would suggest, *The Governess* is forward-looking, but not toward the kind of feminist revolution, subversion, or even protest later registered by freethinkers such as Catharine Macaulay and Mary Wollstonecraft. Rather, in its delineation of proper female education, it anticipates influential feminine icons such as Rousseau's decorative, compliant, and self-effacing Sophie as portrayed in his educational tract *Émile* (1762), and the idealized middle-class women urged upon young readers by Thomas Day, a devout disciple of Rousseau, whose *History of Sandford and Merton* (1783–89), an excruciatingly didactic book for boys, was popular, not only in his own time, but throughout the nineteenth century. The enthusiastic reception in England of both Rousseau and Day suggests that they were tapping into prevailing ideological currents;[9] indeed, the female images they offered were to flower in the next century as the Victorian "angel in the house," the ideal woman as conceived by men—"a model of selflessness and purity of heart" who "lives a life without external events."[10] My purpose here is not to suggest that Fielding directly influenced Rousseau or Day. Rather it is to show how the underlying themes in her mid-eighteenth-century instructional narrative for young girls encoded a set of gender expectations that were later more explicitly elaborated by authors such as Rousseau and Day who articulated an increasingly influential bourgeois value system in educational works that proved to be vastly appealing to the late eighteenth- and nineteenth-century reading public. Thus, while Fielding's novels for adults reveal that she did chafe at the restrictions placed on women, it is, ironically, her least rebellious book that is, in retrospect, most prophetic.

* * * * * * * * *

The Governess is a slim volume that comprises, remarkably, twenty distinct narratives. The word *use* appears often, since the stories told in the female academy are, above all, conduct lessons meant both to reform wayward spirits and to be immediately applied to everyday situations. The preface itself contains two stories calculated to improve the reader's use of the book. The lessons invariably teach humility, self-effacement, and the virtue of putting the interests of others above one's own. The very first story, a fable-like explanation of why no bird except the magpie can build its own house completely, is a warning against the presumption of knowledge. That a young girl's judgment and knowledge must be distrusted is a theme that is iterated throughout the book.[11] The second prefatory story reminds young readers and their parents that reading is a waste of time unless the ideas gleaned thereby are organized and properly stored by the mental faculties, to be retrieved effortlessly at the right conversational moment. Notably, the first practical lesson for young female readers of this novel is a social one: to be able to say the right thing at the right time. Failing to do so is to risk "exposure" and to "become a Laughing-stock to [one's] companions" (97).

The eighteen ensuing stories comprise a melange of genres, incorporating a wide variety of narrative conventions: the fairy story (one of the girls reads aloud two fairy tales, one of which has two other narratives embedded within it); spiritual autobiography (each of the nine schoolgirls tells the story of her "life," each largely a confession of "faults"); the romance novella ("Caelia and Chloe" as narrated by Dolly Friendly and the briefly narrated melodrama of Lady Dison); the plot summary of a play, "The Funeral, or Grief a la Mode"; a recollection of personal experience turned into a corrective of pretension to wisdom; and another aviary fable containing an extended verse meditation. Thus the primary "action" of the book is one of recounting, listening, and drawing explicit morals. Little is learned from direct experience; rather, hearing the experiences of others is the primary means of education. Moreover, the girls are taught that any vicarious pleasure they may derive from the imaginative or adventurous elements in the stories can never be an end in itself; the real value of such stories, they are frequently reminded, is the moral imperative to which each may be reduced. Invariably, the lesson is that just as vice, folly, and misery are found together, so are virtue, prudence, and happiness. Virtue is manifested by self-effacement, humility, and, above all, the ability to keep one's temper. In the constant war between "passion" and "duty," duty must always prevail. Passions are almost always bad—"violent" (235), "tumultuous and tormenting" (243), "raging" (277), "restless" (278). In two separate narratives, a woman literally dies of an excess of the wrong kind of emotion—Lady Dison of envy (206) and Sybella's mother of anger (235). Even when passions appear to be good, they must never be pursued at the expense of duty (253–54). Duty is owed to the rules and maxims passed down by older women (mothers and other teachers), who follow *their* duty in socializing young girls appropriately.[12]

The structure of the book suggests that this socialization is accomplished most effectively through the art of storytelling, the only female "art" that is not viewed negatively. Artlessness is conventionally associated with innocence and modesty, the latter being the sign of the former. In *The Governess*, active arts (those that involve action rather than, like storytelling, simply precept) as practiced by a female are associated with "wickededness"; they are pressed into the service of passions such as envy and vindictiveness, just as "Designs," which are creative and imaginative, are evil in intent.[13] Great beauty, of course, only adds to a woman's ability to be wicked, since a beautiful woman can seduce powerful men to do her bidding. "Good" females, in contrast, withdraw as much as possible from activity and thus from "Arts and Contrivances." They know how to value a "safe Retreat from Noise and Confusion" (241) and understand the importance of "true Obedience," which "consists in Submission" (242). *The Governess* teaches that the only art that females appropriately practice is that of recounting stories that conserve the very values intended to prevent a wider range of options, stories that identify activity, creativity, and imagination with wickedness.

Significantly, these stories are not composed by the young girls, but are found in books or have been given to them, apparently in manuscript form, by older relatives. The one exception is a story that, at the volume's conclusion, we are informed will be recounted to later students of Mrs. Teachum—the story of the incident with which the book opens. In the only real action at the school, the girls physically fight over who will receive the largest apple, and Jenny (who, at fourteen, is the eldest student) succeeds in reconciling them to each other by convincing them that there is virtue in submission because it leads to happiness. This incident is itself destined to become yet another story used to socialize the young charges of the governess. Since Jenny has been the primary role model througout the book, the message is that not only adult women, but adolescents as well, will, ideally, become complicit in their own oppression. Jenny does this by actively intervening in the lives of others in the only approved way, by teaching others that not to repress one's own desires and impulses is almost always selfish. Thus, by the end of the book, Jenny's life is reduced to yet another story used to maintain "Union and Harmony in this well-bred society":

> And if any Girl was found to harbour in her Breast a rising Passion, which it was difficult to conquer, the Name and Story of Miss Jenny Peace soon gained her Attention, and left her without any other Desire than to emulate Miss Jenny's virtues. (342–43)

Although each girl takes a turn telling the "story" of her life, these brief narratives are mostly confessions of faults and errors (indeed, they are even called such), each ending with the admission of former self-indulgence in an inappropriate impulse or emotion and with a resolution to reform or with an expression of gratitude for reformation accomplished through attendance at the boarding school. Monotonous and strikingly lacking in detail, plot, or drama, these narratives are hardly stories in the usual sense. Overall, the girls' passivity and lack of creativity, the constant instruction of their elders to reduce to unvarying moral lessons the mildly entertaining fictions that they hear, and the repeated cautions about "artfulness" (along with the untimely demise of "designing" women) reflect the mythology of opposed female characteristics that, according to Sandra Gilbert and Susan Gubar, acquired its greatest power during the Victorian period: the Queen versus Snow White, the angel in the house versus the wicked witch. The Queen

> is a plotter, a plot-maker, a schemer, a witch, an artist, an impersonator, a woman of almost infinite creative energy, witty, wily, self-absorbed as all artists traditionally are. On the other hand, in her absolute chastity, her frozen innocence, her sweet nullity, Snow White represents . . . the ideal of contemplative purity. An angel in the house of myth, Snow White is not only a child but (as females always are) childlike, docile, submissive, the heroine of a life that *has no story*.[14]

Because Fielding's girls are not even allowed to risk the temptations that the witch offers to Snow White, they have even less of a story. That is, their lives have a beginning and an implied end, but no middle, no experience through which they can grow, develop, and form individual identities.

Fielding herself could not have been unmindful of the repressiveness of her fictional portraits. Although biographical information about Sarah Fielding is relatively scanty, we know that she attended boarding school while in the custody of her grandmother and later acquired enough ancient

Greek under the tutelage of the Reverend Arthur Collier to translate Xenophon's *Memoirs of Socrates.* Her commitment to classical studies, traditionally possible only for men, suggests a defiant attitude toward the limited opportunities for learning available to women.[15] In *David Simple,* the character of Cynthia must have been voicing Fielding's sentiments when she lamented that intellectually curious women are admonished to "mind [their] needle work" since "reading and poring on books would never get [them] a husband," and that bright, ambitious girls are denied knowledge while their dull brothers are "cajoled or whipped into learning."[16] Such comments notwithstanding, academic rigor and intellectual challenge receive short shrift in the "little female academy," where the curriculum consists of "Reading, Writing, Working [i.e., needlework], and . . . all Proper Forms of Behaviour" (99) and the only specially trained instructor mentioned is the "Writing-Master" (183). That *The Governess,* Sarah Fielding's overtly educational book, is essentially conservative seems undeniable. Indeed, it circumscribes the role of young women in ways that would have surprised and disappointed earlier female writers like Mary Astell, who complained in her appendix to *Some Reflections Upon Marriage* (1730) of the unfair educational advantages given to boys, or Sarah Egerton, who protested in her poem "The Liberty" (1703) of being Condemn'd for ever, to the puny Curse, / Of precepts taught, at Boarding-School, or Nurse."[17]

* * * * * * * * *

To understand the reasons that such circumscription would have been at least overtly endorsed by a woman as clever and as well educated as Sarah Fielding,[18] one must look to the shifting social and economic currents of the time. It is a commonplace that the eighteenth century witnessed both the rise of the middle class and a marked increase in the number of women who wrote and published. The increasing power of middle-class values, however, both idealized and marginalized women. Historian Isaac Kramnick has shown how children's literature of the eighteenth century increasingly embodied bourgeois values in purposeful opposition to aristocratic ones. By the end of the century, writers for children such as Sarah Trimmer, Thomas Day, and Maria Edgeworth were explicitly contrasting middle-class virtues, including honesty, industry, punctuality, practical training, and successful entrepreneurship, with the idleness, luxury, and wastefulness of the aristocracy. Day, in particular, whose immensely popular and influential *History of Sandford and Merton* was based on the tenets of Rousseau's *Émile,* showed, as Kramnick has observed, that "primitivism [that is, the cult of the noble savage] and industrialism could come together because there was a common enemy, the idle and unproductive aristocracy."[19] In the ideal bourgeois family as portrayed in this period, men were productive capitalists who contributed to the growth of science, technology, and industry while women remained in the home despite the decline of domestic production that naturally accompanied increased industrialization. The connection between decreased domestic and family industry and the relegation of women to the home (or, in the case of lower-class women, to hard, poorly paid labor) has been detailed in Alice Clark's classic study, *Working Life of Women in the Seventeenth Century*. According to Clark, traditional dogmas that dictated the natural inferiority of women to men were not as useful when women were an essential component of economic production. However, increasing specialization and a growing emphasis on the individual, as opposed to the family, as an economic unit created a congenial climate for the old patriarchal myths:

> If women's want of specialised training had been prejudicial to their capacity for work in former times, such training would not have been withheld from them merely through fear of its weakening the husband's power, because the husband was so dependent upon his wife's assistance. There was little talk then of men "keeping" their wives; neither husband nor wife could prosper without the other's help. But the introduction of Capitalism, organising industry on an individual basis, freed men to some extent from this economic dependence on their wives, and from henceforward the ideal of the subjection of women to their husbands could be pursued, unhampered by fear of the the dangers resulting to the said husbands by a lessening of the wife's economic efficiency.[20]

Thus the roles of women in general, and of middle-class women in particular, became more and more distinct from those of men. Lacking training and education, they could not compete with men in the marketplace, and their "natural" role became that of a sweet-tempered, dependable helpmate responsible for maintaining the moral and spiritual values of the home, shunning decorative excess while remaining graceful, attractive, and nurturing. Moreover, the growing influence of middle-class values encouraged women to identify themselves primarily on the basis of gender, since the circumscribed role of the woman in an entrepreneurial world would naturally cut across class lines.

Although she can hardly be identified with the cult of primitivism that her male successors found congenial, Fielding is careful to deflate the pretensions of the titled nobility; in a satire of those who would affect "Superiority of Station," she ridicules the vanity, snobbery, and self-consciousness of two young girls who, through the death of an uncle, have acquired the title "Your Ladyship" (281–85). The lesson here, a warning against vanity and affectation, falls short of erasing all social distinctions while ridiculing those who appear to think such distinctions make a real difference. This sort of education, enhanced by the gender-specific peer pressure exerted within the "little female academy," mitigates any impulses toward individuality and also any tendency to define oneself in terms of class privilege. It is worth noting here that both Rousseau's Émile and Day's young boys are trained by private tutors, a practice recommended by Locke to protect gentlemen's sons from the "Roughness and ill Breeding" of lower class or less refined boys who might be mixed into the group.[21] In the middle-class world of Fielding's little academy, however (as in the fictions of Rousseau and Day), the traits to be avoided come from "above" (young ladies who insist on deference to titles) rather than from "below."

Conformity to gender expectations is the essence of the boarding school experience described by Fielding, and these expectations grew as the century progressed. Mary Poovey, in her study of late eighteenth- and early nineteenth-century writing by women, argues persuasively that the ideal of the "self-made man" implied a complementary woman whose own individuality, assertiveness, and sexuality had to be repressed:

> [T]he very translation of sexual control into "duty" is perfectly in keeping with the tenets of individualism: a woman's social contribution was, in essence, self-control, just as her primary antagonist was herself. . . . Because of the need to protect their virtue, they [that is, women] were advised to acquire knowledge only indirectly—by reading history, perhaps, or by talking to an older female friend. . . . Women were also urged to think of themselves collectively—not as a political unit, or as beings possessed of individual talents, capacities, or rights, but simply in terms of the universals of what Richardson's Lovelace called "the sex, the sex."[22]

It is true, of course, that a vision of female community, or sisterhood, often informs feminist writing, and that a feminist epistemology has evolved around this collaborative model of learning. Since Fielding insists upon the importance of friendship among the schoolgirls, this aspect of the book might be interpreted as an indication of her feminist ideology.[23] I would suggest, however, that in the context of the kind of socialization and education exemplified in the book as a whole, female friendship and community become yet another aspect of enforced passivity and submission. In addition to acquiring knowledge primarily through listening to each other's stories with almost no complement of direct experience, the girls are never encouraged to cultivate personal talents or to see themselves as individuals apart from the group. Indeed, one cannot help noticing that their greatest "adventures" during the nine days of the book are two walks to the dairy house, where they are praised for their ladylike behavior.[24]

Portrayals of male-female relationships within the narratives that comprise *The Governess* explicitly promote the circumscribed aspects of the female role described by Gilbert and Gubar and by Poovey. Three of the embedded narratives describe love relationships that lead to marriage. In the first instance, a fairy-tale/romance called "The Story of the cruel Barbarico, the good Giant Benefico, and the pretty little Dwarf Mignon," the gentle Amata, beloved by the shepherd Fidus, is a stereotyped romance heroine, twice called the "fair disconsolate," who is prone to tears, fainting, and a swelling bosom, and who remains "retired and pent up within her own apartment" (161) until Fidus comes to tell her of the bad Giant's defeat. "The Story of Caelia and Chloe" (185–99) recounts a trial imposed on two best friends by a suitor named Sempronius who, unable to decide which one to marry (since these young women are—remarkably—indistinguishable), devises a test of their virtue by tempting each to betray the other in order to win him. Chloe, intent upon marrying Sempronius, suggests that Caelia's character is mildly tainted by artfulness and envy, but the paragon Caelia, who would rather lose her beloved than cast any doubt upon the perfection of her friend, says only good things about Chloe, thus proving her great virtue and earning herself a husband. Chloe's deceitful behavior is attributed to her passions, which are "naturally stronger" than Caelia's. The repentant Chloe, deeply ashamed of her behavior and so tormented by her lapse that she is driven nearly mad, almost dies of a violent fever. A death-bed confession to her friend clears the way for her recovery, and she finally conquers her passions sufficiently to accept the marriage of her best friend to the man she herself loves. Perhaps more surprisingly, she even agrees to a kind of chaste ménage à trois, as, we are told, "they lived all together." The message is not subtle: As Amata in the earlier story is rewarded with Fidus because of her delicacy and passivity, Caelia wins her prize because she is artless and—at least on the surface—dispassionate. Two more marriages take place within the "The Funeral, or Grief a la Mode," the comedy read to the girls by Jenny and recounted to Mrs. Teachum by Sukey Jennett. When Mrs. Teachum reminds Sukey that her plot summary has omitted important commentary on the characters of two young ladies who figure in a sub-plot, Sukey rapidly recovers the essential details:

> "Indeed, Madam (said Miss *Sukey*) I had forgot that; but Lady *Charlotte* was a very sensible, grave young Lady, and Lady *Harriott* was extremely gay and coquetish; but Mr. *Camply* tells her how much it misbecomes her to be so; and she having good Sense, as well as good Nature, is convinced by her Folly, and likes him so well for his Reproof, that she consents to marry him." (300)

Lest the young schoolgirls (and the young readers of the book) have any remaining doubts about what makes a good wife, Fielding's concluding story is a fable, "The Assembly of Birds," about an aviary contest, reminiscent of Chaucer's "Parliament of Fowls," to decide which bird is most fortunate and admirable and thus happiest. Only the dove, "who had no Ambition for a public Preference," declines to participate. The eagle, who is chief judge, finds the dove "hovering over her Nest, waiting the Return of her absent Mate" and overhears her song in praise of her children's "gentle sire," whom she calls "the Lord of my Desire, / My Life, myself, my Soul, my Sire." (Sarah Fielding, we may recall at this point, never married.) While the mother dove broods over her young, her husband is out risking life and wing to gather food for the family. His return to their "spotless

Bed" inspires a scene that can only be characterized as the epitome of middle-class family bliss, as papa feeds the ecstatic fluttering babies with the "Wheaten Spoil . . . won with Toil," and mama "on her Lord and Infants smiles" (331–34). Needless to say, the eagle pronounces the dove winner of the contest. The "spotless bed" is, I think, an especially interesting touch, since in this context it reinforces the common observation that middle-class values and notions of female "purity" are mutually supportive. Historian Alice Browne reminds us that the double sexual standard and the categorization of a woman as "good" or "bad" depending solely on her sexual behavior were most characteristic of the middle-class, since "many working-class people tolerated pre-marital sex, or never bothered to marry, or left their spouses and formed new unions [and] aristocratic women had considerable freedom once they were married."[25] Never trusting to the story alone (even one so pointed as this) to convey the message, Mrs. Teachum advises the girls to "imitate the Dove; and remember, that Innocence of mind and Integrity of Heart, adorn the Female Character; and can alone produce your own Happiness, and diffuse it to all around you" (334).

* * * * * * * *

Fielding's school story manifests bourgeois social and political attitudes that gained momentum throughout the eighteenth century and are explicitly promoted in the works of such authors as Jean-Jacques Rousseau and Thomas Day. While there is no reason to claim *The Governess* as a source for Rousseau or Day, a brief comment on the similarities between their work and hers can be useful in situating Fielding on a continuum that persists well into the nineteenth century.

The ideal woman of the mid- to late- eighteenth century is epitomized in Rousseau's Sophie, Émile's beloved, who, like Sarah Fielding's good girls, "souffre avec patience les torts des autres, et répare avec plaisir les siens." According to Rousseau, women are innately suited to tolerate injustice, whereas young boys naturally rebel against it; moreover, women must be shown the necessity of embracing their subordinate position, since marital contentment depends upon such acceptance. In general, manliness is defined as self-assertion and femininity as willing submission.[26] A very limited education is, of course, requisite to promote such "natural" feminine tendencies; therefore by the time Émile begins to court Sophie, she will have read practically nothing: "elle a du goût sans étude, des talents sans art, du jugement sans connaissances" (520). In this, perhaps, she is not very different from the young Émile, for whom reading is considered secondary to experience. Sophie, however, can look forward neither to the kind of education (e.g., systematic study of selected ancient historians) nor to the kind of experience (e.g., the requisite travel abroad) that are planned for Émile. The closer her mind is to being a *tabula rasa*, the more easily her husband can form her as he wishes: "O l'aimable ignorance!" exclaims

Rousseau. "Elle vaudra mieux pour [son mari] que si elle était savante; il aura le plaisir de lui tout enseigner" (520). In book 5 of *Émile*, Rousseau repeatedly and unapologetically attacks the notion of gender equality and mocks women who pretend to the sort of wit, judgment, and literary understanding that men possess. A woman who neglects household duties to read and write deserves what appears to be Rousseau's idea of the worst sort of punishment—perpetual maindenhood: "Toute fille lettrée restera fille toute sa vie, quand il n'y aura que des hommes sensés sur la terre" (519). But it is not enough to keep women ignorant; unlike boys, young girls must be trained early, carefully, and consistently to deny the legitimacy of their own feelings, to accept restraint, and always, before speaking or acting, to consider what others will think of what they say or do.[27] In all of this, Rousseau seems to have missed the contradiction that women need to be carefully trained to be what they are "naturally" meant to be and to resist innate impulses that make them "unnatural" although these same impulses are virtues in men.

Coming at the end of *Émile* as it does, this oppressive dogma confounds the modern reader all the more because of the egalitarian attitudes already expressed in the book with regard to social hierarchy. Rousseau would teach Émile to admire the industry and simple tastes of those who must earn their bread and to scorn the idleness, dullness and vanity of the leisured. Although Émile is rich (27), he is trained to cope with poverty, to be, if necessary, another Robinson Crusoe. He does not need to work with his hands, but he is trained in carpentry, and, since "il n'y a point d'honnêteté sans l'utilité" (229), works for wages when his skills are required. Moreover, while the young woman must always seek social approval, the young man's virtue is in ignoring what others think. Those who look down upon tradesmen are blinded by prejudice, and their opinions must be disregarded: "Pour vous soumettre la fortune et les choses, commencez par vous en rendre indépendant. Pour régner par l'opinion, commencez par régner sur elle" (227). While Émile conquers Fortune and reigns over public opinion, Sophie, like the charges of Fielding's governess, thinks always of public opinion and conquers only her own caprices.

It seems clear, then, that the late seventeenth-century shifts documented by Clark—the decline of domestic production, the beginnings of a modern capitalist economy, increasing emphasis on the bourgeois virtues of individualism and independence, and the growing importance of specialized knowledge from which women had been traditionally excluded—inform Rousseau's very influential educational tract.[28] Clark's study also makes intelligible the dramatic disjunction between, on the one hand, enlightened attitudes toward social class inequalites and, on the other, reactionary views of the proper role of women. The mythology was so powerful and so persuasive that we can understand why "good" women accepted it and why even an intelligent, educated woman like Sarah Fielding endorsed many aspects of it in her pedagogical fiction.[29]

Nowhere is this ideology so clearly revealed as in the life and work of Thomas Day (1748–1789), a devotee of Rousseau, whose powerful influence is evident both in Day's life and in his writing. According to Percy Muir, Day's industrious Harry Sandford is "as close to being Émile as an English background and a somewhat clumsy English hand can compass."[30] The triumph of middle-class virtues over the negative qualities associated with the aristocracy forms the theme of *Sandford and Merton*. In addition, Day cultivated the idea of the noble savage and, as a fervent opponent of slavery, idealized the black man in a kind of reverse stereotype.[31] In view of the thesis developed here, we should not be surprised to find that despite his progressive attitudes on issues of race and class, Day considered women distinctly and irremediably inferior to men. What Day admired in women are the qualities valued in a society increasingly dominated by the middle classes, qualities that would certainly be approved by Fielding's Mrs. Teachum: "modesty, frugality, a love of retirement, the faculty of blushing, [a desire for] virtuous obscurity."[32]

Rousseau—and Day through Rousseau—had borrowed heavily from Locke's treatise on education (1693), which had been intended only for the sons of gentlemen, but they had carefully accommodated the seventeenth-century scholar's ideas to emerging middle-class values.[33] In both cases, women were debarred both from economic productivity in the public sphere and from authentic intellectual activity of any kind. While Day disdained the leisured lifestyle that bred women to be delicate and "indolent," and instead insisted that young girls be inured to physical hardship, his portraits of properly educated females (the kind Miss Simmons [2:226–29] and industrious Selene [3:205–8]) reveal his dedication to a patriarchy firmly cemented in bourgeois values.[34] Notably, two of Locke's ideas that Rousseau and Day depended upon most heavily—the importance of direct sensory experience in the education of children and the recognition of developmental stages with particular methods appropriate to each—appear to be essential only to the rearing of boys. Experience, because it can expose her to risk, sully her reputation, and foster inappropriate ambitions is inadvisable for a female. Similarly, a girl's academic education should remain superficial and dilettantish, both because her mission in life will never require complex analysis or in-depth knowledge and because her husband is her most important teacher. The philosophical writing to which she is exposed is selected by men less to enlighten her than to reinforce, through historical "examples of virtuous women," the nature and justness of her subordinate role.

Popular well into the nineteenth century, the educational texts of Rousseau and Day captured an important social perspective of their time and appealed to the increasingly powerful middle-class ideology that I have argued is integral to Fielding's novel for girls. Percy Muir, who called *Sandford and Merton* a "feast of nausea" because of its interminable moralizing and oppressive didacticism, marveled at its longevity, noting that he was given the book as a Sunday-school prize in 1883, a century after the initial publication of the first volume.[35] Historian Cornelia Meigs, equally nonplussed by the persistence of Day's novel, observes that it "established itself as the model book for the young and was thus to have a stubborn influence" on the children's literature that followed.[36] If my reading of *The Governess* is persuasive, there can be little doubt that the education of Sarah Fielding's young girls would well equip them to emulate the social ideal that Rousseau and Day subsequently delineated to such great effect. As we have seen, this ideal reflected a redefinition or at least a dramatic refinement of the proper roles for women to accommodate increasingly influential middle-class values.

* * * * * * * *

Are there, then, no subtexts or subversions in Fielding's book for girls, no recognition that the price of "goodness" is confinement and oppression? I would suggest that there are at least three ways in which the overt lessons of the book are undermined, although they are not nearly powerful enough, even taken together, to provide the sort of interesting tension one finds in Fielding's novels for adults. First, a possible critique of the prevailing ethos is noticeable in certain elements of the interpolated stories, in which gender stereotypes are occasionally modified in unconventional ways. In the story of the good and bad giants, for example, the good giant seems super-fluous to the plot, as it is the dwarf Mignon who actually defeats the bad giant through courage and ingenuity. Because the diminutive Mignon is de-scribed as gentle, sweet-tempered, and "one of the Prettiest" of men, because he turns out to be Amata's long lost brother, and because he chooses, along with Fidus and Amata, to stay with "the generous Benefico" at the end rather than seek a wife or a new adventure, the character of Mignon suggests that traditionally "male" characteristics (courage, ingenuity, and the willingness to take physical risks) and traditionally "female" characteristics (relatively small stature and lack of brute power, softness, sweetness, and the enjoyment of domestic pleasures) may indeed dwell together in the same breast. Mignon's choice to live communally with his brother, sister-in-law, and others becomes important as part of a pattern of atypical or non-idealized characters who avoid marriage. Another of these is Chloe, mentioned above, whose self-assertiveness and intensity of emotion identify her as less than the perfect woman; as noted, she ends by living with her best friend and her best friend's husband, once her own beloved. Finally, there is the princess Hebe, protagonist of a long, involuted fairy tale, and the only woman in the book who ends up happy and virtuous in the public domain. After learning the conventional lessons of "Humility and Distrust of herself" and begging to be allowed to avoid temptation by leading a private life, the princess, at the behest of her mother, accedes to her Father's throne, since "she thought she could not innocently refuse the Power that would give her such Opportunities of doing Good, and making others Happy" (90). Significantly, Hebe remains single. This pattern, I would suggest, implies Fielding's recognition that marriage within her society requires capitulation by both men and women to strictly defined roles that repress the development of individual character or ambitions.[37]

The second sort of subversion I have in mind is suggested by Fielding's decision to create a book through a variety of narrative forms and voices. Although the narratives themselves promote an oppressive ideology, the multiplicity of the female voices, and their effectiveness in transmitting culture suggests that women's voices can and do acquire power through story-telling. What women lack, the subtext implies, is not the ability to create and to articulate, but rather the opportunity to write their *own* stories and to shape their own lives. This brings us to the third and perhaps most significant qualification of the text's lessons, and that is the fact that Sarah Fielding successfully wrote, published, and sold her little book for girls. Writing for money as did her brother Henry, Fielding most likely composed a book for children that would appeal to the adults who would decide whether or not to purchase it.[38] That the book remained in print for more than one hundred fifty years reflects the skill of its author in articulating the emerging values that were to gain so much strength in the next century. It is not so puzzling after all that the well-educated, assertive, and unmarried Sarah Fielding should have endorsed, in her book for children, qualities and values that seem to counter the evidence of her own life and, to a degree, of her other writings. I have discussed elsewhere a similar kind of disjunction, in the work of Henry Fielding, between the complex and provocative epistemologies of the novels, on the one hand, and the surprisingly conservative arguments of the social and legal writings, on the other.[39] Like legal decisions, literature specifically intended to educate children—and to attract their parents and teachers—is generally written not to subvert or disconcert, but to transmit mores perceived as desirable because they preserve the sanctity of particular cultural values and socio-economic relationships. As the first fictional book in this tradition, Sarah Fielding's *The Governess* helps us to understand both the shifting culture of mid-eighteenth-century England and the development of late eighteenth- and nineteenth-century didactic children's literature, a remarkable body of work for which her little volume must certainly be considered a prototype.[40]

NOTES

1. C. Woodward, "'Feminine Virtue, Ladylike Disguise, Women of Community': Sarah Fielding and the Female I Am at Mid-Century," *Transactions of the Samuel Johnson Society of the Northwest* 15 (1984): 64.

2. Deborah Downs-Miers, "For Betty and the Little Female Academy: a Book of Their Own," *Children's Literature Association Quarterly* 10 (Spring 1985): 30–33.
3. Sarah Fielding [and Jane Collier], *The Cry: A New Dramatic Fable*, intro. Mary Anne Schofield (Delmar, NY: Scholars' Facsimiles and Reprints, 1986), 5–6. Clive Probyn has recently offered persuasive evidence that Collier was the sole author of *The Cry*. See *The Social Humanist: The Life and Works of James Harris 1709–1780* (Oxford: Clarendon Press, 1991), 134.
4. Lisette F. Carpenter, "Sarah Fielding: A Mid-Century Link in Eighteenth-Century Feminist Views" (Ph.D. diss., Texas A&M University, 1989).
5. Jane Spencer, for example, points out that the traditional portrayal of the learned Octavia in *The Lives of Cleopatra and Octavia* (1757) so severely qualifies what might have been a vigorous argument for the value of female intellectual accomplishment that the result is rather a deferential curtsy to "conventional morality." *The Rise of the Woman Novelist: From Aphra Behn to Jane Austen* (Oxford: Basil Blackwell, 1986), 94–95. Similarly, in Fielding's *The Countess of Dellwyn* (1759), the social satire that would incline the reader toward sympathy with the seduced heroine is undercut by the narrator's strict moral judgment of women who fail to guard their reputations (ibid., 122)—and, I would add, of Lady Dellwyn's "criminal Vanity." Sarah Fielding, *The History of the Countess of Dellwyn* (1759; facsimile reprint, New York: Garland Publishing, Inc., 1974), 2:130. Parting company with Mary Anne Schofield, Spencer sees *The Cry* as tentative and limited in its call for change: "They [i.e., Fielding and Collier] criticize the romantic illusion that obscures masculine power, not the power itself." *Rise of the Woman Novelist*, 208.
6. Dale Spender, *Mothers of the Novel: 100 Good Women Writers Before Jane Austen* (London: Pandora Press, 1986), 189; Spencer, *Rise of the Woman Novelist*, 94.
7. Sarah Fielding, *The Governess or Little Female Academy*, intro Jill E. Grey (1749; facsimile reprint, London: Oxford University Press, 1968), 39, 64 ff. Page references, hereafter parenthetical within the article, are to Grey's facsimile edition; *The Governess* is also available in contemporary typography as part of the Mothers of the Novel series (New York: Pandora Press, 1987), intro. Mary Cadogan.
8. Jill E. Grey, in her introduction to *The Governess*, places Fielding's book in the context of adult fiction at the time: like the novels of Defoe, Richardson, and her brother Henry, *The Governess* was an attempt to meld "verisimilitude and formal realism . . . with romance." Moreover, "Mrs. Teachum's nine scholars are the first attempt in juvenile literature at creating fictional children in a contemporary setting," with careful attention to particularities of time and place, a recognition of child psychology, and original plot details that were to influence generations of children's authors (78–82). More recently, Deborah Downs-Meirs has discussed the neglect of Fielding's book by historians of children's literature and has persuasively defended its right to be called the first children's novel. My essay, however, takes issue with her view that *The Governess* portrays an "extraordinarily positive image of active women in positions of

power with a most convincing realism." "For Betty and the Little Female Academy," 32.

9. For a discussion of Rousseau's influence in England, see F. J. Harvey Darton, *Children's Books in England: Five Centuries of Social Life*, 3rd ed. (Cambridge: Cambridge University Press, 1982), chap. 9. The influence was reciprocal: Thomas Day's *History of Sandford and Merton* (1783–89), inspired by Rousseau, was translated into French in 1798. Dorothy Gardiner details the responses of both men and women in England to Rousseau's system of female education. *English Girlhood at School: A Study of Women's Education Through Twelve Centuries* (London, Oxford University Press, 1929), 448–60.

10. The term "angel in the house," taken from Coventry Patmore's poem by that name, refers to the nineteenth-century ideal of womanly goodness, defined by its relation to the satisfaction of male desires. The second phrase is from Goethe's *Wilhelm Meister's Travels*. I have borrowed both references from Sandra M. Gilbert and Susan Gubar's discussion of male attitudes toward female self-assertion and creativity in the nineteenth century, *The Madwoman in the Attic* (New Haven: Yale University Press, 1979), chap. 1.

11. In the fairy tale, "The Princess Hebe," for example, the princess is endangered when she "determin[es] . . . to think for herself and make use of her own Understanding" (261). Another instance occurs when Jenny Peace is asked by Mrs Teachum to articulate the "moral" of the play: "Miss Jenny being thus suddenly asked a Question of this Nature, consider'd some time before she gave an Answer; for she was naturally very diffident of her own Opinion in any-thing where she had not been instructed by some one she thought wiser than herself" (301).

12. Cf. the following from Fielding's preface to *The Countess of Dellwyn*: "Nothing can give us so strong an Idea of the Misery of a Woman, as to suppose her under the Power of her own Passions, in such a manner as to bear a Resemblance to the Top, which is whipped about at the Will and Pleasure of the Boys" (xxx). Ironically, the ill-fated countess owes her downfall not to her submission to passion but to her attempt to live by superficial social values that encourage women to agree to unsatisfactory marriages. In a study of the portrayal of adolescence in literature, Patricia Spacks has observed that "the many eighteenth century novels by women about girls concentrate in particular on acceptable disguises for passion" and that in these novels "the passionate proclivities of the young seem especially threatening when they belong to women." *The Adolescent Idea* (New York: Basic Books, Inc., 1981), 113, 119.

13. Examples of "designing" females in *The Governess* who are presented as negative examples include Brunetta and her mother in "The Princess Hebe" (233–39) and, in the narrated plot of "The Funeral" (297–300), Lady Brumpton, whose "wicked arts" ultimately reveal her duplicity.

14. Gilbert and Gubar, *Madwoman in the Attic*, 38–39; italics theirs.

15. Grey, in her introduction to *The Governess*, 1–38, presents a careful chronology of the influences and events in Fielding's life insofar as they are known or may be inferred from the unfortunately sparse evidence. Spender's discussion is also helpful. *Mothers of the Novel*, chap. 10, 180–93.

16. Sarah Fielding, *The Adventures of David Simple*. Originally published in two sections: 1744, 1753. Reprint as 1 vol. (London: Oxford University Press, 1969), 54.

17. Mary Astell, appendix to *Some Reflections Upon Marriage*, reprinted in *The Other Eighteenth Century*, ed. Robert W. Uphaus and Gretchen M. Foster (East Lansing, MI: Colleagues Press, 1991), 46; Sarah Fyge Egerton, "The Liberty," reprinted in *The Other Eighteenth Century*, 139.

18. The contradiction between a woman's advocacy of submission and the evidence of her own assertiveness and independence of spirit is not anomalous and probably became more apparent toward the end of the century for reasons that this paper suggests. A well-known example is Hannah More (1745–1833), a woman remarkable for her initiative and productivity as an author and educator, who was nonetheless deeply disturbed by women who imagined themselves equal to men. In a tract on female education published in 1799, More relied on traditional Christian arguments to buttress her argument: "Is the author then undervaluing her own sex? No. It is her zeal for their true *interests*, which leads her to oppose their imaginary *rights*. It is her regard for their happiness, which makes her endeavour to cure them of a feverish thirst for a fame as unattainable as inappropriate; to guard them against an ambition as little becoming the delicacy of their female character as the meekness of their religious profession. A little Christian humility and sober-mindedness are worth all the empty renown which was ever obtained by the misapplied energies of the sex." *Strictures on the Modern System of Female Education*, 1799. Reprinted as vol. 3 in *The Works of Hannah More*, 6 vols., (London: Henry G. Bohn, 1854), 3:200.

19. Isaac Kramnick, "Children's Literature and Bourgeois Ideology: Observations on Culture and Industrial Capitalism in the Later Eighteenth Century," in *Culture and Politics From Puritanism to the Enlightenment,* ed. Perez Zagorin (Berkeley: University of California Press, 1980), 231. As Samuel Pickering has shown, the popularity of the Cheap Repository Tracts initiated by Hannah More in the 1790s (intended to counter the influence of the older, more vulgar chapbooks) indicates a growing recognition of the need for the "right" sort of reading for the increasingly literate masses. For a study of the genesis and character of this literature see Pickering, *John Locke and Children's Books in Eighteenth-Century England.* (Knoxville: University of Tennessee Press, 1981), chap. 4. Especially relevant here is the point that the more sober, realistic stories (promoted in place of the imaginative, adventurous chapbook fictions) served an ideological purpose, "making children the fathers and mothers of moral, and indeed politically safe, men and women" (137). The increasing emphasis on politically correct literature is evidenced by Mary Martha Sherwood's publication, in 1820, of a revised version of *The Governess*, omitting the fairy tales and other passages considered detrimental to children. See Percy Muir, *English Children's Books 1600–1900* (New York: Frederick A. Praeger, 1954), 99.

20. Alice Clark, *Working Life of Women in the Seventeenth Century* (1919, reprint, New York: Augustus M. Kelley, 1968), 302. Bridget Hill's *Women, Work, and Sexual Politics in Eighteenth-Century England* (Oxford: Basil Blackwell, 1989) provides carefully researched corroboration of Clark's theories. Chapter 4, "The Undermining of the Family Economy," is particu-

larly pertinent to the argument of this essay. On the connection between industrialism and the rise of children's literature, see Kramnick, "Children's Literature," 213.

21. Evidently, fear of bad influences at school is at least as old as the seventeenth century. Locke wrote: "Vice, if we may believe the general Complaint, ripens so fast now adays, and runs up to Seed so early in young People, that it is impossible to keep a Lad from the spreading Contagion; if you will venture him abroad in the Herd, and trust to his chance or his own Inclination for the choice of his Company at School." James L. Axtell, *The Educational Writings of John Locke: A Critical Edition* (Cambridge: Cambridge University Press, 1968), 169. In Thomas Day's description of a young man's education a century later, the class bias is reversed (now it is the working and middle classes who must be protected from the decadent aristocracy), but the complaint about schools is strikingly similar: Master Compton "had almost finished his education at a public school, where he had learned every vice and folly which is commonly taught at such places, without the least improvement either of his character or his understanding." *The History of Sandford and Merton*, 3 vols., facsimile reprint, ed. Isaac Kramnick (New York: Garland, 1977), 2:241. (Citations hereafter are to this edition.) Recall that in *Joseph Andrews*, Parson Adams blames Mr. Wilson's misspent youth on his education at a public school: "Public schools are the nurseries of all vice and immorality. . . . Joseph, you may thank the Lord you were not bred at a public school; you would never have preserved your virtue as you have." Henry Fielding, *Joseph Andrews/Shamela*, ed. Martin C. Battestin (Boston, MA: Houghton Mifflin, 1961), 194–96. Adams' vehemence, however, is shown to reflect his own vanity as a private schoolmaster, and Joseph's spirited reply in defense of public education seems to be closer to the view of Henry Fielding, who attended Eton.

22. Mary Poovey, *The Proper Lady and the Woman Writer: Ideology as Style in the Works of Mary Wollstonecraft, Mary Shelley, and Jane Austen* (Chicago: University of Chicago Press, 1984), 27.

23. Woodward's analysis, for example, suggests that the portrayal of women in groups in Fielding's novels (including *The Governess*) inevitably camouflages an attack on patriarchy and advances a feminist argument (in varying degrees of "disguise") for the value and power of female community. "'Feminine Virtue, Ladylike Disguise,'" 57–71.

24. While the noncompetitiveness required among the girls in the "little female academy" helped to mold women well suited to a patriarchal system, it is worth recalling that the relationships among boys and between boys and their masters in the English public school environment hardly constituted an ideal that women would be tempted to emulate. See Lawrence Stone, *The Family, Sex, and Marriage in England 1500–1800* (New York: Harper & Row, 1977), 439–44, 448–49.

25. Alice Browne, *The Eighteenth Century Feminist Mind* (Detroit, MI: Wayne State University Press, 1987), 141. On the connection between social class and attitudes toward sexuality in the seventeenth and eighteenth centuries, see Stone, *Family, Sex, and Marriage*, 281–82.

26. "La femme est faite pour céder à l'homme et pour supporter même son injustice. Vous ne réduirez jamais les jeunes garçons au même point; le sentiment intérieur s'élève et se révolte en eux contre l'injustice; la nature ne les fit pas pour la tolérer." Jean-Jacques Rousseau, *Émile ou de l'education*, ed. François et Pierre Richard (Paris: Garnier Freres, 1964), 502. Citations in the text are to this edition.

27. See *Émile* 461–62, 471 for examples of Rousseau's strategies for educating young girls.

28. On Rousseau's enormous influence in England, see, in addition to Darton and Gardiner (noted above), Sylvia Patterson, *Rousseau's "Émile" and Early Children's Literature* (Metuchen: The Scarecrow Press, 1971), which suggests the nature and extent of Rousseau's effect on late eighteenth-century authors of fiction for children.

29. Patricia Meyer Spacks has described how, by the end of the century, a good deal of popular fiction by women promoted a vastly restricted and particularized female role, emphasizing "the badness of assertive females, the long-term profitability of docile virtue, and the limitation of feminine possibility." *The Adolescent Idea*, 137. Mary V. Jackson makes a similar point with regard to literature written specifically for children by "reformers" such as Mary Ann and Dorothy Kilner, Lady Ellenor Fenn, and Sarah Trimmer: "Self-expression heretofore considered appropriate or even becoming was now forbidden respectable females, so as to mold them into guardians and weathervanes of social morality in general and of men's morals in particular, by 'soft persuasions' only, however." *Engines of Instruction, Mischief, and Magic: Children's Literature in England from Its Beginnings to 1839* (Lincoln: University of Nebraska Press, 1989), 139.

30. Muir, *English Children's Books*, 91.

31. For a discussion of Day's anti-slavery poem, "The Dying Negro," see George Warren Gignilliat Jr., *The Author of Sandford and Merton* (New York: Columbia University Press, 1932), 102–10. See also the incident in Day's *History of Sandford and Merton* in which the boys are saved from a raging baited bull by a "grateful black" (2:300–306); the black man's subsequent narrative of life in his native Gambia (3:270–95) reflects Day's idea that the refinements of civilization, particularly as abused by the upper classes, corrupt the capacity for true manliness.

32. Gignilliat, *Author of Sandford and Merton*, 335. Day was unalterably opposed to female authorship; his influence upon Maria Edgeworth's father, the socially progressive Richard Lovell Edgeworth (with whom Day maintained an ongoing dialogue on the subject of female education), kept Maria from publishing her work until after Day's death. Equally revealing and more dramatic were his pathetic attempts to mold two young girls, whom he had adopted from orphanages, according to the prescriptions of Rousseau (Day considered the instruction afforded by *Émile* second in value only to that of the Bible). The plan backfired badly, as neither girl turned out to be the ideal mate he had hoped to cultivate through precise methodologies (this experiment an example itself of bourgeois values applied to the formation of human personality). Day's treatment of the two girls (whom he named Sabrina and Lucretia) is recounted by Gignilliat, 54–57 *et passim*.

33. On Locke's intended audience see Axtell, *Educational Writings of Locke*, 51. Pickering clarifies the nature of Locke's virtually universal appeal to eighteenth-century educators and philosophers, including his "indirect" appeal to the middle-classes. *Locke and Children's Books*, 9, 13.

34. Miss Simmons' uncle is praised for teaching her to disdain "useless" upper-class arts like French and singing and "to believe that domestic economy is a point of the utmost consequence to every woman that intends to be a wife and mother." Singing is simply "the science of making a noise," and as for French, the uncle does not permit his niece to learn it "although he knew it himself [since] women, he thought, are not birds of passage, that are to be eternally changing their abode" (2:228). The description of Selene as related by her father, Chares, in one of the many didactic and illustrative stories Day interpolated into his novel, is similarly unequivocal about the subservient role of women. Like Miss Simmons' uncle, Chares wishes to endow his daughter Selene with a mental and physical "vigour" uncommon among women. What this means is that she works hard at "husbandry and gardening," much to the gratification of her father, whose attitude toward her explicitly recalls that of Rousseau toward his paragon Sophie:

> With what delight did I view her innocent chearfulness and assiduity! With what pleasure did she receive the praises which I gave to her skill and industry; or hear the lessons of wisdom and the examples of virtuous women, which I used to read her at evening, out of the writings of celebrated philosophers which I had collected in my travels. (3:208)

35. Muir, *English Children's Books*, 91.

36. Cornelia Meigs et al., eds., *A Critical History of Children's Literature*, rev. ed. (New York: MacMillan, 1969), 92.

37. Contentions that Fielding rejected sex-role conventions are more persuasive when supported by texts other than *The Governess*. See, for example, Downs-Meirs' interesting argument that David Simple is a man "whose central beliefs are feminist" and who embodies "the feminine virtues." "Feminine Virtue, Ladylike Disguise," 64. Nevertheless, to characterize Fielding as a proponent of "cultural androgyny" (Carpenter, "Sarah Fielding," 12) is, I believe, very misleading. Certainly, the students at Fielding's "little female academy" are not encouraged to pursue the kind of independent (i.e., "male") lives that Mary Wollstonecraft envisioned some forty years later or to draw, as Wollstonecraft did, the radical conclusion that domestic virtues are best nurtured in a culture of political equality: "How many women . . . waste life away the prey of discontent, who might have practised as physicians, regulated a farm, managed a shop, and stood erect, supported by their own industry. . . . Would men but generously snap our chains, and be content with rational fellowship instead of slavish obedience, they would find us more observant daughters, more affectionate sisters, more faithful wives, more reasonable mothers—in a word, better citizens." *A Vindication of the Rights of Woman*, (New York: Source Book Press, 1971), 182–83.

38. Fielding's concern for both the reception of *The Governess* and the marketability of a projected tract on education is indicated by Jane Collier's response to a textual emendation proposed by Richardson. Disagreeing with Richardson's advice to clarify the unspecified punishment meted out to

the quarreling girls by Mrs. Teachum (*The Governess*, 108), Collier offers two reasons to leave the text unchanged: First, "as this book is not so much designed as a direction to governesses . . . as for girls how to behave to each other," young female readers should suppose the punishment "to be the same that they themselves had suffered when they deserved it." Second, leaving the punishment unspecified protects the author from being charged with either excessive leniency or unnecessary harshness. Taking care to offend as few people as possible, Fielding and Collier hope that both those who advocate whipping and those who do not will "be engaged in favor of this other book," i.e., the proposed volume on education. See Anna Barbauld, ed., *The Correspondence of Samuel Richardson*, 6 vols. (London: Richard Phillips, 1804), 3:62–64. Another incident in *The Governess* indicates Fielding's hesitance to take a firm public stand on corporal punishment, which she seems to have personally opposed: The model student Jenny reluctantly approves when a woman "severely" beats her eight-year-old daughter for lying. (The child's screams, audible across the garden wall, have drawn the young students to investigate.) The mother defends her action as a last resort reserved only for the "vile Fault" of consistent dishonesty, and there is no indication that such punishment is cruel or inappropriate (177–79).
39. See Arlene Wilner, "The Mythology of History, the Truth of Fiction: Henry Fielding and the Cases of Bosavern Penlez and Elizabeth Canning," *The Journal of Narrative Technique* 22 (1991): 185–201.
40. On the influence of *The Governess* on children's literature of the late eighteenth and early nineteenth centuries, see Grey's introduction, 62–77.

Contributors to Volume 24

PAULA R. BACKSCHEIDER is Pepperell Eminent Scholar at Auburn University and a former president of ASECS. Her most recent book is *Spectacular Politics: Theatrical Power and Mass Culture in Early Modern England* (Johns Hopkins University Press, 1993). She is the author of *Daniel Defoe: His Life* and other books and articles.

JEFFREY BARNOUW has written numerous articles on the intellectual history of the seventeenth and eighteenth centuries. He teaches English and Comparative Literature at the University of Texas at Austin. His essay was first presented at the 1993 ASECS meeting.

LESLIE ELLEN BROWN, Associate Dean for Academic Services, College of Arts and Architecture, and Professor of Music at Penn State University, has published widely in the areas of eighteenth-century French opera, aesthetics of the Scottish Enlightenment, and eighteenth-century bibliography. She edited volumes 19 and 20 of *Studies in Eighteenth-Century Culture* and is the co-editor of *Hanoverian Britain: An Encyclopedia* (Garland). Her essay was first presented at the 1992 joint conference of the East-Central American Society for Eighteenth-Century Studies and the Eighteenth-Century Scottish Studies Society.

PAMELA CANTRELL is a Ph.D. candidate at the University of Nevada, Las Vegas in literature and art history. Her work on Smollett and Hogarth forms the beginning of a larger examination of the analogy between the arts from early modernism to the postmodern. She is currently working on the affinity between Henry James and James McNeill Whistler. Her essay was originally presented at the 1991 NWSECS meeting.

PATRICK COLEMAN is Professor of French at the University of California, Los Angeles. He is the author of *Rousseau's Political Imagination* (Droz, 1984) and the editor of Rousseau's *Discourse on Inequality* (Oxford, 1994). He is currently completing a book on the French pre-romantic novel. His essay was presented at the 1993 ASECS meeting.

ROBERT P. CREASE is a Professor of Philosophy at the State University of New York at Stony Brook. He is the author of *The Play of Nature: Experimentation as Performance* (Bloomington: Indiana University Press,

1993). His essay is a revision of a paper presented at the 1992 NEASECS meeting.

WILLIAM F. EDMISTON is Professor and Chair of the Department of French and Classics at the University of South Carolina in Columbia. He is the author of *Diderot and Family* (1985) and *Hindsight and Insight: Focalization in Four Eighteenth-Century French Novels* (1991). A version of his paper was read at the 1992 EC/ASECS conference in Philadelphia.

JAMES M. FARRELL is an Assistant Professor in the Department of Communication at the University of New Hampshire. He was trained in rhetoric and public address at the University of Wisconsin (Ph.D. 1988), and has published articles on eighteenth- and nineteenth-century American public address, classical influences on American rhetoric, and eighteenth-century rhetorical theory. His essay is derived from a paper presented at the 1993 ASECS meeting.

MOIRA FERGUSON is the James E. Ryan Chair in English and Women's Literature at the University of Nebraska-Lincoln. She is the author of *Subject to Others: British Women Writers and Colonial Slavery, 1678–1834* (Columbia University, 1992); *The Hart Sisters: Early African-Caribbean Writers, Evangelicals, and Radicals* (University of Nebraska Press, 1993); and *Jamaica Kincaid, Where the Land Meets the Body* (University Press of Virginia, forthcoming). A version of her essay was presented at the 1993 ASECS meeting.

MAUREEN HARKIN recently completed her Ph.D. at Johns Hopkins University. Her dissertation is on Smith, sympathy, and the sentimental novel. She has published on Henry Mackenzie and the sentimental novel in *ELH*. She is Assistant Professor of Literature at New College of the University of South Florida. Her essay is derived from a paper presented at the 1993 WSECS meeting.

CATHERINE INGRASSIA is an Assistant Professor of English at Virginia Commonwealth University. This essay is from a longer study entitled *Paper Credit: Grub Street, Exchange Alley and Feminization in Early Eighteenth-Century England*. She presented her paper at ASECS 1993 in Providence.

PHILIP KOCH, Professor Emeritus of French, University of Pittsburgh, has a long standing interest in the seventeenth- and eighteenth-century theater of France, Italo-French literary relations, and the "commedia dell'arte." He is at present engaged in the preparation of a critical edition/translation of Bartolomeo Rossi's Renaissance pastoral *Fiammella*, a project closer to eighteenth-century concerns than might at first appear. His essay was first presented at the 1993 ASECS meeting.

WILLIAM LEVINE has published articles on mid-eighteenth-century poetry, Johnson, Coleridge, and Wordsworth in *SEL*, *Criticism*, *The Wordsworth Circle*, and *Philological Quarterly*. The current essay is part of a work in progress on the history of civic obligation in English poetry and cultural criticism from 1740 to 1830 and was originally presented in 1993 at WCECS.

THOMAS E. MARESCA is Professor and, currently, Chairman of English at SUNY Stony Brook. His work in the eighteenth century includes numerous articles and the books *Pope's Horatian Poems* (Columbus: The Ohio State University Press, 1966) and *Epic to Novel* (Columbus: The Ohio State University Press, 1974). He has for some time now been engaged in a lengthy study of allegory in, before, and after the eighteenth century. His essay was presented at the 1992 NEASECS meeting.

BETTY RIZZO, Professor of English at the City College of New York and the CUNY Graduate Center, has published many articles on the eighteenth century and two writing textbooks, is co-author of two books on Christopher Smart, and author of *Companions Without Vows: Relationships among Eighteenth-Century British Women* published by the University of Georgia Press in 1994. Her paper was read at the 1993 ASECS meeting in Providence.

ZEYNEP TENGER is Assistant Professor of English at Berry College. She is co-author of "'Impartial Critic' or 'Muses Handmaid': The Politics of Critical Practice in the Early Eighteenth Century," to appear in *Essays in Literature*. She is currently co-authoring a book-length study, *The Culture of Criticism: the Social Roles of Criticism in England, 1662–1835*. Her essay was jointly presented with Paul Trolander at the 1993 SEASECS meeting.

PAUL TROLANDER is Assistant Professor of English at Berry College. He is co-author of "'Impartial Critic' or 'Muses Handmaid': The Politics of Critical Practice in the Early Eighteenth Century," to appear in *Essays in Literature* and author of "The Politics of the Episteme: The Collapse of the Discourse of General Nature and the Reaction to the French Revolution" to appear in *New Essays on the French Revolution Debate* (Contemporary Research Press, forthcoming). He is currently co-authoring a book-length study, *The Culture of Criticism: the Social Roles of Criticism in England, 1662–1835*.

JAMES GRANTHAM TURNER is Professor of English at the University of California, Berkeley, and in 1993 was a National Endowment for the Humanities Fellow at the Newberry Library. In addition to editing *Politics, Poetics and Hermeneutics in Milton's Prose* (1990), Robert Paltock's *Life and Adventures of Peter Wilkins* (1990), and *Sexuality and Gender in Early Modern Europe: Institutions, Texts, Images* (1993), he has written numerous articles on seventeenth- and eighteenth-century culture and two books: *The Politics of Landscape: Rural Scenery and Society in English Poetry, 1630–1660* (1979) and *One Flesh: Paradisal Marriage and Sexual Relations in the Age of Milton* (1987). His essay is derived from his 1992 paper delivered at the Seattle ASECS meeting.

ARLENE FISH WILNER earned her Ph.D. in English literature at Columbia University, specializing in the eighteenth century. An Associate Professor of English at Rider College in Lawrenceville, NJ, she has published articles on Henry Fielding's fiction, travel writing, and legal pamphlets; on William Steig's books for children; and on Cynthia Ozick's place in the American literary tradition. Her essay was originally presented at the 1993 NEASECS meeting.

Executive Board, 1993-94

President: LAWRENCE STONE, Dodge Professor of History, Princeton University

Past President: PAULA BACKSCHEIDER, West Point Pepperell-Harry M. Philpott Eminent Scholar in English, Auburn University

First Vice-President: RONALD C. ROSBOTTOM, Dean of the Faculty and Professor of French, Amherst College

Second Vice-President: BARBARA STAFFORD, Professor of Art, University of Chicago

Executive Secretary: JEFFREY SMITTEN, Professor of English, Utah State University

Treasurer: BARBARA BRANDON SCHNORRENBERG, History, Birmingham, Alabama

Members-at-Large:

JANICE FARRAR THADDEUS, Head Tutor, History and Literature Program, Harvard University (1994)
DORA WIEBENSON, Professor of Architectural History, University of Virginia, Emerita (1994)
JULIA EPSTEIN, Barbara Riley Levin Professor of Comparative Literature, Haverford College (1995)
ROBERT E. SCHOFIELD, Professor of History of Technology and Science, Iowa State University, Emeritus (1995)
JEFFREY MERRICK, Professor of History, University of Wisconsin at Milwaukee (1996)
GORDON SCHOCHET, Professor of Political Science, Rutgers University (1996)

Administrative Office:

Accounts Manager: HAILEY BRADY, Utah State University

Office Manager: KRISTINE FREEMAN, Utah State University

Institutional Members

of the American Society

for Eighteenth-Century Studies

American Antiquarian Society
John Carter Brown Library
Carleton University Library
Case Western Reserve University
Claremont College
Clark Memorial Library
Dalhousie University
Early American History &
    Culture Institute
Evansville University
Folger Institute
Fordham University
Georgia State University
Harvard College
Herzog August Bibliothek
Indiana University at Kokomo
McMaster University
National Library of Australia
Northern Illinois University

Rutgers University
SUNY at Binghamton
Swarthmore College
Towson State University
University of Cincinnati
University of Connecticut
University of Kansas
University of Pennsylvania
University of Rochester
University of Southern California
Univ. of Southern Mississippi
University of Tennessee
University of Victoria
Utah State University
Washington University
Westfalische Wilhelms
    University
Yale Center for British Art
York University

Sponsoring Members

of the American Society

for Eighteenth-Century Studies

Carol Barash
Jerry C. Beasley
Emmett G. Bedford
David Blewett
Thomas E. Blom
Thomas F. Bonnell
Martha F. Bowden
Leo Braudy
Morris Brownell
Martha L. Brunson
John L. Bullion
Marilyn Carbonell
David W. Carrithers
Ralph Cohen
Michael J. Conlon
Brian Corman
Louis Cornell
Howard Coughlin, Jr.
Patricia B. Craddock
Nora F. Crow
William Cunningham, Jr.
Marlies K. Danziger
Alix S. Deguise
Pierre Deguise
William F. Edmiston
Jolynn Edwards
Antoinette Emch-Deriaz
David Fairer
John Thomas Farrell
Bernadette Fort
James D. Garrison
Josephine Grieder
Diana Guiragossian-Carr
Madelyn Gutwirth
Roger Hahn

Karsten Harries
Phillip Harth
Donald M. Hassler
Daniel Heartz
Emita B. Hill
Charles H. Hinnant
J. Paul Hunter
Kathryn Montgomery Hunter
Adrienne D. Hytier
Malcolm Jack
Regina Mary Janes
Thomas Jemielity
Loftus Townshend Jestin
Frank A. Kafker
Martin I. Kallich
Frederick M. Keener
Shirley Strum Kenny
Charles A. Knight
Philip Koch
Gwin J. Kolb
Colby H. Kullman
Manfred Kusch
Catherine Lafarge
John E. Larkin, Jr.
Maynard Mack
David D. Mann
Robert Markley
Steven D. Martinson
Alan T. McKenzie
David McNeil
Linda E. Merians
Ann Messenger
Michael Mooney
Dewey F. Mosby
Maureen E. Mulvihill

Patrons

of the American Society

for Eighteenth-Century Studies

Paul Alkon	Donald C. Mell, Jr.
Mark S. Auburn	John H. Middendorf
Paula Backscheider	Earl Miner
James G. Basker	Virginia J. Peacock
Barbara Becker-Cantarino	Jane Perry-Camp
Carol Blum	R.G. Peterson
Theodore E. D. Braun	James Pollak
Patricia Bruckman	John Valdimir Price
Joseph A. Byrnes	Ronald C. Rosbottom
Chester F. Chapin	Lawrence A. Ruff
Robert Adams Day	Treadwell Ruml II
Susan H. Elias	Howard Schiffman
A.C. Elias, Jr.	Richard B. Schwartz
Frank H. Ellis	Elaine C. Showalter
Roger J. Fechner	English Showalter
Dustin H. Griffin	Patricia Meyer Spacks
Phyllis Guskin	Susan Staves
Basil Guy	Elizabeth Stewart
Edward P. Harris	Keith Stewart
Steve Holliday	Mary M. Stewart
Robert H. Hopkins	Ann T. Straulman
Annibel Jenkins	Masashi Suzuki
J. Patrick Lee	Connie C. Thorson
Geoffrey Marshall	James L. Thorson
H.W. Matalene	David F. Venturo
Helen Louise McGuffie	James A. Winn

Index